BOYHOOD RITUALS
IN AN AFRICAN SOCIETY

Boyhood Rituals in an African Society

An Interpretation

SIMON OTTENBERG

University of Washington Press

Seattle & London

Library of Congress Cataloging-in-Publication Data
Ottenberg, Simon.
    Boyhood rituals in an African society: an interpretation
    Bibliography: p.
    Includes index.
    1. Igbo (African people)—Children.
    2. Igbo (African people)—Rites and ceremonies.
    3. Socialization—Case studies. I. Title.
    DT515.45.I33O88   1988   392'.14'089963   87-21701
    ISBN 0-295-96575-4

Designed by Audrey Meyer
All photographs are by the author; part title illustrations
are adapted from Ottenberg, *Masked Rituals of Afikpo* (University
of Washington Press, 1975). Line drawings are by Margaret Davidson.
Composition, printing, and binding by Braun-Brumfield, Inc., Ann Arbor
Text type: 10/13 Galliard with Galliard display
The paper used in this publication meets the minimum requirements
of the American National Standard for Information Sciences—Permanence
of Paper for Printed Library Materials, ANSI Z39.48-1984.

In Memory
Nora Clarke Ottenberg
1926–1977

Contents

Illustrations

Photographs

Preface

THIS STUDY FOCUSES ON THE PEOPLE OF AFIKPO VIL-lage-Group in southeastern Nigeria, one of a large number of Igbo (or Ibo) groupings in that country. I did not go to Afikpo to study children or initiations, but kinship and descent and traditional local-level politics (S. Ottenberg 1968, 1971). As was the case with the material that I collected on Afikpo masquerades (S. Ottenberg 1975), I have come to write about Afikpo boyhood many years after the field work, and after outlining the main social forms.

The "present day" of my study is now history. I carried out research at Afikpo between December 1951 and February 1953, between September 1959 and June 1960, and during occasional visits through December 1960 and in the summer of 1966. Many changes have occurred since, including those brought about by the Nigerian civil war—in which Afikpo was directly involved—and by the changing political and economic conditions in the country.

I make no apologies for employing information from my time in Afikpo. I do not think that this makes my interpretation any less useful. Nor do I apologize for stressing the older, more traditional forms of childhood experience at Afikpo to the neglect of the factors of change, of a new economy and politics, and of the influence of schools and the missions. I have occasionally indicated some features of change, but I believe that these external influences had yet to become important for children at the time of my research. In writing of Afikpo childhood tradition I have the advantage of having worked through Afikpo social organization in my previous publications (S. Ottenberg 1968, 1971), and of myself having gone through a long period of anthropological and personal maturation. What I have written, then, is a reflective interpretation of a past time, a gathering together of certain threads growing out of my Afikpo experience (1985).

The data in this book, in fact, form a rich background to the subsequent changes which have occurred at Afikpo since the 1950s and 1960s, including the further truncation of initiation rites for both sexes, the effects of sending many more children away to school, the changing status of women in the family, and the diminuition of male secrecy as a form of social and political control as new forms of control and power are introduced.

I wish to thank the Social Science Research Council and the National Science Foundation for financial assistance that made possible the research on which this study is based. In the field I was greatly assisted by Nnachi Enwo, Thomas Ibe and the late Chukwu Okoro, the late Nnachi Iduma, and the late Chiefs I. Isu, Ndukwe Azu, and Nnachi Omeri. They opened their doors to me, led me to new events and perceptions, and introduced me to other people.

This book is primarily a study of boys' childhood experience; I collected much less information on girls. My former wife, Phoebe Ottenberg, now Phoebe V. Miller, carried out field work at Afikpo over much the same period as I did (Miller 1982; P. Ottenberg 1958, 1959, 1965), and has considerable data on female children. When I refer to girls it is usually to contrast their experience with that of boys, and I draw on her disseration and rich store of published and unpublished data. I am very much indebted to her for ideas discussed over a number of years, and for access to her research materials.

My late wife, Nora Clarke Ottenberg, encouraged me to start writing about children–a long-standing interest and concern of hers. During the summer of 1982 I carried out eight long interviews in Seattle with Matthew Okpani Alu, from Mgbom Village; he had been a small boy when I had focused my research on his community. His comments and suggestions (though not touching on secrecy matters) and his enthusiasm were helpful in enriching my data and in guarding against the inevitable retrospective falsification that occurs after field research has been completed. Professors Gilbert Herdt, Beryl Bellman, and Warren d'Azevedo all made very helpful comments on the manuscript. The figures were done by Margaret Davidson, for which many thanks.

Simon Ottenberg

Seattle, 1988

Introduction

THIS IS A STUDY OF THE TRADITIONAL ASPECTS OF BOY-hood in the Afikpo Village-Group, one of many groups that comprise the Igbo people of southeastern Nigeria (see Map 1). I originally intended only to analyze the boys' initiations at adolescence, but I soon discovered that I could not meaningfully accomplish this without considering their earlier childhood experience. So I here provide detailed accounts of infancy and childhood and then link these to adolescent initiation; I look to the whole of boys' lives in one society.

I believe that infant experience establishes certain patterns and sets forces in motion and that during the remainder of childhood, not just during adolescent initiation, the child must deal with the consequences of these early features. Initiation is important, symbolically, socially, and for other reasons, as scholars in various disciplines have often pointed out.* But it is only one of a series of rituals, activities, and events that children go through that mark their personal evolution from infancy to adolescence. Many of these pre-initiation features speak to the same issues as initiation rites and even foreshadow initiation patterns (Schlegel and Barry 1980).

In addition to the impact of infant experience, I consider that the latency period (about 6 to 11 years of age) is a key time in boyhood in the society under study, not only as a reworking of infancy and early childhood experiences, but as a crucial time when the child is sufficiently knowledgeable to absorb many of the basic rules, sym-

---

*See Barry and Schlegel 1980; Bettelheim 1962; Brown 1963a, 1963b; Cohen 1964; Eliade 1965; Gluckman 1962; J. L. Henderson 1967; Herdt 1982; Morinis 1985; Norbeck, Walker, and Cohen 1962; Paige and Paige 1981; Precourt 1975; Schlegel and Barry 1979, 1980; Van Gennep 1960; Whiting, Kluckhohn, and Anthony 1958; and Young 1965.

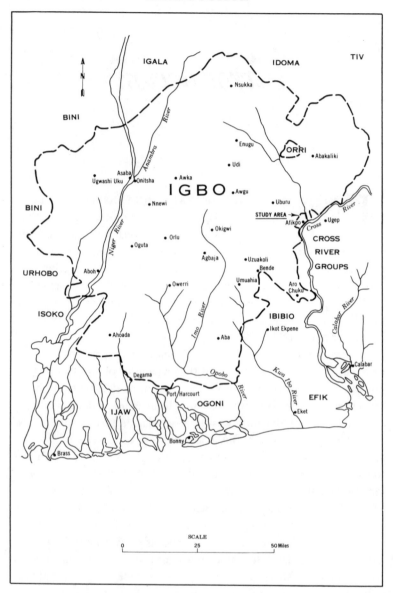

Map 1. Igbo country (*after D. Forde and G. I. Jones 1950*)

bols, and values of his culture. The initiation itself draws heavily on the cultural knowledge and experience that the boys have acquired during latency: technical, manual, social, religious, and aesthetic, as well as emotional and experiential. While the initiation provides links to psychological issues raised in infancy and early childhood at the time of sexual maturation, it also draws heavily on the experience of boys in latency.

The initiation of adolescents is sometimes approached without a thorough understanding of this earlier experience (Allen 1967; Gluckman 1962); the child is viewed as entering the "bush" as a social blank, a tabula rasa which will receive all or almost all of its contents during the initiation. Alternatively, initiation is viewed almost entirely from the viewpoint of its relationships to infancy and early childhood. Rather, initiation should be seen as one of a series of events, rites, and activities which are interconnected psychologically, symbolically, and experientially (Whiting, Kluckhohn, and Anthony 1958; Young 1965). Initiation is neither the beginning nor the end of maturation. Indeed, the period between initiation and marriage has rarely been studied, though it is during this phase—which may be some years in length—that the forces supposedly resolved through initiation are first put to work.

Children are more than passive followers in the initiation rites; they are very active elements. They bring with them considerably developed egos and superegos, and what they have learned from exposure to social, religious, and technical matters. They are not such novices as they may at first appear to be. I believe that placing the initiation in the context of the children's earlier lives provides for a richer and more meaningful understanding of these rites. This leads me to focus on the whole maturation process, on the extent to which children emulate adult behavior, on the question of the existence of a separate concept of childhood, and on the relationship of infancy to childhood experience, as well as on other matters.

In viewing children from birth to maturation I also employ a view of parents as developing, changing beings, not as static persons. As children grow, so do the parents' lives and behavior alter as a consequence of changes in their children, as well as for other reasons. At Afikpo success in producing children who remain alive, and their passage through key rites as they grow, adds status to the parents. In turn the status concerns and activities of parents help move their children along in the maturation process. The two generations are inescapably bound together. The children's initiations are but one of many stages of this involvement.

In order to discuss boys I will treat two pervasive and interrelated themes in Afikpo social life: gender distinction and secrecy. These themes are deeply intertwined and loom large in the experience of all Afikpo and other Igbo groups. No understanding of initiation and its antecedents in childhood is possible without examining both of these features in depth.

Afikpo is a society with very marked and distinctive gender behavior (P. Ottenberg 1958, 1959; Miller 1982). What males and females do in work, in the family, in general social life, and in aesthetics and rituals differs greatly. There is physical separation of the sexes, marked by separate living quarters for husbands and wives, distinct eating arrangements, generally different roles in farmwork, as well as separate and differing boys' and girls' initiations. These gender differences have major implications for childhood experience. They influence the pattern of infant care and the imprinting of psychological features in the infant. They affect the manner in which children learn their own sex roles and the rules of gender behavior and interrelationships. In turn, the child's experiences with sex roles relates to the way he or she handles initiation, as the gender experience of adults influences the manner in which they behave toward children.

Secrecy is a major differentiating feature of the sexes at Afikpo. For men, the societal functions of secrecy are exemplified in the village secret societies, which all adult men join, and the boys' secret societies. This form of secrecy is, paradoxically, a very public thing— what Goffman (1959:142) calls "strategic secrets"—in that there is a certain flaunting of the presence of secrecy. Everyone knows that the men's secret societies exist, although knowledge of the contents of the secrets is more limited.

Female secrecy is of a different kind. Here we find Goffman's "dark secrets," where the presence of secrecy itself is not proclaimed, although it may be suspected. Women's secrecy is very private and is not associated with formal organizations. Such secrecy guards occurrences which are not sanctioned, and is itself frowned upon. Men have "dark secrets" as well at Afikpo—sexual liaisons with women married to other men, and some economic and political affairs—and these too are generally frowned upon.

It is on the strategic forms of secrecy that I will focus in this work. Public secrecy at Afikpo is associated with males, and with their sexuality and physical and political power, and its absence among females is a major differentiating feature of the sexes. Gender behavior is not only distinctive, it is unbalanced; men dominate the political and religious life, and key aspects of the economy (Miller 1982; P. Ottenberg 1959), though females have certain social and economic mechanisms of control over males. In this atmosphere of male predominance their characteristic form of secrecy plays crucial roles.

Secrecy is a subject that was brilliantly analyzed by the sociologist Simmel (1950) at the turn of the century. Other early scholars carried out useful comparative work, particularly on secret societies, but unfortunately their conceptualizations were speculative (Schurtz 1902; Butt-Thompson 1929; Webster 1908). Only in recent years have social scientists again intelligently turned their attention to this topic (Goffman 1959; Bellman 1984; W. P. Murphy 1980; Tefft 1980). I have particularly drawn from Bellman's (1984) rich insights. I am concerned with how children acquire knowledge of secrecy, how they experience it, and how these relate to the developing gender relationships of the young. I will also view gender and secrecy and their ties to one another in the light of the emerging sexual maturation of Afikpo children. Outwardly, at Afikpo, gender distinctiveness and secrecy separate the sexes, while sexuality, through interest and taboo, both associates and separates them. In fact, the issue is more complex. Secrecy is not simply a way for people to withdraw from each other. It is, paradoxically, a form of communication (Bellman 1984), a specific way in which people can relate to each other. Secrecy in its major form at Afikpo is a generating force in social relationships, not an absence of relationships. It is way of sending messages, and the meaning lies as much in the form of the message as in its content. The very phrase "public secrecy," an oxymoron, suggests that the form or frame of communication—what Bateson (1972) calls metacommunication—is as important as what is or is not communicated.

The sexual theme appears in the child's oedipal phase (about 3 to 6 years of age), and then seems to go away, only to reappear at adolescence, yet the awareness of gender differences and of secrecy behavior steadily grows and solidifies during the maturation of boys, a long haul of continuous development. Secrecy and gender issues interplay with sexuality in its two main childhood periods, all three finally integrating in the second period, particularly through the initiation rites.

Certain other general features of Afikpo social life are important to this study. The village-group's culture is both cumulative and complex: cumulative in that the Afikpo take on new ritual forms and types of social organization without necessarily discarding old ones, and complex in that this has led to a remarkable degree of organizational intricacy for a noncentralized, nonstate society. The village-group, which at the time of my research comprised some thirty thousand persons in twenty-two compactly settled villages on the west bank of the Cross River (see Map 2), was probably originally a small-scale non-Igbo-speaking matrilineal society into which came over time—in the nineteenth century and possibly earlier—groups of patrilineal Igbo settlers from the west, south, and northwest, who merged into the village-group while conquering it. During those times and into this century Afikpo was sometimes at war, at home and in the surrounding area; even today some of the key rituals and events in a boy's life are associated with physical strength and skill. Out of these contacts of migration and warfare developed the present system of double unilineal descent, with patrilineal residential nonexogamous lineages as the underlying social frame for the village political organization, and nonresidential exogamous matrilineal clans and lineages as the basis of most farmland holdings (S. Ottenberg 1968a). The villages vary in size from over two thousand members to less than several hundred persons. Most settlements concentrate on farming, but a few are fishing communities as well.

Afikpo is a gerontocracy. Village and village-group leadership depends on well-developed age sets and grades, formed on a residential basis and given increasing authority with age. The hierarchy of power is democratized to the extent that decision-making tends to be by groups of elders, rather than by individuals (S. Ottenberg 1971). I concentrated my own field research on the centrally located farming village of Mgbom, which had, at the time, a population of nearly two thousand persons. Although I carried out a great deal of work in other Afikpo communities, I will draw mainly on my data from Mgbom for this analysis.

Patrilineal groups form the basis of compounds in the villages, which are the seats of the ancestral shrines. The matrilineal groupings are dispersed, though each has a central shrine. Polygyny is prevalent, each wife usually having her own house separate from her

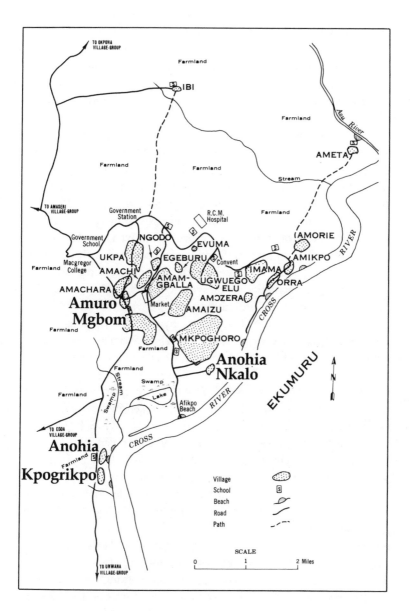

Map 2. The Afikpo Village-Group (*1960*). The five Itim villages are indicated in boldface

husband, somewhere in the same compound but not necessarily next to his. Co-wife conflict is endemic, and only in those rare cases where co-wives are friends or sisters do they readily cooperate in child care and in other matters (P. Ottenberg 1958). Females generally marry into other compounds in the village or to other Afikpo settlements, though there is no strict rule of exogamy (as there is for the matrilineal clans).

As a consequence of the considerable in-migration of people over the years, Afikpo has acquired or developed different forms of male village secret societies. These have merged in many of their activities but they have kept their separate forms of initiation; there is not one initiation at Afikpo but a number of them, differing in some features though exhibiting some similarities in underlying meaning, symbolism, and the order of events. The groups that moved into Afikpo also brought with them shrines and rituals not associated with the secret societies. These, added to those already present, yielded a rich panoply of religious activities in the village-group, with considerable choice and variation (S. Ottenberg 1968a, 1970).

Afikpo social life is also characterized by the taking of titles. There are about fifteen titles for men and several for women. They confer status at compound level, village level, or village-group level; some men's titles are associated with the secret societies, while others are not. Titles are taken by those who have the necessary wealth. Most are open to all adult males; some must be taken in a certain order, while others are acquired as each person chooses. Titles bring prestige to the title taker, but rarely carry political power.

Afikpo, like much of Igboland (LeVine 1966; Ottenberg 1959), stresses individual achievement and entrepreneurship, of which title taking is just one aspect. And the term for title, *meme,* may be applied to almost any major undertaking for an individual. Males in particular are expected to make their own way in the world without relying too heavily on parents and descent groups. At the same time, strength and striving are recognized and supported by social groups. In this egalitarian, active, verbose, and hard-working society, childhood—especially for boys—becomes a training ground for achievement and entrepreneurship within approved social frameworks.

Patrilineal and matrilineal descent groups, age sets and grades, village and village-group political organizations, secret societies and their various initiations, shrines and their associated rituals, and a plentiful number of title societies—all these, in conjunction with gender distinctions and secrecy, serve to constitute a cumulative culture. This is not surprising, since Afikpo has a high population density—some five hundred persons per square mile in 1963 (S. Ottenberg 1971:4). Although this complexity does not touch deeply on all aspects of childhood experience—rarely on the matrilineal groupings, titles societies, and in the political sphere—the child grows up in a crowded and intricate organizational world, whose features he has to learn. The population density means that in most Afikpo settlements, except the very smallest, there are enough children about to allow for a great deal of interchild contact, and for the presence of organized children's peer groups of some size, often by sex. Group experience looms large for Afikpo children, especially for boys.

Complexity suggests the existence of alternative choices. While traditional Afikpo is primarily tropical root-crop farming country, with a few fishing villages, and there is not much selection of occupational roles, most being determined by age and sex, the social and religious complexity allows for a good deal of personal and group manipulation of other individuals and groups, and allows for some choice among alternatives—which title to take, which initiation to put a son through, which land resources to develop, which shrine to sacrifice at, and so on.

There is a strong sense of growth and achievement at Afikpo, which colors the experience of growing boys. The village-group has clearly been a center of population growth, with expanding villages and descent groups. The increasing use of more and more land for farming and the enlarging movement of fishing and trading groups up and down the Cross River, and the pottery trade from items produced by Afikpo women down this river, has increased the wealth of the community and allowed for the enrichment of ritual activities, including those involving boys. The establishment of a District Office at Afikpo in 1902 brought a European touch as well as stranger Africans to the area and subsequently a number of schools. Although in the context of the much larger Igbo society of which the village-group is only a small part, Afikpo is seen as being marginal and less progressive, it generally views itself as a growing and enterprising community.

The sense of success of the Afikpo is coupled with the typical Igbo emphasis on personal achievement (S. Ottenberg 1959; Uchendu 1965), on making one's own way in the world regardless of background while employing kin and other group ties in doing so. The mark of success for a man is a large family, many children, control of substantial farmland, political influence, and wealth, often in the form of membership in title societies. For a woman it is having children and making money that she can call her own (not her husband's) through trade. Entrepreneurship of all kinds is encouraged at Afikpo, and verbal assertiveness is the mode; this is an active and a talkative culture for both sexes.

The complexity of Afikpo society and its alternative choices, in association with strong achievement values and a general air of success in Afikpo life, suggests that childhood training for both sexes will emphasize strong ego formation at the same time that the child becomes linked to social groupings, particularly those based on descent and residence. A lively quality of interest and assertiveness is evident in the children, even upon first meeting them. A strong sense of self develops in them; in males it is evident from about the age of five. In this work I will explore some of the experiences that make for this personal strength.

When I carried out my research the population of Igbo country was about eight million (Nigeria 1953–54). Afikpo, with its thirty thousand persons, was only one of some two hundred formerly relatively independent village-groups (Forde and Jones 1950). There is naturally a great deal of variation within this Igbo area. Matrilineal groupings, for example, occur only in the region of Afikpo and its neighbors, and there the age grade system is also particularly strong. For comparison I will draw on some materials from other Igbo areas, but I want to make it clear that my analysis of Afikpo does not necessarily fit other Igbo peoples in detail, although I believe that it does in general principles.

In this study, I will refer to specific stages of social maturation: *infancy* (birth to 2 years), *early childhood* (2 to 5 years), *growth* (5 to 13 years), and *adolescence*. The years given here are only approximations, which correspond roughly with Afikpo concepts of growth; they have terms for these periods of early life, although their view is not simple and they employ other terms for periods which crosscut these. I also make use of a psychoanalytic maturational framework, one that is not culturally specific: *pre-oedipal stage* (birth to 3 years), *oedipal stage* (3 to 6 years), *latency* (6 to 11 years), and then the *genital period*. I take this outline from Erickson (1963), without necessarily accepting his interpretations of the content of each period.

There is a pretty good congruence between the Afikpo framework and the Freudian one; what really differs is the point of view. Because I agree with Spiro (1982; see also Paul 1980; Devereux 1978) that a psychological focus and a sociocultural view need not diminish one another, I shall try to integrate the two approaches at key points in my discussion. My background and experience has been primarily anthropological, not psychoanalytical, and the weight of my interpretation is on the sociocultural side; nevertheless, I have found the psychoanalytic approach to be helpful to me where certain events and elements in Afikpo infancy and childhood are difficult to understand through an anthropological view alone. A social or cultural approach may appear to be more superficial than a psychoanalytic one—a descent group is somehow easier for me to "see" than an Oedipus complex—but the sociocultural view has crucial underlying logics and understandings of its own. I have grounded much of my analysis in this sphere.

I will place my writing in the ethnographic present, using the expressions "today" and "modern times" to refer to the 1950–60 period. This is done not to fictionalize the work, but to convey some of the immediacy that I felt when carrying out my research. When describing certain ritual events, I will in many cases report the words spoken by participants. At Afikpo, ritual pronouncements are not scripted and may vary according to the individual and the occasion; except where noted, what I am reporting is a typical, hypothetical utterance, not a formula or a verbatim account. I have conceived this work as a study of boys and their developing relationships to others as human beings, under the restraints, inducements, and challenges of a particular social and cultural milieu different from our own. I have had to generalize their experiences in order to analyze them. In so doing, I hope that I have not diminished the sense of the life and experience of the boys.

A note on pronunciation

Although Igbo is a tonal language, I have not indicated tones. The final "e" is pronounced in Igbo. "Kp" (as in "Afikpo") is a single implosive consonant, the "k" and the "p" being spoken at the same moment. "Gb" (as in "Igbo") is the voiced counterpart. I will employ the following phonetic symbols:

ϵ as in b*e*t
ɔ as in th*a*w
ɵ as in r*ou*gh

Part I
In the
Beginning

Part title illustration:
Mba mask of the uninitiated boys,
made by Chukwu Okoro

I

Infancy

I T IS ESSENTIAL TO HAVE CHILDREN AT AFIKPO. FOR A man it is particularly important to father sons in order to have status in society. Through sons men can acquire important titles. Without them a man is shy to speak up at public meetings and he finds it hard to be a leader and to hold religious positions. If he lacks a son he has to "borrow" a boy to initiate into the adult secret society in order to establish his own social standing. And without daughters to marry off a man has difficulties cementing relationships with friends and other families. A childless man will marry and remarry, and take on additional wives to try for offspring.

A woman marries at a young age, in middle or late adolescence. To have offspring that survive is the most important success in her life—nothing matches it. Her marriage or marriages may fail, her farms may spoil, her cooking may be terrible, she may lose money at trade, but if she has children who survive she is a full woman, with status among females and respect from men. A woman without children leaves her husband, tries another, and yet another, but has not fulfilled the ideal of womanhood; she is inadequate (P. Ottenberg 1958).

Both sexes are very conscious of the need to produce children for their descent groups, males particularly for the agnatic line, females for the uterine one. As Uchendu (1965:57), himself an Igbo, though not from Afikpo, writes: "A woman—and worse still a man—who has no male child contemplates old age with particular horror." And as LeVine (1973:135) suggests for agricultural societies south of the Sahara, "in the husband-wife relationship, babies are thought of as material goals for both spouses: a husband 'gives his wife children' and she bears children 'for him.'"

It is not surprising, therefore, that the Afikpo pay a great deal of attention to young children and show much interest in them.

3

Women commence childbearing shortly after marriage, abstain from sex while nursing for two years or more, wean the child and start to sleep with the husband again, hoping shortly to become pregnant. Women continue thus until the menopause; the maximum range of years of fecundity are used, although once a woman's daughters start bearing she is expected to stop. Birth control techniques exist and abortions occur, but both are probably rare. As a rule men marry for the first time in their middle or late twenties, and older men often marry adolescent girls, so that females go to a male adult authority figure who dominates the family. Men say that adolescent girls are "childish" and need the guidance of an older man.

Interest in the survival of children is strong in a society with a high rate of miscarriages and death of infants and the young. The Afikpo see continuous baby production as necessary to maintain the society and its descent groups. There is considerable anxiety that children may die or become seriously ill.

Women work hard: at the farms, cooking, and housekeeping. A pregnant woman remains active until the birth. She may use medicines and employ sacrifices to prevent a miscarriage, but physical activity during pregnancy is considered desirable in terms of producing a healthy baby as well as simply being a function of her role as a wife. Sexual activity continues almost to the time of birth; this is considered healthy and normal, although there is no belief that this behavior helps to form the child as in some other societies (Herdt 1982).

The birth of a child reflects the unity of aims of the parents and also a diversity of interests. While both sexes place a high premium on children, and need them for status purposes, mothers prefer daughters, who will help them with household tasks and farming and be companions in ways sons will not, and fathers prefer sons for their role in the fathers' social advancement. There is a descent factor in this distinction as well (S. Ottenberg 1968a). Girls produce children who will carry on the mother's uterine line, while boys produce offspring who will continue the father's agnatic line. While each parent has ties to the opposite-sex descent line—the mother to her patrilineage, the father to his matrilineal groupings—these ties do not figure prominently in concerns over the gender of children (though they do in regard to land and other matters).

Birth

A birth evokes joy, anxiety, secrecy, and even at this stage sex distinctiveness is emphasized. If the baby is a boy, this event starts the father off on a series of activities and rituals which continue until the child grows to manhood, matters which advance the boy's status but also bring prestige to the father.

The child is usually born while the mother sits on the ground or on a low stool in back of her house, or in a neighbor's yard if her own house has no backyard or if it is too small. She is living in her husband's compound of birth, where she has taken up residence upon marriage. At this time she is attended by several female friends and relatives; even other wives of her husband, traditionally jealous of one another, will assist. A midwife is often present. The woman's mother does not appear; it is said to be too anxiety provoking for her. No males, not even herbalists or other medical practitioners, are there; the child is born into an exclusively female environment.

The baby is born onto the ground. It should cry; this is taken as a sign of health and vitality (Henderson and Henderson 1966:18; Okafor-Omali 1965:42; Uchendu 1965:58). When the placenta appears the umbilical cord is cut by the midwife or another female. The child is then rubbed with sand to wash it, or often nowadays with soap and water. The skin is smoothed with palm oil and white chalk is put on it. The chalk cools the skin and it is also employed at Afikpo as a multivocal symbol of good health, fertility, good life, and happiness. The placenta and cord are buried in the courtyard—a practical procedure which also connects the child with the spirits of the ground, *ale,* associated with human welfare and fertility. The mother bathes in a special solution of water in which certain leaves have been soaked. A secret ritual is performed over the child by the women present. I could find no male who knew it, nor did any female inform me of what it was about. Men are forbidden to view it. The rite differs according to the infant's sex; and so begins the lifelong recognition of the importance of gender and of secrecy at Afikpo.

Mother and child move to her residence, normally her own house where she has been living, separate from her husband's home but in the same compound. Occasionally she resides, especially if a new wife, in the house of a senior co-wife. Then a ritual is performed, *osisa era* (wash-breast) on the mother's breasts by the midwife or another female to make the milk flow and to take out any bitterness in it. Before entering the house this woman breaks a calabash on the ground in front of the dwelling. Symbolically, this appears to mark the end of the uterine period, for the gourd resembles the uterus or vagina; I was told only that it is the usual practice to do this. The rite also signals the end of sexual activity for the mother during the long nursing period; her uterus and vagina become dormant.

The mother and child remain in her house for four days in isolation from men, excepting the father, who usually only visits briefly. The Afikpo say that this separation is necessary because she is likely to be bleeding and unclean during this period. As menstrual blood is contaminating to men and spirits at Afikpo, so is this blood. Friends, relatives, and co-wives cook for the mother and help her with her needs. These first four days of the child's life, an Igbo week, occur in an almost exclusively female environment. The very close mother attachment lasts a number of years. For boys, a major problem of maturation is to move away from this intimacy; for girls, it is how to adjust to and live with it. For the father, the birth signals an end to physical intimacy with the wife for several years, the nursing period, because of the post-partum sex taboo. The wife shifts her physical attachment from husband to child for two to three years, and then back again to the husband, though sharing it with the growing child, repeating the process again and again in her fertile years.

When the infant is born the women attending the mother shout "*okokoroko,*" which appears to have no specific meaning other than as a signal, and then they ululate. This is followed by "*oooooo*" and then by certain phrases. If it is a boy they may call out "*onyokem*" (person-boundary*-my) and if it is a girl "*onyinyum*" (daughter-my) or "*nde nyum*" (person-female). These gender indicators may be preceded by a phrase, "*iro bie kele naow naicha*" (enemy-come-greet-morning good morning), which states that everyone, whether enemy or friend, must greet the one who is born. The phrase implies that even enemies of the mother (most likely hostile co-wives) should act in a friendly and supportive manner at this time. People wait to hear these first shouts to know whether it is a boy or a girl. Individuals,

---

*That is, someone who will become a member of the compound for life, and will form a section with others.

especially women, come to the compound where the child has been born to hear this; even at birth gender is important.

The shouts are repeated intermittently during the day. Interested women from the compound rub themselves with white chalk and some of them form a singing and dancing group. They play about the compounds and visit the wife's mother and sisters in other sections of the village and other communities of Afikpo to announce the event, shouting the birth phrases and singing humorous songs and phrases. Female relatives and female friends of the mother and the wife's sisters join the women's group for a while. Friends and relatives of the wife give presents of small sums of money to the singers, who divide this among themselves and buy native salt with their shares, much valued at Afikpo for use in foods and also as a sign of wealth. In the past it was also sometimes used as money. And, traditionally, when two persons end a dispute with one another they were expected ritually to eat salt together as a sign of peace. After a birth, salt symbolizes prosperity through having borne an infant, and the hope for peaceful relationships in its life.

The songs reflect the status change of the parents. The women sing, "If your father sends you to do work for him, do it!" or substitute the word "mother" for "father." Again they sing, "If a woman is under nursing and the soup does not taste, then you know that she has no firewood," that is, she cannot boil it well for she is not in a position to obtain the wood, as she has just given birth. Or they may ring out, "If a woman gives birth she does not think again, all the thinking goes back," i.e., all her concerns focus on the child. When Ogeri had her first child women sang that she resembled her mother, who also only had one child. When Ogeri had a second child, after some years and much difficulty, her mother came and sang this refrain as a happy joke—a way of reminding people that this was really the second child.

The father acts in a different style. As an Afikpo man said of his son, "From the moment that it is born you have to do something for it." When the father's first child is about to be born he procures yams and dried fish; these he presents to his wife's helpers after the birth. They cook them and the compound women and female visitors have a feast—men do not take part. The husband also pays the midwife and gives small presents of money, native gin, and palm wine to those who helped his spouse and to those who sing. He rubs his face and neck with white chalk to show his pleasure and shoots off a gun to announce the event to the village. The gift giving and use of chalk are optional, depending on how he feels.

In most Afikpo villages the father, after the birth of a son, places a bunch of ripe palm kernels and another of unripe ones in front of the main village rest house or his ward rest house. The men sitting there munch on both types of fruit as they desire; these are delicacies at Afikpo. This announces the event to the male adults of the village, and symbolically to the adult secret society and its spirit, for these men's houses are associated with this organization. The birth of a son is thus proclaimed to the male world. In many Afikpo compounds when a girl is born the father places bunches of kernels at the wife's house for the women to eat, to thank them for their assistance, proclaiming to the female world that a daughter has appeared. But there is no women's meeting house, and for a girl no kernels are placed at the men's house. As one man put it, "What is the use of calling the birth of a daughter to the attention of the men's house? She will never have anything to do with it, she will never be able to join the secret society."

These events are characterized by a separation of the sexes, yet both are involved—a deep-rooted ritual pattern at Afikpo. And they show how the father commences his duties for the child. These lead to praise of him if well done; if not, he will be ridiculed by friends and agnatic kin.

The theme of whiteness pervades these events. There is the white chalk put on the baby's body, on the female singers, and on the father, and the salt is white. Milk, fertility, wealth, and hope for good health and peace are all symbolized, counterbalancing the dangers of birth and infancy. The joy of the parents and others expresses the hope that the difficulties are past, that the mother will not die, that the child has not been born dead or sickly and will survive.

There are also the dangers of "unnatural" births. Impure children must be done away with. As late as the 1950s, children born feet first, twins, and other multiple births (but not albinos or children with body defects) were taken to the "bad bush" (ɔtoto ɛja), a burial ground just outside the village, and left there in clay pots to die. (Women who died in labor or within four days of childbirth were also placed in this bush, instead of being buried in the floor of their homes, as in "normal" deaths.) There was no announcement or singing, but a strange quiet pervaded the village, for the birth was seen as a terrible abomination, a sign of spiritual unrest, directed against the mother. The husband was informed, and others came to know of the matter, though it was not discussed publicly. A complex and expensive purification sacrifice, *ɔhoha ekwu ukwɔ* (squeeze-leaf) was performed, paid for by the husband, who took part in the rites. The mother was isolated for seven Igbo weeks (twenty-eight days) and kept in a special hut away from the village; there she was cared for by women who had passed the menopause, whose childbearing capacity would therefore not be affected by contact with her. No male, not even her husband, was allowed to visit her. Her home was torn down and destroyed, and ever after she was viewed as impure. She could no longer sacrifice directly at any group shrine, though others could perform sacrifices for her. The woman returned to her husband after her period of isolation, but her relationships in her compound and village were never the same, even if she later bore other children.

Modern "progressives" succeeded, in the 1950s and 1960s, in ending the killing of such children and reducing the punishment of the mothers. By the 1960s, such women were merely confined to their own homes, often for a shorter period of time. Yet even today shrine priests are afraid to touch such women; this would contaminate them, and they believe that they will suffer, die, or become unable to help others. Priests of important shrines are reluctant even to go to market, where they might unknowingly have contact with this type of person. It is believed that such a woman may affect other females of childbearing age; women in her compound may refuse to fire pots with her or cooperate in other activities. She may not carry mud for house-building, and she does not prepare food for general groups, in case a priest or diviner eats part of it. There are other restrictions and forms of isolation as well.

The father faces no restrictions or punishments; in matters of unnatural births, children born dead, or deformed children, it is the woman who is thought to be at fault. It is a fundamental Afikpo belief that misfortune is caused by improper behavior, and unusual births are attributed to the breaking of taboos or customary rules on the woman's part. The father is not generally blamed, certainly not at first. The belief concerning birth defects reflects gender distinctions in relation to misfortune. The woman at Afikpo is not only blamed for unnatural and other unfortunate births, but if she fails to conceive the onus for a long time will be placed on her. A man may have a number of wives who do not produce children and yet Afikpo men will blame the women and demand that they take ritual steps to purify themselves. Only after a long while will the husband and others accept the fact that he may be the source of the difficulty. These ideas suggest that the primary role in molding the child in pregnancy is the woman's, and the man is less involved. The woman is not simply a passive receptacle for the spontaneous growth of the child created by her and her husband.

Unnatural birth is not a subject which is openly discussed, except by those who work to reform the system of infanticide and punishment. I once abruptly stopped all conversation in a village men's rest house in Mgbom by mentioning twins. They are referred to indirectly by the term *agbolo ozɔ* (miss-road), those who miss the main way. An important feature of Afikpo culture is a strong sense of the right way, the right order in which things should be done. Afikpo life is a progression of rituals and actions carried out in proper sequence. They are not highly rigid individuals; as we shall see, there are also avenues of choice. But they have a deep sense of correctness and of order.

The Afikpo explain their attitude toward twins by saying that the mother will have only enough milk to nurse one child, but this does not account for the intensity of the response to twins. Afikpo ideas about twins imply that their very existence will lead to tension between them; it may be that in a highly age-graded society such as Afikpo the presence of two persons vying for the same age position—especially of the same sex and from the same parents—suggests too much conflict; there is the psychological consideration, similarly, that sibling rivalry between twins is likely to be intense, with two persons fighting over the same role in the family. Even this explanation, however, does not account for the killing of both twins. Although the Afikpo never expressed to me directly the idea that twins and other unusual births are in the realm of the animal rather than the human, I am not certain that this view is entirely absent. Uchendu (1965:58) remarks on its presence for Igbo culture in general.*

Whatever the explanation, the idea of a female contaminated from

---

*There are some children living at Afikpo now who are twins or who were born feet first. To my knowledge, none of the coming-out rites (described below) were performed for these children.

"unnatural" birth is also linked to menstruation, when women are restricted from association with religious figures, shrines and sacrifices. These features add to a sense of the difference between men and women. Women are dangerous, or potentially dangerous and non-harmonious, because of their physiology and their breaking of social rules, while men are dangerous because of their violence, selfishness, and greed.

Given the considerable chance at Afikpo of a stillborn or "deviant" birth, and of a sickly child, is it any wonder that a normal infant is greeted with joy, song, and public announcement? Yet the first four days of the child's life is a liminal period. The mother and baby are excluded from society at large. The child as yet has no public name. The four-day week itself has ritual associations; these days are referred to and marked with four white parallel chalk lines at certain sacrifices. The week is a unit of ritual as well as social time.* The period of seclusion is said to protect the child so that it will grow strong; it must not be too soon exposed to society.

Coming Out

Four days after a birth the mother and child come out.† The male child is not again so fully isolated until he has his secret society initiation, usually in his adolescence, when he is separated from others for a period of from a day to a number of months. The first seclusion is in a female world, with the father as outsider, the second in a male environment, with the mother external to it. And there is also a kind of coming-out rite in all male initiations, when the boys first masquerade, which has analogies to the infant's coming out. Such similarities suggest a strong connection between birth and initiation. The time between these two isolations marks the transition from being mother's boy to father's son, a period of a growing relationship with the father and a lessening one with the mother. It is the time when the son develops a distanced air toward females, learns how to create and to keep secrets, and becomes strongly in-

---

*As we shall see, four is an important symbolic number at Afikpo. However, it does not seem to be particularly associated with males, nor is the number three particularly associated with females, as in some other West African societies.

†In other Igbo areas the seclusion period is longer (see Henderson and Henderson 1966:20; Shelton 1969:237; Okafor-Omali 1965:44).

volved with male age mates in peer-group relationships. But in infancy the ties with the mother are very strong.

For a girl there is no secret society initiation, but in former days there was a time in her early adolescence, shortly before her marriage, known as the "fattening period," when she remained in a largely female world, eating well, doing no work, and preparing for marriage. In the period between birth and fattening, daughters largely remain female centered; the father is a distant figure compared to the mother.

The father is responsible for the child's coming out, but if he is away from home a brother directs it for him. Men call the event *itayi osi* (chew-pepper), which refers to the pepper given the male child. Women call it *ekwɔ ɛka* (wash-hand), for it marks the end of the mother's confinement, when she washes and emerges from her home. The rite has three parts. In the first, the father, in the early morning, provides his wives (but not usually the child's mother) and other compound women with yams to cook for the feast. The food is then molded into fufu balls by one or more male patrilineal relatives of the child, while the compound women who have cooked, and other interested females of the compound, gather together and perform a rite, alike for boys and girls. A knowledgeable old woman of the compound usually leads this for all children born there. An oval wooden tray, *ɔkwa mgbɔ* (tray-cutting), with a handle and a raised flat surface near its center for cutting on, is produced. Chalk and water are put in it, along with kola tree leaves and a special leaf for a male child (*ɔborɔta nwoke,* name of leaf–male), or another leaf for a female (*ɔborɔta nwanyi,* name of leaf–female). The old woman soaks and squishes the ingredients; the mother takes off her upper cloth and this elder rubs the mother's waist with the mixture, saying that it should be cool (her waist should not pain her). "We rub this chalk for your betterness," she may say. Then she smears the mother's breasts, face and forehead in a like manner. The female elder and other women present do the same to themselves for health and sometimes for fertility—so do any adult women (but not girls or males) who enter the house on that day. The women are then fed the yam fufu and fish by the husband to thank them.

This is a ritual reentry into the world for the mother. The rite asks for health and strength for her and for the other females present. The white chalk stands for blessing and welfare, as we have seen, and for fertility. The kola is for greeting; the special leaf refers to the child and is medicinal. The coming out for the mother suggests her return from her liminal state to everyday compound relationships, including co-wife hostilities and jealousies.

Now the second part of the rite begins. For a male child the father calls together the adult men of his compound, especially the elders, in front of his wife's home. These men are usually agnatically related; they belong to a single major patrilineage (S. Ottenberg 1968a: Chap. 2). Although at Afikpo there is double unilineal descent, matrilineal relatives from outside of the compound do not arrive to take part in or to witness the event. They are absent at many rituals for a growing boy or girl. However, the mother is often present at this rite. The eldest male in the group, or perhaps the priest of the patrilineal ancestral shrine, sits down on a stool, placing the boy in his lap. He takes the traditional yam knife, *mma ji* (knife-yam), which seldom is used today, and touches it to the child's right hand near its handle. He may say, "Here comes *mma ji*. Whenever you grow up and plant yams let them be better." Yams are the major male crop at Afikpo, a status food, and symbolic of the penis. Then he takes up a number of other items, the order and type of which vary, depending to a large extent on what is at hand. One of these, *ɔpia,* is an ancient form of knife used in bush clearing and in warfare. He touches this also to the boy's right hand and says, "Here is your *ɔpia* for clearing the bush. If you go out to the field let your right hand be up. Let you be the first man to cut" (i.e., the first to take a head in warfare). He speaks similarly using another knife, *mpama,* employed in bush clearing and fighting, and also *arua,* a thin three-foot-long spear of iron or of iron and wood. The tools are touched to the right hand, for Afikpo is a right-handed society; children who favor the left are trained out of it. The right hand symbolizes strength and endeavor.

Then the man takes up *agbo,* the fiber belt used in climbing palm trees to reach the fruits and to tap for wine, and he touches it to the child saying, "Here is *agbo* for you to grow up and climb with. Any palm tree that you climb, you will not fall from it." Only males climb trees at Afikpo. Then taking hot pepper he chews it in his mouth with dried fish and yam, which are popular traditional Afikpo foods. Then he touches a bit of this mixture to the child's lips, which may make him grimace and cry. Pepper, a favorite condiment at Afikpo, is given at shrines to "wake up" their spirits and to get them active. Here it is employed to "wake up" the child, to make him lively. The yam and fish are the first he has tasted; they are popular traditional

Afikpo foods. Sometimes a whole yam is touched to the child's hands to "show it" to him. Cassava is never used although commonly grown at Afikpo; it is considered too recent in origin and it is a women's crop. In the Afikpo fishing villages of Ozizza the handle of a canoe paddle (*apopa*) is employed instead of yam.

In this rite the symbolism is simple, direct, and instrumental, befitting an infant. Maleness, adult activity, and strength are stressed. Strong aggressive tools are employed. Iron is valued for its durability and strength, qualities hoped for in males. Iron objects are produced only by men.

Then the elder in charge prays for long life for the child, a common request at many Afikpo rites. He takes water (representing palm wine) in a calabash and pours it on the slanting roof of a nearby house, touching the calabash to the child's feet and then to the ground. This is done four times, to represent the four days of the Igbo week. I was told that the upward thrust of the calabash is to make him fearless and unafraid of heights and that the touching of water to the roof refers to rain and wetness, which the child is then symbolically experiencing. Water is also what makes the crops grow, of course. The ground, *ale,* is what the newborn child first touches when born, a sacred, spiritual element at Afikpo associated with the growth of crops, human fertility, and other matters. The actions with the calabash refer to the opposing qualities of the creator god, *Chukwu,* and the ground spirit, *ale.* The former is male, "high up," the world creator; the latter is female, "down," and directly concerned with sexuality and fertility. Men say that males "go high" in status at Afikpo and that women do not. The boy is now ritually associated with both spirits—the first of many that he will meet as he matures.

This male ritual stresses connections with the past, for the tools employed (except for the climbing rope) are obsolete in everyday life, and fighting and warfare are events of yore. Yet the rite stresses important contemporary male values, including physical ability and skill. It also is associated with yams, a male crop; roofs, which are made and repaired by males; and palm tree products procured only by males. Females are forbidden to climb up roofs or trees. (The reasons given vary; it is not women's work, or one should not see their sexual organs.)

Now the mother takes the male infant away and the third and last part of the rite commences. The father feasts the adult males of the patrilineage, particularly its elders, with yam fufu, fish, palm wine, and sometimes native gin. A portion of yams is given to the boys of the compound as yet not initiated into the adult secret society to eat as a separate group; they do not normally eat with adults in public. The last of the wine is poured on the ground for the patrilineal ancestors by an elder, who says a blessing. In one instance he told the father that good things should come his way, that he should live long with his son, and that his wife should have seven issues (an ideal number for an Afikpo woman and often referred to in sacrifice). Then he prayed that "the boy will follow Tom [the father] and not miss following him," that is, that the father should die before the son, and not the reverse—another expression of the sense of the proper order of development at Afikpo. This feast and prayer symbolically bring the newborn son into his agnatic group.

Thus the coming out of a boy stresses thoroughly male elements rather than things common to both sexes or to early childhood. The separation of the sexes and the marked differences between boys and girls is symbolized by this rite. Of course, one could not say that the boy is aware of what is going on, but clearly the ceremony states male values to others taking part.

A girl's coming out is shorter and simpler. The wife and compound women feast on yam and sometimes fish given by the husband, but often there is no palm wine. The mother squats or sits and holds the child while the oldest female in the compound takes a bit of yam fufu, touches it to the child's chest and throws it out, perhaps saying: "This is your food so that you will eat when you grow up." This is done four times. Then she touches the head, face, and waist of the mother with white chalk to bless her, again four times. The four days of the week are referred to here, giving a sense of completeness, of wholeness. Then, sometimes, a pot or other cooking utensil is touched to the infant girl to "show" it to her.

The differences in the complexity of the coming-out ceremonies, in food served, in ritual acts, and in statements made, reflect the greater control of males of Afikpo ritual life, and the lesser status of women as traditional Afikpo men view the matter. As at the time of birth, adults of each sex largely carry out their activities apart.

Later on during the day, or on a subsequent one, a sacrifice is made at the fertility shrine, *nsi omɔmɔ* (spirit–give birth), to thank its spirit for the successful appearance of the boy or the girl and to ensure its continued health. This major agnatic shrine in the compound, with its own priest, generally an elder of the group, is employed by both men and women to ensure fertility (S. Ottenberg 1968:68–69) and for children's health. In this sacrifice the mother and child are absent; the priest represents them. He brings two bowls of soup with dried fish in it and two calabashes of yam fufu. Taking hot pepper and a certain leaf, *ngwu*, in his mouth he chews them and spits them on the shrine pot to "wake up the spirits." *Ngwu* is associated with general welfare and the growth of social groups at Afikpo. Then he circles the pot rim with white chalk or places four chalk marks on it, for the days of the week, and gives the blessing. In one case he said, "Here is the chalk for you to rub. The wife of Ibe gave birth. Today is the day he [Ibe] performed the ceremony of birth. Therefore we want you to follow her and rub your own chalk [on her]. Let her live in peace." Then he threw a chalk stick into the pot, as a fertility symbol, followed by several bits of yam fufu dipped in the soup, a bit of fish from the soup, and water to represent wine (see S. Ottenberg 1968a: fig. 5). Meanwhile he said something like, "Here is fufu for the newborn child. This is your own food, they [the parents and relatives] have taken their own." One bowl of soup and fufu was given to girls and women who were about the compound; the other was for boys and men. In both cases it was mainly children who devoured the food, but any passing person was welcome to take some, thus participating in the blessing.

The sacrifice serves multiple purposes. It thanks the spirit for helping to produce a new child, blesses the mother and ensures that she will have more children, and keeps the newborn healthy. The living and the spirit world eat together in this rite, as people do who are at peace with one another. The rite is the same regardless of the baby's sex. No distinction is made except in the manner in which some of the shrines are divided. Sometimes the shrine, which consists of one or more pots, has a "male side" and a "female side"; if so, the priest uses the side which corresponds to the child's sex, though he may also throw a bit of food into the bowl representing the other sex, so that its spirit will not feel neglected. There is a sense of good wishes for all children, regardless of gender.

On this day, or a few days after the coming out, the woman's mother and her full siblings each bring her presents, perhaps a large dried fish and some yams, to greet her for bearing a child. This is called *ɔgba okoreeko* (run-cry or run-shout for a new child).

The birth rites introduce key spiritual elements in the future child's life: the spirit of the ground, so important in human and crop fertility; its counterpart in the sky, who created the world; the ancestors, who are believed to have much to do with the health and welfare of those living in the compound; and the human fertility spirit. While these are not by any means the only key spiritual forces at Afikpo they are fundamental ones. They form a web of protection for the growing child. But the child learns as he matures that they can also turn against an individual if he violates rules associated with them, and even if others close to him violate these rules. These spiritual projections of human, largely parental, authority thus have an ambiguous quality to them, perhaps reflecting attitudes toward parents. The ancestors are believed to look as they did at the time of death, only healthy in appearance. The other spirit beings at Afikpo take no particular shape or form and are vaguely "around," or at their shrines.

These coming-out rites spell out both the gender distinctiveness of the newborn and their unity as infants. The compound and its patrilineage looms large, as it does in the daily life of the child. Fertility is a major theme. There is no secrecy in these coming-out rituals, no hidden aspects; the events are open, publicly proclaiming the existence of a new human. But until the child is about five years of age it is little talked about, especially to strangers, for there is a rational fear of its death, especially through the action of strangers (in former times outsiders kidnapped children and sold them into slavery). Infants do not appear in the genealogies of the anthropologist. If a child survives to the age of five, perhaps it will live to adulthood. Silence reflects parental anxiety over the child's health and the hope that it will survive. Since misfortune at Afikpo is often attributed to women breaking rules, the husband is concerned about his wife's behavior; this adds to his anxiety, and certainly to hers if she has violated any taboos.

Names and Childhood Terms

There is no ritualized naming ceremony at Afikpo for the newborn. Either the parents announce at the coming-out rites what the two names are, or nothing is made of it, though if a first son or daughter is given a special name the father usually states this at the coming out and he may explain why. For example, he may choose the first name *Chukwu* (God), given to thank God for successful birth after years of failure, suggesting that the creator god plays a role in reproduction. This is a name commonly given to boys at Afikpo. Or the child may be named in honor of a friend of the parents, or some special event that occurred at the time of birth. In any case, the two names provide the child with its particular identity, so that it is appropriate that they be made public at the coming out. Except for the occasional later use of nicknames, such as *Enwe* (monkey) and *Onye ocha* (white person, for someone who behaves like whites), the names follow the child throughout his or her life; marriage does not alter them.

The parents have considerable freedom to name their children, though the names, especially the first of the two, are generally sex specific—one more feature that makes for gender identity at Afikpo. The parents of the mother and father expect not to be entirely neglected in the naming of their grandchildren. There are general rules as to which parent names which child, which come down to a general equality for the parents, with a slight edge for the father, and there is cross-gender activity, as the mother names some sons, the father some daughters.

Children may be named after either living or dead persons—that is, for living kin and for close ancestors, who both still play important roles in the life of the living. The first name a man gives to his first son is generally his father's father's first name and the second name his father's first name, stressing the agnatic line. For the first daughter of a woman the first name is that of her father's mother, and the second that of her father's father, joining both uterine and agnatic lines. Thereafter, odd-numbered sons of a wife are named by her husband, even-numbered ones by the wife, although the rule is not always followed. The wife names her second daughter and thereafter the father, if he wishes, chooses the names of the wife's odd-numbered daughters, and the wife does so for the rest of her girls. If a father is a strongly assertive person, however, he may select most of his children's names, especially his sons'. The child is not expected to develop any special relationship to its namesakes.

After the first son is born its father is no longer addressed by his first and/or second name, for teknonymy occurs; he is called "father of ——," as in *"Nna Oko,"* and his wife "mother of ——," for example, *"Nne Oko."* When the first daughter is born a similar situation applies, for example, the phrases *"Nna Ogeri"* and *"Nne Ogeri"* are employed in addressing father and mother respectively. Later on the names of their other children may be employed but the tendency is to call a father by reference to his first son and the mother her first daughter, reflecting gender differences and the importance of the first children. Teknonymy underscores the significance of having children. Never to be called "*Nna* ——" or "*Nne* ——" is to have failed as an adult.

The first son, and to a certain extent the first daughter, are objects of great interest and concern to their parents. Much is made of them; their illnesses are a cause of worry and their successes of jubilation. The relationship between a father and his first son, and between a mother and her first daughter, is particularly intense; this division stresses the sex roles. Thus naming gives a child an individual identity, while at the same time indicating his or her place in the family and reinforcing the child's connection with older generations and ancestors.

Terms referring to children reflect both their physical maturation and their social position relative to the (older) speaker. For example, *nwa* means an infant or child of any age, but a mother may use it when addressing her own adult son or daughter. The term for a nursing baby, *ngerere*, corresponds roughly to the first stage of childhood growth, but it is also used idiomatically, drawing on its literal meaning, "little" or "helpless." A common Afikpo expression, "Are you helpless?" uses the same word, and the expression "*ibugughu ngerere*" (you are not a nursing baby) conveys the message "You can do it."

While speakers do not always use these terms to refer to the specific divisions of childhood listed here, the terms nonetheless indicate which features are seen as important at Afikpo. A nursing baby who is not yet locomotive is *nwa ohuhu* (baby-new). When it starts sitting up it is *ino odu* (be-sit), perhaps three or four months old. At about seven or eight months it becomes *igbe igbe* (crawl-crawl), and a little later *iguzo mpe* (stand-up), as it begins to walk in wobbly fashion. When it gets its teeth it is *ifuteleze* (grow teeth). When it is about one year old it is *ijije* (able to walk) and a little later *igba ɔso* (fire-gun), when it runs and moves well, meaning that it is now capable of being assertive.

These terms represent physical stages in the two-year nursing period, well recognized at Afikpo. They do not distinguish the sex of the infant, perhaps because all infants are handled pretty much alike by parents; their sex does not determine the care they receive. *Nwa nwoke* (child-male) and *nwa nwanyi* (child-female) may be used for nursing children, or older ones. *Nwantakeɾɛ nwoke* (small child–male) and *nwantakeɾɛ nwanyi* (small child–female) are often employed for children beyond the nursing stage up into adolescence, although *nwantakeɾɛ*, like *nwa*, is also a relative term suggesting the speaker's age seniority. There is no word for childhood. It is referred to indirectly, for example by *"mgbe mburu nwantakeɾɛ,"* meaning "At the time I was a child," or in plural form, *"mgbe mburu umuruma,"* "When I was one of the children."

Is there a concept of childhood at Afikpo? Ariès (1962) raises the question for medieval Europe, where he claims it was absent. But at Afikpo early life is clearly distinguished from adulthood, with initiation serving as the point of demarcation for boys, and marriage for girls. Despite the lack of a specific term, there is definitely an Afikpo concept of childhood as a period when one is dependent on family, unknowledgeable, sexually immature, and lacking a full sense of social responsibility.

Nursing

The Afikpo say that a mother should breast-feed a child for two to two-and-a-half years. She is expected to abstain from sexual relations during this period—a rule which in practice is sometimes broken after a time. The abstinence is said to allow the mother to give her baby full attention, without the interference of a pregnancy and another child to feed. Some Afikpo believe that if a mother has sex while nursing her milk will dry up (cf. Henderson and Henderson 1966:20; Uka 1966:44–47). Infancy is ideally a long, close, warm, and nurturing period, during which an intensely strong mother-infant relationship develops, with the father in the background. This is consistent with the view that two sons of the same parents should be born at least three years apart. Sons of the same parents are not permitted to belong to the same age set, and since the age sets are of roughly three-year span (S. Ottenberg 1971), this "proper pattern" of births not only permits the mother to recuperate between babies (Stephens 1962:4) but also integrates smoothly with the village age organization.

ɔmɔgɔ, or nursing, is a critical time for the mother (*nne ɔmɔgɔ*). No one blames her for not doing things she would otherwise do, as she is with her child; this contrasts strikingly with her pregnancy period. She carries the baby in cloth at her side or back. She does not go often to market. She nurses the child on demand and comforts it when it cries. She leaves it only briefly. The Afikpo have an expression, *"Mie ye ka nne ɔmɔgɔ"* (Do it as fast as a nursing mother), which expresses the shortness of time that the mother is away from the infant.

The physical contact of mother and child is considerable. The mother carries the baby a lot, nurses it a good deal, and they sleep together in her home, generally in body contact, or at least on the same bed. The father sleeps in his house. My observations indicate that mothers are playful with their infants and rarely scold them, that they enjoy them greatly. When a child cries its mother will usually pick it up to appease it; if she is not there another person will do so. Mothers seem to treat their infant children alike regardless of their sex. It is a golden age for mother and child, a period of liminality from the usual demands of everyday life for the mother.

The nursing period, with its post-partum sex taboo, acts as a cultural mechanism for reducing potential conflict on the mother's part between her emotional interests in her husband and her child. It may be that the long weaning and nursing period actually turns the mother's sexual interest to the child, who becomes a sexual object for her, and that she unconsciously seduces the infant in handling it, perhaps arousing the childs' own sexual interests and focusing them on the mother. However, it may simply be that the mother puts aside her sexual needs during the nursing period, as Parin, Morgenthaler, and Parin-Matthey (1980:153) suggest for the Anyi of the Ivory Coast.

The Afikpo claim that the long nursing period prevents sickness and the death of the child. In one Afikpo village in 1952–53 about half of the children born died within a year; the childhood mortality rate is assuredly high there, as it has been in other Igbo areas (Basden 1938:180, 200). Though the Afikpo attribute much of this misfortune to supernatural forces, J. M. Whiting (1964) sees a connection between poor diet in tropical areas, the avoidance of pregnancy during nursing (post-partum sex taboo) to prevent loss of a good milk supply, and polygyny (the husband seeks another spouse for sexual pleasure and to continue procreating). An inadequate protein diet occurs at Afikpo and may be related to long-term breast-feeding. In any case, breast-feeding is a protective measure against certain illnesses—malaria, dysentery and other intestinal diseases, pneumonia, and so on—problems to which poor diet contributes. At Afikpo the strong desire to protect infants is expressly related to the long nursing period and the post-partum sex taboo—prime conditions for the growth of the Oedipus complex (Spiro 1982).

The home of the nursing mother is the first home and the primary place for the child. The mother remains much around the house, and here the child is in a largely female milieu of co-wives, daughters, and friends of the mother, with only occasional intrusions of her husband and other sons, unless she has another small boy. Her husband, who lives nearby or next door, visits her in or outside her house, and fondles and plays with the infant; men often delight in doing this. This may also occur at his home when she brings him his food or comes to visit. But the father's contacts with the child are limited and he is an outsider in a largely feminine world, having to look elsewhere for sexual pleasure and physical affection—either to his other wives, if he has any, or to the less certain world of other men's wives (dangerous for him), divorced or separated women, and unmarried girls (also of some danger). Since the father too is the product of a long breast-feeding period with close emotional ties to his own mother, the effects of which he has had to struggle to overcome, he must carry ambivalent feelings of love and annoyance for the child, and perhaps its mother. This pattern must occur again and again with husbands and their wives throughout the child-creating years. The effect on the adult male is that he will never have a regularized and very close relationship with any female over time. The mother may miss the sexual excitement and affection of her relationship with her husband, but she has the child to love and to turn her attention to; her affective situation is stable. Of course, both parents share the joy of having made a child, the status that it brings, and the contribution to the descent lines of each. But the impact of the long nursing period, with the isolated father and the strong mother-child relationship, as well as the events that follow the termination of nursing, have dramatic effects on a child and his father.

Teething and Reincarnation

Teething brings physical discomfort, perhaps the first major unhappiness the Afikpo child feels, if it has been fed well and is healthy. Also, now the child can bite the mother's breast and she may, as a consequence, display gentle avoidance behavior. But teething at

Afikpo has other consequences, which are fraught with danger for the parents—particularly the mother—and by extension for the child. These relate to the proper order of physical development and recall the anxieties over improper birth; once again there is a tendency to blame the mother for irregularities.

The appearance of teeth brings spiritual matters to the fore. A child's lower teeth are expected to appear before the upper ones; this is a feature commonly desired in many cultures (Kanner 1935:13–15), and is generally the normal occurrence. The reverse is considered an abomination at Afikpo, requiring a major rite of purification on the part of the parents. Since the irregularity is associated with the ground spirit, *ale,* a complicated sacrifice is made at its compound shrine. The sacrifice is called *isi ɛko ɛsa* (head-wealth-seven). Seven items are sacrificed, including a young tortoise, a small chicken with ruffled feathers, a hairy female goat, a hen, and a cock. The sacrifice is lead only by men of certain Afikpo patrilineages.*

The mother may rub the gums of her baby's lower jaw with salt or some other substance in the belief that this will hasten the growth of the lower teeth. If the uppers appear first, she may conceal this fact until the lower ones are evident. If the incorrect order occurs the mother, not the child, is often suspected of some misbehavior: adultery, or too early sexual contact with the husband or with some other male while nursing. She is not brought to trial in the compound unless there is clear evidence, though the sacrifice is still necessary. Generally no stigma is attached to the child, though in some cases it is said to have done a "bad thing." There are no rites and there is no danger involved when a child loses its deciduous teeth, when it may be referred to as *nwa enwo eze* (child-change-teeth).†

When a child is born it has three spiritual forces in it: a personal spirit and two reincarnated ancestors. The personal spirit is called *owa* in males and *ɛgɛro* in females, and is believed in some vague way—the Afikpo are not very articulate about it—to come from the high god, *Chukwu.* Every newborn child has two ancestral spirits within it, known as *ma.* The Afikpo are not consistent in their ex-

---

*Henderson and Henderson (1966:23) say that Onitsha Igbo feel that a baby that cuts its upper teeth first must be thrown away as this signifies its aggressive intentions. See also Basden 1938:184. Among the Akatta Igbo the wrong order is believed to be caused by an evil spirit (Duru 1980:105–6).

†In a recent paper (S. Ottenberg 1988) I have discussed the significance of teeth on Igbo masks.

planations of how these spirits are chosen for the infant; sometimes it is believed that they choose themselves, that they wish to appear together, particularly in a close relative.

The reincarnators (*ma*) may reincarnate in more than one person at a time, and therefore are not altered in status with the death of any individual. The personal spirit (*owa* or *egero*), however, changes in status during a specific person's lifetime. If a child dies at any age after teething, the personal spirit becomes an ancestral *ma* and can help or hinder the living, especially matrikin of the deceased. If the person dies after reaching sexual maturity, this *ma* can also reincarnate.

Nothing is done about the personal spirit or the two ancestral spirits at the time of birth, but shortly after teething an effort is made to discover who the two reincarnators are and to establish regular ritual contact (through the parents) between the child and these two forces. After the child is weaned and starts walking, ritual connections are also developed with its personal spirit, which will be discussed at the end of this chapter. The child will be increasingly associated with these spirit forms throughout its life, and these actions are part of a gradual process of establishing contact with them. Although the Afikpo discuss these rituals as spiritual responses to physical changes—teething and learning to walk—there is a social aspect as well. Both are responses to new skills and assertiveness in the child; biting and chewing are associated with the ancestral spirits, and walking is associated with the personal spirit. In both cases, increased ability and assertiveness must be guarded by spiritual forces that have parental qualities.

A few weeks or months after the child's lower teeth appear a diviner is consulted—a ritual specialist that the parents select—to discover who is reincarnated in the infant. This is an important matter at Afikpo. The visit may be put off for a while but if the child becomes ill this will be done sooner, because the trouble may be related to one or both of the *ma* of the child. This consultation can even occur before the teeth appear if the child is sick. The usual belief, however, is that since the child can itself become a *ma* if it dies after its teeth have appeared, that it is time to discover who is reborn in it so that these spirits may be ritually approached to protect the infant.

Reincarnation is no simple matter at Afikpo. One reincarnator is said to be from the father's side—it may be from his patrilineal or matrilineal kin, or a friend of one of these. The other is from the mother's side—from the mother's matrilineal relatives, her mother's patrilineal grouping, or a friend of one of these. The ancestral spirits are of the same sex as the child, must be deceased persons, and can enter more than one living individual at a time. (The Afikpo say that full siblings of the same sex never have the same two reincarnators, and only very rarely one of the same. To do so would be to have them appear as the same person, as twins.) One often finds that the first son of a male has his father's father and his mother's father reincarnated in him, and a first daughter of a woman her mother's mother and her father's mother. Other children follow more varied patterns of reincarnation.

The consultation with the diviner, *ɔkuku owa* (tell–personal spirit), is not normally led by the parents, although one or both may attend. The parents ask older relatives of the child to go, for the parents may be too young and not know enough about possible kinship relations to handle the divination properly. Those who consult the diviner tend to be older women, one from the father's side, another the mother's. More than one individual may go from each side.

The child is taken along naked; others who consult wear everyday dress. A calabash neck filled with water (representing palm wine) is carried along, indicating to the diviner that a reincarnation consultation is needed. The neck, the part connecting to the vine or bush, symbolizes the umbilical cord of the infant. The liquid has been poured onto a roof and then collected into the container, suggesting symbolism similar to the water or wine employed in the coming out of the male child—the high god, *Chukwu* is involved. Here, however, this is done regardless of the child's sex. The diviner employs the liquid in his ritual and keeps the calabash neck. He probes possibilities, suggesting places of residence and possible relations, and is guided by the responses of those who consult him, who suggest names of specific individuals and play a role in determining which ancestors are involved. Whether a boy or girl child is brought to the religious specialist, the father's side is divined first. The ritualist also suggests what initial sacrifices should be made by the parents to the two reincarnators to please them. The father usually pays the diviner's fees and provides the items brought to the rite.

There is no necessary connection between reincarnators and personal names; one does not specifically name a child after its reincarnators, or choose its reincarnators from the child's name. Yet there is some relationship. A man's first son often is given one of his father's father's names, as we have seen, and a first daughter one of her mother's mother's names; if these individuals are deceased they are likely reincarnators. The child does not necessarily inherit the personality, illnesses, or troubles of a reincarnated ancestor, although if it has a physical defect, mark, or some mannerism similar to a deceased relative the parent will assume that it is reincarnated from that individual even before consulting a diviner, who may confirm it. The idea that character and behavior are *not* inherited through reincarnation is consistent with Afikpo (and Igbo) conceptions of self, and the strong belief that individuals make their own way and, in a sense, form their own personalities.

When the delegation returns to the child's parents they inform them who the reincarnated spirits are and what sacrifices the diviner has proposed at ancestors' and sometimes other shrines. A parent is often pleased to know that a certain relative has returned in the child; this confirms a sense of unity in human relations. For a male child the father goes to the patrilineal ancestral shrines (*ma obu,* reincarnated spirit–house) of the two male reincarnators and, with the aid of the priest of each, performs the rituals requested by the diviner. One of these shrines is often located in the father's compound (for example, that of the child's father's father) but the other may be elsewhere in the village or village-group, or even in a neighboring Igbo group. This shrine is where rites for this ancestor were performed at his death, usually in the compound where he lived. In the case of a girl it is necessary to locate the *adudɔ* shrines of her female reincarnators (S. Ottenberg 1970:46–47). The shrine is normally established for a newly deceased woman by her eldest daughter at the latter's residence and usually moves with her; since women marry to different parts of Afikpo, and may remarry and move again, the *adudɔ* are widely dispersed. The sacrifice, in this case, is normally the responsibility of the child's mother, although the father usually pays for it.

The reincarnators become the child's important guardian spirits and are sacrificed to at regular feast days, such as the New Yam Festival, as well as when the person suffers misfortune. The Afikpo believe that these ancestors should not be neglected by their "owner" or by his or her parents; they remain important to a person throughout life, and they are able to bring illness and troubles, health and success, and sometimes death, according to how they are treated by their "owner." If a child is sickly after this consultation and does not recover, or if sickness prompted this consultation but was not cured by it, the parents may conclude that the diviner erred and they will seek another one to determine the true reincarnators.

Reincarnation is an internalization of parental control, expressed in spiritual terms. In Afikpo children, and even adults, conceptions of reward and punishment from these guardian spirits parallels views of parental behavior. The Afikpo will attribute success and misfortune to the influence of reincarnators, just as people will thank or blame parents for their assistance, or failure to assist, along life's way. The parents may die, but parental influences stay with a person for life; they live on in symbolic form represented by one reincarnator from the father's side and one from the mother's.

Thus the two reincarnated spirits and the child's personal spirit, *owa* or *ɛgero,* form the oedipal triangle in spirit form: father, mother, and child. The reincarnators are believed to interact with each other only rarely, and they relate to the child separately, not in consort. One may cause trouble while the other remains uninvolved or supportive. Perhaps, in a strictly gender-divided society such as Afikpo, children unconsciously view their parents this way, denying the sexual, conflictual, and other relationships between them which they do not wish to see.

However, if a woman repeatedly loses children at birth or when they are young—not a rare occurrence at Afikpo—this is attributed to conflict between the two ancestral spirits. It is said that one of the two reincarnators does not wish to reincarnate, but prefers to go back to the spirit world (whose exact location is not specified by the Afikpo); if the resisting spirit wins this conflict, the child will die. These beliefs suggest the unconscious idea that a child needs both parents to thrive and grow; rejection by one parent causes conflict with the other parent and misfortune for the child. In such cases, the diviner's task is to placate the dissatisfied spirit so that it will remain; alternatively, he may attempt to drive it away after the child's death, so that it will not return to plague the mother's next child with its ambivalence and another spirit can replace it.

The Personal Spirit

When a boy begins to walk about the compound he starts to visit the house of his patrilineal ancestral shrine, *ma obu* (ancestor-house) (Ottenberg 1968a:46–55). Next to the actual shrine there is a section with mud benches for resting, meeting, and eating. This is open only to males, and here the men relax and talk and discuss lineage business, while females go to the house only to offer sacrifice. Here boys play and nap, but a taboo forbids them to eat at the shrine house, especially items cooked there for sacrifice. When sacrificial food is distributed, care must be taken to whom it is given. At Afikpo sacrifices it is believed that the spirits and the humans eat together, a sign of peace and mutual support. Until a certain ritual has been performed for the boy he is not considered a member of the sacrificial community; he cannot eat with the ancestral spirits.

This rite occurs not long after a boy begins to walk. The rite has been described elsewhere (S. Ottenberg 1970:27–30); only a few salient points are mentioned here. The patrilineal ancestral shrine contains a sacrificial pot for each dead male ancestor of the major patrilineage, the group forming the basis of the compound. A pot is also placed there for the personal spirit, *owa,* of each living male member of this residential group. During this rite for a young boy, a pot is placed for him in the patrilineal ancestral shrine for his own *owa,* the personal spirit. *Owa* is not quite the same as the personal soul (*ci* or *chi*) for both sexes found in other Igbo groups (Meek 1937:55–62; Talbot 1926: Vol. 2, 285–95; R. N. Henderson 1972: Chap. 4). Unlike the *ci, owa* can reincarnate as an ancestral spirit after a person's death, and it is not associated with the idea of predestination. It is a personal guiding spirit for a male, with which he is born. The placing of the pot establishes the boy as a member of his major patrilineage, which is also his father's. It is a key ritual step, symbolizing the transfer of identity of the boy away from the mother and toward the father, and expressing male qualities in the boy.

The rite is carried out by the boy's father and the ancestral shrine priest, who is a senior member of the major patrilineage. The boy is present only for the first part of the rite. A cock is sacrificed and numerous other materials are used. The sacrificial items are put in a special pot which is then placed in the ancestral shrine. The priest advises the ancestors that this is being done and asks for long life for the child. The boy is now the owner of the pot as well as the *owa* spirit. At any time after this the boy and his father can sacrifice to the child's *owa,* on the advice of a diviner or by choice. The owner can do so throughout his life. When the owner dies, if the proper funeral rites are performed the *owa* pot becomes and ancestral spirit pot (*ma*); i.e., the *owa* becomes an ancestral spirit of the deceased and can reincarnate. However, while a male is alive he will not often sacrifice to his *owa*; more often, sacrifices will be made to his ancestors, who are frequently believed to be angry or upset about the actions of patrilineage members, and therefore to cause illness, barrenness, or other troubles to fall upon them.

The greater ritual use of the ancestral pots suggests the greater importance of parental figures throughout life. But the personal spirit is important: it is an aspect of every Afikpo male. It is believed to reside within him, as do his two reincarnated ancestral spirits. (Other ancestral spirits are believed to be external to him.) However, in order to sacrifice to his own *owa* or to one or both of his reincarnated ancestors (*ma*), he must offer the sacrifice externally, at his patrilineal ancestral shrine.

The ritual which establishes a shrine for the boy's *owa* occurs about the time that he begins to move away from the intense early bond with his mother and into a more distant relationship with her, toward his father and toward a world of other boys in the compound, especially boys his own age. The father's role in the *owa* rite guides the son closer to him and to the male world. The mother may have a role in moving her son away from herself; in some Afikpo compounds she must give peanuts to the boys of her son's age, to roast and eat, before he will be allowed to play with them in the ancestral rest house or sit on the benches there.

A girl, too, has a personal spirit which provides her with a direct link to the spirit world. It is called *egero,* and it is for females only; I never heard of an Afikpo male having one. Like *owa,* it is different from the *ci* personal soul that some Igbo groups believe in, but it is not directly linked to the ancestral shrine, although the girl is a member of its major patrilineage, which is interested in her welfare. There is no shrine for the *egero* at the ancestral shrine, but if the girl is ill or has other troubles, her mother can establish an *egero* shrine for her at the side or back of the mother's house, with or without the advice of a diviner. The girl sacrifices there, or her mother or an older female does so for her. When she marries, she moves the shrine to her new home, where she can also establish a married woman's personal shrine for similar purposes (S. Ottenberg 1970:45–46).

While a boy's *owa* shrine marks a degree of independence from his mother, the establishment of *egero* for a girl symbolizes her continuing close contact with her mother and other females. True, as she learns to walk she begins to move away from her mother and siblings and half siblings, to meet and play with other young girls, and to some extent boys, in the compound. But she remains mother-centered in a female milieu until she marries. She does not go to the patrilineal ancestral rest house except when a sacrifice is made there for her if she is ill. Boys, on the other hand, are tied to the patrilineage through their personal spirit and their two reincarnated spirits. In short, boys are linked to the corporate body comprised of living and deceased males, while girls are linked to females and to a personal rather than a group shrine.

The rites of *owa* and *ɛgɛro* symbolize the beginning of strong gender distinction at Afikpo, which has already been presaged in the differing behavior toward male and female children in the coming-out rite four days after birth. In oedipal terms, the actions associated with *owa* and *ɛgɛro* suggest a defense against the attraction of boys to their mothers and girls to their fathers, turning the boys to a male world and girls to a female one. While directing the child toward its proper gender identification, this paradoxically also creates tension with the same-sex parent. We will see that later, during the latency period, boys tend to flee this paternal association, while girls accommodate themselves by identifying with the mother, her home, and her domestic life.

Commentary

The long period from birth to weaning for children of both sexes is characterized by a very strong physical and emotional bond with an extremely nurturing mother. The father is very much in the background during this period, both sexually and in terms of his general behavior and influence, though he visits the child, plays with it, and is ultimately responsible for its welfare and all the rituals performed on its behalf. These features of early life are an important key to understanding the experience of children growing up at Afikpo and the structure and symbolism of adult culture there. For boys, the close, nurturing mother and distant father relate to a pattern which appears in various forms in other cultures (Gilmore 1986; Parsons 1969; Saunders 1981), where problems occur in the separation-individuation of sons from their mothers as they mature, and where there is subsequent male ambivalence toward women in general. With the support of certain cultural institutions, the maturing male child must struggle with the influence of the strong mother-infant bond and the minimal father-infant relationship.

Strong gender distinctions at Afikpo are among the culturally instituted devices which support the boy's struggles for separation, so it is not surprising to find gender differences occurring during the nursing period, though the child cannot be aware of the significance of these. The infant receives its male identity through naming, rituals which are different for females, and the discovery of reincarnators—actions which carry more meaning for the parents at this time than for the child. During this period the mother, in daily interaction with her child, commonly views and treats it simply as a baby, regardless of its sex.

The child is associated with rituals, although hardly cognizant of them: those of birth, the coming out, the reincarnated ancestors, and the personal spirit. By the time of weaning a boy has spiritual associations with the high god *Chukwu,* the earth spirit *ale,* his own two ancestral reincarnators, and his own personal spirit; he is spiritually well protected. He has associations with spirits who are projections of his parental figures (reincarnated ancestors and perhaps also the male high god and the female earth spirit), and with a personal spirit that represents his own ego. All these beings associated with the boy involve controls and taboos; all have superego associations. Similar conditions occur for girls.

At Afikpo there is a strong sense of the proper and correct order of development of persons as natural beings. The child should not be born feet first, or as a twin; his lower teeth should come before his upper ones; weaning should occur after teething and not before; the mother should deny her sexuality during nursing and the father turn his sexual interests elsewhere; and the ancestors reincarnated in the child should be ritually contacted before the child's personal spirit. There is a certain religious fundamentalism to the Afikpo world, which is not unassociated with its achievement orientation. Violations of the proper order can lead to serious consequences which have to be redressed in the spirit world as well as in the human. Of these features some can be controlled and some cannot, some lead to the need for strong spiritual restitution while others do not, but the prevailing sense of proper and orderly development is an important background to the maturation of the child. Proper physical and physiological growth is equated with proper social growth. In adults this pattern continues; improper social behavior angers the spirit world which creates physical misfortune, such as illness, cutting oneself with a machete at the farms, or falling down a tree. Afikpo beliefs strongly associate the human body, social behavior, and the spirit world. This reinforces my view that the Afikpo spirits are projections of human relationships.

Secrecy is a theme that I will stress in this work, but there is very little of it in this early childhood period. Rites for infants are mostly public, as are the child's two names and the names of its two reincarnating spirits. True, undesirable occurrences, physical or social, may be kept secret: a "bad" birth, improper order of teething, or sexual activity on the part of the nursing mother. Secrecy is most evident at the birth itself and in certain rites of that time, from which all males are excluded; this establishes female control, especially through the nursing period. The child spends the first few years of life in a sort of external womb, the mother's home the uterus, her breasts the umbilical cord. The later life of boys is largely an attempt to move away from this experience, and of girls to adjust to it. Boys are supported in this by their fathers and other males, and by the culture of maleness; girls are supported by their mothers and other females, and by female norms and behavior. Secrecy later becomes a device to assist boys in achieving separation from their mothers; since separation is not intended during the first few years, it is understandable that secrecy is not a major issue then. When the time comes, mothers will assist their sons by not clinging to them as they mature, and even by gently pushing them away; fathers aid girls by arranging for their marriages out of the family.

2

Two to Five

MATURATIONAL CHANGES OCCUR IN THE IMMEDIATE post-infancy period of a boy's life. At its beginning he is weaned and he leaves off living with his mother toward its end. In between he is exposed to important events which shape the direction of his person.

Weaning occurs gradually over a period of time, rather than suddenly, sometime after the child is two years old, well after teething. The mother gently forces or entices the child to eat solid food—yam and cassava fufu or cassava meal (*gari*), bits of meat or vegetable. She may also put a bitter substance on her nipples to discourage suckling. Perhaps she wishes to continue nursing, to maintain her close relationship with the child which is sometimes so satisfactory to her, but the husband wants to have sexual relations with her and create another child. Or she may tire of nursing and wish to return to intimacy with the husband. At any rate, she stops nursing and starts coming to her husband's house at night. She does this in rotation with his other sexually available wives, if he has any, each for an Igbo week of four days in turn, the usual arrangement. His home is not far from hers in the compound, but they may be out of sight of one another, separated by other houses. She often brings her baby with her at first, though it may sleep on a different bed. The Afikpo, as well as the Onitsha Igbo, do not believe that it bothers the child to be sleeping in the same room with sexually active parents (Henderson and Henderson 1966:26), but the effect undoubtedly creates oedipal feelings (Spiro 1982:92–95) in the child, who now has to share its mother with another person in intimate fashion, often in darkness. The child may instead stay at home without the mother, cared for by an older female sibling, and suffer the temporary loss of its mother. Either way, the onset of these changes coincides with the withdrawal of the breast.

It would be hard to think of these events as anything but traumatic for the child, although Afikpo do not conceive of them this way, but rather as natural and logical happenings.* These changes mark the beginning of the second stage in the child's life, which terminates at its upper end more distinctly for boys than for girls. It is a time of loose relationships among children, before much organized play is involved, and a period of lessening the intimate mother-child ties for boys. The phase is not marked by a special Afikpo term, although *nwa, nwantakεrε* and *umuruma* can be employed as well as the gender designators *nwoke* and *nwayni* (see pages 19–20). It is the time of the child's first substantial physical and social exploration beyond the mother's home world, when gender roles clearly begin to emerge. Yet the boy still lives and eats at his mother's home; it is his base for exploring the compound, ward, and village.

After the mother has weaned a child she may leave her children during the day to go to the farms or to market. Young children usually do not accompany their mother far from the compound. She places them in the care of a "baby-mother," a woman who is breast-feeding an infant and thus pretty much restricted to staying home. This surrogate mother is often a friend living in the compound. It may be a co-wife, if she is on friendly terms with the mother, but co-wife hostility is endemic at Afikpo and she is more likely not to be (P. Ottenberg 1958). The young child will be with the baby-mother's own children and perhaps still others that she is watching, and will not be at a loss for company. At other times when the mother is busy she puts an older daughter or a son in charge of a young child; young persons at Afikpo are often under the care of older ones. This is usually a friendly and protective relationship. The older child acts as teacher and guide to the younger, sometimes carrying it or leading it about.

Young Afikpo children are very much indulged, a feature which J. M. Whiting (1961:358–59) believes is characteristic of extended and polygynous families. When they cry, a parent, sibling, or other resident of the compound picks them up to pacify them, and if they still cry they may be given food to quiet them. There is a common Afikpo belief, not always followed, that if a child wakes up hungry at night it ought to be fed. Children may be scolded by almost any adult or

---

*For a useful discussion of weaning among the Anyi of the Ivory Coast, see Parin, Morgenthaler, and Parin-Matthey 1980:318–20.

older child, though this is gently done. Children soon learn that any grownup can rebuke them and has authority over them. Thus not only is there a baby-mother or two, and older siblings, in the lives of small children, but, in a sense, all adults are parents. A child is very rarely left alone. As Shelton (1969:239) writes, "The child must follow his mother (or other elder, as the case may be) or he will find himself alone—an extremely unpleasant if not downright horrible condition for the rural Igbo, for aloneness means danger." As parenthood seems easily generalizable to the spirit world at Afikpo, so does it readily spread to other persons. In this way children begin to learn the importance of age differences in respect to authority, which will be so meaningful throughout their lives. Only occasionally, if a father is angry at a child, will he take a whip to its bottom; the mother practically never does this for the father is the ultimate family authority.

Children are indulged out of more than love. The infant's two reincarnated ancestors must be respected, for Afikpo believe that they may withdraw (let the child die) if the child is abused or neglected. And Shelton (1969:237) quotes an Igbo from the Owerri area who suggests that "many parents show an excessive indulgence toward their children on the grounds that they will be dependent upon their children for nourishment and their status both in this world during their old age and in the next world after death." Parents also need children to have status as adults. Afikpo parents are as dependent upon their children as the children are on them.

As in the case of weaning, toilet training is a gradual process, generally nontraumatic, and leads the child from home. At first, a corner outside the house is designated as a spot for the young child to use. A child who goes in the house is spanked on the bottom or back with a cupped hand; this creates more noise than pain. Eventually the children are shown the adults' log-pit latrines in the village, one for men and one for women. Children go in a corner of the latrine at first, for their parents fear that they may fall in the trench if they squat on the log. Gradually they learn to do this.

In psychoanalytic terms this period from two to five encompasses the anal phase of development and goes well into the oedipal stage, when the child first copes with its sexual self, and its sexual feelings toward parents and siblings (Erikson 1963:48–108). Ties to the mother, while not as close as in the nursing period, are still intimate; she still is present a great deal of the time. She carries the child at times, even to the farms, feeds it often and well, and is indulgent of any upset or crying. Yet during this age period, particularly towards its end, she may become pregnant again and bear another child—a further loss to the first child of its motherly attention. The child does not shift its dependency needs to its father (though, if a boy, he is likely to spend time with him during the day, at the father's house or elsewhere within the compound). Rather, as children learn to walk, they begin to explore the compound, often a place of numerous houses and persons (from some fifteen to five hundred people), and to acquire friends of like age of both sexes.

Circumcision and Clitoridectomy

Circumcision (*osise ɔnɔ utu,* cut-mouth-penis) is performed some-time between the time the boy "comes out" (four days after birth) and early adolescence.* It is an Afikpo rule that circumcision must precede adolescent initiation into the adult secret society, but it is not a part of it. In earlier times at Afikpo it was done toward the age of this rite of passage, but since about the 1930s it has been per-formed before the child is more than five years old—previous to, but not necessary for, joining a boys' secret society. It is a simple matter; there is no shrine or sacrifice associated with it. The father is respon-sible, and it is a title (*mɛmɛ*) for him, albeit not a major one. He obtains a specialist, *onye nɛsɛ ɔnɔ utu* (person-cut-mouth-penis), not usually a diviner or herbalist, but a man who picks up gifts and a little money for the work. He is usually a member of an agnatic line with at least one practitioner in each generation.

Circumcision practices vary, but if the boy is young the event is usually held in public outside of his mother's house, where he is living. He will be held by one or more of the father's male friends. The mother is not present, nor need the father be; the Afikpo say that sometimes it makes him feel ill to watch and he absents himself. This may reflect his own castration anxiety; perhaps it is a reminder of his feelings about his own circumcision. Or it may relate to am-bivalent feelings toward the boy (Nunberg 1949:54), of love mixed with dislike for the child who will ultimately replace him in life. The

*In other Igbo areas it is also performed quite early (see Henderson and Henderson 1966:21; Nzimiro 1962:251; Okafor-Omali 1965:43).

father's absence is consistent with his absence from the bush when the boy is initiated into the adult secret society. For the boy the operation identifies him with his father, for he now has a penis similar in appearance, though smaller. But there is also a negative aspect since the boy is aware or soon realizes that it is the father who arranges for the operation (Nunberg 1949:2), with all its castration implications. Circumcision, even in its nonritual form at Afikpo, calls to the boy's attention his own penis, making it important in the eyes of others, and thus also to him (Nunberg 1949:22).

Children are usually shooed away from the event; women are not excluded but they usually do not watch. The circumciser manipulates the penis a bit to make it larger and then pulls forward the foreskin, cutting it off and letting it fall into a small hole in the ground, which is then covered up. There is no special knife and nothing particular is said. The circumciser then rubs medicinal substances on the penis: palm oil, one or more leafy preparations, or kerosene. The boy then returns to his mother. He may be checked every day for a few days by the circumciser to ensure that the cut is healing well. The blood on the ground is washed away with water. The boy may be given a small broom to ward off both chickens and insects. In former times the boy spent four days inside his house and then bathed in a bark and water preparation before emerging again, but this is rarely done today. This was viewed as giving the wound a chance to heal, but it also echoes the isolation of the first four days of life, also in the mother's home. Both are times of physical transition. Isolation also occurs, of course, in adolescent initiation into the adult secret society; this form of separation marks major maturation processes in the boy.

The circumciser is paid a shilling or so (worth about twenty-five U.S. cents in 1960), and is presented with palm wine and yam fufu by the father; he may also be given uncooked yam and dried fish to take home. If the father is wealthy and it pleases him he kills a male goat, giving one leg to the circumciser, and feasts with his family, the helpers, and other compound men. This is called "feeding the child"; although the boy gets some food it is the adults who really eat. If the father does not provide a goat he should at least serve some yam fufu, soup, and wine to these people. Among the northern Afikpo villages of Ozizza the father often feasts his village age set and they sing out in praise of him, for it is pride to the set as well as to the father's patrilineage in the compound to have sons. The words go something like this:

hwɛrɛ hwɛrɛ jao
hwɛrɛ hwɛrɛ jao
[no literal meaning]
ma kawo hwɛrɛ hwɛrɛ jao
and hand [no literal meaning]
ma ukpao hwɛrɛ hwɛrɛ jao
and leg [no literal meaning]
ma isiwo hwɛrɛ hwɛrɛ jao
and head [no literal meaning]

The references are to physical strength and bravery in warfare; the sense of the song is that you should catch anything that you can—the enemy's hand, leg, or head. At a deeper level the song suggests that the father should do whatever he can for his son. Catching and cutting off body parts in warfare is a metaphor for cutting off the foreskin—the boy is symbolically both victim and warrior.

Circumcision is an agnatic matter involving males—the father's patrilineal group and friends and often his village age mates. Women are excluded and matrilineal relatives of either father or son are not involved (unless they are also patrikin, which some will be). If we find the close early mother-son tie at Afikpo, we should also find the other half of the oedipal triangle, a particularly strong, if latent, father-son tension or hostility. This appears to be minimized by the mild circumcision rite, sometimes even with a father absent from the event. As we will see, the father's role in the boy's adolescent initiation is also diffused by his nonappearance in the initiation bush.

Circumcision is vital to the maturation of the male. The boy is not expected to have sexual intercourse before this excision; this is one reason, the Afikpo say, that they like nowadays to circumcise boys at a young age, for boys are believed to be more promiscuous than in former times. Adults say that nowadays it is harder to control the boys' sexual life, and that the operation is less painful if done at an early age. Since the boys are not now preparing for warfare, learning to endure pain is not as important as formerly.*

*I have several records of surviving twins being circumcised, so it is possible to find someone to do this for them. The rationale is that if they are to be permitted to live they must, like all males, have this essential step performed. Possibly this is also done to protect females, who are forbidden to have intercourse with an uncircumcised male.

A violation of the sexual taboo against intercourse before circumcision is a heinous offense to the ground spirit, *ale,* especially that of the boy's compound. In older days an ear of the boy would be cut off, leaving a permanent physical mark, which I interpret to be symbolic castration. Nowadays it is only nicked. In any case the child's father, or father's brother if the father is dead or away, must perform the heavy purification sacrifice of seven items, *isi eko ɛsa,* to the ground spirit at the boy's compound shrine, *ɔma ɛzi.* This is the same sacrifice required in the event of improper order of teething, as mentioned above; in both cases there is a sense of the wrong order of development. This is a standard sacrifice for a number of offenses, especially sexual ones, all of which are considered abominations (*ɔrɔ ale,* wickedness-ground) which dilute the power of something, particularly of land and life. Afikpo also say that in former days if an uncircumcised boy had intercourse and then went to war he would be killed due to weakness. Today this is sometimes said of wrestling—that he will lose—so that circumcision is still associated with a sense of male strength and physical well-being. The age-set songs mentioned above also suggest this.

The association of this ground spirit with circumcision also lies in the burying of the foreskin in the ground. This is a form of sacrifice, a way of informing *ale* of the event. If *ale,* a major female spirit at Afikpo, is also a projection of the mother, the circumcision is a way of indicating to her that the child is now ready for adult sexual experience. If the circumcision is not done any sexuality on the part of the boy is dangerous, for it might be directed towards the mother. In terms of the mother, therefore, the cutting of the foreskin is not as crucial as its being placed in the ground, in the domain of *ale.* But with reference to the father, who organizes the rite, the cutting itself is important, as a symbolic castration which directs the boy's sexual interests away from the family. The male goat killed by the father at the feast following the circumcision also symbolizes the castration. The pain of circumcision for the boy is balanced by the potential force of energy that is released, although he may not have intercourse for years to come.

Circumcision is a necessary prelude both to marriage and in order to enter the village secret society. Marriage for a male usually occurs many years after the start of an active sex life, often in his late twenties. No Afikpo secret society would permit a boy to enter the initation bush uncircumcised; it would be a foolish father who tried to put a son into the society without taking this step. But initiation is not a prerequisite to a boy having sexual intercourse; this is not forbidden by taboo or social custom. Girls, however, are expected to remain virgins until they marry in adolescence.

In former times clitoridectomy (*ubu*—the term is also employed for circumcision) was performed on a girl at early puberty at the house of her future mother-in-law. The operation was done by a skilled woman, in some cases a midwife, employing a locally made knife used only for this purpose. After this the midwife and female friends and relatives were well fed by the girl's future husband and there was singing and dancing by females. The excision was done in private, away from males, and the girl's mother was usually not present, a situation analogous to the male rites. Magical aids were offered the girl to protect her from any harmful effects of the cutting. This was followed by a three-month "fattening" period (the term is used by Afikpo and Igbo), when she lived in the compound of her future mother-in-law and ate well but did little work. She was expected to grow rotund, a sign of beauty and health and potential fertility. She then returned home for a short period, perhaps two or three months, finally going off to live with her husband as his wife.

Nowadays the clitoridectomy is done between infancy and nine years of age, more generally between three and eight (P. Ottenberg 1958:49). This is also the case among the Efik south of Afikpo (Simmons 1960:159). It takes place at the girl's mother's house with the same kind of practitioner as mentioned above and in much the same manner, with magical protection and a feast provided by the mother if there is no betrothed, and a present from her of a large smoked fish. There is also singing and dancing. "Fattening" is almost never practiced and marriage arrangements take a somewhat different form than previously.

The Afikpo offered me little explanation for either the boy's or the girl's excision other than that this was necessary before having intercourse, and that "it is the custom." Some men felt it made females less volatile in behavior and less sexual, i.e., less likely to stray from the husband's bed. It was never said to me that circumcision reduced male sexual feelings or behavior. In both cases the excision is a symbolic castration, initiated by the father for the boy (Reik 1964:105) and by the mother for the girl. In the suggestion that clitoridectomy is done to keep the woman's sexuality under control there is a hint that men are concerned about female sexuality, seeing it as dangerous to men. This is clear in other areas in Afikpo life; for example, a woman's adultery is believed to cause harm to her husband's patrilineage through the action of angered spirits, often ancestral ones. Men at Afikpo feel that they have a problem in keeping women under control, despite living in a largely male-dominated society. This is probably a reflection of the role of the strong, dominant mother in the boy's infancy, although it also appears to have some basis in fact.

If circumcision occurs during the oedipal period, between three and six years of age—when the boy already has unconscious castration fears relating to the father, and when early childhood sexual feelings lie at the surface—then the operation must certainly strike its target. It is not clear what its psychological effect is if done earlier or at a later time during latency. If oedipal feelings are not fully repressed or extinguished by the end of the oedipal phase—as I will later suggest may be true for some Afikpo—the performance of the operation during the latency period may also have a strong impact. In many other West African forest societies, such as the Limba of northern Sierra Leone, where I have carried out research, circumcision occurs as the first part of male initiation, during adolescence. I am not certain why this is not now the case at Afikpo. It suggests an Afikpo desire to minimize conscious antagonism between father and son, and to reduce the impact of adolescent initiation on the son; the father seeks to avoid conscious conflict with his son by having the circumcision done earlier, when it is thought to be less painful, and when the boy is less conscious of his own sexuality vis-à-vis his father.

As in the case of uncircumcised boys, if a girl in former times had sexual relations before her operation this was considered a terrible abomination to the ground spirit, *ale*. If she became pregnant and was unable or unwilling to locate a midwife to help her abort, she had to leave home and endure an unusually severe form of clitoridectomy in the bush, and she was sometimes forced to abort. The house, pots, and other household goods of her mother were destroyed. Her father was responsible for performing a "seven things" ceremony, as in the case of an uncircumcised boy who had intercourse, to ensure that the ground spirit was appeased. The girl was made to live in a special place outside of the village until the birth of her child. Derisive songs were sung about her by other females, sometimes for years. (The songs were still generally known when I did field work). Again we are dealing with an incorrect order of development, and again we see this related to the ground spirit, *ale*. Since girls today have this operation before the onset of menses, this punishment does not occur.

The excision rites thus follow a similar path for each sex, occurring during early puberty in former times, nowadays earlier, with severe punishment for sexual conduct before the operation. Sexual violation involves the same spiritual forces for both sexes. For both, the rite occurs in the absence of members of the opposite sex, and more thoroughly identifies the child involved with its own gender.

The Warrior Ritual

In the nineteenth century, and probably earlier, the Afikpo were a warring people. They fought local small-scale conflicts against their neighbors over land and forests, trade, and women. They raided non-Igbo peoples east of the Cross River. Some Igbo groups fought their way into Afikpo to settle there. The Afikpo were linked to a widespread system of slave trading and military activity by the Aro, an Igbo group south of them, who migrated over much of Igboland (Dike 1956:37–41; S. Ottenberg 1958). Men of Afikpo acted as mercenaries for the Aro, as well as raiding on their own, in order to obtain human heads for prestige purposes. The first to strike a man obtained his head, the second the lower jaw, the third the facial skin. All three were considered to have killed him and all received praise when they returned home. It is said that killing was once a prerequisite to marriage—a matter that I could not verify. On their return from battle the victors carried out a rite, *ɔkwukwɔ iha agha* (face-wash-war) at a village shrine, *ɔbase agha* (god-war), known ritually only to those who had taken a head or killed someone in warfare.

This shrine is no longer employed for this purpose, but it is sacrificed at by male wrestlers before a contest, to ask its spirit for strength and success.

In addition, there are other shrines, usually one for each ward of a village, called *ɔkwanta* or *ɔbase agha* (spirit-war), where young boys carry out a ceremony after killing a bird. This ritual is said to be a childhood version of the older warrior rite. For adults it is a humorous event, and the small boys who do it may be too young to understand it; they may be bewildered by what is going on. Called *ɔgbogba nnɔnɔ* (shoot-birds), it is also known by the term for the head-hunting ritual.

In July or August, when there are plenty of young birds about, the father goes to the bush and brings back a young one from its nest, placing it at the edge of the village for his son to kill. Or an older brother may do this, or an enterprising youth for several boys at once for pennies he will receive from their mothers. Any kind of bird will do. The boys—usually several at a time—are often only three or four years of age, or just a little older. Some of their teeth must have appeared and they must be circumcised; they perform this ritual as a prerequisite to joining the village secret society some years later.

The youngsters are led to the birds by older boys who have performed this rite but are not yet men's secret society initiates. There each youngster in turn is given a small bow and arrow—the bow is about one and a half feet long and of simple design—fashioned by other boys or their fathers. Each lad shoots a bird; he generally misses a couple of times. In fact he may be so young that he cannot hit the target; in this case one of the older boys does this for him, but he is nevertheless said to have done so himself. Then the helpers sing and shout, each "killer" waves the arrow about with his impaled bird, and they all enter the village.

They come to the men's rest house of the ward in which the boy lives (S. Ottenberg 1972). In this structure initiated men of the secret society rest and talk, and greet other people who pass by the commons. Females and boys not yet initiated into the adult secret society are forbidden to greet them first; that would be a direct offense against the secret society, and a flouting of adult male authority. After killing his bird, however, the boy salutes the men sitting in the rest house with a standard Afikpo greeting, often spoken shyly and with hesitation: "*ɔha unuka*" ("people-greetings"). This is humorous to the Afikpo; it is the first time the boy has ever said this to these men there. They answer, "*heh?*" ("Yes?"), and he replies, "I shot once and did not get it, and I shot again and got it!" The boy states this regardless of the ease or difficulty he had in killing and whether he did so himself or not. His claim that he did not kill the bird the first time is to show how difficult it was, as in warfare a man would brag about how difficult it was, though at last he succeeded. The men in the rest house shake his hand in congratulation and also that of the boy who assisted him. After the killing, the boy is allowed to communicate with the men in the rest house, but not to enter this structure; he must be initiated to do so. It is sacred space and objects of the secret society are stored there.

The child's mother, very happy, goes about shouting and dancing and calls other women to join her. If they wish they will put white chalk on their backs, faces, and limbs as a sign of rejoicing. It is a sort of title (*mɛmɛ*), for the boy and both the mother and father are very proud. The mother sings that her son has gone to war and has killed someone. She shouts "*agha muye*" ("war-my") to suggest this. Since more than one boy may perform this killing rite at the same time there is considerable rejoicing by village women on this day. Some of them carry kitchen knives, *mma ekwu* (knife-kitchen), the only form of knife a woman normally uses. The Afikpo say that this suggests that the women too, are ready to fight the enemy, as sometimes occurred in warfare. The mother will give presents of corn and a few pennies to the women of the compound to show her happiness, and some coins to those who sing and dance with her.

After a while the father brings a number of coconuts to the ɔkwanta shrine of his ward and the boy comes with his arrow and bird head and joins him with other boys. A male of the ward who has taken a human head acts as priest; if there is none the son of such a man does so. He opens the bottom of the shrine and pours water into the pot there and he takes the bird's head and ties it to a pole on the inside of this shrine, circular in shape and surrounded with vertical raffia bamboo poles. He also places pieces of red dye prepared from the camwood tree and yellow dye from the bark of another tree, *odo,* in the shrine. Red at Afikpo generally symbolizes blood and aggression, yellow internal body parts and human physiology. These are the same colors used to decorate a warrior who has killed an enemy. The officiator calls out the boy's name and asks the shrine spirit to ensure that he should remain healthy. Four times he dips a hand in the water in the pot and touches it to the boy's face, thus associating the boy with the shrine's spirit. Then he rubs a little camwood and yellow *odo* on the boy's face. If there is more than one lad they are all treated together, rather than one after another. The boys are now fully connected with the spirit of warfare.

As soon as this is done the boys at the shrine scramble for the coconuts their fathers have brought, and carry them away to cut up and eat; these particular ones can only be consumed by boys not yet initiated into the village secret society. The father may also present other coconuts to men sitting in the ward rest house. This sacrifice can be postponed for a few days if the father does not have coconuts on the day his son kills a bird. The Afikpo do not attach any symbolic significance to the coconut; it is simply a gift of food to show that the father is happy. But a coconut, like a human head, is obtained by cutting it off with a knife or machete after some effort—in this case climbing a tree. Coconut is also a popular boy's food.

The Rainy Season Festival (*iko udumini*) occurs every September or October. On ɛkɛ day (market day at Afikpo) of the festival following a boy's bird rite, the boy's father offers food and wine at his ancestral shrine house to the men of his compound in honor of this son. If it is a first son he gives twice as much as for a later one. In one case in Mgbom Village this was, for the first-born male, ten yam fufu balls, two small pots of palm wine, and a shilling (said to be for *ocice*, that is, kola and dried fish, ceremonial food taken when men gather). The palm wine is poured into the very large ceremonial wine pot of the compound, which is likely to fill up since there are often a number of fathers doing this ceremony on this day. Indeed, the fathers are most proud to do so, and if a man desires he may even obtain enough wine to fill up the pot himself. At this time the father greets the compound men. He may announce that he is giving his son a section of farmland, or a small raffia or palm grove, or a coconut tree. On this day the father also feasts his own village age set with much food and drink and sings his son's praises and is merry, for it is a kind of title for him as well as his offspring. He and his age mates sing and dance as at the public events of the lengthy initiation of the eldest son into the secret society. Women are allowed to see and hear all of this but take no part in the events other than to prepare the food—often their lot at Afikpo rites.

Also on this day boys of the village ward about fifteen years of age and younger rebuild the outer raffia bamboo pole edge of the warrior shrine. Those who do this may or may not be secret society members, but they must have completed their own rite. This renews the shrine for a year.

The bird shrine rite stresses concepts of male combativeness and strength. In it the father symbolically encourages the son to prepare for an assertive life. The act of aggression on the part of the "killer" allows him to communicate with, but not yet join, the men of the secret society. The rite separates categories of the young: those who have not done it, those who have but have not joined the adult secret society, and those who are society members. Since the father initiates the rite there is an identification of father and son. The event not only associates the boy with his father but with the major patrilineage to which they both belong, much as putting an *owa* spirit pot in the ancestral shrine did for him at an earlier time. The identification of the boy is extended to the adult men of his ward, establishing the boy's ties beyond the compound, for the village ward is composed of two or more compounds. This process continues through later events in the child's life, to the village and then to the village-group. The boy's contact with the men in the rest house presages his later secret society contacts at initiation; it is a statement to the men sitting there that he exists as an assertive male individual whom they should know will some day be initiated.

The ritual is probably not a reduced substitute for the ancient head-taking rites, for it apparently existed when those occurred. When I asked why the boys' ritual was still carried out today I did not receive the usual sort of reply, which I rather expected, of "it is from former times," but it was suggested to me that strength and physical skills are still important today, and they are indeed. One man even reminded me that Afikpo men go off to modern wars. The rite is also seen as a "test" of strength, necessary before secret society initiation. It has a sexual aspect as well. The bird's head on a stick which the boy carries about can be seen as a phallus; he symbolically exhibits and flaunts his sexuality before the elders. Later, wrapped up, it resembles a circumcised penis, a symbolic replaying of the earlier circumcision rite. Since the boys are so small as to hardly know what is going on, the symbolism is really for the benefit of older onlookers. In this rite three of the four basic Afikpo colors appear: white (on the dancing and singing women) and red and yellow (on the boys and in the shrine). These three colors (along with black) are also prominent in secret society masquerades. Finally, while this is primarily a male rite, and I know of no equivalent female event, the mother and her female friends play a rejoicing role, as they do in the secret society initiation and other rituals. The carrying of knives by women at this event also connects them with the boy; the women are symbolically stating that they too are warriors, are capable of killing, and that they support the boys' move to a male poise. Thus the mothers identify with the boys whom they help to move away from themselves, toward their maleness.

Boys' Houses

In each of the nearly two hundred compounds in Afikpo there are one or more *ulote,* houses where boys and young men sleep at night, both those initiated into the adult secret society and those who are not yet members. It is only in their mid- or late twenties, generally by the time they marry, that men obtain their own homes. In some Igbo areas the *ulote* are special structures in form as well as use, located in the family compound, but at Afikpo these are ordinary houses, not needed as family residences, that have been turned over to the young males. There is sometimes one for initiated but unmarried males and another for uninitiated ones. Initiated males prefer this as they can then discuss secret society matters freely.

An *ulote* is usually owned and looked after by its builder or by a patrilineal relative, perhaps his eldest son, who lives nearby. The owner can turn the structure back into a regular residence if he wishes, but he is not likely to, since he benefits by having the boys present, for they run errands for him. If there is more than one such house in the compound the boys sleep in whichever they prefer, unless one is reserved for the initiated.

Mothers or sisters bring food to the boys in these houses—as they carry food to the fathers in their homes—or the boys, especially the young ones, may return to their mothers' homes to eat. The movement of boys to these houses is associated with the Afikpo pattern of males eating separately from females, which continues throughout life, as well as the practice of members of each sex having their own sleeping quarters; thus crucial gender distinctions are established early in the boys' lives. These youths play in and around the *ulote,* or at the meeting place at the ancestral rest house in the compound, and they gambol about in back of the compound or in the village commons. In former times young boys rarely left the compound unaccompanied, no less the village, for fear of being kidnapped by a stranger or an Aro slave dealer. They went in groups to the village stream or elsewhere. Today they feel free and their parents are less concerned that something may happen to them. Yet for young boys and girls the compound remains the center of most activities.

Mothers not only wean their sons from the breast at the age of about two, but they also wean them from living with them when they are four or five, when they move to the *ulote*. This act follows by several years the association of the boy with the ancestral shrine house, when the pot for the son's personal spirit, *owa*, is placed there. Sometimes the mother simply leads the boy to the *ulote* and tries to get him to stay there, but the father or an older brother may do this. Sometimes the pressure for moving him is that the mother is sleeping with her husband on certain nights and does not wish to have the growing boy follow her when she goes to visit him. Boys sometimes resist this change in their sleeping and living arrangements, a process of emancipation from the very close ties to the mother, to living in a largely male world. If a boy keeps returning home other boys mock him and call him derisive terms, such as "breast sucker" and "mother's tail." The boys are not kept away from their father's dwelling place, and they are free to go and visit him, and they spend some time hanging around his place. But it is not usually the father who pushes the child from his mother's home, although he may support this act.

The move to the *ulote* marks the time when the mother begins to treat the boy differently from girls. Until then she treats her young children pretty much alike, except for rituals, and naming, as we have described. At this age of four or five the sex distinction in social relations becomes important. This is a common cross-cultural pattern (Barry, Bacon, and Child 1957).

The change for boys is a major event in their lives. After weaning it is the next major movement away from the mother-child tie; the third is the adolescent initiation. This residential shift occurs earlier at Afikpo than in many other societies where it exists (Cohen 1964: Chap. 4); significantly, this early move sets the child into weakening the maternal bond during the oedipal stage, when the boy's unconscious interest in his mother is high (Spiro 1982:5).

The boys sleep at the *ulote,* talk, gossip, and play there, especially when it is raining. Each house has its own rules and punishments. In some, if a youth wets his bed (where others may also be sleeping) he has to run between two parallel rows of youths who flog him with sticks (*igba osisi*, run-sticks). The boys' fathers are not involved in supervising their sons' play in and out of the *ulote;* unless there is serious fighting they do not interfere. The move to the *ulote* is not as much a move to closer direct ties with the father as it is away from the mother's influence to a young male milieu, to identification with other males, particularly those of similar ages. It is a gender-related step as well as a way of attempting to resolve latent feelings for the mother in the oedipal stage through avoidance.

Girls remain at their mother's home, so there is physical separation of brothers and sisters at an early age. Young boys and girls, whether siblings or not, still play with one another, often in a friendly way. But now boys have places of special retirement from females, a feature they will possess, in one way or another, the rest of their lives. Girls generally stay out of the boys' houses, except to bring food to their brothers, as they avoid the ancestral shrine house. There is no taboo involved, but if a girl hangs around an *ulote* there is the implication that sexual contact may be going on. The *ulote* are sometimes found near the compound entrance to the village common and close to the ancestral shrine house, the part of the compound where men are most likely to live and to congregate, so that the boy, by leaving his mother, moves into an adult male world as well as a male child's world. The *ulote,* as a place of male rest and refuge from females, has analogies to the men's rest houses in the village wards, recently mentioned in connection with the bird ritual. The patrilineal shrine house and the secret society bush are other places of male separation from females. There is a consistent pattern of male distinctiveness from females that commences in early life at Afikpo.

Girls begin, at a young age, to help their mothers with housework and cooking, and in fetching water from a nearby stream. Boys less frequently assist their mothers, and they do not start to help their fathers with farm work until some years later. Thus small boys have more free time to play and explore than their female counterparts. As adults a similar pattern occurs, for men spend many hours in ritual matters, political issues, and settling disputes—other kinds of "play"—while their wives do physical work.

The young children are relatively free to wander around the compound, except that they must avoid shrines and other sacred places. They can watch most sacrificial rites and other events and they hang around a feast and where food is being cooked following a sacrifice in the hope of getting something; in this they are often rewarded, for Afikpo are generous in sharing nourishment. If adults are dancing and singing in the compound or the village commons, the small children often attempt to do likewise; they are rarely rebuked, but more often are tolerated and even encouraged by amused adults.

These situations suggest that while the boys move to the boys' houses to live, they are not isolated from the world of adults or from girls. The sense of enlargement of space, from home to ward and village, occurs earlier for boys than for girls, who spend more of their time in the compound. Thus gender distinction through spatial experience slowly arises.

There is a lot of fighting among boys, even before they are fully moved to the *ulote,* and a type of "rascal boy" sometimes appears by the age of four or five. Called *ono ghu nte* ("he does not listen with his ears"), or *ono ghu ihe* ("he does not hear"), he is someone who fights for fighting's sake, willing to take on older lads. He may take more than his share of food from other boys when they eat together; he is willing to aggress to gain it. He may steal eggs, chickens, and other sacrificial materials from shrines and eat or sell them. Afikpo adults have ambivalent attitudes toward such boys; they feel that they are acting wrongly, yet these children represent values of strength and daring which are central to social life, and they also admire them. Consequently rascal boys are seldom strongly discouraged or punished. They are the childhood counterpart of the adult "palaver men" (S. Ottenberg 1971:92), towards whom there are also ambivalent feelings, men who play important roles in village and village-group politics at Afikpo who are bumptious, liable to accept or ask for bribes, and who stir up trouble to reach their own ends. Rascal boys do not necessarily grow into palaver men and some palaver men were quiet and unassuming as children. Nevertheless, rascal boys and palaver men are models of a strong and active ego at Afikpo.

Gender-Linked Secrecy

We have seen that at a child's birth women perform a secret rite, excluding males. There are other secret activities and rituals exclusive to groups and to individuals. And certain kinds of knowledge and behavior are restricted to elders, particularly males. As one middle-aged Afikpo man said, "You really do not know many things until you are an elder yourself. They keep to themselves." Age is equated with secrecy.

The first five years of life do not require a great deal of secrecy for the child; he does not gain knowledge which he is expected to conceal from others. He is not likely to be aware of the extent of the elders' special knowledge. Some rituals involving him contain elements of secrecy, but on the whole knowledge of them is public. The gender division of activities in these childhood rites is at this early age a differentiation largely without secrecy, in terms of the child's own personal knowledge.

Of course, secrecy for the small child exists in the sense that much of what is going on around him is unknown; he is in the process of a first exploration of the world of his compound and its members, and to a lesser extent of neighboring compounds. There is a reaching out to get to know siblings and half siblings, relatives of his parents' and grandparents' generations, and other persons of both sexes and all ages.

Yet there is one form of secret organization which even at this early age has an impact on both girls and boys. This consists of the men's village secret society, which all males eventually join, and boys' secret groupings, which most males join after about the age of five. While these societies carry out public activities as well as secret ones, the latter are made much of by Afikpo males as mechanisms for distinguishing themselves from females, and as devices for social control over themselves and over nonmembers—particularly females. The presence of boys' and men's societies helps to maintain a strong role dichotomy between males and females, as well as between men and boys.

The child watches masked events of the adult society in the village commons, held particularly in the dry season (S. Ottenberg 1975). These are usually open to non-initiated boys and to girls to see, and they commonly do so. Young children occasionally show fright at these masqueraders, some of whom have ugly, distorted faces and strange costumes; in fact, one "ugly" masked form is called "frighten-children" (ɔkpesu umuruma). But children take great delight and interest in the masqueraders. The young child also ventures into the back of his own compound and neighboring ones, seeing the houses and activities of the boys' secret societies (discussed in the next chapter), which largely emulate the adult ones. Here the child views masked forms, some of which chase and play with the younger boys, who may chase back. One form, *logholo,* which prances about, wears a mask of calabash, coconut shell or some material other than wood. Another, *ɔtɛro,* dances while girls sing to it and taunt it by calling it "slave, slave" ("*ohua, ohua*"), and the like. There is also a masquerader of the adult secret society, *ɔkpa,* wearing a looped cord costume covering the entire head and body of the male player, which chases after uninitiated boys in the village commons, and some occasions even in the compounds. The player may scoop up a frightened boy and carry him about for a while, in a sort of game. A fiercer adult society form of *ɔtɛro* also appears if the boys roughhouse too much with *ɔkpa*. Girls, while frightened by these forms, are not generally chased by either *ɔkpa* or *ɔtɛro* of the adult society, but they warn the boys that the masqueraders are coming and tease the costumed figures with shouts of "wicked, wicked, wicked," and the like.

Although Afikpo children do not expressly consider these adult masqueraders to be fathers, as the Onithsa Igbo do (Henderson and Henderson 1966:467), I interpret them to be symbolic attacking father images (S. Ottenberg 1982a). They are likely to be of the fathers' age and, of course, the fathers belong to the secret society, as the boys may be aware. In this sense the socially distant "father" of a boy is not so distant after all, for he aggresses against a symbolic son. Yet since he is masked he is distant in another sense.

In Mgbom and in some other Afikpo settlements, on the morning of the day following the short form of adolescent secret society initiation (see Chapter 7), uninitiated boys go to the priest's house at one end of the village common to receive a magical liquid for their protection. But *ɔkpa* masqueraders are in the commons chasing the non-initiates about and trying to bar their way, and the boys, protected by their fathers or older brothers, must get by them one way or another; some boys are frightened, especially if young. Also, during the part of the year when the secret society is active, strange sounds sometimes emanate from the commons at night, reaching the compounds around it. These are in fact title society activities within the secret society, but the child is told by older siblings and parents that they are sounds of the spirits of that society—they are certainly strange and frightening to some young children. At these times, and on some other occasions during the day or night, the commons is out of bounds to all females and to uninitiated boys and they have to remain in their compounds, or pass from one compound to another through the backyards (cf. Henderson and Henderson 1966:30–31).

During the secret society season—from about September to April, when the commons is not specifically closed to them—females must shout "*lɛɛɛɛɛɛɛɛ*" as they approach and pass through and uninitiated boys yell "*looooooooo*." The Afikpo say that these calls are to warn those in the commons that they are coming in the event that any secret society activity is in progress, but the yells also symbolically differentiate society members from nonmembers and reinforce the sense of mystery that surrounds this organization.

Thus by the time a boy is five he has had some contact with the adult secret society and the secret groupings of the uninitiated boys older than himself—exciting and emotional interaction, which must arouse considerable fantasy in him. Fright may be involved in the experience with masked aggressors, and in the mysterious nighttime sounds. The young boy knows that he is expected to show bravery, and in some cases counteraggression in attacking and chasing masked figures. As in the bird-killing rite, the boy learns assertive values linked to secrecy and a sense of mystery. Girls also react with fright, and they are expected to be a bit more passive than boys and to run when masked figures approach them. But they too are often assertive, taunting and egging the masqueraders on in a show of bravery.

Young children learn to differentiate between those activities that they may have access to and those that are restricted for them; they begin to learn rules concerning their inferior relationship to the secret societies of older boys and of the adults. Young boys also learn early that they will some day join these societies and learn their mysteries, while for girls there is a growing awareness that they will be excluded for life, except through knowledge they acquire accidentally or from other females—information that they do not reveal to males that they know (Whiting, Kluckhohn, and Anthony 1958:361). Young children of both sexes are confronted with the excitement of another world than that of their compound, one that they cannot publicly investigate, which they know of through observation and by overhearing the talk of others.

There is a parallel between the young children's knowledge of the secret societies and their sexual knowledge. Young children are sometimes brought by the mother to their father's home at night when the parents sleep together, and they may observe them having intercourse. At a somewhat later age, when the child is not taken along, it may know that its mother goes to have sex with the father at night. Children may also accidentally see other love-making. People live in close quarters and the sounds of love may carry. Children observe animals mating, particularly dogs, goats, sheep, and birds.

It is commonplace to note that in Africa sexual knowledge comes early to children. Fortes (1970:223), for example, writes that the

Tallensi "are not surprised at the comprehensive and accurate sexual knowledge of a six-year-old, though direct instruction in these matters is never given." This could be said of Afikpo, but it really is a very limited knowledge, since the child does not usually experience sex, although he or she may fantasy about it; in the case of sex, as in the case of the secret society, the child is an outsider, one who sees but does not fully understand. He or she may become aware that the mother and other women menstruate, without understanding the process. Any public show of affection between the sexes at Afikpo is rare; it is done obliquely with words rather than through physical movements, adding to the contrast with and the mystery surrounding the private behavior. Also at this young age, in the oedipal period, the child has to deal with sexual feelings toward the parents. These relate to castration anxieties concerning the parent of the same sex, sexual desire for the parent of opposite sex, and aggressive feelings toward older persons; these feelings and wishes lead to repression, denial, and aversion to sexual matters.

The young boy's view of sex is likely to be anything but clear and coherent, as his understanding of the secret societies is also likely to be uncertain. He is unsure of the meaning of the masqueraders' behavior and appearance, although he may play with them; he may not understand his parents and other couples making love, although he may observe them. Like sex, a good part of the secret society activity takes place at night; in both situations there are mysterious nighttime sounds. In each case there is anxiety and curiosity evoked in the observing child, and emotional, aggressive behavior on the part of the participants. The mystery of sex and the societies pervades the entire village: sex in the compound, the boys' secret societies in back of this residential area, the men's society in the village commons at the center of the settlement and in the secret society bush at the edge of the village. Sex and secrecy are associated with all the spatial areas that the child experiences.

The secret societies are a metaphor for sex. There is an interplay between these two distinct areas of mystery, anxiety, and concern for the child. There is the mystery of the functions and hidden quality of the vagina, and there is the mystery of what goes on in the initiation bush; one produces infants, the other men. The child's behavior and reactions in one of these two spheres may be attempts to better comprehend and deal with the other as well. There appears to be considerable crossover between these two areas; the aggressive chasing male masquerader may be viewed by the child as the punishing, castrating father, the beautiful female masked figure—danced by a male and normally nonaggressive—may be viewed as the loving, nurturing mother (S. Ottenberg 1982a), and the sounds of the secret society at night equated with the sounds of love-making after dark.

Of course, there are differences between the quality of sex and of the secret societies. The first involves both sexes, the other only men, although the small child may not at first be clear about the gender of the society members. One concerns groups of persons, the other couples. The compound, where sex generally occurs, is central to the child; the secret society areas are more peripheral. The secret societies aggress against the children through the masqueraders, while the sexual partners assert with one another and not toward the child. Sexual matters are ultimately more fundamental than secret society ones; the latter are more a reflection of the former than the reverse. But these two areas of mystery are clearly bound together for children of this age. We will see how this continues to be true in the latency period, when the boys join the youths' secret societies, and during adolescence, when they are initiated into the adult secret organization.

Secrecy is very important in Afikpo childhood development. It sets barriers for children in interpersonal relationships and guides the direction of their interest and knowledge. But it also leads to action, to activity, motivated by curiosity and desire to gain knowledge of the secret elements, to challenge its holders and to gain control, and thus perhaps also to gain status in the eyes of others. Secrecy is activity-generating as well as activity-separating. At Afikpo some of the generative aspects, as we have just seen, arise through the public functions of the secret societies. And clearly the existence of secrecy, of secret areas of behavior, stimulates thought, leads to fantasy and reflection on the nature of people, things, and behavior. To the young Afikpo child what are those mysterious sounds heard in village commons at night? Are they emanating from spirits, as the children are told, or from animals, or are people producing them? What are the masked figures? Are they spirits or humans? And in the sexual area, what is actually going on in intercourse? What is the meaning of a boyhood erection, of menstruation, of the female lack of a penis? These kinds of questions must occur to young children of both sexes.

I believe that at Afikpo it is through secrecy associated largely with the boys' and men's secret societies, and with sexual matters, that the child is often provoked to thought and action. In this sense secrecy, which by its nature appears to have an isolating and withdrawing quality (Bellman 1984), creates inquiry and assertiveness in the young child in response to it, and this process helps move the child along in maturation—paradoxically, to a clearer understanding of the larger world of which secrecy forms only a part. Secret behavior, like ritual and fiction in our own society, encourages the child to cope with his or her desires, feelings, and lack of knowledge.

The secrecy at Afikpo focuses heavily on males; it is strongly gender-linked through the secret societies. The fact—learned early—that females can never join these organizations, yet all males eventually do, skews the way children of each sex perceive and respond to the secrecy involved. Aggressive behavior is associated with secrecy, so that the differing reactions to nonsexual secrecy of each sex becomes one of the fundamental features in the social behavior of boys and girls, and later of men and women.

Conclusions

By the time the boy is about five or six years old he has gone through two radical changes in life style: (1) weaning, when not only his diet changes, but his mother returns to her husband and he loses some of her affection and interest, and (2) when he moves into the male world of a boys' house and is further removed from his mother. Through much of the first five years of life the father remains a distant, but amiable and nonpunitive parent. Girls go through a similar first change, but there is nothing in their lives which is equivalent to the departure of the boys from their mothers' homes. Girls maintain a strong mother-child bond until they marry, at adolescence. Relations between daughters and their fathers remain distant through these five years.

The second weaning, when the boys move to their separate home, is a physical change but also related to the resolution of psychological issues arising during infancy and the oedipal period. The move, which raises issues of tension and conflict between parent and child, is a necessary prelude to training the boys in aggression and physical endurance, in the warrior tradition of former times. The Afikpo themselves see the move to the boys' house as a mechanism to lessen the dependency on the mother resulting from the years of close contact between mother and son. Striving to weaken the ties to the mother is a major theme in the maturation of boys. The effort to overcome the emotional and psychological issues raised by the strong early mother-son tie is not only necessary for males to derive their own sense of self and autonomy, but, in the past, to adequately prepare them for the life of warriors. We will see how secrecy is employed at Afikpo to further the separation of boys from their mothers. Afikpo adjusted, as did other African societies, to the need for infant health and survival by instituting the strong and long-lasting early mother-child bond. But the society also had a contradictory need to develop vigorous, independent males for warfare and leadership; presumably "mother's tails" don't fight or lead well. The pattern of childhood maturation for boys is an attempt to resolve this dilemma, these two opposing needs for human survival. The two themes at Afikpo represent the universal dilemma that all societies face; the need for adult male vigor on the one hand, yet for childhood nurture on the other.

A further theme stresses the separation of the paths of boys and girls, moving toward highly differentiated gender roles in society. This is expressed through activities that involve one sex and exclude the other (the bird-killing ritual and moving to the boys' houses for males, the domestic duties for girls), and in features that involve both sexes but in differing ways (coming out, naming, the sex of reincarnators, excision rites, and the response to the masqueraders and other secret society activities). The gender dichotomy is also evident in the differing roles that older males and females play in the children's rites, and in handling children in general.

There is yet another universal theme which plays itself out in particular forms at Afikpo. This is the sequence of development that *all* children, regardless of sex, go through from birth, as they mature physically and "get sense" as people say there. At Afikpo this includes coming out, naming, the growth of the first teeth, the determination of the two reincarnators in the child, the exclusion of all children from most adult secret society affairs, and the interest of the young in sexuality and in these secret societies. These features relate to the unity of growth and development of both boys and girls at Afikpo despite gender differences, the sense that there are common and crucial points of maturation for every Afikpo child, marked by special rites and events, and that if errors occur in the natural growth process ("bad" births, upper teeth appearing before lower ones, sexual activity before excision) dire consequences will follow. There is a strong sense of how all children should develop, and considerable worry over their possible failure to do so correctly.

3
Growing Up

AT THE AGE OF FIVE OR SIX THERE IS ANOTHER MARKED change in the life of Afikpo children, particularly boys. This altered state lasts until adolescence, when boys are initiated into the adult village secret society and girls marry. There is no single Afikpo term for this period; the words referring to it vary according to context. It is the time when children prepare for social adulthood, begin to develop a moral sense, make broader contacts in the village and beyond, and when boys further redefine their relationships to their parents.

Boys from about five years of age into adolescence are called *nwa enna* (child-uninitiated; plural, *umu enna*), stressing the pre-initiation state of the child. Younger boys can also be called this, but there is a sense of their being too young yet to anticipate initiation. Girls can be called *nwa ichu* (child–not excised), although this is sometimes a derogatory term, as in the expression, *"ichu erigi ewu,"* meaning "uncircumcised girls do not eat goat." In fact they do; the phrase refers to the goat given to the girl when she is excised. A more common term for girls is *agbogho,* which, while it can also be employed for a female infant, more commonly refers to a child of a least a little maturity who has not yet had her clitoridectomy. A girl at puberty, or even a younger one who makes herself pretty, who has developed self-consciousness about her looks, is referred to as *agbogho obia* (girl-beauty). An adolescent girl is *oke nwa agbogho* (big-child-girl), or just *oke agbogho,* whether the excision has been done or not; an adolescent boy or young man, whether initiated or not, is *oke nwoke* (big-male). Thus there are terms for children that stress the excision as a crucial dividing point and others which play it down in favor of adolescence as a general concept. But even before adolescence gender distinctions in terminology become significant. The terms for children well reflect the interests of the Afikpo.

If children reach five years of age at Afikpo, people begin to feel that they will probably live to adulthood. Parents and other grown-ups are less anxious about their survival and are willing to speak more freely of them to individuals from outside the compound (including the anthropologist). They are regarded more as persons (*onye*) than before, not as adults but as humans that one can communicate with with some intelligence; one can order them to do things and hope for a reasonable response. Afikpo is, in certain ways, a very moral society, and at this age children begin to learn, although they may not understand, its particular standards, including those pertaining to sexual behavior.

By the age of five or six children's basic relationships to their reincarnators, personal spirits, and other key supportive spirits have been established and are assumed to be aiding them. Indeed, Afikpo believe that if this were not so they would probably have become ill or died. By this stage both boys and girls start to join their parents and older siblings in farm work, a major movement out of the village; this brings them into contact with new faces.

For boys, the five- to six-year age level is marked by another change, boys' secret society activities, which moves them during the dry season to the rear of the compound, where they join other lads of their age or those slightly older. This is a major focus of their interest, one which pulls them away from mothers and from other females, and into new relationships. It is a time of a son's considerable autonomy from the father (except when he wishes him to work or to run messages). This is the age of the beginning of strong peer-group experience for males, which in precolonial times marked the beginning of their serious training for warfare—to become men of strength and fighting skill. Peer-group behavior continues throughout their lives, at a later age in wrestling grades and then in village age groupings. These boys' secret societies strongly reinforce and extend the growing gender distinctions and the emphasis on secrecy as a male quality—and its correlates, physical aggression and life outside of the home—as against the nonsecret female home life and domestic activities.

The earlier events of this period, between the age of about five or six and eleven, occur in what is called the latency period (Sarnoff 1976). It is the time when the oedipal conflicts of the previous period are largely put aside, through extinction or full or partial repression (Spiro 1982:164–74), and the child actively turns his interest outside of the family. The oedipal and conflict issues arise again at adolescence, with sexual awakening.

At Afikpo latency is the major period of social growth and the acquisition of culture. The social and cultural knowledge that the child acquires by adolescence forms the bedrock of later behavior and experience. The time from birth until latency is one of physical growth; the mother's concern is to keep the child healthy and to allow it to grow physically, and the child's fantasies are not closely associated with reality. During the period we are now discussing there is, of course, still physical growth, but the focus shifts away from survival and physical maturation to cultural and social maturation, where the child's fantasies are more closely based on, and acted out through, everyday experiences (Sarnoff 1976:11). Here gender differentiation becomes striking in the young, as it does in other West African societies (Fortes 1970:212).

Since for girls the social and cultural maturation continues under the guidance of the mother, in the domestic scene, it would seem logical and complementary if, for boys, this development went on under the guidance of the father. In fact, the father's role at this time is not major; he still remains a rather distant, if friendly and generally nonpunishing figure in the boy's life. What occurs is that a good deal of the living and experience of boys of latency age occurs with other boys of the same or slightly different ages. Peer groups, which play a major role in authority matters, in rule making, in discipline, and in acquiring knowledge, take the place of the relatively absent father. This suggests to me that the conflicts of the earlier oedipal period are not fully resolved at Afikpo, and that the slim contact between father and son at this time minimizes friction between them, as a son's pulling away from his mother minimizes the intensity of earlier childhood ties with her. I believe that the vigorous peer-group activities of boys at this time help to compensate for the loss of the close and intimate links with the mother, and for the failure to develop strong identity ties directly with the father. The links are rather with male peers, and indirectly with adult males, through emulation. This is not to deny that the father keeps an eye on his son at this time, or that the mother continues to feed him and to monitor his activities, but he is away from direct parental control a good deal of the time.

The basis of the children's experience in the latency period becomes the foundation of their adolescence, when children integrate their awakening sense of physical maturation and sexuality with the social and cultural knowledge, skills, and concepts that they have acquired in latency. These form a rich blend that well prepares boys for initiation and girls for marriage.

Boys' Secret Societies

Until about the 1940s boys' secret societies, *egbele umu enna* (secret society spirit-children-uninitiated) or *ɔhia umu enna* (bush-children-uninitiated), were extensive in the Afikpo villages. I will first describe them as they existed before the reduction in their activities and structure which had occurred by the time I carried out my research. There were usually three levels of organization, determined by age. In the youngest level, boys joined up between the ages of about five and seven and remained with the group for five years or so. Nowadays they are already circumcised; in past times they were not. These junior groups were located one to a compound, except in the case of small compounds where two or more neighboring ones formed the basis of organization. Called by various names, such as *isi ulo obu* (head-house-rest-house), they centered on the ancestral rest house of the compound, where the boys met and played. Such a group also sometimes used a clearing in the back of their compound, where they gathered to dance and to play. During the height of the adult secret society season the boys might build a small enclosure or hut at this clearing, where they stayed during the day. Here they carried out their activities, most of which emulated the adult secret society.

The two higher stages of the boys' societies were more thoroughly organized; both were virtually replicas of the adult society. Some Afikpo claim that the two higher stages were subdivisions of one; others state that they were separate.* In any case, each society at these two stages had a well-constructed rest house (*obiogo*), built during the adult secret society season, and resembling the village and ward men's rest houses but smaller in size. There were generally one or more shrines maintained by the boys, including one to their main spirit, *egbele*, a term also employed for the adult secret society spirit. The boys' spirit was also known by a variety of other names.

---

*In some large villages, or sections of villages, there were three higher stages rather than two.

The lower of the highest stages, called ɔsohɔra, ugwugwu, and by other terms, was usually based on a single compound, again unless it was too small in size. It had its own clearing in back of the residential area, where its rest house, shrines, and playing area were located. Sometimes this site was right at the edge of the compound, but in other cases it was back a quarter of a mile or more, in a bush or forest section, comfortably hidden from view. Boys joined this group roughly between the ages of nine and thirteen, and they remained in it five years or so.

The last stage was generally for boys fifteen years or over. There was no special term for this stage; the terms aleady mentioned for all stages of the boys' societies were used. Its area was also in back of the compound. If a compound was large it might have its own society at this highest uninitiated stage, but often boys joined together from a number of neighboring compounds, or from an entire village.

Thus by the time a boy joined the adult secret society in his late teens he had had some ten years' or more experience in the boys' groupings, which generally emulated the adult ones. Before looking at these three stages in detail, let me make a few additional comments.

The father—or a surrogate if the father was deceased or away—had the right to initiate the boy into the adult society at any time, providing that he had taken the necessary preliminary ritual steps, had the resources to do so, and that an initiation was going to occur; boys were sometimes initiated out of the second stage or shortly after entering the third. Thus it was not ritually or socially necessary for the boys to go through all three stages, nor to spend any specific amount of time in each; in fact, they did not have to go through any stage before adult initiation, and occasionally a boy did not. But it was expected that from the age of five or six boys would have some secret society experience, whether in the boys' or the men's society.

Boys moved up through the three-tier system, as well as into it, according to a number of factors. They did so as individuals, not as a group (as occurred in the initiation into the adult society). For each of the boys' societies there was an initiation involving some small expense; the boy generally got his parents, particularly his father, to procure the necessary items, such as peanuts, yams, and kola, though he might procure some of these himself. Every such rite involved not only payment of goods but also a sacrifice at the spirit shrine of the society, conducted by its leaders and involved some of the initiand's items, such as kola. Afterward the boy was whipped as he ran between two parallel rows of the society's members, but tried not to show pain. Each initiation, as in other rites we have already touched upon, was a title (*mɛmɛ*) for the father, albeit a small one, as well as an advancement for the boy. If the initiation items were not given all at once the lad took his initiation in stages, and until he completed it he wore the poorer masks and played the less interesting masquerade roles; he might have to fetch water for the other boys and he could not sit on certain choice benches at the society's house. Until finished he was *nwa efu* (child–low status). The society's leaders were usually the boys longest in the group, and those who had taken its titles; they directed others. When such a leader moved to a higher society stage his status became low again. Leadership was not based on belonging to a particular compound or patrilineage but on interest in the society, titles taken within it, and physical strength—not showing pain when flogged and being able to fight well. And as one Afikpo said to me: "In whichever boys' society you are in you learn from the more experienced boys, the leaders, you do not learn from your father." The process of moving up through the societies was not only egalitarian with respect to birth status and leadership, it also called on virtually all boys to play leadership roles as they acquired seniority and the proper titles at any stage; every child had access to leadership, whether he actively played such roles or not. This is quite consistent with the nature of adult male leadership at Afikpo (S. Ottenberg 1971).

While by today's standards the initiation fee was not high, in earlier times there was less wealth and this might hold up a boy's advancement a little. On the other hand, if a boy was big and strong for his age there was a tendency for his father to push him ahead at an earlier age than otherwise, where he would be able to fight as well as to work with older boys; this enhanced the prestige of the boy and the honor accorded the father. If the child was a man's first son and the father had wealth, he would likely move the boy ahead, for he would wish him to join the adult secret society early, an important title for the father. A boy whose playmates had moved up a stage would want to join them and would urge his parents to allow him to do so; his mates might encourage this by teasing him or beating him up. On the other hand, a boy who became a leader of his group at one stage would want to stay in it as long as possible for he would become a "small boy" in the next stage. A consequence of these numerous factors was considerable variation in the ages of boys in the different stages, and varying lengths of time that a boy remained in a stage.

Each society in a compound or group of compounds was completely autonomous from others at the same stage and from those at the other two stages. Members of one society might observe some of the activities of the others at their own or another stage, especially masquerades, and they might try to emulate those on a higher level, but there was little direct friendly communication between boys in different stages when they were active in their societies. However, a masquerader from one level had to give way to one from a higher stage. A boy entering one stage learned the culture, values, and behavior of the society he had joined and this was passed on to new members as they entered; the particular style of each society at each stage was maintained by peer-group ties, not by the authority of adult males. Of course, boys in different societies had contacts with one another in play, wrestling, farm work, and in other ways, and they borrowed masks and costumes from one another.

The boys' societies were not active the entire year but only during the period when the adult society was functioning in the village, from about October to May. When active there was fighting and tension between some of these boys' societies, good training for later warfare. A lad who ventured into the area of another society in the village, particularly the societies of the last two stages, might be beaten up and chased away, even if the activities of his society and the one he had contacted were similar. There was also a good deal of group fighting between societies within the village; these hostilities extended between villages as well. It is said that boys did not venture into other compounds of their own village or into other villages, except in groups, and that a lot of roughhousing went on among boys of all ages over four or five. Again, note the emphasis on physical strength. These fighting patterns did not occur among the adult societies. Membership in the adult society of one village allowed, and still does, access to the society in other villages, and when inter-village fighting between adult males occurred at Afikpo the conflicts were not based on these secret groups, but on claims to land or tree areas. Adult conflicts were and are oriented around productive property, women, and other tangibles; boys' fighting was and is not. It is expressive rather than instrumental, designed to show physical superiority. For older boys it is also a deflection of growing sexual energies.

Adult males in the compounds did not interfere with the boys' fighting as long as it did not bother them, and adults did not usually direct or guide these societies or act as sponsors or paternal figures for them. Unless the boys annoyed adult men, such as by violating a regulation in some villages against holding their masquerades in the village commons, they were largely left alone to do what they wished. These boys' societies stressed autonomy from parental control, while at the same time emulating male adult activities and values. They represented a vigorous attempt on the part of boys to remain separate from their parents, encouraged by the latter, while, paradoxically, identifying with adult male behavior, including that of their fathers. The societies emphasized the cooperation of boys of like ages within a specifically designated residential area, with hostility to other boys beyond this range; there was a channeling of aggressive tendencies, and a learning of concepts of residence and spatial relations. As a boy moved up through the stages he found that there was increasing discipline and social control within his particular society, well preparing him for membership in the adult one.

Within each society there was frequent fighting among the members as they established and reestablished "pecking orders." Internal disputes often arose over what seemed like petty matters, again suggesting their expressive rather than instrumental quality—over the sharing of food, an argument between two boys as to which was older or who should wear a certain mask. Fighting was with hands, limbs, and bodies, but sometimes involved sticks. Boys developed an ability to whip skillfully and not to flinch or to show hurt when cut or hit hard. Whipping also occured in some adult secret societies at Afikpo in a more organized fashion, but there it was kept secret from non-initiates, who were forbidden to watch it. Yet the boys acted in much the same way.

Occasionally fighting occurred between full brothers, although these were often in different stages of boys' societies due to their different ages. More frequently the roughhousing was between sons of a man by different mothers, particularly if the boys were close in age. The mothers, as co-wives, were likely to be in conflict or tension with one another (P. Ottenberg 1958), living in different houses and sometimes in different parts of the compound, as the houses of a man's wives might be scattered in this residential unit. Thus half brothers might have different friends and live in separate boys' houses. Rivalry between them was sometimes encouraged by their mothers, not only within the boys' societies, but in other activities in compound and village (cf. LeVine 1961:61–62), reflecting co-wife rivalries.

In the early 1950s, when I first carried out field research at Afikpo, these boys' societies were dying out and this was continuing when I returned in 1959. At that latter time there was, in Mgbom village, one society of the second stage and two of the third. There was very little fighting and raiding between them. There were some other boys' societies more casually and informally organized. Those that did exist had a wider range of ages than societies at earlier times. Elders in some villages ordered boys to take part, but with little success. In the early 1940s, in the face of declining interest in the societies, enterprising members of the senior stage in Mgbom village brought the societies together to the point where they cut down their physical conflicts and cooperated in masquerades and in other matters, the older lads helping the younger. Similar conditions occurred in other villages so that age and society distinctions have largely broken down. Before this time, if a boy in Mgbom village helped members of a younger society the members of his own society would flog him for revealing its secrets.

The reasons for the decline in these organizations are complex. There are some primary schools at Afikpo—it is something of an educational center for the area—and children are occupied with school and homework, with less free time. School also brings boys into contact with a wide range of children from their own and neighboring villages at an earlier age than would occur traditionally, and into different kinds of formal and informal play and competitive groups; these occupy a lot of the boys' time and energy. In Mgbom and a few other villages there are student organizations which meet in the evening for studies. Again, as we have already discussed, boys are initiated into the adult society at an earlier age than previously, some as young as four or five years of age. Once initiated, a boy is no longer permitted to take part in the boys' societies, although he may play with the same youths in other contexts. Of course, a like pattern occurs within the boys' societies; once a boy moves to a higher stage he drops all activities at the lower one. There are various other factors involved in the decline of the societies. Some boys are living away from home, often in urban centers in Nigeria, with families or relatives, attending school or working. Furthermore, the Protestant and Catholic missions at Afikpo have been highly antagonistic to the emphasis on secrecy, masking, rituals, and the stress on physical strength. Nevertheless, almost all adult men living at Afikpo at the time of my research had gone through the three stages of the boys' societies and were influenced by this experience.

When we consider adult secret societies in Africa we tend to view initiation as a crucial transition from childhood to manhood, and from a state of ignorance to one of at least partial revelation. Yet at Afikpo, as I suspect is true of some other African societies, the boys know a great deal about the rites and secrets of the adult society before initiation, as they have been practicing them for years in their own groups. Thus I do not see Afikpo initiation into the adult society as a sudden shift from a state of nonsecrecy and lack of knowledge and experience with secrets to one involving these elements. Rather, entrance into the adult society is based on an accumulation of knowledge, experience in handling secrets, and on developed dancing, masquerading, musical and other skills, a gradual transition from an early age to late adolescence. We can even consider that the adult secret society is a fourth stage of secret organized activity, one which has many features of the other stages. It is exclusive of earlier stages, as the third is of the second, and the second of the first. It is roughly age-based, and there are pressures for a male to join it when he reaches a certain age, as exists with the boys' groupings. The adult society encompasses males living in a specific residential area regardless of kinship or descent ties, as do the boys' societies. It is only in more recent years, when boys have been initiated into the adult society at a young age, or without much previous experience, that the adult initiation has come to entail rapid acquisition of knowledge and skills not previously held. These matters will be discussed again in the context of the adult society.

The Junior Stage

The first boys' secret society stage, the least organized of the three, finds the youths learning how to behave in groups. In the old days boys of this age often went naked or wore a loin cloth (*anam ogologho*) purchased from Igbo groups to the northwest; when I was researching they wore short pants, and sometimes a top shirt. They make crude masks of banana leaves, pieces of cloth, coconut shells and coconut tree bark. Wearing crude raffia or leaf dress, they hop around individually and in small groups, trying to imitate what they have seen of the dancing and playing of older boys and adult males in their masquerades, but they are not skilled at it.*

The societies of the junior stage are informally organized, without stable leadership. Once boys start hanging around and playing at the compound ancestral rest house they are in contact with older boys who belong to these secret organizations and the younger ones gradually drift into them. It is an interesting time for the boys, for they are making new contacts and beginning to form close friendships with other youths. Boys who belong to these societies flog lads of their age in the compound who refuse to join up, and they have a small initiation fee—perhaps a couple of pawpaws (papaya) or some peanuts.

The junior society generally lacks a shrine of its own, and while the members may play in their own clearing at the back of the compound, sometimes with masks, they rarely have a shelter there. They store their masks and other paraphernalia under the roof of the compound ancestral rest house, safe from females. Older boys regard these youths with amusement as unsophisticated bumpkins, lacking knowledge of what is proper secret society behavior. Nevertheless, there are taboos on females touching the boys or their masks when they are dressed up, or interfering with their play in the ancestral rest house and in their society clearing area, restrictions that also apply to the older boys' secret societies.

The Second Stage

The next stage marks the boys' full involvement in a well-developed secret group. It is sometimes called *ogo umu enna* (village-children-uninitiated) referring to the wider group than the compound that it may draw its membership from. Most of its activities occur in back of a compound, near a village men's latrine located there, or in the bush behind that. For the period of the secret society season the boys

---

*In the Onitsha Igbo area, the boys start masking as early as age four (Henderson and Henderson 1966:31).

spend little time around the ancestral rest house but are in this place, which is taboo to females. The transition from being a nonmember to membership is a clear one and the initiation is more expensive than for the first stage. In the case of one boy in Ezi Itim compound of Mgbom village, about 1935, this involved giving two pawpaws to the members. The older boys in the group ate much of this, sharing a little with younger members; the former then slapped the skins on the back of the initiand (as I will call any boy who is being initiated into any group at Afikpo, in contrast to an initiate, who is already a member). The initiand also gave the group a medium-sized pot for washing, two small cooking pots, a pot for fetching and carrying water, twenty bananas, a coconut, and a half-penny for permission to play the society's wooden gong, *acha,* which the boys use in dancing and singing. These items were provided mainly by the parents.

The initiation can only take place when the boys' society is active, during the period when the adult society is also in session. The new initiate is subject to rules, which vary from boys' secret society to society; these may or may not be fully explained to him at the time of initiation. Often they include a regulation that all members must wear a loin cloth, or nowadays pants. In Ezi Itim compound, Mgbom Village, in the 1930s, you could no longer sleep in a female's house, be it your mother, a sister, or some other person, thus stressing the male quality of the society. Even today boys sleep in the boys' houses in the compound at night, except for nights after they have worn masks, when they remain in their own house in back of the compound, as members of the adult secret society sleep in rest houses in the commons after masquerading. A violator of this rule has to pass by a line of the society's members, who whip him, a common boys' society punishment.

Another common rule is that you cannot reveal the secrets of the society to nonmembers, not even other boys or relatives; punishment often involves flogging. If you have a dispute with another member of the society you are expected to bring it to the society's leader to settle and not to take it outside, a common principle of group behavior at Afikpo. In Ezi Itim compound the loser of the case had to accept whatever punishment the winner determined. This could be a whipping or the gathering of palm kernels from a tree to feed the society's members. The rules of the society give the boy experience in self-control, the handling of conflict, and punishment outside of his parental setting; the boys in their societies seem less permissive than their parents; it is as if the boys have taken over control of their own destiny in an authoritarian way from permissive and amiable parents.

The members often obtain some of their own food from the bush, or scrounge it from here and there; they are less dependent on their mothers for nourishment than at an earlier age. They also carry out a little simple cooking for themselves. Otherwise their mothers feed them. The boys make simple xylophones of wood and play these and dance to them. This is unusual in that this music and dance is not generally emulative of adult secret society activities at Afikpo, and boys enjoy this play very much. It occurs among adults in only a few Afikpo communities and in neighboring Okpoha Village-Group (S. Ottenberg 1975:171–74).

This stage of the boys' society is well organized. The older members direct its activities and control its shrines and its properties, a common pattern with any age-graded group at Afikpo (S. Ottenberg 1971). Less knowledgeable boys in the society learn from them. As Fortes writes of Tallensi children (1970:211), "every pupil becomes in some situations a teacher." But there is also a great deal of fighting over leadership, which never seems stable for long.

The leaders of a boys' society have usually taken titles that the group controls, again in emulation of the adult secret society. Each title requires payment of small sums of money and often of yams, which a boy may obtain from his father or an older brother. Not only the leaders take these titles but other members endeavor to do so in order to raise their status so that they will be treated well by important members. Titles are crucial to the adult social system at Afikpo; the children well prepare themselves for later life. In some societies a boy without titles is required to fetch water or to sweep out the boys' society house and the clearing around it, or he is forbidden to sit in special seats in front of the house. Fortunately, the titles do not have limited membership; any member who has the resources can take them. The title food and money are shared by the title holders in the boys' society, but the title holders are not addressed in any special manner; it is simply known who they are. Adult title societies, within and without the adult secret societies, are ubiquitous at Afikpo (S. Ottenberg 1971:22–23), and their organization and mode of operation are well known, except for certain secret rituals associated with adult secret society forms. In the case of the boys' secret society there is a shrine near their society house associated with each title, established at some past time. This is sacrificed at by a new title member as he joins up, assisted by the title holders. The boys consider these to be real shrines with power, and respect them as such. Like many adult shrines, each consists of a pot surrounded by stones, often hidden behind hanging raffia strands. Titles and shrines are found in the few boys' societies in existence today.

There is also a special shrine of the spirit of the boys' society; both shrine and spirit are often called *egbele*. My assumption would be that the boys' shrine derives from the adults' secret society one, which bears the same name. This is the way that shrines "travel" at Afikpo; the holders and priest of a shrine allow another person or group to establish it for a fee, with the original owner's assistance. But the Afikpo say that the boys simply established their own at some past time and that they are not directly connected to the adult one, only similar to them. When a child is initiated into a boys' group he offers an egg to *egbele*; group sacrifices are also made at it by the boys at the opening and closing of the secret society season. The shrine has a priest, chosen by the boys from among their members. The *egbele* shrine pot and the title shrine pots, like all adult shrine pots, are made by postmenopausal women, sometimes a mother or grandmother of one of the boys. (Other pots can be produced by younger females.) Because of this, and by their bowl-like (vaginal) shapes, these pots are a metaphor for the female gender and the mother-child bond—a reminder of the reliance of all males on females, for cooked food and for their very existence as humans. But the shrine spirit clearly also represents male interests and values, the male parental figure. Although Afikpo believe that this spirit does not take any particular shape or form, it is viewed as being male and residing in the shrine, although it can move about. *Egbele* is a powerful supporting spirit for the boys, helping them to act with vigor and assisting them to put on fine masquerades. It is the spiritual heart of their society.

The *egbele* shrine is taboo to all females. They should shout "*leeeeeeeeee*" as they pass by the boys' clearing if they think that anything is going on there, as they automatically do in the village commons when the adult society is active. If a girl or woman, even the mother of a boy member, touches something or sees something that she should not concerning the boys' society—for example, the boys putting on or taking off their masks—the boys will insist that she bring materials to sacrifice at their shrine. If she refuses they put on masks and costumes and prepare a mysterious liquid in a pot (*eto isi*, chew-smelling) and blow into this substance through reed tubes in front of her home. The boys say that *egbele* has come to her house. The liquid froths and bubbles in an unsual way and she is frightened and gives in. Then she provides a number of eggs, and perhaps some yams, for a sacrifice, as the lads require. The older boys of the society perform the rite; the whole society shares the yams, but the eggs are left at the shrine. If she refuses to do this adult males will support the boys' claims, for they fear that if she fails to sacrifice some misfortune, particularly barrenness, will befall her later on. Sometimes a girl or a woman who has seen or touched something of a boys' society is not found out and says nothing. Later, it could be many year after, when she fails to have children or is ill or has misfortunes, a diviner may suggest that it is because she has offended the boys' *egbele*; she may unconsciously lead him to this view if she feels guilty about such an act. Then she must provide materials for a sacrifice to the spirit to purify herself. Of course, the diviner may suggest instead that the adult secret society *egbele* is at fault, or some other spirit.

Boys are nominally under the the control of older persons, including their mothers and older sisters, yet in these sacrifices and taboos the situation is reversed. This obvious alteration of the Afikpo sex and age pattern is among the first experiences that young males have in controlling females—certainly exceptional in terms of controlling their own mothers—perhaps thus fulfilling unconscious or conscious wishes. Some Afikpo women fear the ambiguity of the boys' *egbele* and society more than that of the adults. They say that the adults' society spirit is predictable but that of the boys is unsure. For one thing, the boys do not always indicate by certain standard signs whether their clearing area next to their rest house is closed to females or not, as is done in the case of the adult society. For another, there is uncertainty over the power of the boys' *egbele* and the ability of boys to control it properly, evidently a product of ambiguous boy-adult relations associated with these societies, which seem to reverse the normal order of things.

Ritual control over women by males of all ages through the secret societies is endemic at Afikpo. Why even small boys *need* to control women, including their mothers, has to do, I believe, with the desire of boys to gain autonomy after the long early mother-son relationship. It is not a rejection of their mothers, whom they generally love, but an attempt to control them, to bring the mothers symbolically to the world where the youths dominate.

The boys' society leaders control its physical properties. The rest house for the group is usually a low-roofed structure, dark inside, where the boys sit and talk, make costumes and masks, and cook a little food. If they sleep away from their homes in the compound they stay here. As in the adult secret society rest houses in the commons, there are mats and seats and pots for drinking water. The boys repair their structure every year.

In the Itim subgroup of the Afikpo villages (Mgbom, Amuro, Anohia, Anohia Nkalo, Kpogrikpo) the boys' societies also each have a special roofless dressing place called *ajaba* at their clearing, similar to ones found at the edge of the commons in these villages for the adult societies. The boys' structure is composed of a rectangular fence of bundles of raffia palm branches tied together, with a single entrance/exit, and a bench in front. In the adults' *ajaba* there are decorated wooden vertical boards, *imɔrɔ*, at the front wall, but the uninitiated boys are forbidden to make these out of wood; they sometimes construct them of raffia rope and bamboo. These boys' *ajaba* are used only for the dressing and undressing of masqueraders; villages that lack this structure use the boys' society rest house instead.

Toward the end of the secret society season the *ajaba* are burned down, to be rebuilt at the beginning of the next secret society season. The firing is done the day after the adult society in the village burns their own. In each Itim village the process is much the same. The walls are dismantled, leaving only a few markers; the wall materials are placed in piles and fired. In Mgbom, in the boys' societies, each member eats coconut and gives some to men at the ancestral rest house in the compound, and each places coconut shell on every burned pile; this is repeated four times to represent the four days of the week.

Coconuts are associated with boys; they are a kind of metaphor for them. Some boys' masks are made of coconut shell; adult masks are not. Boys climb trees to get coconuts, and they often steal them this way. If adults see this they do not usually trouble themselves very much about it. The rite of the coconuts and the burning are believed to protect women from infertility if they pass too close to the *ajaba* area, an act which offends the spirit of the boys' society. The coconut is an ambiguous symbol. It is gathered by males at Afikpo only from tall objects which have a phallic quality, yet it is breast-shaped and its liquid content symbolizes breast milk. Its association with boys, rather than men, suggests the continuation of an unconscious attachment to the mother.

This interpretation is supported by the fact that coconut shells are not so employed in the adult secret society. In fact, on one occasion new adult initiates in Mgbom, who had not realized this, were heavily rebuked for using coconuts. The priest of the adult society and its leaders were very angry, and they made the young initiates sacrifice dogs to the society's spirit. The use of coconuts may seem to be a small difference, but it is symbolically very important. So is the taboo against the boys' use of wooden *imɔrɔ* boards to decorate their dressing houses, and the rule against boys making masks of wood and performing certain adult masquerades (which will be discussed shortly). These are essential features of the boys' and the adult societies, and are made much of; they distinguish the men from the boys, the truly initiated from the emulative.

One of the major boys' group activities is the performance of a variety of masquerades (see S. Ottenberg 1975 for Afikpo; Henderson and Henderson 1966:31–33 for Onitsha). In former times each society of the second or third stage produced its own, but more recently some or all the boys' societies in a settlement have started joining together to do so. The boys are not permitted to perform certain adult society masquerades, especially those involved with adult initiation, as well as *njenje,* a masked parade which marks the formal organization of a village age set. These restrictions are undoubtedly related to the fact that these particular events involve rites of passage for males older than the boys.

The costumes and masks are made by the boys; in general they attempt to emulate the adult society. Since wood is not permitted in the masks, being reserved for the adult society, except for an occasional part, such as a nose, they are made of calabash, cardboard, cloth, coconut tree fiber and other materials; this has been described elsewhere (S. Ottenberg 1975:57–60). The boys also make their own drums and wood gongs which they teach one another to play and which they employ in some of their masquerades. Girls and women are not supposed to know who the masqueraders are—they are expected to believe that they are spirits or "fairies" (*mma*)—but in fact they are often recognizable, especially to relatives and friends. In some villages the masqueraders of the boys' societies are forbidden to play in the village commons; this is reserved for the adult society.

Of the adult masquerades which are emulated, and several are rarely seen, one of the most popular is a satiric and humorous play, ɔkumkpa (S. Ottenberg 1975: Chaps. 6–8), employing masked players in a variety of costumes and face pieces. The boys act out and sing of events that have taken place or are believed to have occurred in the village, or in Afikpo, naming and impersonating the individuals involved, sometimes adults, sometimes children. Between skits they dance about as other boys play drums and wood gongs. These humorous skits poke fun at members of the boys' society as well as at other children. They also satirize adults of both sexes, even parents of the players, who may be watching and enjoying the performance. This is behavior that the boys would certainly not otherwise carry out in front of older persons; the masks "protect" them. Even those who are spoofed for corruption, greed, foolish or selfish behavior usually enjoy the skits and songs. In a situation analogous to the relationship of the egbele shrine to females, masking enables the boys, in a sense, to control those who ordinarily control them—a reversal of the usual situation. This is no doubt one of the reasons that the plays are so popular. These structured reversals of control allow boys to experiment at being adults, and to aggress against them in culturally acceptable ways. And as boys learn physical aggression through their societies and other activities, so they acquire aggressive vocal and social skills through masquerading.

In the masquerades the boys identify with older figures, including their parents, by taking the role of specific individuals as well as by putting on a type of masquerade that adults also perform. Masquerading also allows the boys to experiment at being female, for they play female as well as male masquerade roles. Since the youths perform in a humorous and derogatory manner, and in the context of the supposed anonymity of the masquerade, which is a conventional illusion (S. Ottenberg 1982a), the play is culturally acceptable to the audience. In Devereux's terms (1971:208–9), the boys successfully bribe their own superegos and those of the audience.

This satiric masquerade, ɔkumkpa, is a major production, requiring twenty to a hundred players. In former times very fine performances were put on by members of the third stage of the boys' society; those of the second stage were also good. As a result of the decline in size and organization of the boys' societies, the plays are not nearly as rich today. They are staged at the clearing of the society, or sometimes in a play area reserved for the uninitiated near the main commons of the village. In the old days men, women, and children attended; nowadays it is largely girls and boys. The players practice in secret for a month or more; the boys' society leaders choose which boys will play what roles. Boys bring stories about villagers to the leaders and gifted youths turn these into songs and acts. The boys don't need the village elders' permission or approval to perform, as the adult society does, again indicating their autonomy from the adult world.

In its best form the boys' *ɔkumkpa* lasts a number of hours, has many skits and parts to it, and is a complex and sophisticated popular entertainment form, requiring skill and imagination on the part of the players. The boys mimic the voices and physical behavior of adults. Since the boys sometimes dress and act as girls and women, always popular with the audience, they reiterate their maleness by playing females, a paradox of gender separation; they experiment with what it is like to be female, in the process of establishing their maleness. At the same time, masking psychologically and socially distances the boys from females by means of the taboos against females touching the masqueraders, seeing them dress and undress, or wearing masks themselves. Masquerading is an aesthetic device, with all its complex symbolism, to separate the growing boy from his mother, who is now on the other side of the fence, as it were. Here art and aesthetics act in the service of boyhood maturation, whatever else they do.

While the boys' society might, at best, produce one or two of these plays during a secret society season, for they take time and energy to prepare, forms of chasing masqueraders, which we have briefly mentioned in Chapter 2, appear, again in emulation of like adult forms (S. Ottenberg 1975: Chap. 11). In one popular type, *logholo,* one to more than ten boys dress up in raffia body costumes and wear a variety of masks. Each boy carries a stick in his right hand as they move about, usually as a group, through the compounds and in the boys' playing section near the village commons. Other uninitiated boys chase after them and try to knock them down, while they fend the aggressors off with their sticks and through body movements. The unmasked attackers may be older or younger boys, or of the same age, operating alone or sometimes in coordination, but they themselves should not yet be initiated into the adult secret society.

Other boys watch, as well as girls and also some adults; bystanders shout encouragement to the attackers or defenders. Boys able to throw a *logholo* player take great pride in this fact and are praised by other lads. When *logholo* players travel through compounds other than their own in the village it is an open challenge and, especially in the old days, fights between boys of different compounds would break out; there would be fierce hitting and whipping.

None of the boy masqueraders described so far can touch or be touched by females, for they wear a leaf (*ɛkike*) from a particular tree in their headpieces which is taboo to females, and like certain other types of leaves at Afikpo is believed to have potent magical properties. If touch occurs, the female must sacrifice at the boys' secret society shrine. And to avoid possible spiritual contamination of females from the power of the boys' *egbele* spirit, which is believed to be in them when they perform, the night of the play the masqueraders sleep in the secret society rest house in back of the compound, rather than in their boys' house. This act, occurring for adult secret society masquerades as well, prevents direct contact with females, again reiterating sex role separation and emphasizing certain religious powers associated with boys which are a substitute for parents. Yet, before a boy masks his mother will be informed by him or other boys and she will bring him fruits and peanuts the morning of the performance. He may eat some then and the rest after the play. Nuture and distancing both occur here.

Two other chasing masked forms, *ɔtɛro* and *ɔkpa,* are not made with this leaf, and boys who wear them can sleep in the compound at their boys' home following the masquerade. These players play with and chase girls as well as boys; girls can touch them although they rarely do. *Ɔtɛro* (S. Ottenberg 1975:180–83) appears in ones, twos, or threes, but not usually more. The costume consists of a banana-leaf body with a bell tied around the waist and a raffia headdress covering the entire face. The masquerader prances around the compounds chasing after both boys and girls. The latter run in real or pretended fright and hide in their houses, for the players will not follow them there, but quickly come out again to follow *ɔtɛro* and to egg the masqueraders on by shouts of "slave" and "wicked." If they should touch or be touched by him nothing bad will befall unless they knock off his face covering, when they have to perform a sacrifice at the boys' society shrine. This lenience also applies to the adult forms of *ɔtɛro* and *ɔkpa;* because these two forms of masquerade are not so closely associated with the secret society spirit, the rules are not so strict. Sometimes small boys are frightened of *ɔtero* and run away, to the amusement of older persons, who may try to get them to face it. A girl who knows a masquerader's identity should never reveal it to males or she will have to make a sacrifice at the boys' shrine. Underlying all this playfulness is a sense of boys controlling girls.

Ɔkpa is a rarer boys' masquerade role, only occasionally seen, and usually only one at a time. The proper dress is a full head and body looped-string affair (S. Ottenberg 1975: Chap. II); a stick is carried in the right hand. It is related to Cross River *ekpe* and *ngbe* figures (Ottenberg and Kundsen 1985). The costume is not normally made at Afikpo but purchased in neighboring markets at some expense—one reason it is not common—but sometimes boys prepare a makeshift one at home. *Ɔkpa* chases uninitiated boys and also girls, but it is gentler and less feared than *ɔtero,* and it mainly dances and prances about the compound, enjoyable to watch. At other times boys just dress up in masquerade costumes of a variety of types and dance and chase among themselves. This is something the adult societies rarely do; their masquerades are almost always regular public performances.

The masquerades are high points in the boys' lives in their secret groups because of their sense of mystery and excitement, the creativity associated with them (even if emulative), because of their aggressive physical and social qualities, and because they lead to interesting interactions with other people. It is in these masquerades that the boys' societies come into most direct contact with the public; otherwise they are largely concerned with their own affairs and with fighting between boys' societies. The meanings of dress and behavior are complex and the boys are involved in symbol-making and symbol-using.

Before masking the boys usually consult their *egbele* spirit shrine, giving it native chalk and kola—common sacrificial items at Afikpo—and each masker wears a small live chick tied in a hidden manner to his costume as part of the sacrifice. The shrine ritual informs the spirit of what they are about to do and asks for success in it; the chicks are believed to carry the society's spirit with the players. As one Afikpo said of the maskers: "They become powerful gods." Later he added, "When you have on a mask it makes you have courage, feel brave, especially with *logholo.* You feel like a strong boy even if you are not one. It is very uncomfortable to wear a mask. It may be too tight, it may be too hot, the player may end up with bruises if playing *logholo*. Everything you wear is considered *egbele* [and therefore taboo] to a woman if she touches it. She will then 'catch' *egbele* and be in trouble." At still a later time he added, "Masking differentiates you from the rest. It gives you spatial distance and puts you above those not in your particular level [of secret societies]." There is a feeling of omnipotence on the part of the masker, of being in charge, and of putting down others, including those normally in control of him (S. Ottenberg 1982a). In this way the boys act out the fantasy of being dominant and omnipotent parental figures.

The boys' masks and costumes are kept in the society rest house, or in the ancestral house in the compound if the society house is not in good repair, as sometimes occurs. But the materials used do not last long and they have to be replaced. Some boys become quite skilled at costume- and mask-making and will later use this ability when undergoing initiation into the adult society and in taking part in its masquerades. Some of the best Afikpo carvers of today obtained their initial experience preparing masks for themselves and for other boys (usually for a small fee) while in the boys' societies.

The boys' societies are not highly innovative; they very rarely perform masquerades that the adult society does not.* Again, there is a certain conning and illusion involved in these boys' groups. They are not supposed to know much about the adult secret society, though they see most of the adult society masquerades. But they emulate even some of the supposedly secret rituals associated with the adult secret society's spirit, and rites of the secret titles of the adult group. If girls were to do these, it would be considered a terrible abomination, but it is not so for boys. When I asked why, the usual reply was that "it is all right, they will join the adult society some day," suggesting that the being male is of importance, and that

---

*At Christmas time I have seen uninitiated boys' groups come to the houses of Europeans and well-to-do Africans, some wearing calabash masks and some wearing wood masks from areas other than Afikpo, while still others, as musicians, wore no masks but hit tin cans and bottles with sticks. Girls' dancing and singing groups do the same, but without masks. This is the only boys' masquerading which is not emulative of the adult society masquerades, and it is part of the emerging new Christmas tradition.

early practice for the boys is not considered undesirable by Afikpo adult males.

If the societies of the uninitiated boys show little true originality from the viewpoint of adult males, they are exciting and vital from the point of view of the boys themselves, or at least were so before modern times. They allow boys a great deal of freedom from parental control to learn, to experience, and to direct their own affairs. The boys may receive parental approval and praise after masquerading, as the mothers often bring further presents of food to their clearing in thanks, and fathers and older brothers praise boys who perform well. The youths are certainly sensitive to and take delight in this praise. But to a large extent the boys are on their own, in a peer-group relationship, emulating what they conceive to be the practices of the adult secret society, and of older boys in the third stage. The boys have both parental approval and a great deal of autonomy.

The Third Stage

Activities of the third stage are the same as those of the second stage; the difference is mainly one of quality. The initiation ceremony is a bit more elaborate and expensive; the rest house and the dressing shed (if there is one) are more elaborately constructed; the masquerades are likely to be better performed, and the costumes and masks more skillfully made. Third-stage boys' societies may have a few more members because they draw their membership from a larger residential area within the village. The boys are rougher and they fight and whip a good deal. But the basic style of behavior learned in the second stage is found here as well.

Thus it is that boys learn many of the fundamentals of secret society behavior between the ages of nine and eighteen, in the second and third boys' society stages, with some preliminary experience in the first. As they acquire skills and knowledge they are entering the age at which their sexual feelings begin to awaken. The boys' society gives no overt expression of this; it is not a group where sexual knowledge is formally learned or experienced, although the boys discuss sex among themselves. The masquerades are not overtly sexual in content, and the boys' groupings appear to lack overt homosexual behavior. But new experiences, the handling of secrecy, male role identity, and ritual and nonritual assertion and aggressiveness all develop coextensively with sexual growth, though these experiences begin in the sexually relatively quiet latency period. Sexual energies are channeled into the societies; they help to maintain Afikpo sexual codes which do not allow the boys much freedom in sexual matters (see Chapter 4). We have discussed the parallelism between sexual matters and secrecy before; we see it here again. As boys mature sexually, physically, and emotionally, so does their involvement in and control over secrecy matters.

Wrestling

Wrestling (*mgba*), like the secret society activities, brings boys together in cooperation and competition, in aggressive actions, and in emulation of male adults. Due to the decline of the boys' societies, in recent years wrestling appears to have come to play an increasingly important role. Unlike the case of the secret societies, here the boys actually join together in direct cooperation with adults; they are not strongly distanced from them, and secrecy is not at the heart of the matter.

Wrestling is a popular sport for young males. In its organized form it occurs in June and July, during the *ɔnwe* or "hungry period," before the new yams have appeared, a little after the end of the secret society season, which to some extent it replaces as a focus of interest. Wrestling carries on the themes of strength and physical skill which pervade male childhood life. In even-numbered years (by our Western calendar), it is only of minor importance, but in odd-numbered ones it is a major activity, with numerous intervillage contests within Afikpo. Village rules pressure young men to return home to take part at this time.

Wrestling is a major sport of adolescence and young manhood, from latency to adult maturity, and of importance to younger boys. Male wrestlers can be either single or married, circumcised or not, members of the adult secret society or non-initiates; the sport cross-cuts these qualities, reaching its climax at about the age of thirty, the age at which, in the past, men were in their prime as warriors. This is also the age at which wrestling groups give way to organized village age sets (S. Ottenberg 1971: Chaps. 3 and 4).

For important matches the wrestlers wear shorts with traditional waistcloths over them and decorate their arms and bodies with chalk. Two wrestlers stand and face each other, each trying to throw the other to the ground by use of arms, legs, and body; the one so thrown loses. Hitting is not allowed, nor grabbing at the opponents' genitals, but grasping, tripping, twisting limbs, and shoving all occur. Skill lies not only in the ability to throw down the opponent but also in displaying a variety of techniques. Speed, boldness, and strength of attack are important. Much praise is given to the wrestler who can put down a larger and stronger opponent, as well as being able to take defeat gracefully.

In organized contests men just past the wrestling age, often once good wrestlers themselves, act as referees (*atamaja*). They match up wrestlers of like ages and, in an atmosphere of considerable excitement, try to keep the players and crowd under control. Often there is argument and disagreement among these leaders as to who should wrestle whom, and a wrestling afternoon has chaotic aspects to it. Before the event the senior wrestlers carry out sacrifices at a number of spirit shrines in the village and compounds to ask the spirit world for success. Drummers are hired by each team for important matches and there are special drumming rhythms connected with the sport. Players, stimulated by the music, dance about and challenge opposing team members to knock them down. Many other males of all ages watch, as well as girls and women, who cheer lovers, brothers, husbands, and friends.

Boys between the ages of five and fifteen are not usually organized into specific wrestling grades, as are older males. They wrestle informally any time of the year, and they enjoy issuing challenges to one another. Their contests sometimes degenerate into fighting, as there are usually no older males supervising them. Young boys have plenty of time to wrestle, and as they can view the organized matches they have the opportunity to observe others at this sport. They enjoy watching contests and talking about the matches afterward; they identify with their heroes, and they have their villains.

As the wrestling season begins, the males of neighboring compounds in a village compete with one another, grouped into three or more organized wrestling ages of youths between the ages of about 15 and 30. Then there are matches between village wards. From these contests emerge the best wrestlers in each wrestling grade, who represent the village in the important intervillage matches.

A boy may wrestle another of a higher age grade if he feels able and the wrestling leaders permit him; to knock over such an opponent brings great acclaim, and is a matter of considerable interest. As one Afikpo said, "If a boy is strong he belongs to the group his strength brings him. If he is weak he belongs to the group his age puts him in." But most boys contest with lads their own age and size.

In interward contests in the settlement, as well as in intervillage competition, the first match (*ibuzo mgba*, first-wrestle) is often of boys in the unorganized 5–15 years category, pitting two good wrestlers together as a warm-up event. Such contestants frequently display more energy and strength than skill. While boys take great pride in being selected by the men involved on each side to do this, and often become, at a later time, the better village wrestlers, this match is something of a joking affair. Nevertheless, Afikpo males often say that the side that wins this contest will win most of the other events of the day.

This match is followed by a general wrestling period, *ɔkpug-hughughu* (roughly meaning "group confusion"). Anyone, from the smallest boy of three to a man of thirty years, can wrestle; many youths come out and compete against one another, often at the same time, while the referees comment on their abilities. Old grudges bring about some challenges. A loser gets up and challenges another than the person who defeated him, which he would not do at an organized competition. Among those fifteen years of age and older only the poorer wrestlers appear at this time; the better ones expect to wrestle in the regular matches to follow. There is an air of humor about these preliminary contests. No one takes them seriously, except some of the participants.

The first organized wrestling grade in Mgbom and many other villages is *mkpufu mgba* (to start off, or to break out–wrestle), made up of boys between the ages of about 15 and 18. In former times this was about the age when they joined the adult secret society. At a match between two wards of a village, or between two villages, only the most skillful will be allowed to wrestle; at the lower intercompound level almost every boy tries out. This is the first age at which wrestling contests are taken seriously and boys work hard to improve their abilities. The winner dances around in happiness to the drums. Youths of this age are not well disciplined; they may not wait to be selected by the referees, but break out onto the field in the commons, challenge others to wrestle, and go right to it.

This is followed by the *isoogu* wrestlers. The term is from *iso*, to grow, and *ogugu*, the growing part of a palm or bamboo tree. The explicit reference is to boys before full maturity who "spread out" (mature); the implicit reference may be to the growth of the penis. This age, often divided into subgroups, includes males of about 18 to 28 years of age, who are usually all members of the adult secret society, and provides the largest number of matches. The side of the winner of the one or two matches between the senior *isoogu* players is considered the winner for the day, even if it loses other matches. But Afikpo also say that there is no official winner for the whole event and that the real interest is in the individual matches. Even young boys watch these contests with excitement and interest.

The highest grade, *ikpo* (iron bell, worn by wrestlers of this class), is composed of men some 28 to 30 years of age. They are considered to be the finest competitors of all. Only a few wrestlers from this group take part at a major match, but every *ikpo* is expected to have thrown someone before he moves out of this age, a reflection of a belief that every male should take part in wrestling, as everybody should join the boys' secret societies. If a contestant is unable to beat someone an arranged match will be set at which another player "takes a fall," or the inept wrestler may pay a fee to the *ikpo* grade as a substitute. The concept of the ideal wrestler is equivalent to an older idea that every warrior should take a head in warfare. Men move out of this grade, and resign from wrestling, when they pass the age of thirty, about the time that their village age set is forming as an official body. Thus wrestling is not only a sport; it is intimately associated with age organization and with male peer-group activity at Afikpo.

Boys' organized wrestling starts some ten years later than the activities of the boys' secret societies. There is a much longer period of unorganized events in wrestling than with the societies, plenty of time for boys to gain experience and develop skills as they wrestle on an informal basis. The organized matches share some features with the boys' secret societies. There is a breakdown into age groupings, with exceptions allowed in both cases for the strong and the gifted. In both cases, the younger males are highly emulative of older ones, watching them with interest and excitement. In both wrestling and the adult secret societies the boys come under the supervision of adults at about 15 to 18 years of age; before then they are largely on their own, in the secret society until initiation into the adult organization, in wrestling until the time of the more senior public matches. We see how adult authority becomes very important in both cases at adolescence, at the time of growing sexual energy, though it does this much more strongly and in deeper symbolic ways through the initiation into the adult society than through the organized wrestling. In both in the wrestling contests and in the secret society masquerades, the boys display their prowess to girls, a kind of showing off with sexual overtones.

As most wrestlers mature they become involved with larger and larger organizations—from compound to ward to village—as in the case of the boys and their secret societies. Both stress strength and physical skill; wrestling used to be directly related to warfare. Both secret society and wrestling activities have many elements of humor about them, and both stress personal skill combined with a willingness to cooperate and follow a set of rules. Both include ritual activities carried out by the boys. The wrestlers do not own the shrines to which they sacrifice, yet of some of these shrines it is said that the wrestlers "take charge of them" during the competitive season (S. Ottenberg 1970:30–34). In both wrestling and the boys' societies music plays an important role.

In contrast to the boys' societies, there is little secrecy to the wrestling (though players or their ward or village guides may consult a diviner before important matches to know what to do to put down an important opponent). For this reason I see wrestling as less an expression of conscious and unconscious feelings and relationships with their parents, than a working out of boys' ties with other males of their age, and perhaps indirectly with youthful females as well. In terms of the latter there is a belief at Afikpo in the power of a virgin girl to influence the course of important matches. For an intervillage contest the village elders consult a diviner a day or so before the event. Elders do not direct the match but they watch it, are concerned that their village do well, and want to know how to defeat the champions of the other community. Coun
charms may be obtained by wrestlers from the diviner. He may say, "Well, the only headache that you have at Mgbom Village is Enwo." The elders ask, "How can we get him?" The religious specialist then asks them to bring a lizard and certain medicinal leaves and roots, and to get something from Enwo's house—perhaps a bit of his cloth. If he is fond of girls, as champion wrestlers are likely to be, being popular with them, the diviner asks the elders to bring a girl from their own village who has not yet started to menstruate. He asks her to hold the lizard, saying, "Well, it is Enwo that you are holding now." She responds, "This is Enwo that I am holding." The diviner tells the girl to say that as she is holding him his power is useless, and that at the match "let the ground be his" (let him fall). He gives the girl a bundle of medicines to store in her house without the knowledge of her mother, who should not touch them, for a menstruating woman will break the power of the charm. It is a common Afikpo belief that the wrestler will then come and have intercourse with the girl and that this will weaken him. For this reason, among others, Afikpo males try to abstain from intercourse the night before a wrestling contest, and also they avoid contact with menstruating women. It is said that the bundle the girl stores represents the wrestler; it is a symbolic seduction, for of course he does not come and often does not know her.

Here there are two conceptions of female power that maturing boys are exposed to: that menstruating females have destructive powers, and that sexually active women can weaken men. Both reflect the attention to and the fear of women that characterize male beliefs about females at Afikpo—the power and the danger. A complementary position is that after males have had close contact with powerful spirits they refrain from sexual intercourse for fear of spreading spiritual contamination to females. In the boys' and men's secret societies, key masquerade players refrain from intercourse the night before playing so as to perform well and all masqueraders are continent the night of the performance so as not to contaminate females with male spiritual powers. Men are believed sexually dangerous to women through their spiritual associations, as women are to men through their physiology. These ideas and associated behavior help to keep the sexes separate and disassociated. I believe that they relate to the early intimate mother-child relation at Afikpo, for these views of female sexual powers reflect the male infant's anxiety over his mother's sexuality. And the danger of the males' sexuality is used to disassociate themselves from females. Through these beliefs boys learn to handle unconscious and conscious childhood wishes toward their mothers.

Girls' Societies and Wrestling Groups

There is no female equivalent of the boys' secret societies, as there is no adult secret society for women. Nevertheless, from the age of about five until they marry in adolescence, girls have an organization, *okpu ntu* (gathering-ashes), in almost every Afikpo compound.

As in the boys' society, girls who do not join are fined small sums of money until they take part. The leadership is in the hands of older unmarried girls of the compound; several interested married women living there act as the group's guides. The members of *okpu ntu* leave it when they marry, which usually draws them into other compounds to live and to other interests.

This nonsecret organization is responsible for the care of the garbage dump and of the latrine in back of its compound. The girls keep these clean and orderly and have the right to fine violators regardless of age or sex, a right backed by the older men, as compound leaders; violators who mess up the latrine or dump, leave trash outside a house, or fail to use the latrine to defecate (except for small children), may be fined by these girls. *Okpu ntu* is called upon by men of the compound to aid in building a home; its members carry rocks and dirt and smooth the walls. The girls fine their members who fail to join in their activities without an excuse. These female tasks are seen by the Afikpo as an extension of their duties in their homes, with some analogies to mothers caring for infants.

None of these tasks is particularly exciting, but the money that is collected in fines is used, every now and then, to put on a dance and a feast, for which the girls purchase, if they don't already have them, outfits of uniform color and design: head ties, brassieres, handkerchiefs, shorts, and shoes or sneakers. Aided by their mothers the girls sew their own costumes. They create their own songs in secret, sometimes excluding the younger females who would be unable to learn them or who might sing them beforehand; part of the enjoyment is in revealing the songs on the proper day. This aesthetic of revelation corresponds to the boys' satiric masquerade plays. Rehearsals take a great deal of time and are a subject of interest and enjoyment. The younger females who are excluded from the singing take part in the dancing, all girls being arranged in line from largest to smallest in size. The songs are commentaries on life and marriage, generally optimistic rather than satirical or derisive, as are those of the boys' secret society masquerades.

This event is an enjoyable nonreligious affair. The girls sing and dance around the compounds and at the commons of their village, for all to see and hear; sometimes they also go to neighboring communities. Friends, relatives, and others present them with small sums of money and food. Then they return home to feast themselves. At

Christmas time, in recent years, some *okpu ntu* societies have taken to visiting the homes of teachers at the various schools at Afikpo, and they also go to the Government Stations area. They sing and dance and receive small presents.

Sometimes one or two young adult men of the girls' compound will take an entrepreneurial interest in the society, encouraging the girls to dance and to make up songs and suggesting where they might perform. Sometimes they dance ahead of the girls to announce their coming. The Afikpo say that without these intermediaries between themselves and their audience, the girls would be too shy to go about outside of their own communities for this purpose. This relationship also illustrates how brief is the period of female autonomy from males at Afikpo; the act of growing up for girls involves switching from a dependency on the mother to dependency on males, where for boys it is from dependency upon to control of females.

These girls' groups symbolize the division of sex roles in Afikpo society, reflecting the domestic orientation of females. Their musical and dancing style is consistent with that which they will do as adults at the Feast of the Tortoise (see Chapter 4), at funerals, at title ceremonies, at the boys' bird shrine rite, and on other occasions (although at some of these they engage in satiric song, for which females are much praised by the men). The creative aesthetic experiences in *okpu ntu* form an important base for later female artistic activity, as the boys' societies do for males.

The girls' dress reflects a unity of females; uniform female performance dress is a common feature of modern southern Nigerian culture. This also expresses the interest in the feminine body and the delight in attracting the eye of viewers, especially parents and, in a different way, boys. The boys' societies also dress to attract, though not in a uniform style, perhaps expressing greater preference for individuality, although at Afikpo persons of both gender appear to vary greatly in personality and behavior. The boys' more secret and esoteric ritualized activities suggest their growing interest in power and authority, in control over themselves and over females as they mature, in knowledge of ritual matters, and in striving for dominance. *Okpu ntu* rather suggests cooperativeness and pleasantness, and is thoroughly secular.

There is girls' wrestling as well at Afikpo, although the absence of warfare conditions and the presence of missionaries has reduced the stress on female strength and assertiveness, and much of this has died out. In former times there was more interest in wrestling between unmarried females, and girls even wrestled with boys—a practice now frowned upon by Afikpo adults. When I was in Afikpo girls wrestled one another throughout the year in play, not only in a special clearing somewhere in or near the village, but about the compounds, the farm paths, and elsewhere. The older unmarried girls, though not organized into formal grades as the boys were, competed at the major village feasts during the "hungry period," the time when males also wrestle. At these more organized contests interested boys matched up the female contestants and controlled the event. At one match in 1952 in Mgbom Village the girls wore shorts or a waistcloth but nothing above (except that some had earrings and necklaces). Boys frequently broke up contests before they were finished, for the joy of it, chasing girls back into the compounds and waving raffia palm leaves at them. The girls returned to be chased again, reminiscent of some of the masked activities of the boys' societies, with their overtones of sexual play. While male wrestling events have a chaotic side, this particular match seemed as much a playful exchange between boys and girls as it was a wrestling contest. It is the older unmarried girls who help train the younger ones and assist in organizing matches, though only a few are usually present at the girls' contests.

The presence of females at male matches is not required, yet girls are often there, have interests in certain boys, and have their favorite male wrestlers. The control of boys over females at wrestling differs from their control over females through the boys' secret societies, but controls exist in both situations; both are expressions of the pattern of Afikpo male-female relationships which the growing children come to experience.

There is more hierarchical control and authority in the girls' activities than in the boys'—wielded by older women, sometimes by a few young men in *okpu ntu* and in wrestling, and by older girls in both. Boys seem to form more purely peer-based organizations than girls, especially in their secret societies, and they are freer of parents than the girls, especially of the mother. This reflects the greater control of mothers over daughters than either parent over sons at mid-childhood. The growing gender dichotomy that accompanies maturation goes with increasing differences in experiences with authority for each sex.

Fantasy

At night, in the period after planting, about May to July, when the rains have started and the new vegetables are beginning to come up, mothers tell stories (*ilu*), usually in their homes, to children of both sexes. Other women are there and adult men are occasionally present. Women cook early so that they will have time for this pleasant pastime. The stories tell how the poor become rich, how an ugly person becomes successful, how yams grow and die and why they are important, with explanations of customs, such as why one should not laugh at the poor or the ugly. Often there is a proverb at the end. Sometimes the tales involve tortoise as trickster; sometimes origin tales are told. It is a time of amusement, reflection, and learning, with adults (especially females) and children together. In the presence of older people, the listening children can let their imaginations wander without fear of condemnation.

A child may be frightened by a tale, but at these sessions there is a sense of harmony and interest among female adults and children of both sexes. For a growing boy, who is pulling away from his mother in other ways, this is a situation of pleasant intimacy with her and other female adults. For girls it is one of many such instances. Also, boys sometimes tell tales to one another in their compound rest houses, or when together in their secret society houses.

Occasionally the stories are about children. One, in rough translation, goes as follows:

The hunter went out hunting, in the night. As he was there in the bush seven ancestral spirits representing themselves as animals met and decided to whom they should go to be born. The first one came up and said that he would go to one hunter and be born as a male child, and he would die immediately he was of marriageable age. The second one came up and selected another hunter and said that he would be born of the hunter as a male child and would die on his circumcision day. A third came and said that he would be born of another hunter, as a daughter, and would die in her fattening room. The fourth came up and said that he would be born of another hunter, as a male child, and would die on the day his first tooth was seen. The fifth came up and said he would be born of another hunter, as a daughter, and would die the very day the four-day coming-out rite of the infant occurred. The sixth selected another hunter and said that he would be born a male child and would die on the child's adult secret society initiation day. The seventh came out and said he would be born of the very hunter listening there, as a male child, and would die after he started crawling, of a snake bite. The hunter was not particularly interested in the others, but that which related to him he was concerned about. He came home.

Not very long after his wife was expecting and the child was born, and it started to grow. Quickly it grew to the age of crawling. One day the child showed signs of unhappiness. He started to cry. The mother was very much upset, not knowing what was wrong with the child. She reported it to the husband, so the two of them kept close watch on the child to know what was really wrong. They discovered that it wanted to walk out of its mother's lap. The father, who knew all about what the child was after, was very cautious and took his gun and loaded it and told the mother to let the child alone. The child started to crawl out, and as he crawled he was no longer crying. He was happy as he crawled. The father watched and saw that the child was going toward a corner. He followed the child. Just behind the corner of the house a big snake appeared. The child quickly crawled towards the snake and the father, knowing that this must be the snake that was to bite the child, fired his gun and killed the snake. The child was disappointed. The father returned the child to the house. He burned the snake and told the mother, "There you are, that is your child, he will not die again." The same evening he went out hunting. When he got to the same spot where he was before he met these animals expecting the seventh to return. They were concerned as the seventh had not come in time and they wondered why he had not kept his promise. What was up? They were very upset knowing that something wrong might have occurred. The hunter fired at them and they scattered. In the morning he saw torches at that spot, burnt sticks which represented the animals that he had fired at. When he came home he told his wife the story of the child. He said to the child, "Well, I have disappointed you, you shall no more die." The child lived. Whether the child lived forever nobody knows, but eventually the child must have died. The moral lesson behind the story is that hunters do know and understand the language of animals; they know all about the secrets of the night.

The tale points to the importance of the crucial transitions of childhood—birth, coming out, teething, fattening, and so on. It is at these times that the Afikpo believe that children are most likely to die; they are clearly times of danger to children. The story also offers an explanation of the difficulty of keeping children alive, due to the nature of the reincarnating ancestral spirits. The hunter, an assertive and strong male who understands the mysteries of the forest, is the obvious hero; his wife plays a passive role. The tale plays on the fear of snakes, and the potentially disruptive and dangerous qualities of this phallic object. Symbolically we have a split father-image: the destructive, killing *pater* (snake/ancestral spirit), and the living protective supportive father (the hunter). These two aspects of the father—the wish to protect and aid the son and the desire to destroy him—conflict with one another. It is an oedipal story as well, in which the evil father figure lures the child from the protection of its mother to kill it. The tale also associates the male hero with secrecy; he keeps his knowledge from his wife, as males at Afikpo do, and thus controls the situation.

Since there are few or no male adults at these sessions, and they usually do not tell tales, there is a return of the child to the mother's home, at night, in darkness. The experience echoes infancy, albeit with numerous children, in a culturally approved and socially bounded setting. This is an unusual situation for boys, for generally they are in the process of separating, and being separated, from their mothers, moving into a male world. The taletelling sessions allow for rich mental associations, including those linked with early childhood, permitting the child to work through feelings of the past in terms of his sense of the present. Women taletellers are real or surrogate mothers, engaging in fantasy and permitting the child to join in this endeavor.

Tales such as these strengthen the rich fantasy life of Afikpo children, spurred by the darkness of the performance situation and the closely packed group of familiar mothers and children (Bettelheim 1977). Afikpo culture does much to encourage fantasy among children, in boys' and adult masquerades, in beliefs in a multitude of spiritual forces and powers (which, like the characters in the tales, embody differing qualities), and in the many rituals that children see. Fantasy involves boys in action, such as masquerading, as well as in passive reflection, as in the taletelling. The boys act out imaginary events in their masquerades; in wrestling they emulate village and Afikpo sports heroes. The actions undoubtedly strengthen their ego formation, providing them with a sense of mastery and control. This powerful fantasy life may involve a sense of danger or difficulty, but it also conveys a sense of human control, of humans employing the imagination for positive rather than destructive ends. The Afikpo do not emerge from their fantasy world as paranoid witch-believers like the Limba that I studied in northern Sierra Leone (Finnegan 1965: 116–22); rather, they develop a pragmatic, bargaining, even entrepreneurial relationship with the spirit world, in which strong individuals (like the hunter in the tale) are believed to be capable of controlling their fates.

Games

In terms of the focus of this book, children's games at Afikpo are more difficult to interpret than wrestling and secret society activities, for the games do not follow any simple pattern. Games involve types of behavior which occur elsewhere in childhood experience, but there is one crucial difference: the games are not emulative of adult behavior and are not usually played by adults. In so far as there is an Afikpo culture of childhood, distinct from adult culture as in contemporary Western cultures (Ariès 1962; Cannizzo 1978; Hardman 1973; Opie 1959, 1969), it seems to lie at least partly in these games, as well as some songs and expressions.

There is an *idea* of childhood at Afikpo which distinguishes children as persons from adults, and there is an active social life for boys, largely separate from their parents, but there is little children's *culture* which differs in basics from that of adults. Much of the boys' behavior is emulative of older males, particularly of young men in the adult secret society, in wrestling, and in farmwork. Girls' actions are imitative of older women's singing and dancing, household, and farmwork patterns. Emulation characterizes other Igbo as well (Shelton 1969:239). As Uchendu (1965:61) writes, "Igbo children participate in the affairs of the adult world with childlike enthusiasm: in their own world they dramatize adult roles and spend their leisure hours doing 'nursing,' cooking, playing father and mother, holding 'play' markets and market fights." Afikpo children appear adult-oriented,* suggesting strong association to parents. Boys are socially separated from parents but culturally emulative of fathers; girls are both socially close to mothers and emulative of them. The social distance of boys from parents protects them from their oedipal and other early childhood conflicts, while the emulative cultural aspects allow them to identify with the parent of the same sex.

Children's games at Afikpo, casually rather than formally organized, are not generally secret. Some are for one sex only, but others involve both males and females. Like many children's games elsewhere they are competitive—not surprising in an entrepreneurial society such as Afikpo. Games tend to be played when there is no

---

*Oppong (1973:51–52) finds this to be true of children's play among the Dagomba of northern Ghana. See also Fortes (1970:204–5) on the nearby Tallensi.

farmwork to be done, generally in the dry season. Parents do not usually organize, supervise, or watch the children play, nor do other adults. Like other children's activities at Afikpo, games have an autonomous quality to them, and generally involve youths of similar ages. The quieter games and those involving fewer players often go on in the compound, while the more athletic ones, and those with a larger number of players, occur in a children's play area, often at the edge of or near the village commons. This is not an area especially designated by adults; it is just an out-of-the-way open space, fitting well the Afikpo pattern that children, especially boys, are not constantly watched by older people.

A popular girls' game is *ɔgbubu azama* (throw-*azama* [a kind of bean]). A number of players each bring a certain number of beans, of a type cooked by females, to the game. They dig a small pit in the ground and take turns dropping beans in it, until one, or sometimes two if they so decide, lands on top of another. The player who has dropped this bean then attempts to grab all of them in the pit with one scoop, to add to her collection. If she fails to retrieve them all she leaves all of them there, and the game goes on. If she succeeds she continues dropping seeds and the game proceeds. The winner is the player who collects most or all of the beans. Boys occasionally play this game.

Girls also play several form of jacks, called *igha ogwe* (pick [as from a tree]-*ogwe* [a type of seed used in the game]). Skipping rope (*ihwe akpe*, to fly–rope) is a common and competitive girls' game, played either by a girl holding her own rope of native fiber or by two girls holding it for a third. I do not know whether skipping rope and jacks are European derived or not; they are carried out in the context of traditional village life. Another female game is cat's cradle (*odɔ ɛka*, string-hand). Girls also sometimes hold foot races in the compound.

Turning to boys, *kuso*, probably of Hausa origin, is played by spinning a conical shell on the ground. *Ɔka mgba* (to pass–wrestling) is a popular and amusing mock wrestling match, where two boys each throw up a grass blade, and the one whose blade lands on the other's is the winner. Other boys then challenge the winner. *Ede* (elsewhere in Africa called *wari*), a highly competitive game, played rapidly and involving moving *ede* seeds in two rows of holes carved in a wooden board or dug in the ground, is largely a boys' game. Occasionally adult males play it; on the whole it is not very popular at Afikpo. Another game for two boys involves one of them throwing a palm fiber ball with a fiber hook attached to it, while the other lad tries to catch the hook in a noose of native string. This is mainly a game for adolescent boys; it is too difficult for younger ones. The English game of draughts is played by two boys, often in the compound, with other young male onlookers. The play goes very rapidly, as in *ede,* and it is interesting to watch.

A game played by both sexes together or by boys alone is *okombɵ* (building-houses), where boys create miniature houses in the sand that resemble the homes of adult males and sometimes of females (slightly smaller); the children may even make a small compound. If girls join in, they procure the sand for the boys but do not build, much as in adult home building. Sticks and leaves and other elements may be employed; more recently match boxes have been used by the boys to mold sand bricks. Other boys may come by and knock down the houses; this often results in fighting. This game, with its emulation of adult house building, has closer reference to adult culture at Afikpo than other games.

This house building game is played by boys from about five to twelve years of age. Sometimes they put grasshoppers, with their wings torn off, in these constructions, and pretend that they are people, creating scenes with them. There is a destructive side to this play, as the insects are often later taken home, roasted, and eaten by the boys. So much for symbolic parental figures and other adults! At other times crickets or grasshoppers are impaled on the ribs of palm fronds, especially by boys, and carried about like trophies of war, as human heads apparently were in the past, and as birds' heads are in the ritual that we have already described. The insects may be taken off the fronds and lined up on the ground, the boys pretending that they are horses. (Horses are very rare at Afikpo, high status animals brought in only to be killed at major funeral rites.) Eventually the insects are cooked and eaten by the boys. Adults do not eat them, a clearly differentiating feature.

Boys find burrows of field mice at the farms and dig them out, catching the animals; this requires cooperation as there are usually at least two tunnel exits from their underground home. Girls may assist in this work. Boys also trap or catch rats. Both mice and rats are cooked (the latter usually smoked); the children share the meat with siblings and parents. The Afikpo do not usually eat the tails of rats or mice. They are believed particularly harmful to the unexcised child, for it is thought that eating them will make blood vessels grow at the point of the excision on the penis or clitoris, and there will be much bleeding when the cutting occurs. Clearly then, the animal tail represents penis and clitoris; the taboo involves refraining from "eating" the genital area, from attacking it, reflecting anxiety over the possibility of uncontrolled bleeding at the excision, and perhaps the consequent guilt of an adult of having damaged a child.

There are other games which may involve both sexes. One is *ili asa* (bury-*asa* [name of game]) in which a circlet of raffia is buried in a small sand heap and each player in turn stabs at it with a stick, trying to enter the object with one jab. A point is given for each success; six points usually wins the game. This is a favorite pastime of small children. Another game, in which the teams may be of both sexes or males alone, but rarely only females, is *obeghile* (no translation). There are two teams of equal number. A soft fiber ball is thrown up in the air by a member of one team. If someone from the second team catches it a member of the first group has to move to the second; this child is called a "slave" (*ohu*). The second team then throws the ball toward the first and the process continues. The play is over when one side has captured all the players of the other.

There is also a game called *igba agha* (catching-war) which is played by twelve-year-olds of both sexes, together or separately. The game is a form of tag, which involves singing and chanting.

These games develop manual skills in both sexes, although they require only simple materials, if any at all. Games involving grasping seem more characteristic of females, throwing and catching of males, and contests involving greater physical exertion are likely to be played by boys. Yet the competitive spirit among children of both sexes is high, and the games are open and nonsecret, unlike some activities associated with the boys' societies. This is yet another face of male experience at Afikpo, contrasting in some ways with the more secret aspects of boys' life, but exhibiting the same competitive drive, with an emphasis on assertive physical motion, skill, and sometimes strength, and some association with warfare and wrestling. There is autonomy from parental supervision, or that of other older persons, as with the boys' secret societies, but unlike some aspects of wrestling contests.

Conclusion

In this chapter I have discussed some of the more organized activities of children during latency and early adolescence. It is worth remarking that the considerable organizational activity at these ages, particularly for boys, serves as useful training for the complex social structural patterns of adult Afikpo life. Boys learn to handle secret knowledge and behavior, and girls to act and react to it. Further, I have noted how the boys' activities in strongly organized peer groups draws them away from their mothers and keeps them at a distance from their fathers; in this process secrecy, aesthetics, and bodily skills all play important roles. It is also a time of rich fantasy development, in which the boys play an active role. In the next chapter I examine the less formal relationships of children to one another and to adults. Both aspects are germane to this study.

4
Social Boundaries

HROUGH THE RITUALS OF CHILDHOOD, THE BOYS'
and the girls' societies, wrestling activities, and some children's games, children develop strong social boundaries on
the basis of age and sex, with recognized and acceptable forms of
behavior within them. The process of social boundary development
accelerates as children mature. But the matter is more complex than
just the separation of the sexes and of youths from older persons, for
very specific kinds of positive attachments across these boundaries
also arise.

Children and Secret Societies

For girls, the behavior that they learn in relation to the boys' secret
societies they also carry out toward the adult men's society all of their
lives. During the adult secret society season all females are surrounded by restrictions; they must be careful of what goes on in the
village commons, on which the compounds front, for adult secret
society activities occur there. Females also regard with caution the
back of the compounds, where the boys' societies are located. Bush
areas around the village are likely to be used by adult or boys' society
members, so females remain on the regular paths as much as possible. Failure to comply with these measures is believed to cause illness
or death, but particularly barrenness, brought about by an angered
boys' or adult society spirit.

But there are also positive relationships for girls with the adult and
boys' secret societies. They see the public masquerades and enjoy
them considerably. They receive blessings from the adult society's
priest at the end of the short form of male initiation, largely to ensure
their future fertility. They help their mothers prepare food for the

boys in the initiation bush. They lend male initiates cloth, plastic beads, and jewelry for masquerades that the adult secret society puts on, as they do for the boys' societies, knowing what the loans are for but not stating so. A girl may indirectly praise a masquerader in either the boys' or the men's society for his performance sometime after it is over, and even give him a gift, but she may not do so at the time of the masquerade, as secret society initiates can do. Clearly, the girls contribute to the success of the masquerades. Thus for the growing female there are possible and expected interactions with members of both the boys' and the adult secret societies, but they are carried out in highly prescribed form. These mirror the relatively distant relationship that girls have with their fathers.

With restrictions and interactions comes knowledge. It is in girlhood that females begin to learn what the boys actually do in their secret societies, and they discover at that time, or later, that much the same kind of activities go on in the adult society. They acquire this knowledge from older girls and adult females and from observation. They may accidentally see and hear things that they should not. They recognize their brothers and other boys in masquerades; not all of the costumes completely cover the body, and the girls' loans of items of dress to boys for these performances gives them information. At the same time that girls fear the spiritual forces associated with the boys' shrine, they know that the boys' activities are carried out by real people, some of whom are their own agnatic kin. At the time that the boys officially learn about their own societies and the adult secret society, girls also acquire information about the boys' and adult secret societies. Some girls feel that it is important for them to learn about these secret groupings for their own sense of their place in the world. But to boys and male adults alike the girls maintain the face of innocence and unknowingness; they reveal what they know only in private to other females.

Boys are forbidden to have anything to do with the adult secret society. Taboo to them are most parts of its initiation ceremonies, its secret title activities, and its whipping contests. They are forbidden to enter the society's priest house (if there is one), the men's rest house in the commons, and the men's dressing structures (in those villages that have them), and they cannot sing adult secret society songs. They must shout their warning call when passing through the commons during the secret society season and stay out of it when it is closed by the society.

The boys are also expected not to allow their own societies to become like the adult one in certain respects. They are not to employ certain terms and phrases of the adult society. In fact, they sometimes use them in their own groups, but not in front of adult males. They cannot perform certain adult secret society masquerades and initiations, as we have noted. They are not to produce certain mysterious sounds which are heard emanating from the commons at night, even if they discover how to make them. In the Itim villages of Afikpo they cannot use wood in making masks or for the decorated boards for their dressing structures. They can produce wooden stools, gongs, and drums, for they are not forbidden to work in wood entirely, but only in those instances where this material is believed to have a mystical association with the adult society and its spirit.

To these rules can be added social restrictions. It is said that in former times a non-initiate into the adult secret society (not then initiated until perhaps eighteen years of age) was not supposed to have sexual intercourse; it is not clear whether this edict was ever strictly followed but it is not today. The boys are expected to eat separately from adult society members at most feasts and rituals—a rule not always followed. They cannot marry until they are secret society members, nor can they take certain nonsecret titles which require initiation. They are not supposed to break wind while in the company of initiates. If they do so they are not punished at the time, but they or their fathers may have to pay compensation at the time of initiation. A non-initiate into the adult society is also restricted from owning certain personal shrines, such as *njoku*, the yam shrine, and *ibini ɔkpabe*, a powerful spirit (S. Ottenberg 1970:41–44), although he may have and use other shrines, such as *nkamalo* (S. Ottenberg 1970:30–35), established for him by another person, usually the father, who performs its rites for him until he is initiated. Initiation into the adult society permits the male to enter more fully and richly into the religious life of Afikpo, while uninitiated males, regardless of age, interest, and talent, cannot do so.

The situation for boys who violate adult secret society restrictions is nowhere near as serious as for girls. For one thing, it normally does not require a sacrifice to the adult society spirit, as in the case of girls and women. For another, a violation is not usually associated with subsequent illness or lack of fertility for a boy, as is likely in a girl's case. A boy will be rebuked by adult males, and spanked as a last resort, as a young boy will be beaten by older boys if he learns secrets of the boys' society above him in age and this becomes known. A boy who fails to shout "*loooooooooooooo*" when passing through the village commons during the secret society season may be cautioned by men sitting in the rest house there. Uninitiated boys living in a compound near the adult secret society priest's house see and hear things forbidden to them, but it is not viewed as a serious matter, for they will be initiated some day. I have seen uninitiated boys walking through a commons where the fence was being built for the first-son form of initiation, but without rebuke, although they should not be there at all. If boys sneak out and see the parts of an initiation ceremony forbidden to them nothing serious will happen. As one Afikpo said to me: "They will be told: Right, you are a non-initiate and you try to be an elder. Wait until you are initiated." Such a boy may be threatened with being beaten when initiated. If he fails to complete a difficult run in masquerade costume to neighboring Edda Village-Group as an adult society member (S. Ottenberg 1975:167–69), or if he becomes weak or faint during his initiation, he may be told, "Well, when you were a non-initiate you ignored things, and now here you are, see what happens!" These comments suggest some mystical connection between the offense and the later situation, but its nature is not explicit and its consequences not very serious for boys. Age and initiation separate boys from men—the markers are clear—but they are all males after all.

If uninitiated boys, as a group or individually, sing adult secret society songs, or ones similar to them, the elders of the village, perhaps prodded by the secret society priest or leaders, may fine them. Their fathers usually pay or try to talk their way out of this punishment. Or if the boys' emulation of adult society activities becomes too striking, as it may in the third stage of the boys' societies, a few young members of the men's society will dress up in the *ɔtero* and *ɔkpa* masquerades and swoop down on the boys' headquarters, tearing down the buildings and destroying everything. They tell the boys that it is time for them to join the adult society, for they are getting too good at imitating it. Some boys may join up, while others rebuild their structure. Such action is rare; it is more talked about than done. What is evident is that the boys know a great deal about the adult society before they join it. The paradox is that adult males really want the boys to acquire secret society skills, to be creative and assertive, yet wish to maintain social distance commensurate with age differences between them. The ambivalent relationship of fathers and sons is symbolized in this way.

If there are expectations that uninitiated boys should refrain from acting as if they are members of the adult society, there are also times when they are expected, if not pressed, to interact with that society. Although not required to, boys generally are eager to attend the public masquerades put on by the adults. While the youths do not form the major part of the audience, they are certainly present, and often scramble to sit closest to the performers. As we have seen, certain figures in the adult masquerades play with boys, much as the boys' society masqueraders play with younger children (S. Ottenberg 1975: Chap. 11). The adult *logholo* prances about the commons and uninitiated boys chase after it trying to throw it, in an aggressive game. The boys are urged on by men sitting in the nearby rest houses or standing about. *ɔkpa* dances about in his looped string suit followed by boys, and sometimes scoops one up in a threatening manner, and *ɔtero* the fierce moves about in a frightening way. Uninitiated boys are exposed to all three forms of these adult secret society masquerades and are expected to react with assertive and brave cooperative play.

The uninitiated boys are also involved in the initiation rites of other lads into the adult secret society. We have already mentioned how all non-initiates in Mgbom village go to the secret society priest's house for a blessing at the end of the short form of initiation, passing by the playful *ɔkpa* maskers. This ritual involves the priest flicking a magical liquid onto all present, which is believed to counteract the effects of anything that they may have seen or heard that they should not during the initiation. Non-initiates are also allowed to view a masked dance, *isiji,* performed by a man's eldest son during his initiation. At certain times during this rite, a form taking some months, uninitiated boys can talk to the initiands and bring them food cooked by their mothers. In Mgbom, before an initiation begins, the initiated boys sweep the commons, while the uninitiated ones clean inside the compound entrances facing these areas. Uninitiated boys in Mgbom are permitted to use the first-son initiation bush area for their own masquerades and play after the adult initiations have ended. Other interactions of boys with the adult society will be described later on. The point is that the social distinction between the initiates and non-initiates at Afikpo does not mean the total isolation of the members of one status from the other, but a partial separation with interaction in well-defined areas, following well-established rules. Secrecy becomes a way of communicating, as well as of separating the initiated and the uninitiated (Bellman 1984).

In this light it is interesting to note the autonomy of each boys' society from the adult one, in terms of internal control and mechanisms for adjudication and punishment. Adult males respect this and rarely interfere. It is true that in the past village elders sometimes tried to force lads to join the boys' societies if they refused to do so. It is also significant that the boys' society buildings are only rarely destroyed in the manner described above, and then only by masked figures of the adult society, who, being unidentified, cannot be revenged. While adult secret society members can walk about a boys' society area and enter their rest house without violating any rule, they usually do not associate closely with the boys for fear of lowering their own status and since there is little reason to do so. Once a drunken man from Amachara village saw an uninitiated boy *logholo* masquerader in nearby Amuro village. Claiming that he had been an expert at throwing this form of masker when a boy, the man became excited and threw him. The Amuro village elders forced the man to sacrifice a dog at the priest's house of their adult secret society, for he was believed to have angered its spirit by acting as if he was a boy, contradicting his adult status. This illustrates the strong respect that adults have for the boys' secret societies.

W. P. Murphy (1980:193) considers that among the Kpelle of Liberia "secrecy separates elders from youths. It supports the political and economic control of the youth." That is, the secret societies are interest groups that assert political and economic control through their exclusive right to particular knowledge. Among the Kpelle there do not seem to be boys' secret societies (although there are secret societies for adult females as well as males), and the demarcation between uninitiated youths and secret society members seems more rigid and extensive than at Afikpo. I attribute the difference to the fact that in Kpelle life the secret societies have strong political controls and authority over productive land, while at Afikpo the adult secret societies control only the land in their bush areas, which are not used for farming, and have only diffuse and supportive political functions (S. Ottenberg 1971: Chap. 5), which makes for a less rigid demarcation of boy-man boundaries. Political and economic controls at the village and descent-group level are largely in the hands of elders (S. Ottenberg 1971). There is a gradually increasing authority rather than a sharp demarcation, from the junior boys' secret societies through the middle and senior ones to the adult secret society, though the greatest cleavage is clearly between the last two groupings. But the uninitiated youths at Afikpo are not really under direct control of the secret society elders, unless they violate its rules. It is the newly initiated who are much under the authority of the secret society elders, although this is largely for ritual rather than for political and economic matters. True, it is often the same elders who direct the adult secret societies who also lead in the political and economic sphere, and boys and young men are very well aware of this, but at Afikpo there is a diffusion of the kinds of male authority in the secret societies and the more secular arena. In Kpelle it is a diffusion of political and economic forces between the secret society elders and the local chief, a somewhat different situation, which seems related to the strong youth-elders contrast there.

At Afikpo relations between uninitiated boys and the secret society mirror those between the boys and their fathers. The fathers' activities are largely separate from those of the boys and are frequently not understood by them, but the relationship between father and son is a friendly one, and the father has ultimate authority if the son misbehaves outside of adult secret society matters, as the adult society has over non-initiates in matters of their society. But boys have a high degree of autonomy with respect to both the adult secret society and their fathers. We will see that initiation lessens the autonomy of boys in both spheres, drawing them closer to the adult world of their fathers and to the village secret society.

The separation of uninitiated from initiated males is restricted to specific behavioral spheres. Initiated and uninitiated boys play and fight together, engage in important wrestling competitions with one another, jointly take part in communal work, and may sleep in the same boys' houses in the compounds. The initiation of one of a pair of friends may alter their ties but they still carry on certain activities together. Similarly, an uninitiated son carries out a whole range of activities with his father, even if he does not belong to his father's secret society as yet. He may help him at the farm, carry messages for him, and spend time hanging around his house.

The different kinds of relationships that boys and girls carry out with the secret societies sharply sets them apart by gender as they mature, helping to move them in different social directions and toward somewhat differing life goals. For the boy this separation through secrecy also assists in drawing him away from his mother's strong influence of infancy and early childhood. But sooner or later the boy will make adolescent sexually oriented contacts with girls while still retaining his distance from his mother. He has to differentiate these two types of females psychologically as well as socially; he cannot distance himself from all females for the sake of separating from his mother. I now turn to these opposite-sex interests.

Growing Together

Before the 1940s neither boys nor girls had their genital excisions until adolescence and boys did not join the adult secret society until shortly after this operation. These facts form an important background to what I am going to discuss here. An unexcised pre- or early adolescent girl would choose a boy of similar age as her special friend in a relationship called *nwa ulo* (child-house).* He would visit her in her compound a good deal, bring her small gifts of food and soap and other things, help pound *fufu* and break firewood for her mother, aid her father with his farms, and protect the girl from advances by other boys on the way to the farms. She would sometimes cook for him but she did not usually come to his residence, though she might help carry water for his mother. She was generally from a different compound or village from her male friend, as is generally the case with Afikpo married couples. There was often a bed at the mother's home where the boy, or the boy and girl, might lie down and rest, but the mother kept an eye on them. The girl's parents called the boy "my son" and the boy called the girl's parents "father" and "mother"; the boy's parents addressed the girl as "daughter." *Nwa ulo* was not a covert or disapproved relationship, and the girl's parents accepted it as normal and benefited from it. It was also not a strongly sexual tie in an overt sense, although the boy might touch the girl's breasts lightly and fondle her a bit. (Kissing was, and is, rare in Afikpo sexual relations. It is largely seen as a European innovation at Afikpo.) The couple were required to belong to different matrilineal clans, as Afikpo matriclan incest taboos extended to *nwa ulo*. "You cannot *nwa ulo* with your sister," the

*The term refers to the boy, but is also used for the girl. My information on *nwa ulo* derives in part from P. Ottenberg (1958:59–62).

Afikpo told me, and if there were sexual relations and a child was born of two parents from the same clan, by Afikpo standards this would be a terrible abomination. Rivalries existed between boys hoping to be chosen by a girl and there was anxiety among some boys over not being selected at all. The factor of female choice seems to me unusual at Afikpo, in a culture in which, at least nominally it is the male who initiates male-female relationships, and where women have been dominated by males in many ways. It may have given a girl experience in choosing which she employed later on as a married woman taking a lover, which did occur and still occurs at times. But her choice in the *nwa ulo* situation was an illusion; it did not lead to marriage.

The girl in the *nwa ulo* relationship was generally already spoken for through arrangements made by her parents, often when she was very young. Her intended was likely to be between some ten to many more years older than her and her *nwa ulo* partner, and he married her shortly after her genital operation and "fattening" period. The families of the girl and her husband-to-be were usually close, as well as that of the girl and her *nwa ulo* partner. The future husband also brought the girl presents and he assisted her father with his farmwork, as befitted a man in his role, but he generally spent less time with the girl than did the *nwa ulo*. In many cases, Afikpo claim, he got along well with the boy, who might run errands for him, but if he did not, and felt competitive about it, he could dismiss him. So the intended kept an eye on the boy and the girl; to some extent he judged the girl's character by how she acted with her *nwa ulo*. After the marriage the boy might continue as a friend of the couple if this was acceptable to all, but sometimes the *nwa ulo* relationship was broken off. Occasionally the boy and girl ran away after the marriage, she divorced, and they became husband and wife. Yet it is said that ideally a boy in a *nwa ulo* relationship never married the girl but could marry a daughter of her marriage. I have no data to indicate whether this occurred or not, although in terms of relative age it would not be inappropriate at Afikpo. The boy in the *nwa ulo* relationship was also often spoken for in marriage by his parents, but his wife-to-be was generally too young for this tie; she might be only a few years old.

The *nwa ulo* link was a sexually sublimated one between adolescents of opposite sex in the face of a system of marriage which directed both partners elsewhere, an attempt of age mates of differing gender to develop and maintain a relationship in a culture which both encouraged and denied this. It was a fantasy courtship between two individuals of the same age who had common orientations and interests, where the girl acted out the idea of choice in a society where she had little at all. It was a playing at courtship that involved not only the couple but both their parents.

Occasionally there was a breakdown and the *nwa ulo* boy and girl had intercourse. If they were caught or the girl became pregnant the intended husband might break off the marriage plans; he did not want a "polluted" girl (*igbari uchu,* you are polluted). Though Afikpo men like to know that a woman is fertile, her intended might be reluctant to marry her; her parents would then pressure the boy to do so. The husband-to-be was also expected to refrain from intimacies with her, for the marriage payments and obligations had not been fulfilled. Probably his own earlier *nwa ulo* experience with another girl helped him to fulfill his role as a restrained husband-to-be with some ease.

The *nwa ulo* tie replicated aspects of the very early relationship of a male child to its mother. In both cases the male spent a good deal of time with the female at her place of residence, in a warm relationship. In both cases there was an older male involved, who eventually "took" the female away (the father his wife after she had weaned the infant; the husband-to-be the girl). The girl was likely to be torn between her affections for her age mate and her commitment to her intended, who was sometimes old enough to be her father, and in his potential authority over her resembled him; likewise, a mother might be divided between her love for her son and her husband. For the boy's part, the girl's parents became surrogate parental figures, but without the tensions and strong emotions associated with his real parents, hence generally pleasant ties arose.

Nwa ulo changed considerably by the time I came to carry out my research (P. Ottenberg 1958:60–62). Boys generally choose girls, and a girl sometimes has more than one partner at a time. Excision for both sexes is performed at a much earlier age, and there is considerably more sexual activity among the young, in *nwa ulo* relationships and elsewhere; this is a matter of concern to parents and elders, who sometimes ban children's singing and dancing in an attempt to control sexuality—with little success. "Fattening" rites for girls have almost disappeared, and changes in the economy have made it possible for a boy to compete with a husband-to-be in gift-giving to the girl, and even to afford to marry her himself. Arranged marriages seem less likely to actually take place, since girls claim a stronger right to protest and to choose, and in this they are sometimes influenced by a boyfriend or a *nwa ulo* partner.

There is another important feature of the *nwa ulo* system. This is a yearly event called *egwu ɔnwa* (dance-moon); in English, the Afikpo call it "Moonlight Dancing." For three or four months of the yam planting season, centering on March and April of each year, Moonlight Dancing takes place on alternate days, which are the farm days at Afikpo. Boys and unmarried girls of all ages from five or so upward sing and dance in the village commons much of the night, led by the senior girls; then the children sleep together there for the rest of the night. It is primarily a girls' dance, with boys protecting their particular girls from other village lads and from aggressive boys of other settlements, and with the protectors joining the girls in dancing. At dawn the senior girls rise and sing and dance one more time. The children then go home where they may sleep for a while, thus the Afikpo expression, "*ilari egwu ɔnwa abale,*" "Did you do moonlight dancing?" spoken in jest to an adult who sleeps late in the morning.

Boys pick the small *odara* fruits from trees to give girls as presents at the dance and to eat themselves, but the children eat little else as they have had a late supper after returning from the farms with their families. The songs, created and sung by the girls, with the boys sometimes joining in the singing, are occasionally humorous, but often refer to farming, to yams, and to the moon; they are not overtly sexual in content. The children sing to the moon as a spirit which is believed to promote the growth of yams. I see this fertility aspect of the song texts as a metaphor for the growing sexual interests of the children: they are growing like yams in the farm; yams and moon may represent phallus and vagina respectively. No shrines or sacrifices are associated with these activities.

Moonlight Dancing, coming at the end of the secret society season, goes on in the same village commons that the adult society employs; secret activities are thus replaced by this form of entertainment, to be replaced in turn by wrestling matches. Moonlight Dancing behavior is cooperative and friendly for the sexes, different in tone from boy masqueraders chasing girls at an earlier time of the year, and from the adult masquerades in the commons. Thus sex role differentiation is followed in time by attraction, though even in the secret society activities there are also elements of flirtation and covert sexuality across gender lines. In Moonlight Dancing limits are set on this attraction.

The form of activity occurring in Moonlight Dancing is specific to children. It involves boys and girls dancing directly together. (In adult dancing at Afikpo men and women move in separate groups in the commons at the same or at different times, and for adult females there is no sleeping on the ground there.) Moonlight Dancing expresses a relationship between male and female children, associated with growing maturity and sexual awakening, the children being "betwixt and between," neither young nor adults.

One may wonder whether there is or has been much sexuality occurring at Moonlight Dancing. Boys are permitted to fondle the breasts of girls and a couple, particularly if in a *nwa ulo* relationship as the older children are likely to be, often sleep together in the commons late at night on a mat of banana or coco yam leaves provided by the boy. Other children sleep here and there in the commons. Parents or other adults do not supervise; the children are on their own, led by the older ones. This is a familiar pattern, as in the boys' secret societies where the lads are largely unsupervised by their fathers. At this nighttime event there is some roughhousing, with boys chasing girls about, and the *nwa ulo* boy is expected to put off these playful and sometimes sexual advances toward his partner, which may include body pinching and fondling breasts.

The answer to my query about sexuality seems to be, from the evidence that I have, that in the past there was very little actual intercourse, despite the lack of parental supervision. Girls wore a native cloth, *ɔwɔwa,* similar in form and name to that worn by boys in wrestling, which went through the crotch and tied around the waist, not a cloth girls usually wore. The mother instructed her daughter not to let a boy poke his finger into her vagina; the cloth was expected to protect her from sexual contact. Girls feared becoming pregnant, which would bring down the wrath of parents, a disgrace if they had had their excision, and a more serious abomination if they had not. Boys wore any kind of cloth or nothing at all, and were sometimes stimulated to the point of having an erection.

The *nwa ulo* sexual behavior can be viewed in the context of adult sexual relations. Touching between adult men and women is not common, even between husbands and wives. A child may have slept with his parents while they were having intercourse, but the public image is puritanical; the same couple will not touch, hold, or hug each other. Children do not see much adult public expression of sexual feeling at Afikpo, though there are forms of speech which are suggestive, and there is the sexually explicit ritual, the Feast of the Tortoise (described below). During Moonlight Dancing there seems to be an unusual degree of sexual freedom, but significantly this occurs "in public" among children only; adults are not present, and it is dark.

Why so much—and yet so little—sexuality? Aside from meeting the obvious need to avoid pregnancy, the Moonlight Dancing behavior seems also to fit the image of public restraint on sexuality at Afikpo. One Afikpo suggested to me that Moonlight Dancing, and by extension the whole *nwa ulo* relationship, provides experience in exercising sexual restraint, which will serve both males and females later in life. The woman as wife will need to exercise control with respect to men other than her husband, and during her period of abstinence while nursing; men will need it during the same period, and also with respect to women who are sexually taboo to them with whom they have close relationships (such as other women living in the same compound, and matrilineal kin, with whom sexual relations are forbidden). Viewed as part of this overall pattern, *nwa ulo* relationships seem not to contradict, but in fact to symbolize and express the development of a moral sense in children, an internalization of sexual controls. For children who have, until now, dealt with sexual feelings primarily through distance, avoidance, and ritualized play—the boys separated from their mothers and the girls remote from their fathers—*nwa ulo* relationships and Moonlight Dancing represent a very different approach; there are still restrictions on sexual behavior, but the context allows a more direct confrontation with sexual feelings.

It was evident, though, at the time of my field research, that as a consequence of Moonlight Dancing some sexual relations occurred on those nights or later. It is also clear, from remarks I have heard, that boys sometimes attacked girls, aggressing against them sexually, particularly if the *nwa ulo* boy was weak or absent. Boys learn both protective behavior toward females, as *nwa ulo* partners, and aggressive sexual patterns toward them. Both behaviors carry over into adulthood, the man protecting his wives against other men and acting sexually assertively toward some other females.

Both the *nwa ulo* relationship and the Moonlight Dancing are aspects of the Afikpo culture of childhood, as are the games we previously discussed. Adults don't carry out *nwa ulo* relationships, although there are analogies to adult courtship, which occurs primarily between a man and a widowed or divorced woman. Nor do adults perform Moonlight Dancing, although there are dances, such as at the Feast of the Tortoise, that both sexes engage in at the same time, although in different forms.

At this two-day Feast of the Tortoise (*ebu mbe,* dance-tortoise), young men in their twenties, who have not yet formed into village age sets, sing and dance together as a group about the commons. There are other performing groups of older young men organized by age. All the males are dressed in good cloths. Mature married village women, wearing fine cloths and with an elaborate hair-do, also sing and dance as a unit; again there is a group of young girls and another of somewhat older unmarried females, as well as one of young married women. All of these units move about the commons, often at the same time, in a running dance, singing the songs that each group has made up previous to the performance, the males moving in a different fashion than the females. Many villagers watch the event.

The songs are descriptive, sexual, derogatory, and leave no doubt as to what is involved; they sometimes name specific individuals in the community and specific sexual attributes. For example, in rough translation:

Men: The woman's privates have red and yellow.

Men: One lady, her bottom shoots up like a white ant. [She is ugly; she has a big bottom.]

Girls: Men are thieves. When their wives sleep they steal up their legs.

Girls: Men, you can give them food, they will take it easily, water after food, they take it, water for bath, they take it. But when you don't give them the vagina they are unhappy, and when the woman gives him her sex she becomes a very faithful woman.

Girls: [replying to the men's first line] Penis has a very beautiful hat on, there is a rope on, there is okra there.

Men: —— is full of sex. She is shy outside but never shy to put the penis inside her vagina.

Men: Woman's privates smell. The vagina smells. [They call the names of women playing leading roles in the singing.]

Women: ——— has a standing penis. It is never down. [They sing other names.]

Girls: It is the men that cause us to be stinking.

Small boys prepare papayas to look like female sex organs by cutting a wedge out of them lengthwise, and carry these about the commons where everyone is dancing; girls carry long pointed red or orange flowers which resemble penises. If asked, the children will tell you exactly what they represent.

The rite is a ritual of reversal (Babcock 1978). Detailed sexual statements are made in public, which is otherwise never done. Much the same words are used every year, though the names change. These outrageous comments, of course, serve to reinforce the norms, by overturning them in an unusual and ritualized manner.

The tortoise is an appropriate symbol for this event, for he is the trickster character in Afikpo tales, who often reverses the natural order of things. He has a double aspect, being associated with both water and land. By analogy, the festival explores a second, and seldom public, aspect of Afikpo life: the submerged, "underwater" side of sexuality. The festival is not a day of sexual license, but it is clearly a time when sexual tensions, resentment, and hostilities are relieved through acting out. In this respect, the singing reminds me of the satirical masquerades put on by the boys' and men's societies. Both involve behaviors which reiterate the norms by reversing them (S. Ottenberg 1975: Chaps. 6–8); both involve ritualized derision of individual community members and their behavior, and public revelation of private knowledge and gossip. The Feast of the Tortoise, however, involves both sexes, while the masquerades involve only men.

The festival occurs during the harvest period. As Moonlight Dancing concerns the maturation of human sexuality expressed in terms of the moon and of yams in Afikpo's springtime, so the tortoise rite is an expression of adult sexuality phrased in the context of the harvest.

My interest here is the considerable exposure of children in the tortoise ritual, either as audience members, or as participants, to an atmosphere of public satire and sexuality. The content of the songs may help children to learn sexual rules and constraints, but they also acquire knowledge of the varieties of sexual behavior and the nature of sexual deviations. This is one of those few occurrences at Afikpo when males and females make direct public statements about sexuality. One can view rite after rite—sacrifices, masquerades, and other public events, as well as male initiations—without hearing or seeing any direct reference to sexuality, although symbols abound. Thus this festival is an unusual outburst of sexual feelings and opinions in public, carried out by children and young adults of the village with great vigor, humor, and interest. No one is bored at this event. Suddenly secret behavior, perhaps gossiped about in homes and in the boys' and men's houses, becomes very public. The impact is strong. And it continues beyond the festival as females and children of both sexes sing the words for months afterwards at the farms, as they work or rest between laboring. Here children take over the songs of older persons as well as singing their own; once sung at the festival the words and tunes are public property, and the youngsters use and reshape them to fit their own interests.

There is a sense of greater freedom to sing derisively at the farming areas in nonritual contexts than in the village, for it is also at the farms that females sing of unmarried girls who have become pregnant, again naming them. Such voicing in the village in nonritual situations is seen as too direct. A major Afikpo cultural theme is the association of earth, the farms, and the crops (especially yams) with sexuality and fertility. Sexual intercourse of the uncircumcised is an offense against the spirit of the earth, as is any sexual activity on the ground at the farms. In Moonlight Dancing boys and girls share the ground together and the dance is associated with the planting and potential growth of yams. In the tortoise rite sexuality is associated with the harvest. The yam is an explicit phallic symbol at Afikpo. Human fertility and sexuality and crop fertility and the earth are interconnected; it thus seems consistent that Feast of the Tortoise songs should be heard at the farms.

I found no evidence of overt homosexuality or of human-animal sexual relations at Afikpo. If they occur they are very secret and quite unusual. It might seem surprising, in a society which makes overt heterosexual activity so difficult for children—particularly for males way past their adolescence, as there are few females available to them—and in which sheep and goats are kept, that sexual relationships of humans and animals does not seem to occur. Furthermore, in a society where boys spend a lot of time by themselves in peer groups unsupervised by older persons, that homosexual behavior should be absent is striking, although some group masturbation occurs. I found no examples of disputes or cases involving either human intercourse with animals or homosexuality; the dark side of Afikpo generally shows up in such disputes. Neither did I find it at sacrifices, where these might appear, especially in rites of purification. It is said by the Afikpo that if homosexuality occurred and the couple were caught that they would be severely punished, certainly ostracized, and in former times possibly buried alive. Again, I know of no Feast of the Tortoise songs or farm songs concerning homosexuality or sexual relations between humans and animals.

Certain expressions used by young men show that they are not ignorant of the possibility of sexual relations with animals or with other males, but rather they are consciously rejecting them. One young man may see an attractive woman and remark to his companions, "I want to fuck that woman!" The statement is said to reflect badly on the speaker, but the companions may say to one another, "Do you expect him to fuck a man or a goat?" This makes it clear that the desire for a woman is a correct and acceptable impulse, while homosexuality and human-animal intercourse are recognized but unacceptable alternatives. (The word "mother" may be substituted for the word "goat" or "man," or both, indicating that mother-son incest is also a recognized, and equally reprehensible, possible behavior.)

Be this as it may, the absence or complete concealment of both forms of sexual behavior is consistent with a society in which the sexual behavior of the young is, or at least was, very strictly controlled and regulated; there is strong morality in sexual matters. It is difficult to determine the degree to which the children internalize the control, as opposed to merely accepting the rules due to outside pressure. Children—and adults—act as if there is considerable internalization, deep conscience and superego controls. However, the rapid breakdown of sexual restraints in recent years, coincident with other social changes (the performance of excisions at earlier ages, the later age of marriage for girls, the declining authority of the traditional elders, the introduction of schools as an authority in the place of parents, and changes in the economy), suggest that in the past that sexual behavior may have been constrained by the fear of punishment, of being shamed and ridiculed publicly in song, and of the anger of parents and elders, rather than by any deep sense of conscience.

The various activities of boys' secret societies serve to distract the boys from homosexuality or relations with animals, and the home situation for daughters also applies controls on behavior that would be considered deviant at Afikpo and that I might consider substitute sexual gratification.

There is a strong analogy between the rules of sexual restraint among children and the rules associated with the boys' secret societies. In both instances there are certain gender-specific norms of behavior involved that are well known by children. In both instances religious spirits are believed to be offended by violations of these rules and to become dangerous to the violators, if not to others—the spirit of the ground for sexuality, and the spirit of the secret societies for secrecy violations. In both cases there are ritual atonements for violators of gender-specific rules. In both cases the rules are superficially nonsexual and gender isolating; they force girls to interact with females and boys with boys. In both secret societies and sexuality there is a strong sense of restraint in male-female relations, with attraction and distancing occurring in highly formalized patterns. This is very clear in Moonlight Dancing and the *nwa ulo* situation. It also exists when masked boys chase girls and in other boys' society activities; most masqueraders cannot even touch or be touched by girls. Furthermore, there is secrecy in children's sexual relations and in the boys' societies. The societies act as a metaphor for sexual relations, phrased in nonsexual terms. Indeed, it is probably because secrecy is a metaphor for sexuality that the secret societies have so little overt sexual content. This allows them to serve as a powerful image of sexual maturation, whatever other purposes they may have.

Children and Parents

About the time that a boy enters the first stage of the boys' secret society, when he is about five or six, he begins to accompany his father to the farm and to help him in his work. At first he does this only occasionally, but then with greater frequency over the years, so that by adolescence he is working pretty regularly. At first his father will be pleased simply to take him along and assign him a task or two, showing him farms that are not too far away. The son also may assist his mother with her farm activities. He carries out food and farm tools and brings back crops and firewood, taking yams to the racks near the village and tying them up there. He places the seed yams on the earth heaps his father has built up. When he is a little older he helps clear the land after it has been burned off by older males. And later still he helps his father with yam heaping, heavy work involving forming large earth mounds in the top of which the yams are planted. Males take great pride in efficient and rapid heaping; if there is no longer warfare to exhibit strength and skill there is still farm work. In a sort of contest an older boy or a young man tries to build a certain number of yam mounds in a day which, if he is successful, often results in a gift of land or trees to him from his father. The boys learn of different kinds of yams and soil conditions and when and where to plant particular crops. The father also shows his son the father's agnatic and matrilineal land holdings, and land of the son's matrilineal group which the father acquired for temporary use when he married the boy's mother.

Farming is an activity, like others at Afikpo, with a considerable division of labor by sex. At the height of the planting period, from January to April, full attention can be given to agricultural work and secret society activities taper off. Women do not often grow yams, although there is no taboo against it, but plant vegetable crops around the yam heaps and cassava (manioc) in separate earth heaps in the poorer soil. They prepare their mounds themselves or their husbands assist them; the women are responsible for weeding both their own and their husbands' fields. Girls help in carrying crops and tools between farm and village, and in weeding. It is largely the task of females at Afikpo to carry heavy loads of firewood back to their settlements.

Children of both sexes play a great deal at the farms, often together. They wade about in the streams where they chase frogs and trap fish. They capture grasshoppers and other insects and snare rodents and birds, which are cooked and eaten. They learn much about plants and animals and other humans. Since contiguous plots of land are often worked by people from different sections of the child's village or from other villages, as a consequence of the system of matrilineal land control (S. Ottenberg 1968a), the child meets youngsters and adults that he or she has not yet come into contact with; there is interest and excitement in these encounters. And because of the dispersed locations of the farms of a given adult, the children may also pass through other Afikpo villages, meeting individuals, sometimes matrikin, from these settlements.

Even though they may sometimes duck work in order to play, children take considerable pride in helping their parents at the farms and emulating their work habits and behavior, and parents love to

have them with them. The generally pleasant parent-child relationships of the compounds continue on the farms, and here boys seem
closer to their parents than in the settlements, in particular to their
fathers. Work brings them together in a comfortable relationship. At
home girls increasingly assist their mothers with domestic chores
such as cooking, fetching water, and tending younger children; for
girls there is no strong break from the mother-child bond, which
continues until marriage. A girl spends a good deal of time at her
home—which is also her mother's and her sisters' home—and in the
residential part of the compound. Girls learn nurturing behavior in
caring for younger children under the mother's guidance. Boys occasionally take care of youngsters, but not as frequently as girls.
Child care duties may start when the girl is six or seven (cf. Duru
1980:138).

Girls assist their mothers and other women in soaking and squeez-
ing cassava and preparing it in cereal-like form (*gari*) for local use or
for sale at the market by women. They help their mothers prepare
palm oil by crushing the kernels in water in rock holes, and assist
them in making both yam and cassava fufu for home use. They aid
their mothers in making and firing pottery, a common activity at
Afikpo through which many women earn cash, for there is an export
industry of pots shipped down the Cross River for sale at Calabar. It
is through the sale of pottery and of *gari* that women earn income
which gives them a certain independence from their husbands; girls
quickly come to appreciate the value of this through their mothers.
Some women become expert entrepreneurs at the pottery business,
good models for girls to follow. Older girls learn the business and
help their mothers selling or buying at the Afikpo market and soon
learn that liaisons and flirtations develop there. Boys, in their spare
time, make mats to sleep on or to sell, and they take part in house
building in their compounds. The woman's yearly work load is fuller
and harder than the man's; this is also true of girls' work in contrast
to that of boys. Girls, and sometimes boys, may go with their mothers when they visit their families and patrilineal and matrilineal relatives. A girl's life is domestically oriented but she does spend some
time away from the house, at the farms, the market, and visiting.

Not only is the work of children strongly divided by sex but so is
the authority over them. The mother is generally in charge of the
daily work of her daughters, the father of his sons. While the father
has ultimate authority over all of his children, a daughter's disobe-

dience rarely results in his punishing her, for the mother does this, but he is certainly involved in the decision as to who the girl marries, generally playing a stronger role than his wife. In earlier times he decided when his daughter should go through "fattening"; today the clitoridectomy is usually scheduled by the mother.

The father has authority over his sons in directing farm labor and other work, although the mother may do so as well. The father largely determines when a boy will be initiated into the adult secret society, and he may have a hand in deciding when a son moves up a stage in the boys' secret groupings. He often arranges a first marriage for a son and sets the time when it will occur. He gains titles by the advancement of his son through a series of rituals, and plays a crucial role in specific aspects of the boy's life, despite the autonomy of this child in the boys' secret societies, in wrestling groups, through his relatively independent living arrangements, and in other ways.

Children have traditionally been disciplined by corporal punishment as well as other means. Flogging with a whip might be done by a parent or an older sibling, usually in the heat of anger. Yet physical punishment has not been frequent at Afikpo. When it occurs it is usually because a child refuses to take part at all in farm work or household tasks, or as a consequence of fighting, lying, or stealing. Denying food to a recalcitrant child is a punishment sometimes employed. Parents fear, however, that if they punish too hard and bear malice toward a child they may later find themselves accused of causing the child's death by arousing the anger of spirit beings associated with the child, particularly reincarnated ancestors. The pattern of infant indulgence continues in childhood. Threats of punishment, seclusion, or banishment from the home are also employed. A very potent force is ridicule through speech and song. Afikpo delight in sarcasm and are expert at it (P. and S. Ottenberg 1964: 39–40).

Though Afikpo has double unilineal descent (S. Ottenberg 1968a), matrilineal relatives of a boy (other than his mother and his siblings) do not play substantial roles in his life at this stage, in terms of authority or affection; the youth does not live with his uterine relatives, nor does he see much of them. But by adolescence it is the responsibility of the father to lead his son to the son's matrilineal relatives, for visits and sacrificial rituals, so that the son can come to know his matrikin and they him. His mother's brothers, who may live in another community, are particularly important; through them he will acquire farmland as an adult, and they will have authority over him in matrilineal affairs. The father (often accompanied by the mother) takes his son to the annual meeting of the boy's matrilineal clan, where he is introduced to the major spirit of that descent line, *nja,* at its shrine, often in village other than the child's own, where he thereafter makes yearly sacrifice. However, unlike the ancestors reincarnated in them, this spirit rarely affects children; it is mainly concerned with the welfare of the matrilineal grouping's land and crops, its health, and the general fertility of clan females.

The father is also responsible for introducing his son to the father's matrilineal relatives. Matrilineal exogamy at Afikpo makes it impossible for the son to belong to this group, but the child helps farm the father's matrilineal land, and even after his father's death may be allowed to use the land as a "son" of the matrilineal group. But a son will have no true claim to this land and his father's movable wealth will go to these matrikin and not to him when the father dies (S. Ottenberg 1965).

The father also, as the son grows, explains to him the genealogy of their major patrilineage, with which they live, and whose members the boy already knows in the compound. Thus the father plays an important role in this period in a boy's childhood, expanding his knowledge about, and contact with, key relatives.

The mother plays a similar role for her daughters. She will see that a daughter meets her matrilineal relatives, particularly the mother's brothers, who will be concerned that proper marriage arrangements have been made for her, and who are hopeful that she will eventually produce offspring to enlarge the uterine group. The daughter also becomes familiar with the *nja* matriclan shrine. The mother also introduces her daughters, and her sons, to her own patrilineal relatives, although this is largely a courtesy as the children do not become associated with these kin through land matters or through a spirit shrine (except through ancestors reincarnated in the child).

These pragmatic matters link the two generations, creating ties that go beyond mere expressions of affection and love. They form the basis of a steady understanding between parents and children when the latter grow up. Such relationships help to balance increasing tensions between fathers and sons and mothers and daughters that arise with children at adolescence.

The Child Prepared

By the time the boy is of age for initiation and the girl for marriage they have developed clear-cut gender distinctions which they maintain the rest of their lives. Afikpo data agree with the study of 110 cultures by Barry, Bacon, and Child (1957:332) which "shows that the differentiation of the sexes is unimportant in infancy, but that in childhood there is, as in our own society, a widespread pattern of greater pressure toward nurturance, obedience, and responsibility in girls, and toward self-reliance and achievement striving in boys." Although at Afikpo there are some important ritual distinctions between girls and boys, before the age of five or six they are largely treated the same.

After this boys move away from the family situation, toward an identity with the father and toward males, while girls remain in a mother-centered domestic environment. Work for boys involves helping grow yams and climbing productive trees for palm products; for girls, growing cassava and vegetable crops and preparing *gari* and pottery, and trading in them. For boys, there is the aggressiveness of the boys' secret societies, away from parents, while for girls there are the more restrained social relationships of the female home, with a good deal of hard work, and sometimes long hours of tedious labor. Strong pressures are placed on children to act their separate roles: gender distinctions are clear by the time children have ended their first decade of life.

Children have also, through their experiences in the various activities that we have discussed, learned that gender dichotomy differentiates but does not create equals. In Afikpo men outwardly rule and females have less of a say. So children learn that the farmland will pass from males to other males, but not generally to females, that the adult secret societies act to control females, and that male physical strength is associated with leadership.

By adolescence each sex has acquired a set of skills which mark it off from the other. The domestic abilities of the girls are developed to the point that in this regard early marriage presents little problem for them; they have also had creative experience in singing, dancing, and pottery making, although the ware is generally without elaborate design. The technical skills of boys are such that they are quite prepared for their initiation into the adult secret society, through considerable experience in producing and using masks and musical instruments, in costuming, in dancing, and in performing sacrifices. Some of them have leadership experience, and have a sense of whether they enjoy leading or not. They have developed physical skills through fighting, games, wrestling, and chasing in masquerades, as well as in farm work; they are toughened up and can stand pain.

The distinctiveness of the sexes is also reflected in age relationships. The life of boys is intensely peer-group oriented, moving from the compound scene to the ward and then to the village. Boys quickly become very sensitive to peer-group ties and come to associate age, and thus authority, with membership in particular peer groups, especially boys' societies and wrestling groups. They explore social relationships with boys of their own age and become used to thinking of males in terms of membership in age-graded organizations; they will experience strong peer-group influences throughout their lives.

The way of girls is more intimately tied into the female hierarchical structure of the family with the mother and older sisters. While girls have their own singing and dancing societies and their occasional wrestling games, their peer-group experience is less developed than boys. They are likely, upon marriage, to move out of their compound, and sometimes their village, and to form new social ties, while boys remain with their male age peers for life. Adult female age organizations and other groups are nowhere near as well developed as those of men (S. Ottenberg 1971).

But boys and girls do not interact only with members of their own sex. As children mature their relationships move from playing games together and chasing one another to overt sexual interest. These attractions also involve considerable restraints. Afikpo is a society which allows adolescent children intimacies, but without sexual fulfillment. There is emphasis on the girl's virginity at marriage and hence there is the difficulty of boys finding sexual partners, though virginity is not required of them after their circumcision. Both sexes have learned sexual constraints to the extent that an event like Moonlight Dancing can occur over many nights without much likelihood of sexual intercourse occurring. There are also constraints against other forms of sexuality, particularly homosexuality and human-animal intercourse. Sexual issues are phrased in moral-religious terms. Children also come to understand that there are dangers associated with sex other than getting caught in the act. Boys come to believe that sexual intercourse may weaken them before wrestling or masquerade performances. Both sexes think that menstruating females may contaminate rituals, shrines, and persons, and that females who interfere with male secret events invite dangers to themselves, particularly barrenness. The growing sexuality of girls is channeled into domestic work and farming, and of boys into secret society activities and wrestling, as well as farm work. There are meticulously worked out codes for male-female interaction not only in sexual matters but in every sphere of a child's life, so that consciousness of one's own gender and that of the other develops strongly in the child.

Gender distinctions can also be seen in children's dependence and independence with reference to parents. For boys a balance is struck; girls tend toward dependency. A boy has a close and warm relationship with his father through farm work and through the aid the father provides during the son's rites. This situation, with the father as authority figure, is matched by the considerable time and energy that boys spend playing with other boys of roughly the same age, free of parental control. This does not mean that the boy can do whatever he wishes; for his father and mother he substitutes the leadership of slightly older, more experienced, physically stronger boys. The *nwa ulo* and Moonlight Dancing experiences are free of immediate parental controls and allow boys some sexual exploration, yet there are constraints in these areas as well. Boys seem to experience equal degrees of paternal support and role model behavior (as well as nurture, especially food, from their mothers) on one hand, and of independence from parents on the other. The combination produces a strong sense of self.

By contrast, a girl is more securely bound to her mother, an immediate and strong role model. She sees little of, and has little to do with, her father. While she has friends her own age and belongs to a girl's dancing group, independence training for her means having less, not more, contact with age mates outside of the home. Even her *nwa ulo* relationship occurs largely in the home, in the presence of her mother. The emphasis on dependence in her experience prepares her well for domestic life as a wife and mother, but it prepares her poorly for leadership in village activities. Such differences are evident in the life of Afikpo adults.

I have stressed the gender issue at Afikpo since there is currently a great deal of discussion and research in anthropology on this topic,* but little has been written by anthropologists on how maturing individuals arrive at a consciousness of gender. It is also clear that persons at Afikpo are very much aware of gender matters. I believe that this is at least partly due to the needs of the processes of separation and individuation for boys following their long and intimate nursing period with the mother. The framework of strong gender contrast makes the path of male development for boys clear, with precise guideposts along the way that assist in preventing boys from moving back to a dependency situation with their mothers.

Secrecy, as well as gender, plays important roles in the lives of Afikpo children. There is secrecy concerning sexual experience, and the children's natural curiosity about the licit and illicit sexual relations of others is given expression at the Feast of the Tortoise and other events, and in their own private sexual explorations. As we have noted, the attractions and constraints concerning sexuality are mirrored by the interest aroused by the secret societies, and the constraint they place on children of both sexes.

Secrecy at Afikpo has three aspects. First, it creates separations between people according to age and sex. Second, it moves the keepers of secret knowledge to action, as in the secret societies. Third, secrecy challenges individuals to penetrate it; it motivates girls to satisfy their natural curiosity about the boys' and men's societies, and boys to learn about adult society, and it motivates children to establish particular kinds of relationships that cross the secrecy barrier, such as boy-girl and child-parent ties. At Afikpo, secrecy stimulates behavior. Secrecy matters are associated with a high level of interest, and teach children much about gender relationships, what it means to be boys and girls. A natural curiosity about parents' and other older persons' behaviors and lives flows in culturally guided ways to other areas of Afikpo life. The songs of the tortoise rite and those subsequently sung at the farms, as well as the skits and songs of the satiric masquerades, make secrets public in creative and amusing ways. Children of both sexes at Afikpo are very much a part of these revelations, which suggests that there is a strong

---

*Much of the literature focuses on female gender issues. For Africa see Hay and Stichter 1984 and Oppong 1983. For more general anthropological works see Bourguignon 1980, Freidl 1975, Golde 1970, Hammond and Jablow 1976, Ortner and Whitehead 1981, and Rosaldo and Lamphere 1974.

morality to be broken at specific times. Children soon realize that the foibles of adults are important, as well as those of children.

Secrecy is a mechanism by which boys distance themselves from their mothers, and by extension from other females. It breaks a sense of commonality with females, leading to new understandings. Since the father is a member of the adult secret society and his son is not, this is also a barrier between them until the boy is initiated, but not as great a one as between son and mother.

As Bellman suggests for the Kpelle of Liberia (1984), the importance of secrecy may not be so much in its content, although this has symbolic and metaphoric meaning, but in the very existence of secrecy itself, in the particular social forms that it takes, and the social settings under which it exists and thrives. By its presence and its forms, secrecy at Afikpo "speaks" of gender differences, age distinctions, sexuality, power, and aggression, almost regardless of its particular content at the moment. Secrecy creates particular ways of relating. As Bateson has suggested (1973), the meaning is in the form of communication associated with secrecy as much as in what is communicated. And, of course, children at Afikpo, in learning secrets, and about the existence of secrets, are acquiring knowledge of social behavior, not only with regard to the actual or probable content, but in terms of its form; they learn how to hold secrets, to reveal them, to deal with the secrets of others. Secrecy becomes a frame, at Afikpo, through which major social relationships are drawn.

Secrecy provides a tension, excitement, and interest in life at Afikpo; it even has aesthetic qualities. Its two major forms at Afikpo are interrelated. Dark secrets (Goffman 1959:141–42), include knowledge and events which others are not supposed to know exist: secret sexual acts of children, adultery, private acts of deviation, and political secrets. The second type, Goffman's strategic secrets (1959:142–43), where the existence of secrecy is known, at Afikpo is found in the male secret societies. The presence of the second form there enhances interest in the first, with which it contrasts, and the first type may become the second (witness the delight in the revelatory nature of the songs of the Feast of the Tortoise). All secrecy becomes a matter of considerable interest, a way of life.

Secrecy at Afikpo is also closely allied with aggression; it provides a framework for it. We have noted that the assertive interests of boys are developed through fighting and wrestling and represent, at least in part, redirected sexual energies. The supposed anonymity of the masquerader allows boys to chase other boys as well as girls, to act in forceful and aggressive ways, to appear omnipotent, and to satirize older persons aggressively. We have also seen how there is fighting within and between boys' secret societies. Secrecy sanctions these forms of aggressive behavior. Boys and girls soon learn that secrecy does not necessarily mean a quiet withdrawal but can lead to public assertiveness.

While for boys there are numerous outlets for assertive tendencies, both in secret situations and outside of them, for girls there are fewer channels—singing at the Feast of the Tortoise and at the farms, occasional wrestling, fighting and chasing, and playing with boys. The Afikpo model for girls is a less assertive one than for boys; young female aggressive tendencies are quieted through daily labor. In neither sex does aggression seem to turn toward the parents; there appears to be little overt adolescent rebellion at Afikpo. For girls aggression is submerged into the family situation and in boys it is directed elsewhere, though in the boys' satiric masquerades hostilities toward parents and older persons appear.

Turning to the developmental features of childhood, there is an obvious sense of the proper order of events. This is not surprising; societies generally have ideas of the correct order in which children should experience things, for both sexes together, and for each alone. But the style in which development occurs differs. At Afikpo it is characterized by six key features: the horrendous consequences of incorrect order, the replication of previous events, a gradualism in development, the extensive emulation of older persons by children, the rich fantasy life of the growing child, and the role of art and aesthetics in maturation.

To begin with the first feature, we have seen that it is an abomination if a girl becomes pregnant before her excision, if a child's upper teeth appear before the lower, if two children are born to a woman at the same time, or if a birth comes feet first rather than the other way around. These terrible events imply spirit anger and unrest, suggest the idea of misbehavior on someone's part, and require drastic purificatory actions. They are not explained by the Afikpo as animal behavior; a simple nature-culture dichotomy is not very helpful here. They are rather viewed as the work of spirits and of humans acting dangerously. These violations are tied to a very strong morality of developmental order. Other transgressions, such as pregnancy after excision but before marriage, and coitus by unmarried children who have had their excisions, are not seen as abominations but rather as social errors, needing correction but not involving the spiritual world to as great an extent.

The emphasis on the correct order of development at Afikpo is not, I think, a sign of a rigidly compulsive people, but of well-organized individuals with strong egos who have a sense of the proper order of the world in which they operate. It is, perhaps, also a way of ensuring the ego independence of growing children, following the early mother-child tie. It is a map of maturation which, if followed, ensures the proper separation of the child from its mother and its development of a sense of independent self. Most of the serious abominations involve females as mothers or as girls; if blame is attached it is usually placed on the female. The Afikpo male fantasy of the uncontrollable female is a pervasive one, and I believe linked to early experience, where the infant son is highly controlled by the mother.

As for the second feature which characterizes development, the childhood of Afikpo individuals involves replication, similar events in different contexts, a sort of continual *déjà vu*. The infant-mother tie is repeated in the *nwa ulo* relationship; the relationship between a girl and her intended husband replicates aspects of the daughter-father tie. Each stage of the boys' secret society repeats the stage before, although in a grander and more skillful manner. The coming-out rite of the boy, in so far as it symbolizes warfare and physical strength, is repeated in different form in the child's bird-killing rite a few years later. The forms of replication are varied and this phenomenon does not always occur. But there is a tendency to ritual and behavioral repetition which provides childhood experience with an underlying continuity; this pattern occurs as well with reference to the adolescent initiation rites.

The third feature, gradualism, means that learning and changes in behavior of children are not expected to be sudden. I take as key examples of this pattern the gradual nature of weaning and of toilet training, and of the moving of young boys to sleep and live in the boys' houses in the compound. Furthermore, initiations at all three stages of the boys' societies can be done in parts, rather than all at once. And, of course, the learning of farming skills for all children, and of domestic techniques for girls, has a leisurely rather than an urgent or sudden quality. Likewise, the time for excision for both boys and girls, for the bird ceremony for boys, and so on, are flexible; they can be done one year or the next, whenever parents are ready.

At Afikpo there is a sense that growth and experience come in their own time, and will occur better without strong pressure. Parents are very patient with the young, not so much because they are "easy-going" as because they understand that children—and parents in activities with children—have varying rates of development and learning. It is true that some events occur as scheduled by the parents, and not according to the child's own inclination (such as the coming-out ceremony after birth, and certain events involving trauma, including circumcision and weaning), but the general pattern is one of gradualism, tied to a sense of the proper order of development. This gradualism appears to soften any potential child-parent conflicts.

The fourth feature, emulation, clearly allows children to strongly identify with the parent and others of the same sex. We have seen that childhood behavior often emulates adult activity, most strikingly in the boys' secret societies, where virtually all that occurs copies the adult secret society. It is also evident in gender role differentiation, in the boys' secret societies and forms of secrecy, in knowledge of farming, and in girls' domestic experience. Very young girls become involved in household duties and children of both sexes in farming. While it is true that there is a limited culture of childhood distinct from that of adults (centering around children's games, Moonlight Dancing, the xylophone dances in the boys' societies, some general songs and expressions, and aspects of the *nwa ulo* relationship), in other areas of behavior the children are very much in the adult mode from the age of five. As I have suggested, Afikpo children are socially demarcated from adults, but their culture is more emulative of that of adults than distinctive from it.

The fifth feature is that Afikpo childhood experience allows for a rich fantasy life. The presence of secret societies, with their sumptuous visual and aural aspects, the ritual activities of children, their exposure to tales and stories, wrestling, and some of their other games, allows them to explore fantasy richly, and to act it out in play. It is not a constricted mental life for the child, but a very full and imaginative one, where the child's individual psyche and experience can play on the culturally constructed world of imagery. Metaphors, analogies, and symbols abound for the child.

The sixth feature of development, clearly connected to the fifth, is that children at Afikpo mature in the context of a rich artistic life, of which they are participants as well as viewers. Youths of both sexes observe the rich and varied masquerades of the adult secret societies and the singing and dancing that occurs at various rites and events. Girls have their own singing groups, and take part in the activities of the Moonlight Dances and the Feast of the Tortoise. While boys also join in these last two events, their artistic activities center on their secret societies, where they make masks, costumes, and musical instruments for the performance of masquerades involving singing, dancing, and sometimes acting. In these boys' societies we see how aesthetics helps the boys to separate from their early mother-child tie, for they act and create in ways their mothers are not permitted to do. Furthermore, they identify with their fathers and other older males through artistic emulation in the masquerades. For both sexes the arts at Afikpo are very much associated with the development of a sense of a skilled self, integrating well-directed fantasy with physical and vocal skills. And artistic roles are for all children, not just for a select few. All boys take part in masquerading; all girls sing and dance.

By the time of their adolescent initiation the boys have acquired many skills that will serve them well in these rites, as well as afterward. They are used to operating in a world of male cooperation, one frequently isolated from females. In the boys' societies they do so largely within their own age group, though in wrestling, games, farming, and in other ways they are involved with males of other ages. The boys have acquired knowledge of, and skills in, making and using masks, costumes, and musical instruments, and they have performance experience. They have operated their own secret society shrine and had other ritual exposures. They have considerable familiarity with the idea of secrecy, in their own secret societies and in relation to those that they do not belong to. They have acquired knowledge of the age-hierarchical structure at Afikpo, although they have not yet experienced its most controlling forms. Thus they have developed varied skills and rich experiences in the maturation process, which prepares them for their initiation.

Many of these experiences at Afikpo, but particularly in their own boys' secret societies, in circumcision, and in their ritual experiences, ready them for initiation not only in terms of skills and experiences, but also psychologically. They are emotionally fortified so that when the initiation comes they are mentally prepared for it, and they are usually ready and willing to be initiated, and not overly apprehensive. There are two aspects to this psychological preparation, one conscious and one more hidden. The first is what Heald (1982) calls the vernacular psychology, the work of psychologically preparing the child for initiation, done largely in a conscious manner by persons in the culture. Heald discusses this with reference to her research among the Gisu of East Africa, where individuals help the boys to prepare for the major adolescent circumcision and initiation rite in psychological terms; thus the children usually come to it willingly and ready to undergo the ordeal. She argues (1982:32), as against a more traditional social anthropological approach, that "the contribution of the communicative aspect of ritual symbols then, is not to carry largely hidden messages about social relations, but to directly structure the psychological field in which the individual is prepared and made capable of acting." Her suggestion concerning a conscious vernacular psychology is very well taken, in that members of societies that have strenuous adolescent initiations must prepare the youths emotionally, in a conscious sense, for the initiation. This is certainly the case at Afikpo, as well as among the Limba of northern Sierra Leone (S. Ottenberg n.d.). The encouragement of fathers to their sons to join and continue to participate in the boys' societies, and the role of the father in the bird-shrine rite and in circumcision are conscious acts clearly connected with the emotional preparation of the boys for initiation, whatever other purposes they serve.

On the other hand, in writing about the maturation of Afikpo boys moving toward adolescent initiation I have made numerous interpretations dealing largely with unconscious factors. Heald might object to this as stressing "hidden messages" of a symbolic psychological kind, which do not explain how the youths are prepared for initiation in a conscious manner. I would argue, however, that the psychologically "hidden" messages, in my study—say in the boys' societies' religious shrine activities, in the boys' masquerades, and in the *nwa ulo* relationships, which center on oedipal issues and on the covert relationships between sexuality and secrecy—are at the very heart of the boys' experiences. Though the boys and others may not be conscious of them, they ultimately also contribute considerably to the emotional preparation of the youths, though at a different level than the vernacular psychology. These two are probably highly interrelated levels. The conscious need, at Afikpo, to get boys to act with ego strength as males, relates to the less conscious need to separate emotionally from the early mother-son emotional tie. The act of circumcision as a necessary preparation for entering initiation, something known consciously to everyone, including females, psychologically tells the boy he can go ahead at a later date. To this conscious level is added the unconscious anxieties and concepts having to do with father-son relationships and conflicts. The integration of the vernacular psychology and a psychology of the unconscious is evident. With these conclusions in mind we now turn to the initiation rites.

Part 2
The Initiations

Part title illustration:
Mbubu mask of the *isiji* dancer,
made by Chukwu Okoro

5

The Initiation of First Sons

T HE RITES OF INITIATION FOR ADOLESCENT BOYS AT
Afikpo are extensive, symbolically rich, and varied. I will
show how they are very closely linked to the boys' previous
experience, as well as indicating something of the knowledge and
insight that the boys bring to the initiations. These rites separate the
boys from a childhood of emulating adults; they become those that
they have emulated, and they in turn will be copied in the future by
yet younger males. The initiations also bring them more fully into
adult life in their compounds and agnatic groupings, establish a
lifelong pattern of a loving but separate adult relationship with their
mothers, are an early prelude to marriage, and are a prerequisite to
full relationships with the boys' matrilineal kin.

There are three major initiations at Afikpo. The rite for the first
son, *isiji,* is found in virtually all the Afikpo villages. Another form,
isubu, for other sons, is also widespread; a third and popular short
rite, composed of two interrelated initiations, *isubu eda* and *ikwum,*
occurs only in certain communities.

The existence of different initiation forms is the result of a history
of different peoples coming into the Afikpo area over time, moving
in on an indigenous people there (S. Ottenberg 1968a). As a consequence, each Afikpo village has either one, two, or three secret societies, each with its own initiation form. One type of secret society
is centralized at the village level, with a head priest, an assistant
priest, and a ritual group; other types are less centralized, being run
by interested elders of a village. One joins a particular kind of society
in a village by taking its initiation. But in practice, once initiated, one
can take part in many of the activities of the other society or societies
in the village (if any), such as in the masquerades, for strict differences are not always maintained. There is no overall organization of
these village societies for Afikpo as a whole; each village maintains its

own society or societies as a separate unit, although members of one society in one village usually have access to the societies of other villages, if they move or wish to take part.

There are no great myths of the origins of these societies or their initiations; rather, there is the historic tale of a particular initiation and society having always been there or having been been brought with a particular group of immigrants, or having been bought from the outside.

There are certain characteristics common to all Afikpo secret societies. Each village has complete control of its secret society. The societies have little economic control over productive resources and only an indirect supportive political role, as indicated in the last chapter. Each village has one or more sacred bush areas controlled by its society or societies, where the initiations partly take place. Surprisingly, these are generally at the very edge of the village, rather than some distance away. Each village society closes the village commons to women and male non-initiates for certain of its activities. Regardless of the type of society present, each village has a series of secret titles associated with its societies, which are part of the larger title system of the village-group, and must be taken in a certain order. Each secret society is active for only part of the year, in the dry season, when farming duties are not heavy and there is food for feasting. Every society is under the control of the village elders as a group, and of two priests as well in the Itim villages of Afikpo. In each society, however, it is a small group among the elders who are most interested and generally are very involved in running the society. They are not necessarily dominant leaders in the secular political world; in fact some of them are only ritual specialists.

Every adult male has to join a village secret society, otherwise he cannot have status and any political power or influence in the village or Afikpo as a whole. Any male from elsewhere who lives in an Afikpo village is likely to be initiated, if only in a brief form. He will generally be encouraged to become a member; otherwise he cannot ever fully take part in his community. The secret society excludes all females, and men say that one of its aims is to control women, "to keep them in their place." Women who violate the rules of a secret society, generally by seeing or touching something that they should not, are believed to fail to become pregnant, or their children will die, unless compensatory sacrifice is made to the offended spirit of the society.

There is one main spirit for each secret society, called by various names such as *omume* and *egbele,* according to the village and the particular history of that society. The spirit is considered to be male, though it takes no special form or appearance. Located at the secret society shrine in the bush, or in a priests' house if such is present, it is believed to work its will anywhere. It is the force which is said to harm women who violate rules of the secret society. I could discover no myths concerning it, but this seems typical of the Afikpo; if myths exist they are either very secret or I simply missed them.

The secret society spirit manifests itself directly in masquerades, where the members dress up and and put on performances, most of them public and well attended by females, uninitiated boys, and other males. Men only masquerade until about the age of forty. It is considered undignified to do so after that time. This is unlike the Liberian secret societies, where senior men with political power use masking to express their influence (Bellman 1984; d'Azevedo 1973; W. P. Murphy 1980). At Afikpo senior men are in the audience watching the performance. To the world of nonmembers the masqueraders are believed to be spirits (*nde mma,* persons-spirits) who are manifestations of the main spirit of the society, and who should not be touched by nonmembers. Masquerading is one of the main activities of these societies. Other than the main spirit and the masquerade spirits there does not seem to be a host of other secret society spirits; but the masquerade spirits themselves take a variety of forms (S. Ottenberg 1975).

All initiations share certain characteristics. Circumcision is a prerequisite. The father must perform certain preliminary activities, but does not go to the bush with his son. The initiation is a secular title, not a secret one, for the father. The boy spends periods of time ranging from one day and night to a number of months in the bush and elsewhere in the village area. Boys are initiated in groups, not singly, and they are still fed largely by their mothers during their rites, through male intermediaries. Some physical hardship occurs during the richly symbolic events, and the boys masquerade in public either during or shortly after the initiation. The initiation tends to involve much of the village during the time that it is occurring. It is in a ritual rather than an economically productive mode; villages spend accumulated wealth at this time, rather than gathering it in. The rites occur during the dry season, from about October to March. This is the period when the level of village activity is very high, when disputes are settled over land, divorce issues, and other matters, when many marriages are held, when the big second funerals occur (the funeral at the time of death being a small affair), and when the various village festivals are held. It is the ritual season, in contrast to the remainder of the year, when farming and fishing dominate activities and the patrilineal and matrilineal descent groups and polygynous family structures prevail rather than village activities. Nevertheless the initiations at Afikpo involve both the village-level organizations and the patrilineal descent groups.

With this background we now turn to the first-son rites of manhood. The Afikpo say that the initiation (*ubu*, from *obubu*, to initiate) of a man's first son should be a special affair; the extensive nature of *isiji* reflects this view. The events reveal the pride that a father has in his first male child, and the real need to have at least one male offspring, if the father is to achieve status in the village.

The father sponsors his own first son, not the first male child of each of his wives, into *isiji*. He does not have to have been a first son himself and to have gone through *isiji;* this does not matter at all. In the unfortunate event that a man has no son he "borrows" a son (but not a first son) of a brother or another patrilineal relative, often one living in his compound, and sponsors him as his own. An older man can even do so if he is not married at the time. Though he may have the resources for the initiation a young male waits until he marries, has a son, and the boy grows to a reasonable age, before sponsoring him.

The first-son initiation, normally the first that a father does for any son, is an exciting experience for both males. The rite symbolizes and reinforces the bonds between them; it reunites the son symbolically and in reality with the father after years of quasi separation. The son becomes publicly identified with the father through the initiation, which also ties the father closer, as a mature adult, to men of his own age. Afikpo say that no man who fails to put a boy into *isiji* has standing in his village; he cannot be a prominent leader or hold an important priesthood. I have elsewhere cited the case of a childless priest of a patrilineal ancestral shrine who refused to put a surrogate son into *isiji* and who subsequently was fined and then removed from office by his patrilineal elders (S. Ottenberg 1968a:43–44). In turn, the first son, like other sons, needs to be initiated in order to have a place in the adult male world of Afikpo, although he does not have to do *isiji.* His status will be only a little diminished if he does another initiation.

The first-son rite honors the boy, whose prestige is considerably raised among his age mates and in his patrilineal grouping, especially if he performs the public masquerade well during the initiation. Father and son cooperatively assist one another to enhance their respective statuses, an ideal Afikpo model of behavior among males.

The father determines when the boy is to be initiated, largely in terms of his own resources. Since *isiji* rites occur in an Afikpo village only every seventh year, there is not much choice of time if the father wishes to put the boy through as an adolescent, as is usually the case. The father is generally in his late thirties or his forties, for men at Afikpo usually do not marry until they are well into their twenties. Because in recent years a man may have the resources to initiate his first son as a young child, the age of initiation has been lowering. Such a father is anxious to get ahead in status himself; on the other hand, he may fear that the young child will be harmed in the bush. Recently cases have occurred where an older boy, a patrilineal relative of the father, has been substituted, the first son later doing one of the other initiations. The surrogate does not have any special claims as first son of his "father" after the initiation. The use of a surrogate first son suggests that *isiji* is as much an initiation for the father as it is for the boy, yet Afikpo speak of it largely in terms of the son. If the father is dead the first son still goes through this rite. He is sponsored by a brother or another patrilineal relative of the deceased, or occasionally by a number of his agnatic kin who pool their efforts. The boy's mother may pay a substantial portion of the initiation costs if she has the resources, but a male is always presented as the sponsor; women cannot be so at Afikpo.

A father can put a second son into *isiji* at a later date than the first one, but this is not done very often today, for men would rather put their resources elsewhere. The food and other initiation costs are reduced after the first time. A wealthy man does this if he feels like it, for it brings him prestige.

A stranger living regularly in an Afikpo village, whether of Igbo origin or not, can put his first son into *isiji.* Such a man has usually joined the secret society in the village where he resides but in a short and less prestigious initiation form; it is not acceptable for adult males to live for long in a village without becoming secret society members. They will not be forced out of the village but they are viewed as strangers until they initiate themselves and their sons.

A father, as the boy's sponsor, is considered to be taking a title (*meme*: S. Ottenberg 1971:22–23), one of the numerous Afikpo titles; this one is called *itiye nwa na ɔhia* (put-child [or son]-in-bush), or *egba ɔhia isiji* (build-bush-isiji [first-son initiation]). The latter term indicates that the sponsors build a certain structure in the initiation bush, although they usually have other initiated males do so for them. The father thus joins the title society of all village males who have put a son through *isiji*.

The son usually lives in his father's home village, though a surrogate son could possibly come from another Afikpo settlement. If a man's first son has moved away with his mother following divorce, the father tries to attract him back to his home village for this initiation and hopes to keep him living there after it is over; tensions between father and stepfather sometimes develop over this matter.

The first-son initiation is called *omume isiji* (perform-*isiji*) or *ime isiji*, a shortened form, or just *isiji*. The term *isiji* has various interpretations at Afikpo. One is "head-yam," meaning that this is an important event, it is like the head of the yam, its growing portion. The term is also a metaphor for the boy as a growing yam, and for his growing penis and awakening sexuality, since the yam often symbolizes the male organ at Afikpo. Yams are also liberally employed in the considerable feasting during this initiation; they are the major Afikpo ceremonial food, grown largely by men.

Isiji was introduced many years ago from nearby Edda Village-Group to the west, a related Igbo people, where it is prevalent. It came to Afikpo by way of the ancient settlement of Ovum, now a deserted compound west of Mgbom village, which is the site for rites of the Afikpo Rain Controller (S. Ottenberg 1971:203–5). This was before Mgbom and some other Afikpo villages existed. From Ovum it spread to the central Afikpo village of Amamgballa and from there to others in the Ahisu subgroup of Afikpo settlements (S. Ottenberg 1971:193–96). The boys in these settlements enter the *isiji* bush on the *nwkɔ* day of the New Yam Festival, the day that the first yams are dug out of the ground, in August or September, during the rainy season. Thus the initiation in these villages is called *isiji udumini* (first son initiation–rainy season). Except for those villages which lack the ceremony (see Appendix 1), the rest of the Afikpo villages obtained their *isiji* at a later date, also from Edda Village Group, through the ancient and now extinct Afikpo village of Ɔorogho. These settlements commence their initiation seven Igbo weeks (28 days) later or more, following the *iko ɔkɔci* (feast–dry season) festival, which marks the beginning of the dry period. The rite, *isiji ɔkɔci*, does not differ essentially from the form found in the Ahisu settlements. The forms of *isiji* in nearby Edda Village-Group are more elaborate and lengthy than those at Afikpo (Marsh 1934; Afikpo 1935). The Afikpo form could not have developed independently, for the initiation shrine must be purchased from an *isiji* performing group, with proper instructions and ritual installations. The Afikpo believe power must be transferred; you cannot create your own shrine independently and have the shrine spirit operate with power; where and how a village obtains its initiation depends upon its political and kinship relationships with other settlements.

History, the particular interests of members of certain villages, and other factors have served to create considerable variability in the year when *isiji* is performed in different villages. Performed every seventh year, it coincides with the farming of the same block of village farmland each time, since there is a six-section land-rotation farming cycle in a village—a convenient way of keeping track of it. In Mgbom this is when Ebe Mgbom land is worked, and the years concerned are 1950, 1957, and 1963. *Isiji* occurs every year somewhere at Afikpo. There is no necessary reason why this should be so, for the resources of one village are not drawn into the initiation in another settlement, and there is no centralized system of control of the initiations. Yet the Afikpo relish the idea that there is a first-son initiation in the village-group every year; this ties in with their sense of its importance.

The initiation can also occur out of regular sequence when one or several men in a village take the highest Afikpo title, *omume*. This is done largely for prestige purposes, for the title carries little political power; it is generally held by about ten Afikpo at any one time, mostly older men, living in various villages, although there is no limit on the number of members. *Omume* involves an elaborate set of rituals and feasts for the title holders and other persons over the course of a year or more. The taker must "buy" the *isiji* bush, that is, establish the initiation bush in his village and put a son through this rite. Sometimes he does so at a regular first-son initiation period, but usually he establishes the bush in an off year, which calls attention to his exploit. He must already have put a first son through *isiji;* here he makes use of another son or a surrogate child.

The title taker is often joined by a small group of other village men who take the opportunity to put a first son through *isiji* at this irregular time, and sometimes even by a man who wishes to sponsor a boy in *isiji* for a second time but who is not taking the title. For the boys, the rites are similar to a regular initiation; this is also true for the men except for the title taker, who has additional numerous and heavy feasting and ritual duties.

Variation is endemic in Afikpo initiations. Sometimes a man "buys" the bush in his village in an off year because he wants to put his first son through in a hurry. In Mgbom village a wealthy man, Ɔkpane Eke, desired to take the *omume* title during the regular *isiji* initiation time in his village, but he had not yet initiated his first son, so he "bought" *isiji* several years ahead of time; unfortunately he died before he had the opportunity to take the title. In more recent times another Mgbom man, Pa Okoce, a contractor who had been working away from home at a time when few Afikpo did so, wished to put his first son through *isiji* right away and he did this three years ahead of schedule. He was a man known for being unusual and powerful. Perhaps also, in this case, pressure to show what he had gained from his experiences away from home at a time when few Afikpo left, played a part in his action. In these cases, as in the *omume* title taking, other men sometimes join the person buying the bush; they are normally repeaters, doing it for a second or even a third time, just because they have the money and want to show their wealth.

Further variations in the initiation rites occur, particularly between villages. These are discussed in Appendix 1. Authority over the *isiji* initiation rests with the elders of each community, rather than any central agency, such as the Afikpo village-group elders, or controls through a strong belief in a set of unchangeable rules for initiations. There is no regular priest for this form of secret society initiation rite. The variations mirror historical factors and the degree of unity of groups of villages and of single communities. The Afikpo are untroubled by these numerous differences. Rather, they delight in them and in the explanations for their existence, of which they are well aware. Modern influences have created even greater changes. Yet the underlying symbolic elements in the various initiations are much alike; this is where unity lies.

I will describe the first-son initiation in Mgbom village (see Map 3), a settlement of the Itim subgroup, and then discuss variations in other villages.

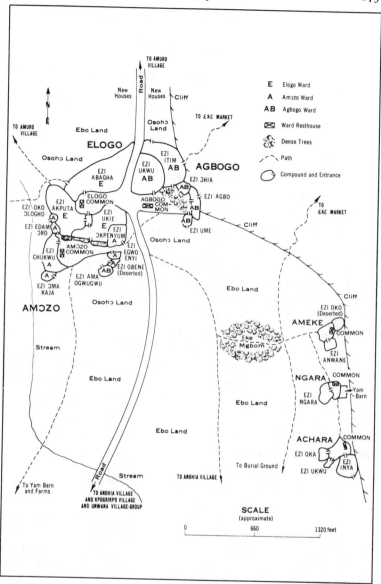

Map 3. Mgbom Village (*1960*)

Preliminaries

A complex set of preliminary events, particularly feasts, gears up the male organizations of the village for the initiation, and ritual sacrifices notify the spirit world of the event. The fathers of the boys to be initiated take the initiative, guided by senior patrikinsmen who have done the rite. The preliminary events often take place on certain days of the four-day Igbo week: *ɛkɛ, orie, ahɔ,* and *nkwɔ,* the first being big market day, the third small market day, and the other two farm days. A boy to be initiated should have gone through the rituals discussed in previous chapters, although only circumcision is absolutely essential. The excision is a physical cutting, the initiation a social one; both are arranged by the father. The first allows the boy to have sexual intercourse without spiritual offense, the second makes him socially a man and permits him to marry. The father has generally informed the boy a few months ahead that he will likely be initiated. The time is the father's choice, not the son's; the boy is responsible to his father throughout the rite. Boys look forward to the initiation even though they may be frightened of it.

There is a prerequisite male title, *ewa anohia* (goat–entrance bush), for the father, the first of many preliminaries to his son's initiation, and one of the first of twenty or so titles that an Afikpo male can acquire. This moves him ahead on a long career of title taking, both within and without the secret society; it may be done many years before the first son is initiated.

An Afikpo man takes a title by feasting and giving money to the title holders in the compound or village or village-group, depending upon how the title society is organized. The title society members share the funds, more or less equally. The person is then a title holder himself and meets with the others of the group when another individual joins; there are no other meetings. Honor and prestige follow joining up; there is usually no special form of address or dress for the title holders.

Ewa anohia is taken in the compound; title holders generally belong to the same major patrilineage. They comprise nearly all the male elders of the compound, some middle-aged men, and a few younger ones. A male goat is slaughtered at the start of the ceremony, and the title taker feeds the title holders boiled yams with goat meat, palm wine and native gin, and other foods. He also gives them the title fee, usually two to five pounds or more (at the time of my research, this was worth about ten to twenty-five American dollars). The title taker also gives meat to other males in the compound, and feasts his village age-set mates in a separate group and his male friends in another.

In killing the animal a sacrifice is made at the compound entrance, which is also its major exit. This is generally done by pouring the goat's blood on the ground, along with standard sacrificial materials: palm wine (for the spirits to drink), kola nut (for greeting), white chalk (for health and fertility), sometimes a small iron piece (*apa*) or a brass rod (both represent wealth and success and were once forms of money), and other materials. The rite is lead by the oldest title holder in the compound. He calls for blessings for the title taker and his first son who will initiate some day. The sacrifice is said to inform the spirit (*ɔhia omume,* bush-perform) associated with the first-son initiation, which is in the initiation bush, where its shrine is found. The bush itself is not used for this sacrifice, for its shrine is closed except during the initiation, when its spirit is active. The Afikpo consider the compound entrance to be a good place to call up spirits, as is a crossroads. The son to be initiated may be present and receive some food but he is not essential to the rite, which is for the father and the compound title holders; in fact, the son need not have been born when this title is taken.

The sacrifice and feast proclaim to compound males, to the father's village age set, and to the bush spirit, that the title taker will some day initiate his eldest son. As one Afikpo put it, "One has to kill a goat to open the gate to the initiation." The goat is a symbol of male strength and vigor.

In recent years very wealthy fathers, after having performed this title and initiated a son into *isiji,* take the title again, in the son's name, rather than waiting for him to grow up and do it himself. The Afikpo say that this gives the son a head start on his own rites when he matures, and shows the father to be wealthy, for even after the expense of initiating his first son he has the resources to do this. The father is praised for his generosity, spending money on the son rather than on himself. This special form of title taking may appear to diminish the symbolic quality and timing of the rite, but this does not bother the Afikpo, who stress the importance of what the father has done for the son.

While this title is often taken a number of years before the father initiates his first son, there are other rituals to be carried out during the year before the initiation. This preliminary time, which has no special name, is characterized by certain feasts given by the fathers of first sons to be initiated, and by gifts from these same fathers to the *isiji* title holders, men who have already done the *isiji* first-son initiation for a son. They are sometimes grouped for these activities at the village level, representing residential concerns, but at other times by compounds, signifying agnatic interests. The son also makes preliminary preparations, and there are some material things to be attended to, such as the gathering of firewood and the building of the initiation bush structure.

The village festivals of the New Yam and of the Rainy Season (in some villages also the Dry Season Festival) are held before the initiation and create an atmosphere of village cooperation which is a useful preparation for the initiation, after the kinship- and descent-oriented farming activities. The rite addresses the overabundance of uninitiated boys in the community, and it does not usually generate or resolve village leadership conflicts. Existing ones are put aside, and there is little difficulty over the initiation and its leadership. (This is not the case among the Ndembu, as described in Turner 1967: Chap. 7.) Outwardly, at least, there is unity and an emphasis on social readjustment and status change. Initiation fits well into this period, with its ritual emphasis.

There are two *isiji* bushes in Mgbom village, representing the two main sections of the community. One bush is located in Agbogo common, at the front part of the compounds of Ezi Ukwu and Ezi Itim (see Map 3), and it is for Agbogo and Elogo wards and the three subvillages of Mgbom. The other is found behind the men's rest house in Amɔzo ward, which uses it, and as well a patrilineal group, Nde Agbagha in Ezi Agbagha compound in Elogo ward, which originated in Amɔzo. The Amɔzo bush is used by about one fourth of the male population of Mgbom; the rest use the other bush area. Some initiation activities are carried out jointly by the whole village, others separately by each section, and still others by individual compounds; this will be indicated below.

When a village has more than one *isiji* bush it is not so much a function of its size as of the particular histories of the community. The *isiji* rites reflect the delicate balance of village unity and the autonomy of its sections. Autonomy is stressed in the ownership of shrines and rituals, in land controls, and in other ways. In Mgbom the Amɔzo ward was settled later than other parts of the village; its founders were blacksmiths, having special shrines associated with their work which they never shared with the rest of Mgbom. In the case of other forms of secret society initiations in Mgbom, which are of later origin, one common bush is employed, or each compound has its own separate initiation area.

Mgbom, one of the largest Afikpo villages, had a population in 1953 of over two thousand persons divided into three wards and three subvillages (S. Ottenberg 1971:41–46). There are twenty-two major patrilineages grouped into twenty compounds. The village is of sufficient size to put on impressive ritual displays, with little internal factionalism to mar the rites, and with a good competitive spirit in reference to other communities. The Afikpo Rain Controller (S. Ottenberg 1971:203–5) lives there. There is a village rule that diviners using certain procedures are forbidden to reside in the community. Therefore, although he is not a diviner, the Rain Controller fulfills some diviner's roles in the Mgbom initiation, but not all.

Preparations for Mgbom's *isiji* begin during the dry season of the year before it is held (see Table 1). At this time the men in a village who plan to put their first sons through the rite begin to meet together. Some already know one another as members of the same village age set (S. Ottenberg 1971: Chap. 3); men of the same ages often perform *isiji* at the same time. Some of the fathers were themselves initiated at the same time. They are also familiar with one another through village politics and agnatic and uterine ties. Since a village age set covers a three-year span and the initiation occurs every seventh year, fathers involved are likely to represent two age sets, though there is variation, especially toward the older ages. There are even a few elders in Mgbom who, for one reason or another, have not sponsored a son into the initiation, and occasionally one of them joins up.

There may be over fifty fathers initiating sons in Mgbom. One among the fathers who is interested—and there are always men who like to put effort into ritual affairs—offers his house and compound as their meeting place. Here they gather at invervals to pool money, for they have to consult a diviner, plan feasts, and carry out other actions. And they take the opportunity to drink and feast among themselves from time to time, for they enjoy the initiation as well as shouldering its responsibilities. Both sections of Mgbom act together to form this group. Later other men may decide to go ahead with the

TABLE 1
Schedule of the *Isiji* Initiation in Mgbom Village

Time Period	Day of Week[a]	Events
Preliminaries		
Any time previous to initiation		Father of initiand takes *ewa anohia* title.
Previous dry season		Fathers begin to meet regularly, consult a diviner, and begin to plan the initiation.
After Dry Season Festival		Fathers send sons to collect firewood.
Between Dry Season Festival and New Yam Festival		Fathers feast title holders of the compound *(nri obu)*; fathers "buy the bush" from village title holders.
Week 1	[any day of week]	Initiand feasts *isiji* title holders in his compound. Corn taboo takes effect. Break-wind feast in compound. Father sacrifices at various shrines, to ensure success for the son. Father selects helpers for the son's initiation (unless they have been chosen earlier).
Week 2	*ɛkɛ*	
	orie	
	ahɔ	Wood and raffia are cut for initiation bush.
	nkwɔ	Poles for bush structure are brought to village.
Week 3	*ɛkɛ*	[Rainy Season Festival takes place.]
	orie	
	ahɔ	Grass is cut in the village commons. Fathers feast all village secret society initiates and, separately, their own age sets.

[a]The order of days in the Igbo week is as follows: (1) *ɛkɛ*, (2) *orie*, (3) *ahɔ*, (4) *nkwɔ*.

TABLE 1 *continued*

Time Period	Day of Week	Events
	nkwɔ	
Week 4	*εkε*	Initiation bush is cleared.
	orie	
	ahɔ	
	nkwɔ	
Week 5	*εkε*	Inner fence constructed inside initiation bush. Fathers feast all village secret society initiates.
	orie	
	ahɔ	Outer fence constructed around initiation bush. Initiands feast compound secret society members.
	nkwɔ	
Week 6	[any day of week]	Father feasts friends and compound men. Father sacrifices at shrines.
	εkε	Father feasts son's initiated friends.
	orie	
	ahɔ	Fathers feast village *isiji* title holders who are senior elders. Rain Controller prepares magical charms.

Bush Phase *(ababa na ɔhia)*

	nkwɔ	Mothers feed sons a fine meal. Fathers give buffalo skins to village *isiji* title holders. Boys enter the bush. Central part of the bush structure is built. Initiands practice dancing. Stick-throwing contest. *Isiji* shrine uncovered. Rules of *isiji* explained to initiands.

TABLE 1 *continued*

Time Period	Day of Week	Events
Week 7	ɛkɛ	*Isiji* costume material is collected. Actual initiation takes place.
	orie	All initiands dance. Father feasts (separately) helpers, his age set, and compound *isiji* title holders.
	ahɔ	Initiands break calabash utensils before mothers. Fathers feast village secret society initiates. Starting on this day, initiands may gather fruit, with bag and machete, on days that they do not dance.
	nkwɔ	
Week 8	ɛkɛ	Fathers feast all secret society members in the village.
	orie	All initiands dance.
	ahɔ	
	nkwɔ	
Week 9	ɛkɛ	
	orie	Sons of the youngest fathers dance; their parents celebrate. Their fathers feast agnates and friends.
	ahɔ	Goat is eaten by initiands, fathers' age sets, and village *isiji* title holders.
	nkwɔ	
Week 10	ɛkɛ	
	orie	Sons of older fathers dance; their parents celebrate. Their fathers feast agnates and friends.
	ahɔ	Goat is eaten by initiands, fathers' age sets, and village *isiji* title holders.
	nkwɔ	

TABLE 1 *continued*

Time Period	Day of Week	Events
Week 11	ɛkɛ	
	orie	Sons of oldest fathers dance; their parents celebrate. Their fathers feast agnates and friends.
	ahɔ	Goat is eaten by initiands, fathers' age sets, and village *isiji* title holders. Title holders meet to divide fees received.
	nkwɔ	
Week 12	ɛkɛ	
	orie	*Isiji* spirits dance.
	ahɔ	
	nkwɔ	
Week 13	ɛkɛ	
	orie	Best dancers perform again. Boys leave the bush, and the bush structures are cut down.

Compound Phase (*Enya ɛgwɵ*)

	ahɔ	Initiands move into compounds.
	nkwɔ	
Week 14	ɛkɛ	
	orie	
	ahɔ	Whipping Day
	nkwɔ	[*Isubu eda* yearly initiation for non-first sons]
Week 15	ɛkɛ	
	orie	[Feast of the Tortoise
	ahɔ	takes place.]
	nkwɔ	
Week 16	ɛkɛ	End of compound phase of *isiji* initiation; beginning of *isubu* initiation.

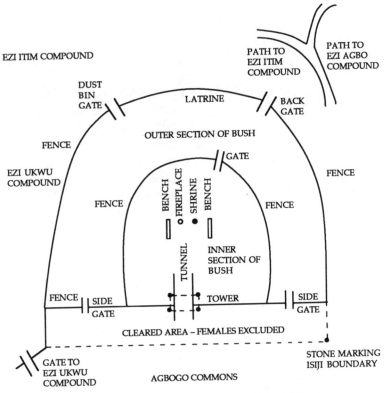

Figure 1. Mgbom Village, Agbogo section, *Isiji* bush

initiation and join up; those who enter late must pay whatever back dues have been collected.

Several months after forming, the fathers' group consults a diviner at their meeting place, to ensure the success of their endeavors. This rite, *egba eja* (consult-sacrifice), is also performed by land-holding groups at the start of the farming season, and by individuals before taking a major title or going on a long trip. If not done it is believed an evil spirit or spirits may act to make for failure. The diviner—in this case an outsider to Mgbom is generally called—is asked what ritual steps should be taken so that the initiation will be "healthy," i.e., so that no one in the bush will become ill, die, or be injured. At a minimum the diviner prepares a magical protective charm, *ekike*, out of various medicines tied together with leaves, which he places in the open section of the southern part of the community, where firewood will be stacked for the rites. He also prescribes sacrifices at various village shrines for further protection, usually done a day or two before initiation, which the fathers carry out. This is to inform major spirits in the community of the initiation and to ask for their assistance in making it successful. Sometimes the diviner tells the men to throw a small chicken and an egg into the *isiji* bush for its spirit, to inform it of the forthcoming rite. The Afikpo say that "this is what the spirit likes." The two items clearly represent fertility and growth, or the potential for growth, a reference to the initiands.

At this diviner's consultation men who are planning to put a son into *isiji* for a second time announce their plans. They have not taken part so far and they do not pay certain fees required of fathers doing this rite for the first time, for they have already done so. After this meeting the *isiji* title members in each Mgbom ward, and again in each compound, call in a diviner and carry out whatever he suggests in the way of rites at ward and compound shrines respectively. Each level of village organization has its own preparations, even though the same fathers are involved, typical of many Afikpo rituals.

Soon after the Dry Season Festival in Mgbom Village the fathers tell the first sons to go out and collect firewood. Then the sons definitely know they are to be initiated; with much excitement they go about their task. Called *nkɔ isiji* (firewood–first son initiation), the wood is grouped into piles representing each of the three wards and each of the three subvillages of Mgbom. There is competition to build the highest stack, reflecting rivalries among the youths from their secret society and wrestling days. Other boys who are not yet to be initiated help out. This continues for about a month, on every fourth day, *ahɔ,* until sufficient wood is gathered, when the fathers stop the work. The wood will be used for fire in the *isiji* bush and in the men's rest houses in the village commons during the initiation. The initiands receive small sums of money from their fathers for this work. If a father decides to put his son through initiation after the wood has been collected, he must pay a small sum, five to ten shillings, to members of the fathers' group of his village section, in lieu of his son's labor.

Between the time of earth heaping and planting for yams (February and March) and the New Yam Festival (August or September) each father feasts the men of his compound who have done *isiji* for a son and pays them a title fee. Called *nri obu* (food–meeting house), the expenses vary from compound to compound; the price and foods

are set by the title holders, in keeping with the considerable autonomy of Afikpo social units. In Ezi Akputa compound in Mgbom, in
1951, each father held a feast on a separate *nkwɔ* day of the Igbo week,
providing one lump of mashed yam fufu for each title holder, and as
a group they were given two ducks (cut up and cooked in soup), one
dried hedgehog, one pot of palm wine, a shilling (a substitute for the
traditional chalk) and two kola nuts. Yam is the staple ceremonial
food at Afikpo, the kola is for greeting, and the ducks and hedgehog
are expensive and unusual items, calling attention to the importance
of the event. The chalk blesses the title holders; it represents peace,
fertility, and health, as discussed above. The title price was ten shillings, which the title holders divided among themselves. In 1951 in
this large Mgbom compound sixteen fathers did *isiji*, so sixteen separate feasts at different times occurred, all taking place at the ancestral rest house in the compound, the general meeting place for the
men. In some Mgbom compounds several fathers give the feast on
the same day. The initiands may be present and receive food but, as
in the *ewa anohia* title, this is basically adult men's business. If a man
is putting a son through for a second time he does not do this rite;
he has already done so.

The *isiji* title members of the whole of Mgbom are also collectively
feasted by the fathers. This takes place on the *nkwɔ* day after the Feast
of Obeyi, usually in June. In this rite, called *ozuzu ɔhia* (buy-bush),
the fathers are said to be purchasing the bush from the village and its
isiji title holders, in order to initiate their first sons. The fathers feast
these titled men at a convenient open place in a compound that the
title holders select. In 1951 they met in Ezi Itim, at the home of a man
interested in initiations and other rituals. The fathers feed the title
members rich food, much yam and a number of ducks in soup (eight
in 1951). Each father provides a small pot of the very best palm wine
and each pays the title holders a ten-shilling fee, the standard price in
Mgbom for "buying the bush." This is done jointly by both village
sections, a splendid and expensive repast which is the public announcement of the fathers' intent to go ahead with the initiation.
The sons are not present though there is no rule against them being
there. Thus each *isiji* title holder receives two feasts and two fees
from the fathers, one in his compound and the other in the village.

About the time of the New Yam Festival in September, on an
nkwɔ day, the initiands each hold a feast for initiated lads and young
men of their compound, to ask for their help and support during the

rites, which these males will provide. The boys' fathers provide the dried fish, meat, palm wine, and corn; the boys contribute by catching field rodents which are cooked and eaten. The young initiated males of the compound are anxious that their boys do well in the forthcoming rite in competition with those in other village compounds and so will assist them; the feast expresses a wish for the solidarity of the already initiated and the soon-to-be initiated in the face of the coming events.

Following this a boy is forbidden to touch or to eat corn until his initiation is completed; this gives the name to this feast, *ntebu akpokpa* (bite off–corn). In some cases the son assiduously sweeps the floor, ceilings, walls, and shelves of his mother's house to remove any corn, for she will cook for him before and during the initiation, as she normally does. She may have contact with corn outside of her home but not when cooking for her son. He will be careful to go only to places, such as the boys' houses in the compound, where he is sure that there is no corn about. Corn ripens in June at Afikpo and there is plenty of it about during the initiation period. Later on I will offer a symbolic interpretation of this taboo; here I comment only that boys are being denied a common food, very popular with them.

On *aho* day, six days after the Mgbom New Yam Festival, materials are collected from the village forest grove (*uru*) for the elaborate fenced structure which faces the commons and serves as a shield for the initiation bush, as well as its entrance and exit. In Mgbom the task is carried out separately by the two village sections. In former times a village age set selected by the elders obtained the wood and raffia, clearing up the commons and building much of the fencing. This was an age set in which no member had yet gone through *isiji*, so there was an incentive for males to do the initiation in order to be free of this labor; it was usually an age set in process of formation (S. Ottenberg 1971: Chap. 4). Nowadays boys are initiated at such a young age that this arrangement is not feasible and the elders simply order one or more village age sets to direct the labor. This set supervises the work, delegating tasks to younger initiated boys.

The crucial part of the bush structure is the center section, some twenty-five to thirty feet high, an important public symbol of *isiji* clearly visible from the village commons, and its top from some of the compounds. It consists of four vertical poles of a special wood, *cigheci*, arranged in a square. On top of each pole is tied a protective magical charm of braided plant material, *ɛkikɛ*, covered with a calabash to shelter it; these are made by a diviner (in Mgbom by the Rain Controller), and are believed to protect the boys from harm while in the bush, as well as the workers preparing the structure. The four poles are supported in place by vertical connecting pieces of *okɔ* wood, which form a sort of ladder, and by crosspieces of another wood, *ɔtero*. The construction of this center section, *ɛnya osisi* (eye-pole) or *obube isiji* (ladder–first son initiation), is aided by skilled carpenters who are not afraid of heights and who volunteer to assist. It is not actually built until the initiation is in progress, but preparatory tasks are done earlier. The work takes several days and is of interest to men, who enjoy watching it go up.

On the second work day, *nkwɔ*, the poles are brought to the village commons. Then the village gong is played, a large hollowed out tree trunk in the rest house in Agbogo ward (S. Ottenberg 1972) in the main village commons, and the fathers come out and dance about, shooting off guns in celebration and offering palm wine to friends and relatives in their own compounds, thus publicly announcing to all persons in the village—here not to any specific groups—that they are going to initiate their first sons.

The following day is the Rainy Season Festival in Mgbom, but nothing occurs in the initiation until two days later, on *ahɔ*, when the age set responsible for the fence work cuts down the grass in the village commons, especially near the initiation bush area; this is called *ɔrɵrɵ enwuwɵ* (weeding-grass). On this day each father, for both village sections acting as one, provides forty boiled yams and forty pieces of boiled corn, to be shared among all secret society initiates in the village, regardless of which form of initiation they have taken. Most of the males of a mature age are there to receive this. The fence builders rate a good share of it for their work, and the village elders get most of the rest. This is a large amount of food and men take it to the rest houses in the commons to eat at their leisure over a number of days. It is said that husbands who have been fighting with their wives are happy at this time for they now have an independent source of nourishment.

Also on this day each father initiating a son, at his home or somewhere in his compound, provides yam fufu, meat, and palm wine to members of his own village age set, to greet them and to let them know of his plans. It is also a call for their support.

Two days later *ɛkɛ*, the age set in charge of the work, directs the clearing of the initiation bush of brush and grass by men and initiated boys, in a rite called *egbuji osisi* (cut–fence poles). Four days later the inner circle fence of bamboo is built (see Figure 1), in an action called *ɔgbobo nguzoghe* (to fence–standing), a term also employed for the fence itself. The spirit of the *isiji* bush is located within this fence. Both spirit and shrine are called *omume*, or *ɔhia omume* (bush–perform). The work is done separately by the two village sections. On this day the village secret society initiates are again fed forty yams and forty pieces of corn by each father in another feast. In recent years money has been given in place of this and the earlier feast. This is a general tendency at Afikpo; many people prefer the funds and see the heavy feasting as a waste.

Two days later *(ahɔ)* the age set in charge of the construction builds the outer fence, *ikɔrɔ*, in the bush. Again the work is done separately by males of the two village sections. And on this day the initiands feast the males in the compound who are secret society members, regardless of their form of initiation. Called *otara ekpoe* (fufu-[a name]), it is again a way of calling for help from the initiated compound males when the initiands are in the bush. Again, the father provides all or most of the food.

Four days later, the fathers of both village sections together offer yam fufu and palm wine to the village *isiji* title holders of the two highest Afikpo age grades, *ekpe uke ɛsa* and *ɔni ekara*. This feasting involves only some five to ten men; there are few senior elders alive. No set amount of food is provided—whatever is seen as proper is given—though the elders, as at many other Afikpo feasts, are not above asking for more if they feel that they are being slighted. The meal is said to be thanks for "taking their time." The rite honors and informs the most senior men of the village of the forthcoming initiation, among a people who have great respect for age and whose elders have power.

Also on this day the Afikpo Rain Controller in Mgbom—a diviner in other villages—prepares an *ekike* protective charm to be tied on the loin cloth (*anam*) of each initiand before he enters the bush. It is kept by the parents until that time. A like charm is also made for each mother (or surrogate if the natural mother is dead) to tie around her left arm when the boy is in the bush and in the subsequent *ɔka* stage. The initiand's charm protects him from harm throughout the bush period, and the mother's screens her from contaminating influences from the bush spirit and ensures that no poisons get into the food that she cooks for her son during the initiation. For this work the Rain Controller and his male relatives, who assist him, are given a good feast and a fee by the fathers of the initiands.

On the next day, *nkwɔ*, the boys enter the bush. The day is called *enya osisi* (eye-pole) after the high central fence section, completed after the boys go into the bush. During the entire process of clearing the initiation area and erecting the structures the commons is closed and women and uninitiated boys are excluded, but in fact small uninitiated lads often hang about during the construction without being chased away.

The fathers in each of the two sections separately give eight pieces of wild buffalo (bush cow) skin to the *isiji* title holders to chew on as a final pre-initiation gift. This is an unusual food, rarely given at Afikpo rites. The animal is difficult to find and dangerous to hunt, taking great skill. I obtained no statements as to the skin's symbolism but it suggests a major effort on the part of the fathers to do everything possible for the title holders, no matter how difficult. Metaphorically, the fathers are strong as wild buffalo, as is the hunter of such an animal. The idea of physical danger in the forthcoming rites for the boys is equated with hunting that animal, and an association of animals in the bush and boys in the bush is made.

Several other events occur shortly before the initiation. Some days previous to it the father, with his son in his compound, feasts all the boy's initiated friends. This is to ask them to help protect the boy from harm during the rite. Called *omume ehe* (perform–break wind), the feast is associated with a belief that an uninitiated boy should never break wind before a secret society initiate. To break wind before an older person at Afikpo is to insult him; it is talking out of the wrong end of the body. If a boy does so he will be scolded and may be threatened: "Just wait until your initiation," or "Wait, we will meet in the commons some day," referring to the whipping contests held in Mgbom and some other villages in association with a certain initiation. On the same day the father, in the name of his son, also feasts the father's friends and compound males. These two feasts are said to clear any offense that the boy may have caused by breaking wind in front of initiated persons, so that an offended individual will not demand food during the initiation, as he has the right to do if this has not been done. However, sometimes males from outside of the compound come to the father, demanding to be paid off for this offense. An offended man may keep a boy from entering the bush until he is feasted or given a gift, in a playful way or as a harassment of the father.

In some compounds this feast is not given as a general meal. Instead, at the time of the corn taboo feast in the compound, the father invites any male that the son is aware of having offended by breaking wind. The boy gives a small present—a penny, a cigarette, a yam, or a coconut—to each offended person and says, "Well, here is a gift I give you for once having broken wind." This present may be given to other initiates as well to ensure their support during the rites.

A day or two before the initiation the father sacrifices at his shrines and those of his son in the compound to ask spirits to look after the boy during the initiation. This is generally done at the patrilineal ancestral shrine; at a general welfare shrine in the compound, *nka-malo,* which the son may have as well as the father (S. Ottenberg 1970:30–34); at *ɔma ɛzi,* which is an agnatic and compound shrine to the ground spirit, *ale* (S. Ottenberg 1968a:64–68); and at a shrine for the Aro Chuku oracle, *ibini ɔkpabe,* a high diety at Afikpo (S. Ottenberg 1970:41–45). The father, or if he is busy the mother, should also see that a sacrifice is performed at the matrilineal clan shrine, *nja* (S. Ottenberg 1968a:97–99) of the boy, often located in another village. The parent usually touches a fowl and a piece of chalk to the boy and takes these to the matrilineal shrine where, with the aid of its priest, the shrine spirit is told of the forthcoming rite.

The food given at the sacrifices at these various shrines is believed eaten by the spirits. Often the sacrificers eat as well; the shrine gets the chicken blood and feathers, and those who take part cook and eat the rest. Thus spirits and the living sup together, suggesting that they are at peace with one another.

The father selects one or two young men as helpers, usually from his own compound and thus generally agnates or friends of his or the boy, to go into the bush with the son to guide and protect him. The Afikpo say that it lowers the father's status to go into the bush himself, and only a very poor man who cannot afford helpers, or one who loves the rites, does so. As one man said, "Anytime a father leads a boy there he has no kin and no friends." But there may be psychological reasons as well, similar to those that I have suggested for the absence of the father at a son's circumcision.

Boys may be frightened in the period before entering the bush as to what will occur there; initiated lads deliberately attempt to scare them, telling them how difficult it is and how much they will suffer. But there are also encouragements. A boy considers the younger ones who will be initiated with him and says to himself, "How should I die if there are smaller ones than I who might live?" And his father may encourage him not to be frightened, stating that he will protect the son against the males he has broken wind in front of. Yet the boy usually knows that the father himself does not go into the bush and may have heard of boys getting sick or dying while there, and he is not always consoled. However, he enjoys the preliminary feasts in the compound, and is delighted to be the center of attention. Sometimes boys start wearing the narrow strip loin cloth that is their dress in the bush several days before entering, as part of their preparation. The cloth covers the genitals and anus, is tied around the waist, and one end drops free in front while the other does so in back. Usually of white and blue native cotton material, it is not made at Afikpo as weaving is not done there, but comes from Uburu to the northwest, or elsewhere in Igbo country.

Commentary

The main role in the preliminary events of the *isiji* initiation is played by the fathers. Through a series of feasts and rites they lay the groundwork for the initiation. They activate a range of support groups and individuals, and alert the spiritual world. These things are necessary to "hand the bush over to the son." Table 1 summarizes these events. The son carries out a few activities, but it is the father who plays the directing role. Once the boy is in the bush there is a dramatic reversal; the father's role is more passive, the son's very active, symbolizing the changing relationship of the two.

The father gains prestige through his actions in the preliminary period, especially if he is generous in feasting. To provide large amounts of food and drink at Afikpo is to exhibit wealth and strong kin support. Food, as a resource, is often employed to enhance personal position. Eating together—humans with humans, and humans with spirits—symbolizes harmony. When hostilities exist people are reluctant to eat jointly for fear of being poisoned.

The extensive nature of the preliminary events indicates the importance that the Afikpo attach to the first-son initiation; it is a major activity for the village, and a test of fatherhood. It is a heavy burden for the father. He provides five feasts to persons in the compound, two directly and three on behalf of his son. He also feasts his village age set, and he contributes to four village feasts. The cooking is done by his wives; it is helpful to have a number of them, but if he has only one his brothers' wives often assist. The financial drain on the father is heavy; if he is poor, agnatic kin and his wife or wives assist him. The feasting stresses the totality of organizations in the community. When the fathers feed persons at the village level the members of the two village sections join together. What they do separately are technical operations, such as collecting building materials and preparing their own bush areas. The presentation of food recognizes the village as a whole, its *isiji* title members, the male members of the village secret society, the eldest village males, and the village age sets of the fathers. The whole community is apprised when the village gong is sounded and the fathers dance. All these groups are "begged permission" to perform the rites, as some Afikpo put it. The major male organizational structures of the community are activated. No village priest or other religious official exists for *isiji*, no secret society officials are involved. The power to control *isiji* affairs rests with the *isiji* title holders, and among them the elders as leaders (S. Ottenberg 1971: Chap. 4).

The heavy burden of feasting for the father suggests that the first-son initiation is a kind of initiation for him as well as his son. Both "suffer" in the initiation, though in different ways. Their common fortunes link them, as both advance in status through this initiation; the initiation rites themselves also bind them together. There is a strong interdependency of the two, and these features help the son to work out an adult relationship with his father and other males, and the father to work out a more firm relationship with senior males in the village at large. The feasting also suggests a certain conning of the fathers by title members and older males, to get as much out of them as they can; in turn, the fathers will do the same when they are older. This is much like the situation in the bush (described below), where those who give the initiands the hardest time are often those who only recently were initiated themselves. There is an "it's my turn now" attitude involved.

When jointly feasting any of the village groups (except the age sets), the fathers also eat as a separate group. A camaraderie develops among them through these repasts and through their other joint activities, which will be echoed by the ties of their sons to one another when in the bush. In fact, some of the fathers are friends and were initiated together when they were young. Again, when a father feasts a group in his own compound he does not eat with them, but with his own friends and relatives. In both village and compound feasts the father uses other adult men as intermediaries between himself and those he feeds.

The same man may be feasted by a given father a number of times, in different contexts: as an *isiji* title holder in the village, as a village elder, as a member of the compound of the father, as an *isiji* title holder of the compound, and as a friend of the father. We note the meticulous care with which each male village organization is treated, and that no women's group is so indulged. Women are involved in the initiation, cooking and also eating the food that they have prepared, as well as carrying out other activities, but their roles differ from those of the males.

The feasting moves back and forth between village and compound, expressing the father's interests in the two important organizational levels for most male rites and activities at Afikpo. Few events are organized at the level of the village ward or at the level of the village-group, that is, of Afikpo as a whole. The father has been active in both compound and village for some years. While the *isiji* rite for his eldest son moves the father further into village affairs, a major theme of his life until he dies is the interplay of compound and village, of agnation and residence.

That the son's own feasts and other activities (except for the gathering of firewood) are held in the compound is logical; the compound is where his life has centered until now. Excepting for wrestling contests and some boys' secret society activities in the highest stage, he has not yet really entered village affairs. The initiation moves him into the larger community of men and involves him in the fine dialogue of compound and village activities in which his father is already involved.

A man's relationship with his village age set is very special. His feast for this group during the *isiji* preliminaries is similar to the feasts he gives them in connection with any important title he takes, and for his marriages. He has a reciprocal relationship with these men, who often were his peers in the boys' secret society and during his own initiation. He feeds them to show what a big man he is, but his success in the initiation will, in turn, reflect well upon them. It is a "strong" age set, Afikpo say, whose members have all done *isiji* for their first sons when the members are young, and a poor one whose age mates all fail to do this; these facts are often publicly known. And the age set assists the father with resources should he need help in the initiation. For other titles his age mates give gifts to help him whether he needs it or not, but here he is expected to pay for himself if at all possible. This age grouping also joins in the *isiji* masquerade dance (see below).

At the village level the preliminary events appear leaderless. Secret society religious officials are not involved. The rites occur automatically every seventh year; nobody orders them. No one tells the fathers to play their roles; they simply gather together and do so. It is true that the village elders choose an age set to direct the bush construction, and have the right to postpone the initiation for a year or two, but the numerous events seem to flow in a regular schedule without authority, simply through the efforts of the fathers. The elders hypothetically oversee matters—any troubles or problems ultimately have to be resolved by them as the village authority—but I found no serious cases of grievance or hitch in the rites. As sons have autonomy in their own boys' societies activities, the fathers here have considerable autonomy from the elders, their symbolic (or actual) fathers. No one gains political capital out of the *isiji* initiation except the fathers, through enhancing their status.

This noncentralized pattern continues into the bush period where the initiands and young initiates, to a large extent, run their own affairs; the latter, somewhat older in age than the former, act as guides and helpers rather than as strongly authoritarian figures.

The matrilineal groupings play no role in the *isiji* preliminaries and in the initiation as a whole other than at the father's (or mother's) sacrifice at the son's matrilineal shrine. No mother's brother of the initiand appears at the feasts or other preliminary rites; this person does not even have to be informed by the father that the rites will take place, although the sacrifice is an announcement of it. Neither are matrilineal relations of the father involved, unless they are also patrikin. The initiation is a patrilineal and residential affair, like so many Afikpo rites.

The mother's links with the boy, through their mutual ɛkikɛ charms and through her cooking, symbolize her continuing tie to him and to the world of men. The boy, already living away from home in a boys' house and the boys' secret society area, still is and will continue to be fed by her during the initiation. Both observe certain taboos, particularly with regard to corn. While the father's other wives, and sometimes other compound women, also assist in the cooking, it is the boy's mother who shoulders the main share of the kitchen work, a fact well recognized in Afikpo but not ritually or symbolically rewarded. She is happy about her son's impending initiation and gathers females together to share the work and her feelings. They have their drink and food together at various times during the rites, as do the men.

The initiands often know one another. The preliminary rites are public and the boys are aware of who is to be initiated; some are friends, relatives, or age mates. They take joy in knowing that they will go through the rites together, and often keep in touch with one another over the course of the preliminary events. They carry their friendships and enmities into the bush.

In the Bush

The initiation is divided into two periods (see Table 1). In the first, *ababa na ɔhia* (run-in-bush), twenty-eight days long, the bush area is used and the initiands sleep in the men's rest houses in the village commons at night. In the second, *enya ɛgwɵ* (hang on–raffia), lasting the same length of time or less, the bush is closed and the initiands live, under restrictions, in boys' houses in the compounds. In describing the bush period in Mgbom village I remind the reader that the activities in the two bush areas are separate but occur at the same time; they are substantially alike. The activities inside these bush sites cannot be seen from outside of them.

On *nkwɔ*, the day that the son enters the bush, his mother prepares fine soup, perhaps with duck in it, and other foods, and feeds him. It is said that the boy can ask for anything that he wishes to eat at this time, though this does not always occur. It is a farewell feast; both mother and son are likely to be at least a little anxious, and certainly excited, about the initiation. It is not only the father's first experience with initiating a son, it is also the mother's. Again we note the symbolic importance of food.

At about noon the wooden village gong sounds, hit by its usual players, interested young adult men. Young initiated males go into the bush through a side gate; they remain in its outer section (see Figure 1), where they roughhouse a lot, shouting, wrestling, and hitting one another with their elbows. Included are most of the initiated boys in the village and some of its young men; the village elders sometimes state what ages should go in in order to have an impressive rite. These males look forward to the play and exuberance; to them the initiation is not a serious thing. They have not all gone through this particular initiation themselves; they may have taken another form (though the brief one, *isubu eda*, is not acceptable here). They may remember not too long ago the tribulations and excitements of their own initiations, when they were both guided and put down by boys older than themselves. It is their turn to do this now.

The commons are now closed to females and uninitiated males. Some young initiated boys still in the compounds fight, chase, and play around, raising a ruckus; this is designed to scare the initiands and their mothers. Then these males, the initiands, and the initiands' helpers move into the *isiji* bush outer section by the same gate the others used. Those of one compound usually go together, although there is no set order; they go when the initiands and their helpers are ready. The one or two helpers or guides for each initiand have been well fed and advised by the fathers; they are males who have been through this particular rite themselves. They come and get the boys, who are sitting, in their loin cloths, at their father's home or at a boys' house in the compounds.

In a village the size of Mgbom there may be as many as one hundred initiands and several hundred helpers and other older initiates in the outer part of the bush area. The initiands have now penetrated the mysterious bush, but only its outer part. The initiands are lined up by their helpers, facing outwards, with their backs against the outer side of the inner fence; if there are too many some are placed against the inner edge of the outer fence. They hold onto the fence with their hands above their heads while the initiates continue to horse around. In some other villages, such as Mkpoghoro, the boys sit on rocks, again with their arms up.

Keeping the arms above the head also occurs in other Afikpo initiation rites. I was told that it is a form of hardship, and that at this time it is taboo for the initiands to touch the ground with their hands or arms. In Mgbom the ground in the bush area is often wet or damp, but this is not the reason for the restriction. I believe that the taboo is a metaphor of the helplessness of the initiands. They cannot protect themselves against initiates hitting them, which they threaten but rarely do. The initiands are physically defenseless. A father sometimes holds back a very young son from the bush as long as possible for fear that the roughhousing and the difficulty that boys have of keeping their arms up for a long time may be too great.

At this time interested initiates construct the high center portion of the *isiji* structure, with the aid of carpenters, but the initiands keep their heads down; they are not allowed to see this done, to know its secret at this time. The initiand's costume of a loincloth with a protective charm tied to it is rarely seen in Afikpo today; boys usually wear underpants and khaki shorts. Some boys' thighs chafe and become sore from wearing the old style cloth. The boys' bodies are not chalked or otherwise marked, though in some villages their hair is cut in a particular manner to indicate their status; this is not usually done in Mgbom. The helpers and other initiates wear any clothing they choose, European or African.

Toward evening the initiands, now with their arms down, accompanied by the other males there, come into the commons in front of the bush; the commons is now off-limits to nonmembers. Here the initiands practice, without costume, the masquerade dance that they will perform in public two days hence. In many villages, as in Mgbom, this is the only chance to practice; in a few communities there is also a pre-initiation session on ɛkɛ day of the New Yam Festival. After a while the initiands go to the men's rest houses in their commons, usually to those of their own ward or subvillage, where they remain for a while, and where they will sleep and eat during this first month of rites. These *obiogo* (S. Ottenberg 1972) are the meeting and resting places for secret society members; it is here that masks and other secret society equipment are stored. In Mgbom an extra house, *obiogo Ɔmaka* (rest house–Ɔmaka [a man who was fond of resting and sleeping there]), normally a storage house, is also used by some initiands. This is the first time that the initiands have ever been inside of these structures. It marks their changing status from the time when, as small boys, they first approached the elders there in the bird-killing rite. While the boys rest, the initiates return to their compounds and eat, and make merry. The fathers are at home entertaining friends; it is a happy period—except, perhaps, for the initiands themselves.

In the evening these boys are assembled by their helpers and other interested initiates and led in front of the high part of the *isiji* structure on the commons side. The commons remains off-limits. Here true first sons only engage in a contest, each throwing a burning stick, taken from a fire in a men's rest house, over the high entrance and into the inner enclosure. The goal is to throw it as close to the *omume* spirit shrine in the bush as they can, although at this point they do not know exactly where it is. Initiates in the outer section in the bush report where the sticks land by looking through the inner fence. They shout "No!" if the stick hits in the outer part, and they run through a side gate to report a good hit. To do well in this event is quite a feat, for the structure is high. The best marksman among the true first sons becomes priest of the *isiji* bush and the head of the initiands, the next best the assistant priest. Surrogates and sons other than first sons are thus excluded from formal leadership.

In Mgbom, the choice has usually been made before this time through discussion among the fathers and the village *isiji* title holders. In the larger of the two Mgbom village bush sections one leader is usually from Ezi Agbo compound and the other from Ezi Akputa. The patrilineal groups in these compounds claim to have brought *isiji* to Mgbom, and to be the founding compounds of the village. The two priests should be large, strong boys. If there is a man in the village taking the highest Afikpo title, *omume*, his son automatically becomes the senior priest even though he may not be a first son. If he is young and weak a very strong first son is chosen as his assistant. In other villages these leaders are chosen in other ways; for example, in Amachara and in Ukpa through divination before the initiation. But even here the selection often reflects the wishes of the consulters.

Now the first sons, with the two initiand priests, are led by their helpers to the outer bush section from whence all but the helpers move into the inner area to locate the *isiji* shrine in the ground. The helpers remain in the outer section advising these initiands, looking through the fence. It is said that if the helpers went into the inner area, they would have direct contact with the shrine and would then have to stay inside through the entire rite. There is a one-time quality about this shrine that gives it a sense of special power; it is only opened at this initiation, and is only for the initiating boys. The *isiji* mask and costume also do not appear at other times. Meanwhile, the initiands who are not true first sons remain in the commons outside. The prestige is clearly with the first sons, as in other aspects of Afikpo life; there is both a symbolic and a real separation of these two classes of boys.

The senior priest searches for the shrine in the ground with his hands while his assistant starts a fire, which is sacred and is maintained day and night by the initiands for the month of *isiji;* it symbolizes the power of the bush and its shrine spirit. It is believed that if it dies out harm may come to the initiands. One man said that if those outside do not see the smoke rising in the bush then they know that the fire has ended and that all the boys there are dead. The fire symbolizes human life in the world of nature and spirits. There is a log bench on each side of the fireplace on which only true first sons can sit, although later other initiands enter this sacred area. The priest does not know where the shrine is; he has been told by the initiates to search for a stone on the ground. When he finds this he digs it out and probes for the shrine below, the neck of a lidded pot. In the Agbogo-Elogo section of Mgbom no one knows where the rest of the pot is anymore; only the neck exists. When the priest has done this he is told by the initiates standing in the outer part of the bush structure to take the stone in his hands and kneel down and groan as if he were lifting a very heavy weight. He produces a variety of groans until he gets it right. It is a very strong moan, as if he were engaged in a hard task, and the Afikpo say that a large boy should be priest so that he will make this sound well, an illusion which focuses on the importance of the shrine. The initiates will tell the boy priest when he makes the correct sound. Sometimes they remind him that he must have heard the sound in the bush seven years earlier (the last time the rite was done) or at other times in other communities, and he should imitate it now. Actually, the priest may know the sound, but he hesitates because he does not wish to reveal how familiar he is with it. When at last he lets out the anticipated loud moan, the old initiates and the initiands in the bush and the commons join him in shouting "*hwoh hwoh hwoh hwoh hwoh*" innumerable times. This is the yell for all forms of Afikpo adult secret societies.

Then the priest removes the clay lid from the pot neck and the spirit of *isiji* is said to be out. The lid and stone are left on the ground beside the neck. The shrine is opened whenever there is a special event in the initiation, such as the *isiji* dance. Otherwise it is closed. Men of Mgbom say that the shrine spirit, with its strong medicines, is located where it was placed by the agnatic ancestors of the two compounds that brought it. Popularly called *omume,* the spirit has no specific form, human, animal, or monstrous. It is the pot, the bush, and the force associated with this secret society.

The priest sacrifices an egg, provided by his assistants, by placing

Girl carrying water pot past men's rest house, Mgbom Village

Title taker dancing in front of his compound's
ancestral shrine house, with boys joining in

Mother and child

Boy wrestlers at a match

Boys at a market

Boys eating yam fufu at feast celebrating first day of construction
of a new patrilineal ancestral shrine house, Mgbom Village

Decorating the panels for the men's
secret society *ajaba* dressing house

Whipping day activities preceding the *isubu eda* initiation

Logholo player resting. When he is seated the other boys do not chase him. He is a new initiate into the men's secret society.

Adult *ɔtero* player of the kind that chase the initiands

Uninitiated boys' *logholo*, chasing and playing with the boys

Uninitiated boys' *ɔtero* playing with girls

Boys' secret society shrine house and area, Mgbom Village

Girls dancing on New Yam Feast Day, Anohia Nkalo Village

Ladder entrance to the initiation bush, with two
initiands dancing in masquerade in the background

First-son initiands in their calabash masks and raffia costumes

it at the shrine; the Afikpo say that this is what *omume* wants. It symbolizes the birth, or more correctly the rebirth, of the bush and its spirit. Then everyone returns to the commons, which remains closed to non-initiates. There is more shouting of the *isiji* cry, and there are other cries and singing and dancing.

The initiates gather the initiands in the commons, which remains closed to others, and explain to them the taboos and regulations that they will follow during the initiation period. Some initiands already know them, having been told by friends or even by their fathers. They must never let their shrine fire go out or they will die. They must employ certain terms instead of the usual words when in the bush or the closed commons in talking with one another, or with the initiates, terms the latter use in talking amongst themselves. The initiands are to use a temporary latrine located in the outer area of the bush enclosure. They should not touch any calabashes other than the one that they eat out of and its calabash spoon, and the calabash mask that they will wear in their *isiji* dance. The Afikpo gave me no reason for this, but I believe it is because the calabash is associated with women in everyday life and symbolically represents the vagina and/or the uterus, and the initiation is a time of social separation from females. They should not play any drums or gongs during the rites; this is for the initiates to do. When in sight of women and non-initiates in the open commons or elsewhere they should never expose their penis or their teeth; they should have no physical contact of any kind with females. So they must not smile nor talk to females and they may only converse with uninitiated boys with their mouths covered by their hands or with their backs turned. I have already remarked that the initiands' mothers do not talk to anyone while cooking for them when the boys are in the bush. No reasons for the silences were provided by the Afikpo, other than that of tradition. But the silence of boy and mother symbolically link the two, as does the charm that they both wear and the corn taboo. It is said that if a mother were to talk while cooking for her son she would be forbidden to cook any more during the rites. And a menstruating woman should not cook for her son—a general taboo extending to feasts and rituals. The helper does not talk to the initiand when he brings him the food that his mother has cooked, usually to a men's rest house in the commons, where he rests and sleeps. Any hardships the boys suffer do not concern food; they eat lots of yam fufu and special soups. Afikpo say that the secret society spirit would not like it if any of the taboos were broken; it would be angered and endanger the initiands.

On the second day in the bush, the commons remains closed to females and uninitiated boys, and the initiation actually takes place. Now all of the initiands go through the tower-like structure to the shrine, where a sacrifice is performed for each of them.

In the morning initiates, especially helpers, go out and look for a certain reddish orange seed, *akpǝrǝ atǝtǝ* umuruma (seed-clitoris-children), said to resemble a clitoris, which is used in headdresses in the *isiji* masquerade, starting the next day. Raffia is collected by the helpers and other initiates to use in the costumes. It is common for the father and his friends together to go to the boy's mother and tell her that they need money to obtain wool for the headdress of the costume, for the seeds look like wool from a distance. She has seen it worn by other initiands in past years. Anxious to have her son well dressed, she gives something, not realizing that the material is locally procured. Possibly she knows this but gives the money so as not to reveal knowledge that the men do not want her to have. There is symbolic irony here, for women have their clitoris partly or completely excised by a society which is under male control. The conning of women by men here reflects male control of females and their sexuality, the taking of sexuality from females to give to males.

On this morning the initiand priest and his assistant go again into the inner bush area, taking two other first sons whom they select from among the initiands. They take yams which they roast in the sacred fire, the only thing permitted to be cooked there.

In the afternoon the two priests appoint two big and strong first-son initiands to stand in the inner enclosure at each side of the back of the tower. The rest of the initiands are lined up in the commons by the helpers, facing the bush structure, the taller boys first. Here no distinction is made between first and other sons. The first in line is told to climb up the tower on the outside and down the other side, and that if he has violated *isiji* restrictions since the preliminary corn feast he will fall down and injure himself. He starts to struggle up, but they soon tell him to go under it instead. He goes through a tunnel-like arrangement, coming out near the sacred fire in the inner enclosure. The initiands have been previously led to believe by initiates that they would have to climb this structure; the impact of not letting them see it during its construction heightens its fearsome qualities. The lining up of the initiands by size, and thus by strength, reinforces this idea. In fact, the weaker and smaller boys are put at the rear of the line for another reason. Once in the bush they are subject to a test of endurance the rest of the day, so the later they go in the shorter will be this period for them.

After the first boy has attempted to climb the structure, the rest of the boys realize that they will not in fact be made to climb it. Nevertheless, each is told to attempt the climb, and does so. He is then called down and sent through the tunnel instead. As he emerges from the tunnel on his hands and knees, one of the two strong initiands stationed there takes his hands and pulls him forward and upward while the other hits him lightly four times on the rump with the flat bottom end of a palm branch. The two initiands have been told to do this; they know little of what is going on themselves. Initiates in the outer enclosure watch the sacrifice through the fence and advise the two priests and their assistants if they fail to act properly. One of the two assistants, holding the boy's arms up, leads him to the priest, who stands beside the shrine. The initiand is told to kneel down, which he does, keeping his arms above his head. The assistant priest cuts small pieces of roast yams, handing them to the senior priest. The priest four times dips a piece of the yam in a small pot of palm oil beside the shrine, circles it above the boy's head counterclockwise and throws it on the shrine. He repeats this act three more times. The fifth time he does the same except that instead of throwing the yam he gives it to the boy to chew. The priest then gives the initiand a pot of water, said to represent wine, to sip from. Then the priest lifts the stone cover of the shrine and touches it four times to the boy's chest. As in many Afikpo sacrifices, the repetition by fours here stands for the days of the Igbo week, representing a totality of time and life.

The sacrifice in the bush associates the bush spirit with the initiand, the force entering through the head, the mouth, and the body. Both boy and spirit eat yam, a symbol of masculinity. In other secret society and nonsecret rites only one or two places of spiritual entrance to the body are usually employed. To use all three here stresses the importance of this spiritual sacrifice. The boy priests have no trouble doing their work. They have either been priests in the boys' societies or cooperated with other boys who have, although the specific operations at the initiation shrine differ somewhat from those in the boys' societies.

The boy for whom the sacrifice has been done is then passed from the shrine to the outer section of the bush with his arms over his head. Two initiates sprinkle a liquid on him from a pot; it is made from reddish camwood dye and water. The boy's arms remain high. His helpers take his loincloth and tie his hands together with his arms up, wrapping the rest of the cloth around his neck. He is then led out, with genitals exposed, through a side gate of the bush to the commons. He passes the line of boys waiting to go into the bush, to whom he looks bloody and weak, which is said by Afikpo to be why camwood is used. Some of the boys in line are frightened. Meanwhile other initiands are going through the tunnel, the sacrifice, and the sprinkling, one by one. As each finishes he goes to the rest house of his ward where he remains until he dresses for the masquerade the next day. He is fed with his hands above his head by his helpers, sitting or standing, or he is temporarily untied so that he can eat. Some boys manage to sleep a bit, but it is difficult to do so as it is forbidden for them to touch the ground with their hands or arms. However, they can lie on mats if they are careful, and most of them do. The Afikpo say that if they should touch the ground nothing will really happen to them, that it is merely a hardship; they do not phrase the restriction in spiritual terms.

The masquerade begins on *orie,* the next day, and continues on subsequent *orie.* The initiands appear in costume and mask and dance in public in the commons, as gentle spirits of the bush (*nde mma,* people-spirits; see S. Ottenberg 1975). The first day brings all of them out in masquerade; this is their first appearance since entering the bush. Mothers and fathers are jubilant on seeing their sons— the mothers especially, for they have had little knowledge of their boys since they went into the bush, unlike the fathers who have been in touch with the helpers; mothers worry about how their sons are faring. Parents, relatives, and friends usually have little difficulty in recognizing the boys in costume.

On the second *orie* all the boys dance again. Attention is paid to the quality of the movements and the best performers are noted by the helpers and initiates. On the next three *orie* the masquerade continues and each initiand dances on one of these days; at that time the boys' parents celebrate and feast. On the sixth *orie* there is no dancing or other activity. Some say that on this day the spirits of the bush (also called *nde mma*) dance and that this is their day, but others deny this. On the seventh *orie* the very best dancers appear again. The next day the bush is closed and this phase of the initiation is over.

Each time a boy dances his helpers help him to dress. Here men from his compound join in, either sent out by the father or simply out of interest. The helpers do not have to have done *isiji* themselves; they may even be from other villages. All that is required is that they be secret society initiates and have the proper knowledge. It is considered a reflection on the compound and its agnates if a boy is poorly dressed, implying lack of interest on their part. There is considerable intercompound competition over this. The costume is called *isiji*, as is the calabash mask (S. Ottenberg 1975:55–56, 189–94). The mask should be well made; an old one can be used or a new one obtained by the father on order or loan from a carver. The raffia in the body costume must be fresh; it is cut the day before each time that the boy dances. The seed headdress projects up in back of the mask and covers the sides and back of the head. The initiand must have proper bracelets and anklets, and he wears raffia coils on his upper arm. A coral necklace (*ase isiji* bead–first-son initiation) of European origin, is tied tightly around his neck, and worn from this time until the end of the *isiji* month. Necklaces are not usually worn by males; the coils and necklace have no magical power. They are markers of the boys' status. This is the first time that the boy wears a mask as an adult secret society member. Perhaps to signify its importance this mask and seed headdress are worn only here; they do not appear in other masquerades, nor is calabash used for other Afikpo masquerades.

The mask, made from half an oval gourd with horizontal slits on its center face, has a gourd neck at its top which curves upward and forward. Light brown in color, the calabash is painted over its central section and to the side with black, white, red, and yellow, the basic colors of Afikpo masks. It is the most nonrepresentational face form at Afikpo, suggesting no particular human or animal features, although the late art historian John Donne (personal communication) thought it represented an elephant face turned upside down; I am skeptical of this. At Afikpo these four colors stand for important elements of life: white for health, peace, and fertility, red for blood and aggressiveness, yellow for body processes, and black for illness and death. The colors do not correspond to the four days of the week, but again we see the number four associated with a totality.

The mask signals the return of the boy from the bush to the world of humans, but as a spirit.

On the first masquerading day the helpers prepare the costume in the morning and dress the boys in the afternoon. Before dressing the initiands go to the bush shrine and the boy priest performs a sacrifice; this is done for all who dance on each *orie* day. The senior priest touches a chicken egg, supplied by the boy's helper, four times to the boy's head and puts it on the ground. Each initiand picks it up in turn and does the same to his own head. It is taboo to hand the egg directly from the priest to the boy, or from boy to boy. People say that in former times one never gave an egg directly to another individual in any circumstance. Transfer has to be blessed by putting it on the ground, where *ale* the earth, the ground spirit of sexuality, fertility, and growth, blesses it. This sacrifice renews the boy's contact with the earth; he can now touch the ground again, for he is symbolically reborn. After all the initiands have finished the rite the priest breaks the egg over the shrine, praying that the boys will do well in the dance and in the initiation, that they will not get hurt, and that no other harm will befall them.

After dressing, the initiands come out to the commons from the bush with their helpers, the former emerging backwards, symbolizing their distinctiveness from the rest of the village. This is also another endurance test, as it is difficult for them to move wearing masks. Then the commons are opened, announced by the playing of the village gong. Men, women, and children pour out and sit down on benches, chairs, and the ground, separated by sex, as is usual, except for young children, and also to some extent by age. The dancers remain near the bush. In front of the rest house of the main commons of the community, where the elders sit, is a group of some fifty or more young adult males, wearing ordinary cloths and led by a middle-aged expert singer. Seated on the ground in a circle, they are divided into two groups: the singers, who tend to be mature, and young men and older boys who only clap to the songs. All are secret society members and some are helpers to the boys. No musical instrumentalists are present, although from time to time the village gong is played, more to stir up excitement than as a musical accompaniment, for its beats do not keep time with the songs.

Each initiand in turn—there is no specific order—comes out from the masquerade group and dances for a short while in front of the musical circle in gentle and well-ordered movements, which contrast with the roughhousing that has been going on in the bush. There is nothing to indicate to females and uninitiated boys that there has been any hardship. The dancer then returns to his group and another steps out. While masked, these performers do not vocalize, in keeping with their speech taboo, even though their face and teeth are hidden.

Unfortunately, I gathered little information on the songs. Some praise farmers in Afikpo—not just in Mgbom village—who raise plenty of yams; their names are given. This, of course, is the yam harvest season and yams play a major role as food in the initiation feasts and sacrifices, and are also a phallic symbol. One song concerns a certain woman's actions during the time the initiands were in the next initiation after *isiji,* which is called *ɔka.* There is a leaf, *okpete,* which initiands throw at noninitiates as the former pass by; women can watch this, but one female picked up a stick and threw it back at the initiands, which she should not have done. The song ridicules her for acting like a male. Other songs are comments on females who violate other rules of the secret society. None of the songs are of a sexual nature. Some songs use the expression *ahe* and *ahehe* over and over again, words without apparent meaning, accompanied by the clapping of the musical group.

The fathers of the masqueraders are gaily dressed in fine shirts and pants or waistcloths, with canes and fancy hats. When his son appears, a father and his friends and age mates come out and dance and strut and sing about. Even the mother may dance a bit, and there is much noise and milling about in the commons, for the parents are happy. The performance goes on for three or four hours in Mgbom until all the initiands have had their turn. Then the singers chant "*he he he he he*" a number of times and the females and uninitiated boys know that it is time to leave; they do so quickly, without looking back. When they are gone the masqueraders rush to the side gates of the bush with their helpers, trying to be the first to go in. Sometimes one or more of the boys gets knocked down and a mask may come off, which is one reason the uninitiated have left. The boys change to their bush loincloths and return to their rest houses; the commons remains closed for the night. The initiands need not hold up their arms anymore; the sacrifice and masquerading has released them from this.

The helpers see that the boys are fed and at this time there is also much eating in the compounds. Every father feasts those who have assisted in dressing his son with wine and cow skin to chew on (sometimes money is substituted for the latter), and he feasts his village age set and the compound males who have put a son through *isiji* at other times. In Mgbom in 1960 the latter included a pot of palm wine, ten yam fufu balls, and ten shillings, another title fee. The merrymaking in the compounds goes on for some time; the father is very pleased that his son has danced. Some boys perform the masquerade dance with skill, others without it; every father likes his son to do well, but this is not as important as the fact that he has appeared, was well dressed, has danced, and his initiation is going satisfactorily. Of course, the initiands have had considerable masquerade experience in the boys' societies, although not with this particular mask and dance, nor as such a focus of attention.

On the next day, *aho,* the fourth day of the first *isiji* week, the fathers, including those putting a son through for a second time, feast all of the secret society initiates in the village, regardless of which form of initiation they have taken, with yam fufu, but no other foods. This is done separately for the two village sections. Called *ekwɔ eka isiji,* it is said to be equivalent to the coming-out ceremony for a child four days after it is born, also sometimes called *ekwɔ eka* (wash-hand). Men say that the *isiji* spirit has been born and must be given the coming-out ceremony after four days, as with all children. There is no explicit concept here that the initiating boys have been reborn, but the "birth" and the "coming out" of the spirit are clearly metaphors. Some men say that this feast is just an excuse, like many other initiation feasts, to get more things out of the father; there is truth in this assertion.

On this *aho,* the day after the boy has danced for the first time, he returns to his mother in the compound with a helper, bringing his calabash food dish and spoon that he has been eating from. His helper puts these on the ground. The boy breaks them with his feet and goes away without a word; the verbal taboo still exists. Afikpo say that this tells the mother that the son left her on *nkwɔ* day but is still strong. This is one of the few times that the child comes into the compounds during the twenty-eight-day *isiji* phase. It is a clear symbolic statement of the separation of mother and child. The symbolic rejection is twofold, of the mother's food and of the mother herself, as a producer of the son, for the calabash symbolizes the uterus or vagina, as we have stated. The act also represents rejection of the mother as a sexual being, a symbolic turning away from oedipal concerns on the part of the boy. Yet the mother continues to feed the boy.

Also on this day each initiand collects from the village grove a cluster of ripe palm kernels and another of unripe ones. If he is too small to climb a helper does this for him. The initiands carry these to the bush where the ripe ones are roasted and eaten, the unripe ones chewed on. Any male in the village who has taken this form of initiation can join them in eating; both forms of palm kernels are a favorite taste delight.

From this time until the end of the bush period the boys have freedom to move about, except on masquerade days. The commons is only kept closed before and after these performances. The initiands continue to sleep in the men's rest houses, and their mothers to provide their food. A helper gives each initiand a double-edged machete (ɔtake), a walking stick (akpoto), and a long raffia bag which the boy wraps up and ties to his loin cloth. He is free to cut and eat palm fruits, bananas, and other fruits anywhere that he wants and to take some of these to his parents in his bag. The boys are told by their helpers that this is permitted stealing, only they should take the fruits quickly. Initiates sometimes playfully accuse the initiands of theft and take the fruits from them to eat themselves, as harassment, chasing them away. The initiands bring edible leaves to their mothers, but no ground-growing foods (considered the most vital for life at Afikpo). The mothers are especially pleased if brought ripe palm kernels, as they prepare palm oil from them. The son puts the food in back of his mother's home and asks uninitiated boys to let her know; he can speak to them but not to her. Or he knocks about with his walking stick to inform her.

The initiands assist their parents with farm and other work, but they always follow the restrictions against showing their teeth, talking, and exposing their genitals to females. They charcoal their faces, which makes them look glum and serious, wear the usual loincloth and coral necklace, and carry their walking stick, which makes a noise when it strikes an object. This is their "mouth," the Afikpo say, used to call attention to something or to warn females that they are coming and to let them pass. In some villages, such as Mkpoghoro, but not in Mgbom, the initiands cover themselves with the reddish camwood dye. In any case they are not expected to linger about the open village areas; if they fetch water for themselves they do so hurriedly.

During the days that the boys go about they are not permitted to eat anything when the *isiji* yell of "*hwoh hwoh hwoh*" is made. If initiates see the helpers bringing food to the boys they give this cry. The boys must get out of earshot before eating; consequently they often go with their helpers to the farms to eat, and may leave scraps of food about. Women working at the farms see these and think that the food that they have prepared for their sons is being wasted or eaten by the helpers to whom they have given it, although this is not usually so. It is considered bad form for helpers to do so, especially since they are often close agnatic kin. Nevertheless, some helpers do this to harass the boys. Though the initiands are under restrictions and are bothered by the initiates when not in masquerade, it is a leisurely time for them.

On the sixth day of initiation, *εkε*, three days after the first masquerade, the fathers, including those putting a son through for the second time, again feed all males who are initiated into the village secret society in any form. Both Mgbom village sections do this together. The feast's name, *otara enya osisi* (fufu-eye-stick), refers to the bush structures and the twenty yam fufu balls which each father provides. Each also presents six shillings to the village *isiji* title members; if this is the second time the father is putting a son through the initiation, he gives only six pence. The fee name, *nkpɔla urwu akparata* (rod-trunk-tree), refers to a large tree in Agbogo common which fell down sometime before 1952, under which title members sat and were paid, formerly in metal rods. The money is still given where the tree once stood.

The second *orie* day of masquerading is much like the first in many Afikpo villages, including Mgbom, although in some communities only the better dancers are selected by the initiands and their helpers to perform. In Mgbom all initiands dance, and the father's friends and age mates again come out and move about as a son dances, but there are no feasts or payments.

The masquerading differs for the three following *orie* days. In Mgbom, the day on which a boy dances depends on his father's age. On the first of the three days sons of the fathers of the youngest village age set sponsoring initiands, and of the two sets above it in age, are involved. The last two sets are included even if there is no one from one or both of them doing the *isiji* for a son (the implication is that there should be). On the next *orie* the sons of fathers in the next three higher sets dance, and on the third *orie*, called *mgbaci* (close up), the sons of fathers belonging to any older village sets dance, as well as the two boy priests.

On the day that a particular initiand appears his parents again celebrate, this time especially well, stressing the parent-son relationship more strongly than in the earlier two days of general masquerading. While the son dances, the father, his friends and agnatic kin, and his age mates come out, sometimes moving in male dance steps, sometimes in mock imitation of women's dancing. The father is splendidly dressed, often with a wool cap with a feather in it, and he may carry a horsetail whisk or a cane in one hand. In past times the feather indicated that the man had taken a head in warfare, but now it simply indicates that the father feels himself to be a big man in what he is doing for his son. Likewise, the horsetail should indicate that the man has taken titles and is a prominent person, whether in fact he is or is not.

The father's age group and other men praise the father in song; the mother of the boy sings that the father is a rich man. The father and friends shout "*kwe kwe, ha ha*" and the like and run about merrily. Gun shooters hired by the father discharge their weapons. Other masked initiands who will dance individually that day with their own parents may join the father and his followers in dancing for a while. The father and his age mates give coins to the singing and clapping group sitting on the ground to thank them for their help and because they are pleased and wish to show generosity; this is said to be the pay that they receive for their work. The father and his friends, to show their wealth, happiness, and generosity, throw pennies about the commons; women and small children rush to get these. The father's friends bring out two goats on their shoulders—usually female, but male if the father is rich. One animal is for the son and the other initiands to feast on, with one leg reserved for the father's village age set. The other goat is said to be given to the singers, but in fact it is eaten by the *isiji* village title members. In former times the father gave a large number of pieces of corn to the title members in his compound, but nowadays he gives them twenty-five shillings on the next day, when he feasts them. The *isiji* masquerade thus calls attention to both father and son, uniting them in status increase.

The women of the boy's compound, including the mother, come out and dance, wearing the Afikpo women's ceremonial hairstyle, peaked from front to back along the head's center. Wearing typical ceremonial dress—nothing on top but with a fine waistcloth, ivory or bone bracelets, and carrying a colored handkerchief in one hand—they dance in women's styles. The mother and the other dancing women throw pennies out to show their happiness and the mother gives a small sum to the musical group, said to be for a cock; again this does not go to them but to the title holders in the village. In former times, despite the taboo, she would send out four hundred pieces of corn for the village title holders, but nowadays she provides ten shillings through the singers. At this time the boy's mother has the privilege of imitating his *isiji* dance steps. This is the only time that she, or any other woman for that matter, is permitted to emulate male secret society dances without censure. Only a few mothers do this, for most are too shy or do not feel capable of performing well.

During the proceedings the father presents palm wine or native gin to the elders sitting and watching in the rest house nearest the dancers. His age set gives him and his son each a good sized yam, and the father's wives give him presents of money, beer, gin, tobacco, and so on. The extensive exchange of presents on this day is characteristic of many Afikpo rites; public display of kinship, descent, age set, friendship, and other ties in this way is considered appropriate and desirable at these times. The first-son initiation is a chart of a man's agnatic, affinal, and village ties. It brings all these relationships into action.

During the masquerade, certain age sets of young adult men in the village—what I call the executive age grade (S. Ottenberg 1971: Chap. 4)—are delegated by the village elders to control the crowd at the masquerade, which on occasion gets a bit out of hand. Women and children scramble for the coins that have been thrown out, and a father's group may become quite noisy or refuse to give way to another group. The executives pressure young initiates that they spot in the audience to come out and join the clapping and singing group, threatening to fine them if they do not, and they move about waving small leafy branches as a warning to behave properly.

No one is much concerned with how well the father and his friends dance, nor the mother and the compound women, although skill is always appreciated. However, if the initiand dances poorly, the audience may laugh and yell at him. The ridiculing of masked dancers occurs at other Afikpo masquerades; this criticism is not taken too seriously nor is it said to spoil the event. Yet if the boy dances well this reflects positively on his compound, patrilineage and his father. The audience is active and talkative; its members move about, and sometimes they rise up and dance.

If an initiand is a very good dancer, while he is performing in masquerade the leaders of the musical group sing out a question and the boy responds with his feet, tapping out the rhythm of a word or phrase. For example, the leaders sing out, "If I come into your house and you don't give me something I will tell your mother," to which the masquerader taps out, "Please don't." Or the leader sings, "Who has a hunchback?" and the initiand taps out the names of hunchbacks he knows. This game only occurs in some villages, including Mgbom; it is not essential to the initiation, but it is much liked by viewers and participants.

The initiands who do not dance on a particular *orie* day remain in their loincloths, their faces charcoaled, as at other times when they appear in public. They sit with the musical group but they make no sound, nor do they clap, talk, or show their teeth. Every once in a while, when the crowd becomes noisy, one of them runs up and throws dirt at people or waves a stick glumly at them. Or he chases after uninitiated boys in the audience of his size or bigger, threatening them with dirt or his stick but maintaining his deadpan face. The boys may flee in fright, to the delight of the aggressor, who at this time can chase bigger boys than himself who are not yet secret society members; thus he sometimes settles old scores.

The initiating boys may also make broader movements. At one masquerade I saw a charcoal-faced youth grab the hat off an old man standing in the audience and throw it to the ground. It is said that the boy felt it was an offense—an insult to the *isiji* bush—to see a man wearing a hat at such an important ceremony (although men often wear hats at major rites). Later he threw down an umbrella that another elder was holding over his head, and he waved a stick around to scare other older persons. These kinds of aggressive acts are permitted here and are viewed with humor, though not always by those acted against. In other circumstances such behavior would be forbidden; the boy's actions would be considered offensive and he would be punished and his father fined by the elders.

In this part of the initiation, reversal is a major theme: men imitate women's dancing, mothers dance secret society steps, and the initiands aggress against the elders. The glum, hostile, charcoal-faced initiands are in evident contrast to the gentle dancing of the masqueraders in their bright costumes and the enthusiastic movements of the father, mother, and their friends and relatives. The charcoaled boys are symbolically inert in appearance. They too are in a state of reversal, not showing their teeth, with black faces, and speechless. Reversals carry the interest of the rite along, attracting attention by their novelty; they state what is right by doing blatantly what is normally wrong. In the context of his most important rite, the reversals emphasize for the maturing boy the proper quality of behavior that the will have to adhere to.

In the evening of the day his son has danced on his own, the father feasts friends and agnatic kin in the compound. The next day, *ahɔ*, his wives and other compound women cook the goat given when he masqueraded. The initiands in the bush receive all but the leg, which goes to the father's age set along with a good deal of palm wine and yam fufu. If a number of men from one age set are taking the title at the same time, which is likely, the legs are all given and shared, but the feasting with yam and wine is done over a number of days; it is too much for one sitting. The Afikpo say that the food is given to thank the age set for coming out and dancing with the father.

On the day that the sons have danced, their fathers also feast the village *isiji* title holders and give them money for the corn, to add to the ten shilling payment from the mother and her payment for the fowl. The feast includes yam fufu and palm wine and the second goat. (If the father can afford only one goat, the age set gets the foreleg, the title members the mid-section, and the son the remainder, to share with the other initiands.)

This feast is held jointly by both sections of Mgbom Village, informing the title members that the sons have done their dancing. In earlier times, each mother of an initiand in Mgbom feasted her village age set after the son did his particular dance. But sometime before 1951 the village men stopped this, feeling that the women were using too much food at these feasts for other women, for the title is for males, not females. Although quite busy with cooking, the mothers still find time to feed female friends and relations. And after the son dances the mother usually gives her husband a bar of soap, a bottle of native gin, cloth, or money—whatever present she wishes. His other wives, if he has more than one, will also present him with gifts.

The *ahɔ* day after the fifth *orie* masquerade day the *isiji* title members gather separately, by the two village sections, at the residence of a member, and divide the funds received from the fathers, generally in equal shares.

On the seventh and last *orie* day, when only the very best dancers appear, their fathers again come out and dance and sing with friends and relatives, but there is little feasting; the rites are drawing to a close. The senior priest of the initiands is usually the last to dance. He carries a raffia bamboo stick in his left hand and throws it over the high central portion of the *isiji* structure to the inner bush, as he did in secret days earlier with a flaming stick. It does not matter whether he succeeds or not. Everything is public now. In some villages the stick is hoisted to the top of the tower and left there. The use of the left hand in throwing, rather than the usual right is yet another reversal; it occurs in other Afikpo rituals.

On the evening of this day the initiands leave the bush, saying good-bye to its spirit. The fathers supply their sons, through the helpers, with thin brownish white yams, *abo*. Each boy cuts a yam in half crosswise with a knife, in front of the shrine. He tells the shrine spirit that he is leaving, that it should not come out for him or near him. Calling the *isiji* spirit by its name, he leaves the two pieces of yam there. The cutting of the yams symbolizes the end of the direct relationship between initiand and shrine spirit. After the sacrifices the shrine is closed by the priest and the raffia costumes worn in the dances are piled on top of it, and left to rot. The masks are stored in the men's rest houses in the community. The sacrifice makes for closure with this powerful bush spirit. Even so, boys sometimes dream of the initiation after their return to the compounds, and are said to call out the name of the shrine spirit in their sleep.

The boys leave the bush by climbing over the fence; they do not use the side gates nor the tunnel under the tower; the latter is only employed once in the rite. They spend the night in the men's rest houses in the commons, closed to non-initiates. Initiates, especially those who have helped to build it, tear down the tower and other sections of the structure. The sticks and raffia are left piled there, as is the front fencing on each side of the tower; the gates are closed up. In Mgbom, some of the poles and wood are used in building up dressing sheds for a later initiation, *isubu eda* (see Chapter 7), and as firewood in the men's rest houses in the commons. The wood cannot be taken into the compounds, for it is associated with the initiation and its spirit will pollute females.

During the rest of the year the bush area is not considered sacred.

Uninitiated boys play there and they run there to hide if chased by secret society maskers, but it is not used much by boys, and females avoid it. If an initiand dies while in the bush (which occurs only rarely, from causes unknown to me) he is buried there; afterward his parents carry out the usual funeral ceremonies for him in the compound (S. Ottenberg 1965:79–80). Regardless of the apparent cause of death, it is said that the spirit of the secret society has killed him.

If a mother of an initiand violates the corn taboo, or other *isiji* restrictions, and it comes to the attention of males, initiates rush to her compound and demand money from her. With this they purchase a laying hen, touch it to the woman's body, sacrifice it at the *isiji* bush area, and cook and eat it there. The fertile chicken symbolizes the desire that the woman's reproductive powers not be harmed by her act, whether intentional or not, through the force of the *isiji* spirit. Women must be careful not to walk too near the bush shrine when the commons is open. There are usually stone markers set out several feet from the front corners of the bush to indicate lines that should not be crossed.

When a woman, or even a man, sees the *isiji* masqueraders in the commons he or she is not supposed to point at them with a crooked finger. To do so is said to imitate the crooked neck top of the calabash mask. If the violator is a woman, it suggests symbolically that she has acted as if she were a male and has a penis; if she does so the initiates take a dog, or a chicken, or a duck, or some other thing from her compound to sacrifice at the bush shrine to "cool" the matter. If the violator is a man he is chided by other men for acting as if he were being initiated.

Violations on the part of an initiand are not taken as seriously. If he touches or eats corn, smiles, or otherwise shows his teeth, he will be reprimanded by the initiates, but no sacrifice is done. The matter rests on him; if he later becomes sick, has an accident, or dies, an explanation is at hand.

The Compound Phase

The second major period of the first-son initiation is also called *isiji*, or *ɔwuwu ɛzi* (return-compound), or referred to as "putting on the raffia" (*enya ɛgwɵ*, hang on neck–raffia), for the necklace worn at this time. The initiands live in one or two boys' rest houses in their compounds, depending on their number. The fathers choose these homes; other boys move out. If there is only one initiand in a compound he may live with others in a boys' house of a neighboring compound. Any traces of corn must be removed from these structures, for the taboo still holds. The initiands continue to wear the loincloth and charm, but on the morning when they go to the compounds, the coral necklace is replaced with a raffia one. I could discover no meaning for this new necklace other than what the Afikpo say, it indicates who the initiating boys are and in which stage they are in. They no longer blacken their faces but their helpers cut their head hair to the skin in a particular style; the design varies from village to village. In Mgbom a round cut of the hair is made at the right temple and the left rear of the head by the father or the boy's helper. This indicates their status, clearly differentiating them from other boys living in the compound. In some villages, such as Mkpoghoro, the boys cover their bodies with camwood dye; this is not done in Mgbom.

In those villages that have their initiation in the rainy season the compound phase lasts twenty-eight days. In communities which take *isiji* later on, the period is shortened so that the boys can take part in another rite, for both first and other sons, ɔka, four days after the start of the Feast of the Tortoise. In Mgbom this means that the boys are in the compounds for only eleven days. Afikpo do not consider the compound period to be as significant as the earlier phase, when the boys were introduced to the bush spirit.

Indeed, it is a quiet time. The initiands maintain the restrictions on talking, showing their teeth, having anything to do with corn, and exposing their sexual organs. There is no formally selected leader among them. They are in closer contact with people in the compound than in the earlier phase, yet a female cannot touch them or enter the boys' houses, or else she must sacrifice a chicken to *isiji* in the manner just described. This, of course, means that no sexual contact is possible for the boys in this phase, a condition similar to the first phase. While the initiands cannot talk to females they can, with their teeth hidden, converse with their helpers and with the uninitiated lads who bring them food from their mothers. Uninitiated boys must not walk out of the house backward after putting the food dish on the house floor; initiands would refuse to eat food presented in this manner, for it is believed that the server is imitating the *isiji* masqueraders, who entered the commons backward from the bush. The mother continues to cook for her son, and he still gathers fruit for his parents and for himself, using his bag, machete, and cane.

Now the two village sections in Mgbom are inoperative; everything is on a compound basis. Fathers do not hold feasts and the title members do not meet; there are no rituals. The bush has been closed and the initiands do not enter it. In Mgbom it is a period when many people are busy at the farms, bringing in the remainder of the harvest, and the initiands help, although the taboos are maintained.

The initiands use the regular village latrines in back of the compounds, but these have been fenced by initiates at this time so that there is no possibility of females seeing the boys' genitals. As the lads move about they appear easily angered if there is a lot of noise or talk around them, perhaps because of their own restricted condition, but certainly because they are expected to act this way. They throw sand or dust at noisy persons, much as at the public dances of *isiji*.

The initiands visit back and forth a great deal in the compounds of their village. They talk freely with each other, exposing their teeth. They inquire as to how others are getting on with preparations, for their task is now to construct the structure in which they will live in the rear of the compound in the next initiation stage. They tell stories and discuss their bush experiences. Each boy makes a hunting net from palm leaves *(ɔgbo nta)*, about six feet long and three feet wide. The boys tie a number of them together and take this out of the village to drive animals into, which they kill and eat. It is a period with little or no tension. The initiands live in the compounds and yet they are separated from secret society members and from females. They have survived what for some of them has been an anxious but exciting period.

The boys cannot go to the Afikpo market, where they might be in contact with women or corn. In the Itim villages, including Mgbom, they cannot go to the commons from four days before the Feast of the Tortoise until it is over; they are forbidden to see this event, with its salacious singing, its Whipping Day activities, and another initiation form, *isubu eda*, which occurs at that time, although they watch and take part in aspects of this festival the years before and after their initiation.

These boys are in a transitory period; they are neither non-initiates nor initiates. When they walk through the commons they do not shout "*loooooo*" as non-initiates do (perhaps because of the restriction on exposing their teeth), yet they are not yet free to enter the men's rest houses in the commons until the end of the next initiation phase.

In this period the boys make the raffia costume that they will wear in the next initiation stage and prepare the special enclosure in back of the compound where they will reside then; friends and helpers assist them. This involves building fences and a tree platform, making wooden beds to use there, and collecting firewood. These activities keep them busy at least part of the day. Toward the end of the boys' rest house period, anxiety, anticipation, and excitement build up again, for the next initiation stage is more active and ritualized.

Commentary

Isiji consists of three markedly different but interrelated phases. In the preliminary period feasting and sacrifices are employed to activate village, agnatic, residential, and age groups and the major spiritual forces. Social obligations are met by the fathers, and expectations are aroused in the community without creating political tensions. The initiands are psychologically activated, and magical protective measures ensure that no harm comes to them. The father proves his readiness to sponsor his son by completing the preliminaries.

In the bush phase the initiands symbolically change status through the typical initiation patterns of liminality and communitas (Turner 1967, 1969), with physical and social isolation, and some hardship, in a rich symbolic environment. A dominant theme is behavior reversals, and another is rebirth.

In the third period, the initiands are reintegrated into their dwelling areas, yet without being free, a time of "betwixt and between" (Turner 1969). It is a quiet period of adjustment following the excitement of the bush, without elements of secrecy or sacrifice.

The rites reiterate the importance at Afikpo of a man's first son, who will be a guide to other sons as they mature. If the father dies young the first son takes charge of the family when he is old enough. And as we have seen, a son is necessary for a father to become prominent; if he does not exist, he is created for *isiji*.

The first-son initiation is one of the first important rites that the father performs as an adult at the village level; marriage is rather a compound and kinship matter. The initiation of his first son comes before the father takes the most important titles and usually previous to playing an active leadership role in village affairs. It allows him to move ahead to these. For the son it is his first major move into village life, preceding marriage, taking titles, and a career as a grower of yams, with which so much of male life is concerned.

Isiji is an initiation for both father and son, playing parallel but coordinate roles. The father's activities center around the compound and village feasts and the directions he gives to the boy's helpers. The main part of the son's actions are in the bush. It is true that if a father is poor, or if he enjoys rituals, he can go to the bush and act as his son's helper rather than having others do this, whom he must then feast many times for their work. But a man who is his son's helper loses prestige; the better status comes from remaining in the compound and directing matters from a distance. In this way he fulfills the prototype of a typical Afikpo elder, administering well while keeping a sense of social distance between himself and others. The symbolic rewards are in the cooperative but separate activities of father and son rather than in their intimate association. There are psychological rewards as well; tensions between the two are minimized. Some Afikpo say that if the father were in the bush, under the emotional conditions existing there, conflicts between him and his son might break out into the open and disrupt the ritual; we have seen how the father is also often absent, though in charge, at his son's circumcision. And the Afikpo told me that tensions might arise between the father and the initiates running the initiation over the treatment of the son, which the father would see if he were in the bush. The father may fear for the son's welfare, and the son may feel restrained by his father's presence, or resent being led directly by the father into a ritual involving hardship and constraints. The son's adolescent feelings of love and hostility for the father, and the father's ambivalent attitudes towards the growing boy—who as the first son will eventually replace him—are kept under control by the distancing of the two in their separate ritual roles. The separation of father and son is symbolized by the apparent leadership role in the bush of the initiands and the young initiates. This is an illusion; the real leadership is in the hands of the fathers and ultimately of the village elders, though carried out by young adult secret society initiates.

For the son's part, his being distant from his father is symbolized by the attacks he may make on senior men when he is in his charcoal-faced condition, while other initiands are masquerading. This appears to be aggression against a symbolic father, a putting down of him, albeit playfully. Also, when the initiand masks, this very act separates him from his father, even though the father dances with friends and others at the same time. Father and son are together, yet each has a separate role. They normally meet in the bush stage of initiation only when one is masked and the other is not.

Yet despite the distance between father and son, and the minimal contact of mother and boy, the initiation is very much a family affair. It is true that the son is physically away from his compound and parents in the bush stage—the first time that he has ever been away for any length of time, as a rule—and that he is also restricted in relating to his parents in the compound phase. The sacred bush, the taboos, the men's rest house in the commons where the initiands sleep, the boys' house in the compound, all provide spatial as well as psychic separation from the parents. Yet the initiands are not isolated from their parents by a great distance or over a long period of time. As before initiation, the mother cooks for her son with food provided largely by the father. The son does not only live off of what he collects and cooks himself; indeed, the son provides fruits for the parents. Further, the father feasts close agnatic kin a number of times during the initiation and they actively cooperate in the son's rites as his helpers and in other ways. There is much of a sense of family involvement; the *isiji* rites symbolize family unity and cooperation. The initiation has a double message: the boy becomes an autonomous adult and yet remains very much a family member, though with changed relationships.

In the years before initiation, as the son takes part in the boys' secret societies and in other boys' activities, he pulls away from family life. The initiation draws him back, it reiterates the importance of family and of agnatic ties. The rites prepare the boy not only for entrance into village social life but also into the adult life of his compound, with its familial and agnatic links. The initiation publicly states that there are first sons in the compound who are reaching maturity and who will play leading roles in this patrilineal and residential unit in the years to come. It broadens the boys' social contacts with the village and deepens existing ties in the compound, necessary for a male to become a full adult at Afikpo.

The initiation symbolically separates the boy from his mother, the child returning home a different social and psychological person. When the son comes to her after the first few days in the bush and

breaks his calabash dish and spoon in front of her, this act symbolically negates his dependency upon her, as does his subsequent collecting of fruits to feed himself and even to feed his parents. The
breaking of the calabash, a symbolic uterus or vagina, marks the
hoped for end of his psychological dependence upon his mother. It
has analogies to the crushing of the calabash before the mother
enters her home with her newborn child, indicating the end of the
gestation period.

On the other hand, there are continuities in the initiation. The
mother and son share a common restriction involving corn, both
observe speech taboos, and they wear a like type of protective charm.
The mother feeds the son generously during the initiation, and the
rite of breaking the dish and spoon does not change this; all males at
Afikpo are fed by females. Since the child has been living apart from
his mother the initiation situation does not represent a sharp shift.
The bush is an elaborate and ritualized boys' house. Although symbolically the rites represent separation at a crucial age of sexual development, in fact they are part of a process of disengagement that
begins at a very early age in the boy's life.

It may be that at Afikpo—as in other matrilineal societies that have
adolescent initiations—the need for psychological separation between mother and son conflicts with the practical needs of people
with strong matrilineal descent interests. This would explain why the
break between mother and child is not as severe as in societies with
other kinds of descent concepts. The rites establish the boy's independence from his mother in symbolic ways, while carefully preserv-
ing the ties between them so as to protect legal rights, property, and
inheritance (S. Ottenberg 1968a). What is clear is that during the
initiation the boy is separated from his mother physically and symbolically, at the same time that contrary statements about the
mother-son tie are also being made.

Food is a major form of wealth at Afikpo. Until recent years there
was little money; that which existed was in the form of cowry shells
and brass and copper rods, to a large extent in the hands of slave
traders from Aro Chuku and their local associates living in the area.
For most Afikpo men the expression of wealth has been largely
through feasts, often associated with rituals such as initiation.
Wealth is the consequence of being enterprising farmers and skillful
land manipulators, and choosing hard-working wives. Feasting is
not wastefulness or idleness; it is a valued ability, associated with

personal achievement. Having the resources to provide sumptuous meals in the initiation rites is a reflection of the wealth of a man in the number of wives to farm and to prepare food, and of good relations with agnatic kin, for no man prepares a fine meal alone.

The initiation feasts are strongly associated with the yam, the major male crop and ritual food at Afikpo, only occasionally grown by women. This root plant is explicitly a symbol of the penis, as is evident in the songs of the Feast of the Tortoise. The heavy use of yams in the initiation feasts, and by the initiands at the bush shrine, mark the male nature of the rites; it is a thoroughly appropriate symbol for the adolescent boys. For the son, sexuality and achievement (of the initiation) are linked together in the rites, while for the father these two come together in the feasts he is involved in, which celebrate both his farming skill and his past procreative ability.

Although considerable pretense is made to scare the boys and their mothers, the initiation is surprisingly free of physical hardship. The initiands spend little time in the bush, sleeping and resting in the men's houses during the first month, where they are secure and where roughhousing is never allowed at any time of the year. If there are restrictions on the boys there are also the helpers who bring them good food, and the boys have the opportunity to collect fruit as they will. If holding the arms over the head is uncomfortable, if throwing the stick over the tall structure of the bush is a difficult test of strength, and if on the first day in the bush there is some shouting and shoving, still the physical side of the rites is mild. There is no circumcision or scarification, beating, or serious test of endurance. The bush is not a nasty and brutish place; that illusion is developed by initiates. The pretense of suffering satisfies the needs of the Afikpo.

It is said that the initiation was harsher before this century, in pre-European times, in keeping with the emphasis on warfare, the rites serving as training in physical fitness. The mock attitude toward physical endurance in *isiji* today reflects the change in realities. The initiation is a conning at the same time that it is very real. The initiands and their mothers are led to believe that they are going to be more brutally treated than they are. The boys are fooled about climbing over the high bush structure, and through the use of camwood to represent blood. The mothers are conned into paying for the red part of the initiands' masquerade headpieces, and into giving money to secret society members to protect their sons. A mother is expected to believe that her masked son is a spirit. The father is rarely involved in the conning, perhaps because this might arouse latent hostilities between father and son or father and mother—the Afikpo particularly seem to want to avoid the former situation at all costs— but, of course, the father is indirectly implicated since he initiates the ritual and is heavily involved in it. Conning adds an element of delight and creativity to the rite, which is both serious and humorous, a playing with and a playing on father-son and mother-son ties.

Two of the most uncomfortable elements of the initiation are the restrictions on the boys' exposing their teeth and on speech. Afikpo are great talkers and the ability to speak well is highly prized and an important attribute of leadership (S. Ottenberg 1971). Facial animation in speech is desired; a lively interesting face adds to good talk. The taboos severely limit this. The speech taboo prevents relaxed and animated talk for the initiating boys except when they are alone. This adds to their sense of communitas, as it separates them from others. And the initiands cannot eat with initiates for they would show their teeth; the importance of eating together has already been discussed. Showing teeth is sometimes a mark of aggression, and even disrespect at Afikpo. Hiding the teeth reflects being under control.

The charcoal employed on the face when out in public during the first month of the initiation deadens, rather than highlights, facial qualities. At first I believed that the charcoal symbolized death, although no one provided me with this interpretation; the boy dies to be reborn as an adult. This is in keeping with Eliade's (1965) idea of initiation as death and rebirth. Charcoal is a transformation of living wood through fire to something inert, as the boys are transformed, through the fire of the spirit of the bush, into temporarily inert beings. But now I am less certain that the charcoal faces represent death. The timing in the ritual is wrong for this interpretation, since the initiands appear in this way at the later masquerading periods and beyond, when not themselves in costume, and their first masquerade appearance I have interpreted as an analogy to their coming-out rite four days after their birth. I do not find that there is any symbolization of death in these rites, aside from the fact that the seclusion from parents and the public when the boys enter the bush is a kind of temporary social death.

I see mainly rebirth. The initiands emerging from the bush into the village commons after first contacting the shrine is their rebirth.

They hold their arms above their heads, symbolizing the helplessness of infants. They are painted with red dye, suggesting the blood and liquid on a newborn infant. The initiands waiting to go into the bush see the red colored bodies and are expected to be frightened; this is a conning of them and perhaps a reminder that birth is a very physical and dangerous thing. The bush is a symbolic womb.

The charcoal face, coming sometime after these events, has other referents than death. It relates to the infant under restraint with its mother, not adult enough to express true feelings, restricted to its mother as the initiands are to older men in the bush. It is part and parcel of the taboos on expression, on talking and on showing the teeth. It does make the boys' features look inert, but it does not make them look dead.

It should also be noted that the color black on the face is a reversal. Normally infants are rubbed with white or pink chalk, often by their mothers, to keep them cool. White has references to peace and health. Black, in at least some Afikpo secret societies, is a taboo color; it has the idea of danger associated with it. Further, in some Afikpo secret society masquerades (S. Ottenberg 1975) not associated with initiation, dark and black masks are used to portray evil, greed, and foolishness, particularly among men, while white is employed as a positive color, associated with females. Black is linked to ideas of non-normative behavior. The charcoal face is a kind of mask. It has associations, therefore, with danger, breaking norms, maleness— literally the dark side of life. It is a metaphor of the struggling and unhappy male side of the boy's infant life, as white is for the peaceful and motherly side.

The constraining taboos on showing the teeth and talking, and the use of charcoal, affect important areas of behavior. The initiands are forbidden to speak like men, to eat with others as men, as they are denied sexual expression. The hiding of the genitals and the teeth from females is analogous; the boys cannot talk to, aggress toward, or have sex with females. The initiands' assertive tendencies are chan-neled into the bush rites, into gathering fruits, masquerading, and other activities which are seen as manly. Such restrictions induce the boys (and others) to contemplate the value of talk and of sex in everyday life.

The initiation draws heavily on earlier childhood experience. It is not so much a rich learning situation as an application of past ex-perience, knowledge, and skills. The rites replicate some of the events of the earlier birth rituals. There is the time of isolation and the coming-out ceremony in both; there is the smashing of the gourd on the ground in both; there is the birth in one and the rebirth in the other; there is the secrecy of birth in both cases. The first-son initiation thus returns the boy to the birth situation where he was originally surrounded by females, but this time he is in the company of men, to break the remnants of the mother-son tie and to allow for a richer father-son relationship. The initiation uses elements drawn from the first event but arrives at different conclusions; it is a re-writing of the primal birth.

The initiation builds upon the boys' past rather than departing from it. Gender role definitions, already clearly worked out for boys and girls, and for males and females, are reinforced. Male aggression away from the immediate home and female domestic labor at the home are reasserted. The use and significance of male secrecy, as a gender marker and as a metaphor for sexuality, continues. Male peer-group activity, so strongly embedded in the boys' societies and other boys' activities, also is found, in modified form in the communitas of the initiands and the position of the initiands' own priests as leaders of a sort. The boys living separated from the parents with a distant but supportive father and a nourishing mother are familiar social roles. Physical strength and the ability to endure hardship are stressed in the initiation as well as in the earlier experiences of boys. The *isiji* builds on the religious knowledge and technical skills of boys, rather than being a marked departure from them. A new mask and new masquerade dance, yes, but drawing on developed skills in dancing, masquerading, music, and costuming, on the boys' abilities to hold secrets, and on their already developed ritual skills in sacrifice. The rich fantasy life of boys, as we have discussed, prepares them for the initiation experience, with its mystery and exoticism. Yams, chalk, kola, the four days of the week, and the four basic colors have appeared before in the boys' lives, in their own secret societies, in the bird-killing rite, and elsewhere. From the initiands' point of view the *isiji* spirit of the bush, a vaguely defined powerful male force, replicates the spirit of the boys' societies, looking at the matter developmentally, although adult males would say that the boys' spirit emulates the adult one. The boys may be novices in the initiation, in that they meet new situations and experiences under the control of their seniors, but they face the events with a wealth of knowledge and experience that allows matters to flow smoothly, rather than to stumble, without very strong outward authority on the part of others. Indeed, this is one reason, along with anticipatory excitement, why such authority is little needed; the boys are already knowledgeable and skilled and emotionally prepared. They are prepared in both unconscious depth psychology and in the more conscious vernacular psychology, as we discussed at the end of the last chapter. It is almost as if they are initiating themselves—but like many things concerning the Afikpo secret society, of course, this is an illusion. Men control the bush.

In the initiation, as in earlier periods of the boys' lives, aesthetics play an important role in maturation; there is continuity between the boys' earlier aesthetic experience and the initiation. There is masquerading in both, with dancing to music, and in both the uninitiated are expected to believe that the masqueraders are spirits. However, there are differences as well. The initiand wears a type of mask that he has never worn before. He does not have freedom to create his own performance, to emulate adult masqueraders, to dress and perform as he wishes. And while some of the boys' secret society masked dances are critical of other boys and of adults, this does not occur in the initiands' masquerade. Thus the aesthetic qualities in this rite build upon earlier experience in the boys' lives, yet have new features that largely represent the initiands' coming under the direct authority of older males. It is an aesthetic of control rather than of freedom and emulation.

The lack of genuine physical hardship is coupled with a surprising lack of outward authority in the initiation, in the bush and in the compound phase. Perhaps strong authority is not needed; the initiands are psychologically prepared through anxiety and anticipation to accept direction, and they are used to cooperation from the days of their own boys' societies. Initiands who violate taboos are rebuked but not severely punished, as younger boys also are not; the initiands are not even required to perform compensatory sacrifices. If they become weak or sick or die in the bush this is explained in terms of violations of taboos, with spiritual retribution, rather than as the consequences of human punishment.

The helpers direct and keep an eye on their charges; these older males are father surrogates and sometimes the fathers' close friends. By virtue of their age they have authority over the initiands under normal conditions; life in the bush is an extension of this situation.

But they are protectors and helpers rather than harsh authoritarians. There are no omnipresent religious officials; the two priests are initiands themselves, and not much older than the other initiands, if at all. The boys cooperate with one another under mild leadership; there is no evident concentration of authority, although this ultimately exists in the power of the elders, as distant authority figures, and in the fathers of the boys. The initiands easily learn the rules— some they already know and some they come to know as events occur. They need even less direct supervision in the final, compound phase. The initiation draws on a pattern of peer-group behavior, with slightly older and stronger males in leadership roles, established in the boys secret societies, thus avoiding parental-child tensions as much as possible.

There are few conflicts among the initiands or with their helpers and other initiates. Boys shove one another going into the bush at the end of a masquerading day, and this may lead to fights, broken up by their helpers. They compete by throwing sticks over the central tower, though the leaders have already been chosen by their fathers and the secret society members and it takes some of the sense of competition out of the event if the boys know this, as they sometimes do. The initiands compete to collect the largest pile of firewood before the bush is opened and to dance their best at the masquerade. In the bush there is some petty fighting among the initiands over minor but irritating matters. Yet there is little need for authoritarian figures to resolve serious antagonisms. The frictions which develop do not mirror village political or social conflicts, although tensions among initiands in the bush sometimes reflect rivalries between compounds of the settlement. The boys who have already been fighting one another before initiation continue to do so, but are restrained by initiates. The initiation has elements of aggressive behavior, not inconsistent with that which initiands have been exposed to in their earlier lives, but these do not seriously mirror village conflicts as a rule.

The lack of conflict in the bush, and the ease with which events transpire there without strong leadership, suggest that communitas is operating for the initiands, bound closely together by sentiment, and that this sense of togetherness makes strong controls unnecessary. It is true that there are distinctions among the initiands in the bush—first sons as against other sons, priests as against others, and the older boys as against the younger ones. These differences play important roles in the activities in the bush, but they do not override the sense of unity.

Experience in their own secret societies admirably prepares the boys for the rule-guided nonauthoritarian milieu of the bush. They are familiar with running secret matters on their own. They have had their own priests, shrines, sacrifices, isolated bush areas, taboos, and masquerades. The boys' societies emphasize many features stressed in the first-son initiation: strength, aggressiveness, endurance, and skill. The first-son initiation does not represent a sharp break in behavior from earlier experiences. Rather, it represents an expansion to the wider social horizon of the village.

What differs strikingly is that the boys' societies are operated by themselves with tacit parental approval, while the *isiji* rites are organized by their fathers and other men, under the authority of the title holders and village elders—often the same persons. Ultimate control and direction of the initiation is out of the boys' hands; the secret elements in the initiation are, in theory, unknown to them, especially matters concerning the shrine and its rituals, and the tower and tunnel. These elements are absent from the boys' societies.

The youths, without authoritarian behavior of a direct and strong sort, are brought under the control of fathers and male elders through the initiation, men who are not themselves in the bush. These men do not have to be there; the shrine and its spirit, and the bush itself, stand for this male adult authority, as do the rest houses in the commons which the boys can enter and sleep in for the first time during the initiation. The spirit of the *isiji* shrine symbolizes fathers and elders—the adult males of the community—whose authority the boys must accept in becoming adults. This spirit is believed to be very much more powerful and mystical than that of the spirit in the boys' societies. The high entrance structure to the bush, so visible from much of the village, stands for maleness, the male penis. Thus the bush has major opposing referents; it is a mother's womb, out of which the initiand is born, and it also stands for the father. The bush, its structures, and its shrine represent both parents.

But this is not all the symbolism involved. One feature marks these rites by its apparent absence: the lack of overt reference to sex. Yet this is a time when the boys are awakening sexually. What do we make of this fact? There are no other rites for the first son which markedly represent sexual maturation, yet sexuality seems immediately absent in the initiation. Even the holding of the arms over the head denies the boy the pleasure of playing with his genitals and of masturbation, which is common for boys of this age. The boys refrain from all contacts with females. There are no songs or dances which refer to sex, and no explicitly recognized sexual symbols exist; even the male genitals are hidden in public.

Yet I find it hard to believe that sexual references do not exist. I believe they are present in symbolic form, in the sexual restrictions themselves, in the extensive use of yams in feasting, in the headdress and masks of the masquerade costume, in the structure of the bush, and in the manner in which it is used.

The denial of communication of the initiands with females, the holding of the arms over the head, the shielding of the male genitals, all suggest that there is something to control, something to prevent, and of course, that is sexuality. The very taboos themselves express sexuality by their denial of it.

I consider the two circular fences in the initiation bush to be vaginal lips, the tunnel to be the vagina, and the inner bush, with its shrine, to be the uterus and womb (as we have already discussed the womb in terms of the idea of rebirth). These female structures in the bush are secret, in contrast to the phallic entrance structure; this mirrors the attitude toward the male and female genitals in everyday life. When the initiands first enter the bush they do not go through the tunnel under the tower but through another gate to the outer area. Here their hands are tied and they then leave the bush for the day. I see these actions as symbolizing sexual foreplay, to which intercourse is denied by older males. Their helpers, representing the fathers, are the ones who tie up the boys' hands and make them hold them above their heads, who do not let them see the tower being built (the male erection denied), and do not let them enter the inner bush at this time.

At the time of their actual "initiation," as the Afikpo call it, the initiands are released from this control and they try to throw shafts over the tower into the inner circle, i.e., they attempt intercourse. The shaft is burning, as the penis is "hot." But they do not know how to do it and they must be shown the way through the tower; that is, they are still dependent upon older males for permission to be effective sexually. The most successful shaft throwers—in theory, but not always in practice—are rewarded by becoming priests. Symbolically the most sexually assertive ones, they direct the initiands through the tunnel, into the inner circle. Here the lighted fire represents sexual feeling and heat of the uterus. Then a sacrifice is performed which connects the boy with the spirit of the shrine; the association is with sexuality, with female sexual organs and activity. The "female" is passive, the male assertive, as often occurs in Afikpo sexual relations. The rite is a symbolic act of sexual intercourse. We have the introduction of the initiand to adult sexuality symbolically, under gentle guidance, and in an atmosphere of outward rejection of sexual interest. The act is repeated in restricted form in the egg sacrifice carried out before each masquerade. I believe that the egg represents sperm—although no Afikpo stated this to me—or it may represent a more generalized concept of fertility.

Whose womb is it? The bush can be seen as the mother's womb in the oedipal drama, and the rite thus for the initiands a psychological regression to early childhood, in permitted ritual form, a goodbye to the mother. But it can equally be interpreted as the initiand's (symbolic) first sexual experience as a maturing adult, or a looking to such a future real experience. The initiand thus looks both forward and backward in sexual feeling and experience in a metaphoric manner. The initiation also strives to direct male sexual interests away from the mother, to other females, to end oedipal feelings aroused as an aspect of the growing sexual awareness of boys, at the same time that it suggests the Oedipus complex. The rites become particularly important in this regard because of the long and strong early mother-son tie. The initiation helps the boy by renewing a sense of the punishing father, no matter how distant, and by conveying the idea that the events confer sexual manhood on the boy, in turning him away from the mother to other sexual interests, which he can then pursue. The bush, as symbolic mother, is both womb to the infant and sexual object to the maturing boy. Infancy and sexual maturation are united in the drama of the ritual.

Thus the shrine has multiple symbolic referents; it symbolizes both mother and father and also male authority, rebirth, and past and future sexual concerns. There is a remarkable unity, then, in the initiation, of ideas of birth, incestuous wishes, awakening sexuality, and the acceptance of male authority; conflict and contradiction between these elements are minimized in the presentation of the initiation as a unified activity. It is the appearance together of these diverse metaphors in one setting which gives the initiation its human interest and strength.

The boys appear in public for the first time during the initiation in

masquerade, in an exotic costume and mask, laden with sexual referents. The red berries on the headdress are said by Afikpo to represent the clitoris. They appear as a costume element at this masquerade only, as far as I know. The neck of the calabash suggests a
phallus in the midst of a clitoris. In two Afikpo villages, Anohia and
Kpogrikpo, the gourd neck is absent, but there is a very tall wood
construction, again phallic (Jones 1985:65, top plate). (The gourd
neck may also represent the umbilical cord, as it does during divination of the boy's reincarnating ancestors; this especially suggests
the idea of rebirth.) The *isiji* mask itself is also employed in only this
one rite at Afikpo, its body signifying the vagina or uterus. I interpret the costumed figure as being androgynous; later initiation rites
make the boy fully male. It is interesting that the mask is the most
abstract Afikpo type (S. Ottenberg 1975); one cannot tell whether it
is a male or female, as one can usually tell for other Afikpo masks,
particularly by indicators such as hairstyle. The *isiji* mask can represent either or neither sex. It is not even clear that it is a face, though
the Afikpo speak of it as such. This suggests that the masked boy is
in an intermediate status; he has a faceless, genderless visage. His
identity as a social person is not yet clear. The androgyny is also
hinted at in the masquerader's performance, when his father and
friends dance as women do and the mother moves about in men's
secret society style. At the public appearance of the initiand he symbolically "comes out" four days after being reborn, but his status is
still ambiguous. Perhaps this echoes the fact that for the mother, in
caring for a newborn child, it is not immediately very significant
whether it is a boy or a girl. Only later does this become important.

The numerous red clitoris-like seeds on the headdress have yet
another meaning. The boys have captured female sexuality and now
control it, as Afikpo men believe that they should control female life
and sexuality. The conning of the mother into paying money to the
father and his friends for "wool," which is in fact these seeds, reflects
this aspect of control.

When the initiation is over (or when subsequent ones end, if the
initiands continue with other initiation forms), the boys are expected
to go out and to have intercourse, preferably the first time with a
stranger or a harlot. Some boys do this and some do not; it is not
obligatory. If the initiation has no sexual reference, which it outwardly does not, why would the Afikpo expect the boys to do so?

The metaphoric association of sexuality and secrecy, as represented in the secret society initiation, is a continuation of an earlier tie between the two that we have already discussed, here in greatly enriched form. The secrecy of the womb and of the bush are joined, the mystery of human birth and social rebirth are linked. The metaphoric association of sexuality and secrecy, which began in the earlier life of boys, continues to be meaningful after initiation.

Thus I interpret the rites, among their other meanings, to be an expression of sexuality. It is sexuality in its symbolic forms, under full male control, with a symbolically passive but powerful female acquiescing to male penetration without the potential conflicts which may occur in real life, with an assertive, hostile, withholding, resentful, dominating, or uncooperative female partner. There is male mastery and control as men desire in their everyday lives over females. In this sense the rites not only suggest the positive, nonconflicting aspects of mother-infant relationships, where the mother accepts the infant's demands, but also the idealized adult male view of gender relationships, where there is male potency and sexual control.

The initiation continues the pattern of gender role distinction that we have observed in earlier social ties of the boy, and in boy-girl interactions. In fact, this distinction is present in almost every act of the initiation, from the separate supportive roles of mother and father, the isolating of males from females, to the paradox of the mother who dances the steps of the *isiji* masquerade (which, by its exceptional nature, reiterates her female role). The secrecy of some of the rites also reinforces gender differences.

The meaning of initiation then is not so much in its form as in the fact that it is done at the time of sexual and social maturation, that attention is called to it as widely as possible by involving virtually all the major groupings and individuals in the village and many of the important spiritual forces, and that it has multiple referents, all grouped together—to birth and infancy, to the Oedipus complex and to adolescent sexuality, to male control and father identification, to separation from the mother, and to gender identity. It is this rich symbolic interweaving of elements that makes the rites so interesting and important, a summing up, as it were, of the adolescent boys' lives so far, as a preparation for their future new and changing roles. These references appear to be layered, from the most explicit to the deeply unconscious, with the association to males and father identity as the most visible, along with the separation from the mother, then the adolescent sexuality theme, then the rebirth metaphor, and at the deepest level the oedipal issue. But different initiands may experience levels of consciousness of these themes in varying ways.

6

The Second Initiation

F OLLOWING THE *ISIJI* INITIATION, MOST NEW INITIATES
perform another rite called *isubu*. This popular subsequent
initiation is open to first sons and others who have not done
isiji; the distinction of birth order loses much of its significance.

Isubu is a contraction of the phrase *isi obubu* (head-initiation,
which the Afikpo say signifies "the finishing of the initiation" (i.e.,
the completion of what was begun in the *isiji* rites). The rite is
divided into two periods. The first is called *ɔka* (fence)—alternative
names for it are *ababa ɔwɔkɔ* (run–enclosed yard), *ababa na ɔka*
(run-in-fence), and *ɔwɔkɔ* (enclosed yard)—and ideally lasts the Igbo
month of twenty-eight days, concluding with a sacrifice at the time
of the Dry Season Festival. The sacrifice is said to constitute the
actual initiation. Since the Dry Season Festival is held on different
days in different villages, some initiands remain in *ɔka* for a longer
period, waiting for it, while in other communities they spend less
time. During *ɔka* the initiands live in a fenced enclosure in back of
the compound.

During the twenty-eight days following the Dry Season Festival
the second initiation phase occurs. It is also called *isubu,* which is the
term for the whole initiation. I will employ *isubu* for the whole rite,
and the term "second stage" for its second part, during which the
boys live in the commons, sleeping in the men's rest houses.* In
many villages their time there is shorter than seven Igbo weeks.

Though the *isubu* commences in the Afikpo rainy season, it is
considered a dry season rite since its major sacrifice is at the begin-

---

*The terminology is complicated, for in popular speech the term *isiji* sometimes refers
to both parts of the *isubu* rite as well as the previous initiation. In this work I use *isiji*
in its more restricted and technically correct sense, to mean the first-son initiation rites
preceding *isubu*.

ning of this period. The *isubu* initiation occurs in every village, the first stage in roughly similar style, while the second varies from settlement to settlement in its masquerades. Those villages or sections of communities which lack *isiji* start their initiation with *ɔka*, having no special initiation for first sons. In the eight northern Afikpo villages of Ozizza, where *isiji* is absent, each community does *isubu* on a different year. As in the case of *isiji*, the central and southern Afikpo villages hold *isubu* in various years and there is no centralization of activities for the whole village-group, reflecting the autonomy of the village from any centralized Afikpo political structure (S. Ottenberg 1971).

The Afikpo believe that both stages of *isubu* are indigenous and older than the first-son initiation, which is known to come from elsewhere. The *isubu* shrines and rites are generally attributed, though it does not seem a matter of great interest to Afikpo, to an ancient and probably non-Igbo matrilineal people, the Ego, who lived in the area before the Igbo arrived (S. Ottenberg 1968a:19–20). The rites were then adopted by successive waves of Igbo settlers to Afikpo. Nevertheless, this initiation today does not have any more of a matrilineal flavor than do the *isiji* rites. The shrines for at least some of the *isubu* events originated in Amɔzo subvillage of the largest Afikpo settlement of Mkpoghoro (also called Ndibe), spreading out from there to other villages. The parent shrine at Amɔzo is employed in a sacrifice by men taking the highest Afikpo title, *omume*, regardless of what village they are from; otherwise only Amɔzo villagers make use of it.

The ideal Afikpo pattern is that the boys who do *isiji* should also take part in both stages of *isubu*. This includes not only true first sons, but also other sons—of fathers using surrogate sons, sons of men taking the *omume* title, and men putting a second son through *isiji*. Afikpo believe that every man should put a boy through *isubu* as well as *isiji*, as should every man taking the highest Afikpo title, *omume*. *Isubu* should be done before a father is said to have completed the title of his first-son initiation, discussed in the previous chapter.

In fact, an initiand sometimes breaks off after the *isiji* rite, if he has to go to school, to work, or if his father is poor. He may return another year to perform the latter part of *ɔka*—the sacrificial rites and perhaps some of the subsequent masquerading—since this often coincides with the Christmas period. In the case of a boy whose father has already done *isiji* for a son and is repeating it because he has the wealth and delights in doing so, the boy usually breaks off after *isiji*, unless the father particularly desires him to go on. But here the father usually has little interest; the prestige comes in directing a boy through *isiji* a second time, and not through the *isubu*, which is less expensive, with fewer feasts, and a less spectacular initiation.

All other boys are traditionally expected to go through both parts of *isubu*, starting with the ɔka stage. They make the ɔka raffia costume in the boys' rest houses, or their fathers do this, while the *isiji* initiands are making theirs in the backyard, during the compound stage of that initiation; those just starting are not subject to the taboos placed on the initiands until they begin the actual *isubu*. They enter the fenced enclosure at the start of ɔka along with the initiating boys from *isiji*. Boys who terminate their initiation at the end of the compound stage of *isiji* do not make this costume; they just leave off without any closing rites, returning to their normal life in the compound, living at the boys' houses until they marry, many years later.

I will again draw my examples from Mgbom village.

The First Stage

There is no division in Mgbom, or in other villages, into two residential sections for *isubu;* most matters are conducted at the compound level, with the masquerades occurring in the village as a whole. In Mgbom *isubu* follows *isiji* every seventh year; it has not changed to being offered every year as in many other villages (see Appendix 2), probably because Mgbom, like other Itim villages of Afikpo, also has its own yearly form of initiation (see Chapter 7).

On the evening of the last day of the *isiji* initiation, ɛkɛ day (see Table 2), the father, or his helpers (initiates who themselves have done *isubu*), lead the initiands from the boys' rest houses in the compounds to a convenient place in the commons, such as the young boys' playground next to Agbogo commons. The helpers shave off the boys' head hair, throwing away the raffia necklace that they have been wearing in the compound phase of *isiji*. The commons is not closed; anyone can watch. Symbolically the boys are reborn again, naked, though wearing their loincloths from the *isiji* initiation. The father or his helpers have made a painted bamboo spear with no iron point (*azua ogugu*), which the boy holds in his right hand, clenching

TABLE 2

Schedule of the *Isubu* Initiation in Mgbom Village

Time Period	Day of Igbo Four-Day Week	Event(s)
October or November	ɛkɛ	Boys go to burial ground, then to the fenced enclosures, where they change dress. Beginning of ɔka stage of *isubu* initiation.
Five-week period		Boys live at leisure inside the fenced enclosures. They are attacked by masqueraders.
	orie	Initiates destroy initiands' cooking pots. Fathers feast compound title holders and consult a diviner.
	ahɔ	Initiates reveal the secret of the ɔkpa masquerade costume to the initiands. Enclosures destroyed by initiates.
	nkwɔ	Boys leave enclosures to live in the commons. Sacrifices made. Fathers feast title elders of the compound.
	ɛkɛ	Boys put on oke aba costume with net mask.
	orie	Dry Season Festival. Boys dress again in oke aba costume; boys watch njenji parade.
	ahɔ	Beginning of the second phase of the *isubu* initiation. Boys change clothes; each boy breaks a calabash food dish before his mother; boys play with masqueraders. Fathers feast agnates and friends.

TABLE 2 continued

Time Period	Day of Igbo Four-Day Week	Event(s)
Two- to three-week period		No particular events or activities.
	ɛkɛ	Last day of *isubu* initiation. Boys perform *logholo* masquerade and visit the Afikpo market.
	orie	
	ahɔ	Boys' hair is shaved off.
Four- or five-month period		No particular events or activities.
June		Boys are considered initiates; they may eat corn and other vegetables, expose their genitals to women, and have sexual intercourse.

the hair clippings in his left. The helpers lead the boys toward the burial grounds south of the village (*ɔtoto ɛja:* bad-bush), where those who die of certain diseases which make the body swell, as well as twins, and dead babies are placed, considered a place of evil and dangerous spirits. Sometimes the boys and their helpers go only as far as an open area near a stream, *iyi inyime,* where Mgbom adult male players practice for their satiric *ɔkumkpa* masquerade later in the secret society season. Along the way uninitiated boys throw roots at them, of a hard inedible type (*nkase balezi*) that look like coco yams. In turn, the initiands threaten the attackers with their spears. One or several of two hostile types of masqueraders appear, *ɔkpa* and *ɔtero,* played by secret society initiates holding sticks in their hands, who threaten and chase the initiands. We have described these maskers before (see pages 102–3). The helpers try to defend their charges. Again and again during *ɔka* these maskers will come out to bother the boys. The Afikpo told me that these hostile acts on this day are not real fights, only playing, which allows the initiands to show their strength. But they are a form of harassment. Thus at this time the initiands are annoyed by members of the social category below them in status (non-initiates) while still under the control of members of the social category above them (initiates).

At or near the burial grounds the boys throw their spears and head hair into the bush and return to the village to enter directly into the fenced enclosures that they have constructed in back of the compounds. The Afikpo say that the burial ground rite rids the boys of *isiji*, including potential spiritual danger outside of the initiation context, and that this clears the slate for the next initiation. The boys have buried *isiji*. Since the burial grounds are where those who die "unnatural deaths," as Afikpo see these, are placed, the rite removes any evil or contamination that might have accrued to the initiands during their previous initiation. The action suggests the initiands' death as *isiji* figures and their rebirth in a new initiation stage. The absence of head hair and necklace are markers of their new status.

In the fenced enclosure the boys remove their loincloths with the charms on them. Their helpers take these back to the initiands' compound dwelling places; the boys are free to wear them after initiation. They dress in a raffia waist costume, *ukpu ekwo* (weave-raffia), dyed red with camwood, which they have made in the previous period; their helpers bring these to the enclosure (see Figure 2a). This has a new *ɛkikɛ* protective charm on it, procured by the father from the Rain Controller in Mgbom, or from a diviner in other villages. The raffia piece looks something like an athletic supporter, with a woven section horizontally crossing the lower stomach and attached at the back with raffia string; the genital area is covered with braided raffia that attaches to the waistband at the front and the back. Loose raffia covers the upper front of the legs, but the buttocks are exposed. The boy rubs white chalk over his body and camwood on his head. The costume, chalk, and camwood, worn throughout the ɔka stage, characterize the boys' appearance at this time, as the two previous *isiji* phases each had their own dress. The white chalk suggests a newborn child, also chalked in this manner, the hairless head birth and/or castration. The red camwood signals aggression; in this initiation stage there is a good deal of fighting.

The fence for the sides and back of the enclosure is some six feet high, and there is a rear gate. The front entrance is set back from a roofed oversection running the entire front. The roof is prepared

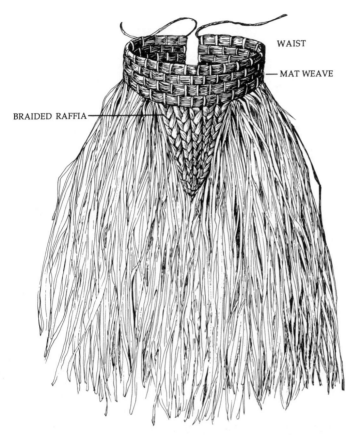

WAIST

MAT WEAVE

BRAIDED RAFFIA

Figure 2a. *Ukpu ekwe* costume for backyard enclosure

from coconut leaves, not usually employed at Afikpo but satisfactory for a temporary structure. The back walls of this front part are often built up with mud. There are wooden benches under the roofing and in rainy weather the boys stay under this cover. They use beds of softwood when sleeping in the enclosure. If only one or two boys in a compound are doing ɔka, they join with those in a neighboring compound, helping to build its enclosure and living there; it is not worth building this structure, called ɔwɔkɔ, for only a few boys (see Figure 2b).

In the open space in back of the roofed area are clay cooking pots, two for each boy, placed on stone tripods; they cook yams and other foods there. Each initiand also has a new water pot, sent down by the father through a helper, for washing and to wet the reddish cam-

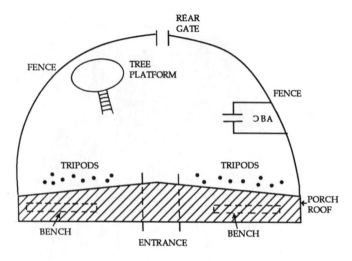

Figure 2b. Ɔwɔkɔ backyard enclosure

wood dye before it is used on the costume and body. Within the enclosure there is a roofless area called ɔba, where the boys store their yams. The boys' ɔba is also a latrine, a bathing spot, and a place of refuge from the ɔkpa and ɔtero masqueraders who come into the enclosure to chase them; these players are forbidden to enter the ɔba. In the enclosure there is a high platform with a ladder, usually built between two trees, which the boys' fathers and helpers assist the initiands in constructing. The boys go there when chased, for the maskers, with their costumes, have a difficult time reaching them there. There is no shrine in the entire enclosure. This area is large enough for the initiands to play in and to dance about. Uninitiated boys visit the enclosure but the initiands are expected not to expose their genitals to them, nor to females, who do not appear there at all, but who may see them elsewhere.

In this period the boys are still fed by their mothers. Both mother and son are subject to the corn taboo and the mother continues to wear the original ɛkikɛ charm put on at the beginning of the first-son initiation, if her son went through that rite; the father obtains one for her if not. At this time the boys are at leisure and do little physical work. They eat well and the Afikpo say that they grow to look "fine" by the time they leave the enclosure at the end of ɔka. They drink no palm wine or other spirits; they are considered too young. They are said to be in the equivalent of the girls' "fattening period" before marriage. They do not use feminine clothing or effeminate behavior, but like girls at this stage they are mostly at leisure and they eat well. The array of cooking pots in the enclosure suggests a feminine atmosphere, resembling the array behind a woman's house and fitting into the "fattening" analogy. The initiands' costume gives them the appearance of being large and fat—unusual for boys, who are normally lean; it is older political "big men" who are sometimes large. At any rate, the boys' dress is not an ancient everyday dress, nor a modern one. It is an awkward costume, a form of harassment of the initiands, who do not feel comfortable in it.

The initiands are still under restrictions. They cannot go into the compounds or commons but stay in the compound backyards. They no longer collect fruit, but they visit back and forth from one enclosure to another. Initiated friends call on them and the initiands can talk freely with them. Visitors bring them fruits and other foods. Friends, relatives, and parents send yams, which they cook and eat. However, the initiands still cannot show their teeth to or talk to or have physical contact with females, who see them as they move about, but who move or run away from them. The boys are unhappy that females view their costumes, which they do not consider appropriate for boys, and because their outer thighs and buttocks are bare. They each carry a broom when they travel about; if they see females or uninitiated boys, they drive them away with it. These objects, made by the boys in the *isiji* initiation, are not used in the enclosures. The boys have a sense of social embarrassment in this liminal period. They are not fully male but not female, not boys and not men. They are conscious of their ambiguity, as expressed in their feelings about their dress.

As in the previous *isiji* compound stage, the boys make hunting nets. But now they are restricted from climbing trees, as are females at all times, so they use only the low-hanging leaves in preparing the fibers. Initiates teach them how to make a fibrous cord from palm leaves, which they roll up into balls; some boys know how to do this already. They give some of this cord to their fathers for everyday use, keeping some for themselves to make into net masks which they will employ in the second stage. Wearing net masks will be a new experience; they do not usually make these in their boys' secret societies. Why give a cord to the father? A manly item links the two; the boys are saying that they can do something men do.

The day that the initiands begin the ɔka stage they bring with them a small wooden xylophone (*akware*), usually one for each enclosure. They have made it themselves or someone in the compound has done this for them during the earlier initiation phase. This is a familiar instrument, for they made and used crude ones in the boys' secret groupings. They play it in the enclosure and dance about, practicing adult secret society dances that they have seen or emulated as members of the boys' societies, such as *akparakpa*, which imitates dancing girls during the satiric masquerade, *ɔkumkpa* (S. Ottenberg 1975: Part 2). In addition, they perform a special dance, *ɔgbubu akware* (dancing-xylophone), that is done in the boys' secret societies but not in the adult one. These activities indicate the boys' ambiguous status; they do some things associated with the adult secret society and others with the boys' societies.

The boys' life in the enclosure is peaceful and relaxed, except that they are subject to continual harassment by *ɔkpa* and *ɔtɛro* masqueraders—sometimes one of each, sometimes more—who go from enclosure to enclosure chasing and bothering them. The harassment is done by young adult secret society initiates who volunteer out of interest. This continues throughout the *ɔka* stage, starting the day the initiands go to the burial grounds (as described above) and then occurring every other day (*ɛkɛ* and *ahɔ*), and sometimes on the nights before.

These masquerade figures have been described elsewhere (see pages 103–4 and S. Ottenberg 1975:179–84), but a few comments here may be helpful. *Ɔkpa* is a full head and body costume brown and gray in color, of looped cord, that fits the body tightly so that only the player's feet and hands are visible. He carries a stick in his right hand. *Ɔtɛro* is a body costume of loosely woven brown dried banana leaves with a net mask. The player's arms and lower legs are usually visible and sometimes charcoaled. He dresses in a red or pink raffia fiber cap, and carries a stick or a stiff broom in one or both hands. Each *ɔtɛro* has a metal bell tied to his waist of a kind associated with *ikpo*, the highest wrestling grade at Afikpo, the bell symbolizing male strength and achievement.

The boys are familiar with these figures, having been chased by them as non-initiates, and they have their own form of these costumes in the boys' secret societies. *Ɔkpa* has a hop-and-skip motion. It is quiet; its player makes no sound; its colors are neutral. But *ɔtɛro* shouts as he moves about and as the bells sounds, and is contrastingly brighter. Unlike most other adult secret society masquerades at Afikpo, both are free to move about the compounds and in back of them. They are probably ancient Cross River area types of costumes associated with Ego, the pre-Igbo peoples at Afikpo, as is this initiation (S. Ottenberg and Knudsen 1985). *Ɔtɛro,* the fiercer form, is sometimes considered the "son" of *ɔkpa,* who is the gentler "mother," but the latter is anything but feminine; *ɔkpa,* if strongly attacked by the initiands calls on his aggressive son to put them down. This is a fantasy of mother-son ties, from the point of view of the son, the hero of the drama, and clearly associated with the initiands, even if they are the ones put down.

The masqueraders chase the initiands both inside and out of their enclosures. They disturb them while they are eating, taking away their food. It is said that younger secret society initiates, if they are hungry, dress up just to get at the initiands' food, which is of high quality at this time. If they catch the boys they flog them with sticks or brooms. The boys retreat to the yam storage shed where they are protected, or to their high platform, but their awkward dress makes it difficult for them to move rapidly. *Ɔkpa* is also not an easy costume to move about in, and this masquerader has trouble reaching the boys on the platform, but *ɔtɛro* usually can get up and catch them. The masqueraders also may go to the mothers of the initiands and demand money, stating that if they do not pay that they will flog their sons. The women acquiesce, giving the coins to a male who makes the payment, for women should not give masked figures anything directly. We have seen this form of conning in the *isiji* rites.

The maskers are a constant nuisance to the initiands, an annoyance that they have to put up with at this stage. People in the compound nearby, including women and children, are well aware of the masked men and the trouble that they cause the initiands. They also play around the compounds, chasing uninitiated boys and frightening girls, who run away and then return to taunt them with song, to encourage them to play some more.

There is little need of formal leadership among the boys in the enclosure, and there are no sacrifices requiring a priest. Yet some boys play a stronger role than others, for example, in the boys' dances, or in fighting off the masqueraders.

Some time during the *ɔka* stage the fathers of the initiands in each compound feast the title holders living there who have put a son through both *isiji* and *isubu.* Yam fufu, fine soup, good meat, and fine palm wine are presented along with a title fee. A diviner (the Rain Controller in Mgbom) is called in for an *egba eja* rite (see pp.

152–53), to determine what sacrifices need to be done to ensure that the remainder of the ɔka stage will be successful. In the compounds of Mgbom this consultation is done on the *orie* day before the Dry Season Festival. This occurs late in the process, and suggests that the main concern is with the ending of ɔka, that this part requires ritual protection. The enclosures themselves are not considered dangerous places for the lads, so there is little need to protect them there. No strong spiritual forces are at work there as in the *isiji* bush.

Towards evening of the *orie* day before the Dry Season Festival men of the compound come to the enclosure and tie up its back gate. The boys can no longer leave, nor are the masqueraders allowed to enter. The men break up the boys' cooking pots, knocking over the stone tripods. They act seriously; they swing sticks, do not talk, and leave quietly when through. The initiands are not surprised; they have sufficient knowledge of the rites to know that this is coming. It is a sign that ɔka is ending. The boys are not permitted to cook any-more, but friends and helpers bring them food by the front gate.

The next day the initiands are shown the secret of the ɔkpa cos-tume, a form which differs from all other Afikpo masquerade figures. The boys have known that it is a costume worn by a human being, but this display reveals how it is worn, which some of them may not have known. An adult secret society member, skilled in this partic-ular masquerade, wears the costume into the enclosure. He does not on this occasion wear the hanging raffia waistpiece that ordinarily conceals the opening through which the player enters the costume. The ɔkpa goes to the covered part of the enclosure where the boys sit on benches, walks around these objects four times (again, the sig-nificant number four!), and moves to the center of this outer section of the enclosure. Near the entrance, he pulls off the top part of the costume, puts it on again, and leaves without a word. The boys' helpers have not told them that this was going to happen, though some of them may have known. The act reveals to them the nature of this costume, which is a masquerade form only rarely used in the boys' societies, and then in crude form.

The revelation is not made for ɔtero, which the boys have had in different forms in their own societies. On the evening of this day a number of ɔtero masqueraders come to the enclosure and destroy it. The boys sleep the night in the open.

In the early afternoon of the next day the initiands come out in a line from the compounds to the commons, assisted by their helpers, bringing their softwood beds and other kit with them. Still wearing their special dress, they bring out two new pots for washing and two for cooking, gifts of their parents. The compounds and commons are closed and females and uninitiated boys remain in their houses and do not look out.

Most compounds in a village own a shrine for the *isubu* initiation, called *omume*, which we have seen is also a name for the *isiji* bush shrine, and in fact appears to be the same main secret society spirit. In Mgbom only Ezi Ume lacks its own shrine, and joins neighboring Ezi Agbo, with which it has close relations (S. Ottenberg 1971:43). These shrines are usually found on the outskirts of the village, but not in the *isiji* bush. In Mgbom some are in back of the special storehouse in Agbogo commons, where we have noted that initiands sometimes stay during the first-son initiation. Others are in a bush area to the east of this commons, Eke Mgbom, not far from the clearing where another initiation form, *isubu eda,* is held (see Chapter 7). Still others are in the ancient abandoned compound, Ezi Ovum, west of Mgbom, now used by the Rain Controller and his agnates for rituals. In some Afikpo villages, such as Ukpa, there is only one shrine; everyone uses it. In Mgbom there is a priest for each shrine, chosen by the men of its compound; the role may automatically fall to the oldest active male. Normally only during the ɔka stage are sacrifices made at it.

At or near the shrine the fathers, with their initiand sons, feast the title members of their compound who have put a son through both *isiji* and *isubu*. The size of this repast varies by compound. In Ezi Akputa, Mgbom, in 1951, each father gave one large dried fish, ten pieces of yam fufu, a pot of very fine palm wine, nine large and twenty small uncooked yams, and one *apa,* a native-made iron winged piece used in sacrifices and formerly used as money. With this feast the father is considered to have finished his initiation payments for a first son and to be a titled man, although the son still has much to do. A father who is not initiating a first son also pays his fees by taking part in this rite. If this is not the first time that a man is putting a son into the *isiji-isubu* initiation he gives fewer of these items, for he is already a title holder.

After food and drink a sacrifice is carried out at the shrine in a rite known as *isubu ehugbo* (*isubu* initiation–Afikpo), or *obubu ehugbo* (initiation-Afikpo). The shrine usually consists of some rocks on the ground at the base of a tree or tree stump, with old sacrificial pots about it. The priest wears a white waistcloth but nothing on top, typical priestly clothing at Afikpo where black is forbidden at most sacrifices and white has positive associations, as we have seen. Each initiand's helper brings out a small sacrificial pot, *nja*, with palm oil in it; this has been obtained by the father. The boys and helpers build a small fire and roast small seed yams, one for each boy. Then the priest prays to the shrine, holding a white cock—one is used for all the initiands—supplied jointly by the fathers. The priest asks the shrine spirit to let them hear its voice. When the cock crows it is said that the spirit is talking; asleep for years, it is now awake. Sometimes the cock does not crow; the sacrifice cannot be done until it does. This may take hours, or perhaps everyone has to return the next day, but the fowl may be tickled to encourage it to speak. The spirit of the shrine, like the *isiji* spirit of the same name, is not believed to have any particular form or shape, but to reside in the pot, and to be in the vicinity of the shrine when awake. The metaphor is again of birth; the cock crows as a sign that the shrine spirit is alive, as a child should cry out shortly after birth. In both cases failure to do so indicates trouble to the Afikpo. After the bird crows, the helper of a first son puts the boy's *nja* pot down at the shrine. The boy takes a bit of roasted yam, dips it in the oil in the pot, touches it to his lips and drops it on the shrine. He does this four times, while kneeling down. Thus spirit and boy symbolically eat together, a positive and peaceful sign. After his sacrifice the boy stands up and his hands are tied above his head by his helpers; he is forbidden to touch the ground with them. The other initiands then perform their sacrifice, one by one.

The boys are led back to the men's rest houses in the commons; there they keep their arms up. The cock crowing part is done only once. The cock is returned to the compound when they all leave and is cooked and eaten by the priest and the compound elders. No part is given to the shrine—an unusual procedure, as normally the feathers, blood, cooked liver, and heart are offered. But here the cock is employed not as a sacrifice but to wake the shrine spirit.

The Afikpo say that initiands should not marry until they have done this sacrifice. Nowadays some males do not do the whole of ɔka, or even the sacrifice, and yet they marry; if the rule was followed in the past it is not today.

After this the fathers perform another sacrifice at their compound entrance, *etɵ abobo ɔnogo* (to put out–native iron spoon–compound entrance). In former times a native iron spoon was placed on the ground during the rite and later removed. Nowadays the winged metal piece, *apa*, mentioned above, is employed for each boy instead and is left there. This sacrifice is done by the senior male of the compound, often the same man who performed the earlier one. For each initiating boy he places an iron piece on the ground with pieces of chalk and kola and issues a general blessing for long life and welfare for him. The sacrifice is a general one to all spirits, as indicated by the former use of the iron spoon. We note that this is the second sacrifice at the compound gate associated with initiation, the first being during the taking of the *ewa anohia* title preceding the first-son initiation (see page 145). In both cases the rite announces a change and protects the boy leaving the compound—in the first case to the *isiji* bush, and in the present case his move from compound to commons for the next stage of the initiation.

In the evening the boys are fed by their helpers with food prepared by their mothers. One hand may be let loose so that they can feed themselves. Their hands are then retied and stay up until morning when they are freed. The symbolism appears to be similar to that in the first-son rites. They cannot touch the ground; their helpers bring mats for them to sleep on to keep them off the dirt floor of the rest house, or they sleep on their softwood beds. Also their food and food dish should not touch the floor. The commons remains closed to non-initiates and females until morning. The front posts of the rest houses are colored with camwood dye by initiates to indicate that the initiands are staying there; this is where they live in the second stage of *isubu*.

Early the next morning (*eke* day) the initiands prepare to masquerade, assisted by their helpers. They continue to wear their bulky raffia costume, and they cover their skin with camwood dye. They wear a costume of dark green palm leaves which covers them from shoulder to knee. The helpers prepare the costume from materials collected by them the previous day; the initiands' hands are now free to help with the costume, though they are still not permitted to touch the ground until the day's masquerade has ended.

The net mask they wear is called *oke aba* (big-*aba* [a secret society term]). It may also be called *aba orie eda* (*aba*, a secret society term; *orie*, a day of the week; *eda*, the Edda Village-Group west of Afikpo), or *aborie* for short, though the latter term is also used for a mask that is used with a different costume (S. Ottenberg 1975:56–57). The face, striped dark brown and gray, has a string at its front which the player holds out as he moves in order to see, either through the mask or downward to the ground. But his face cannot be seen by viewers, and there are no eyes or mouth or other facial features pictured on the mask, as there are on wooden ones. It is made by either the boy or his helpers, or both, on this morning, or the boy has prepared it in the last days of ɔka. In any case the twine used is that which the boys produced while in the second stage of isiji.

The boys dress in the men's village latrine near the commons; there is more room and light there than in the rest houses. This is where members of the adult secret society sometimes dress for their masquerades as well. When they are ready they go to the commons, which are then opened to the public, and uninitiated boys and interested females come out. Adult males sitting in the rest house watch the action. The initiands carry okpete, the stem of a bush about five inches long, in their hands, and there are others tied to their clothing at the waist. The boys limp about pretending that they are very sore and awkward, and the red camwood dye on their limbs suggests that they are bloodied, as at one point in the first-son initiation. Then suddenly one of them throws a stick aggressively at uninitiated boys there, who may be surprised, although some know what is coming. Those attacked throw the sticks back, trying to hit the initiands, who continue throwing at them. An initiand may catch a stick in the air, or more likely he tries to pick it up from the ground with his feet; he is still forbidden to touch the earth with his hands. After the initiands have thrown all their sticks they tire of the contest; they just hop about the commons in their intriguing costumes. The act differentiates the initiands and non-initiates; the aggressive actions between the two groups suggests their social distance. The net mask without facial features has resemblances, in its abstract qualities, to the isiji calabash mask. Both are worn after a sacrifice by the initiands. Neither resembles a human or an animal; the faceless quality of both masks suggests that at this stage of initiation the initiand's role is ambiguous. The boy has contacted the spirit of the shrine and exhibits publicly his new status to uninitiated males and to females, as well as to men, but he is still in transition, as an androgynous secret society spirit, not yet a social person.

In late afternoon the boys line up and walk through the compounds of the village, although they do not always go to those of the three subvillages of Mgbom, some distance away. There is a regular order in which they visit, starting with Ezi Agbo, then other Agbogo ward compounds, then Elogo ward, and finally Amɔzo ward. The order is a rough statement of the history of the founding of the wards. We have already noted that historical factors play a role in the initiations in the question of choosing the two *isiji* initiation priests.

The boys walk, run, and play about in each compound, making *"uh uh uh"* noises, but without singing or musical accompaniment, and they cannot talk to anyone. No one gives them presents at this time. This day is the first time that they have been seen in public since their ɔka enclosure was closed off three days earlier. To females and uninitiated boys they have survived a period of isolation and mysterious activities; their movement through the compounds, even if in masquerade form, is a public announcement that they are well and everyone is happy to see them.

Then they return to the commons, which is closed for the night, and they undress in the latrine. They can now touch the ground. They are brought food by their helpers in the men's houses, and they wash in the commons.

Orie, the next day, they reappear in the same masquerade costume in the open commons, but they do not throw sticks or play about; they just sit in the men's rest houses. Every few minutes one of them stands up, hops about and sits down again, but generally they are at rest. The Afikpo say of a man who is quiet that he acts like an *oke aba,* this masquerade form. On this day in Mgbom there is a public masquerade parade of young adult village secret society members, *njenji* (S. Ottenberg 1975: Chap. 9), and the boys watch this event; the players tour neighboring villages and masqueraders come from other settlements and pass through Mgbom. It is also a rite of status change, of young adults forming a village age set. It is the first day of the Dry Season Festival in Mgbom. Towards evening girls from neighboring villages come and visit female friends in Mgbom, to be feasted, and they often remain the night; Mgbom girls in turn go to other communities when they have their festivals. Later in the evening the commons is closed and the boys wash, eat, and sleep there, but this time with the unmasked *njenji* players, who must remain after a performance.

On this day the initiating son of a man taking the high Afikpo title, *omume,* does not dress in *oke aba,* but wears another masquerade costume, *ikpem aja,* with brass rings on his legs and a wooden mask, *mkpere,* used only at this time (S. Ottenberg 1975:27–31, Fig. 7), which has a human face. He walks around the central Afikpo villages, as do the *njenji* maskers.

The Second Stage

In the morning of the next day, *ahɔ*, the parents send fine cloths to their son in the commons, which is still closed. He puts these around his waist in the manner of loincloths worn by wrestlers, setting aside forever the uncomfortable raffia dress. This act indicates his transition to the second half of the *isubu* initiation; the *ɔka* stage is at an end. Helpers or his father cut V-shapes in the son's newly grown head hair, in front, on the sides near the ears, and in the back down to the nape of the neck; sometimes his eyebrows are nicked here and there. Dry camwood is packed onto his head, and camwood dye rubbed on his lower limbs and upper body. He carries a stick of the type he used in playing two days earlier, only longer, like a cane. Going to his mother's house for the first time since the *isubu* initiation began, he places a calabash of soup on the floor of her doorway, which he stamps on without saying a word, and walks back to the commons. If he started his initiation with the first-son rites this is the second time that he has done this and it follows much the same sequence of events—physical aggression and hardships, followed by contact with a secret society shrine, then masquerading in public. Again, this act is a symbolic rejection of his mother as food giver, and as a sexual object in the oedipal drama.

Later in the day the initiand's helper comes and leads him to a boys' rest house in his compound where the helper brings him a fine meal cooked by his mother. But he still cannot show his teeth to females, so the boys eat alone in the house. Usually a duck or a big fish is provided, with yam fufu and rich soup, but no wine; the father feasts his agnates and friends at his own home to thank them for their help and to express pleasure that his son's initiation is progressing.

Now the boys return to the closed commons, and a number of chasing *ɔkpa* masqueraders appear and dance around. Some initiands are apprehensive—they have seen enough of *ɔkpa* in the enclosure stage—but while the masqueraders move about they do not aggress. Then a variant form shows up, usually only one, called *oke ekpa* (big-bag) or *ɔkpa orɔwɔrɔ* (*ɔkpa*–flowing about). In Mgbom it is seen only on this day. It has a looped string costume like *ɔkpa*, of like color and with raffia hangings on it, but it is much looser, and has no covering for the head, arms, and lower legs. The player (any interested society member) wears a wooden mask with human features, of a type called *ibibio* (S. Ottenberg 1975:22–24). The mask, and probably the whole costume, comes from the Ibibio people south of Afikpo, if not from the Cross River area to the east (Ottenberg and Knudsen 1985). In Mgbom the initiands present ɔkpa and oke ekpa with small gifts of yams and money, as if to placate them. As each in turn does this the masqueraders grab the boy and wrestle with him a bit; sometimes they force the initiand down a couple of times. The lad scarcely resists, for this is light play compared to the previous aggressive actions of the chasing masqueraders. The gentle, pleasant, encounter suggests that since the boys have done their recent sacrifice and have masqueraded, they are now on the initiated side of their rites and soon will don like costumes themselves and chase after others.

Masqueraders and boys then move through the compounds of Mgbom in the order that the initiands did two days earlier. The ɔkpa lead; the initiands remain behind oke ekpa, who hollers the secret society sounds as made in the first-son rites. The ɔkpa talk to women in the compounds, especially to the boys' mothers, telling them how fresh and fine the lads look and that anything the women care to give the boys will be welcome. The initiands are silent; they are still under their speech taboo. The mothers usually give generously; so do mothers of children yet to be initiated, who believe that if they do so the society men will look after their sons in the future. Many things are presented—yams, peanuts, money, tobacco—but not corn; the taboo still holds. Then the masqueraders and the boys go out to Mgbom's main commons, Agbogo, where the gifts are placed on mats. The village elders divide them or delegate younger initiated males to do so. While oke ekpa is given the single largest share and the ɔkpa masqueraders each a smaller portion, the bulk of the presents go to the elders. The initiands receive nothing! Again the women have been deceived, or once again they pretend not to know.

For the next two or three Igbo weeks the initiands eat in the boys' houses in the compounds but sleep in the men's rest houses in the commons. They retain their costume, camwood dye, and fine cloth, distinctive of the *isubu* second stage. If their families are poor the boys may have to go out and help at the farms, but generally they are at leisure, making hunting nets and net masks as they sit in the men's rest houses, and they eat well. The restrictions on showing teeth and talking remain.

The end of Mgbom's initiation is on the εκε when the village of Ibi has its Dry Season Festival, two or three weeks after Mgbom's. The day is called *logholo isubu* (for the masquerade form and the initiation form). The initiands masquerade for the last time in the rites, but there are no sacrifices. Two days before, the helpers gather the raffia palm leaves and the day before they prepare the costume and each father separately feasts his helpers to thank them for assisting his son.

The *logholo* costume is one that the boys know, for as non-initiates they played with and tried to throw these secret society masquerade figures. As uninitiated boys they also had their own form of *logholo* to chase even younger boys (see pages 77–78; S. Ottenberg, 1975:184–88). This is a flowing body costume of loose raffia hung from the shoulders to the knees, and a wooden mask of the adult society—any of a variety of masks that are stored in the village men's rest houses in the commons. These have human faces, male or female, rather than being faceless forms. There is also a head decoration of one variety or another. This is the first time the initiands have worn wooden masks of the adult society.

The initiands dress up in masquerade costume early in the morning; they leave the commons as a group shouting "*awa awa awa awa*" over and over again, heading for the Afikpo market, about a mile from Mgbom. Uninitiated boys from any village attack them and try to pull them down, and there is much play, but strong male helpers protect the initiands. The maskers run all around the Afikpo market, which is still quite empty, in a mock announcement to all of Afikpo of the end of their initiation. They return to Mgbom and play around all day in the commons in costume, attacked by non-initiates who, however, are not allowed to go after them while they sit down, as they will do to rest, or when the attacks become overwhelming.

In the evening the masked initiands move about the compounds, dancing a little. Then returning to the commons, which is closed, they change in the latrine where they put on their fine cloths again. They then remain in the commons for the night, as is usual after masking in the adult secret societies at Afikpo.

The commons is opened the next morning and they are free of most restrictions. However, their head hair must be shaved off the following day by their helpers to indicate their new status (hair is never cut on *orie* or *nkwo*, which are farm days at Afikpo; thus the wait). The boys can now show their teeth and talk to everyone. They sleep in the boys' houses in the compound until they marry and obtain homes of their own. They can visit, eat, and sleep in the men's rest houses in the commons as they wish. They are secret society initiates, able to take part in village masquerades during the remainder of the secret society season. However, in Mgbom and the other Itim villages they cannot use the special dressing houses (*ajaba*, see Chapter 7) until they have taken yet another form of initiation, *isubu eda*, so they dress for these masquerades in the men's latrine.

Until the new vegetable greens or corn come out on the farms, about June, and the new initiates eat some of these, they are not supposed to expose their genitals to women. They should bathe privately, and not urinate along the roads or paths as men do. If a boy violates one of these rules he is not punished, nor is it believed that harm will come to him from supernatural sources; he is simply thought to be acting foolishly. In effect, the ban on sexual relations extends for some months after initiation, although it is not always followed. Afikpo do not provide any symbolic interpretation of this post-initiation continuation of the sex taboo; they simply say it is only to make it hard for the boys. After the lad has eaten of the new vegetable crop he is expected to sleep with a "loose" stranger woman, what the Afikpo call in English a "harlot," so that he will know that he is a man, and so that if there is any contamination within him from the initiation rites he will get rid of it by passing it on to her. The anthropologist might also observe that in a society which does not encourage sex with unmarried girls or married women, for a male in such a status the only kind of female readily available is such a one, other than some divorced women.

But some new initiates do not do this and nothing is done to them. Nowadays boys do not often follow this sexual restriction; nobody seems to bother about it. After the initiation they go to the market and buy green tomatoes or vegetables and eat them and they are free; they don't wait for their family's crops to grow.

Commentary

During the *ɔka* stage of the *isubu* initiation there are opposing modes of aggression and leisure. Older initiated males aggress against the initiands through the attacks of the maskers. In the earlier initiation the secret society members have not so directly aggressed against the boys, except perhaps in the excitement of the first days in the *isiji* bush, and in mock actions. But in *ɔka* there are repeated masquerade attacks where the boys are whipped, their food taken from them, and they are disturbed in sleep and in other activities. Personal retaliation cannot later be taken against the attackers, who may be unknown, and in any case are expected to be treated as spirits and not as humans; they stand for the power of the secret society and its fathers, for the influence of the older and more authoritarian males. It is not the last time in their lives that the boys will be reminded of these males in the village, although it is the last time during their initiation.

Nevertheless, during the rites the initiands' role alters; they join those who have been putting them down, as is evident when we examine what happens to them after the *omume* sacrifice at the end of *ɔka*. At that time they act as initiates, being required to wear the *oke aba* net masked costume and then the *logholo* dress, and to play out the associated aggressive roles against non-initiates. With the latter costume they wear masks of wood for the first time, a sign of membership in the adult society. At the next *ɔka* initiation they are likely to be among the aggressive maskers who harass the initiands in the enclosures. For some this is a just revenge for the sufferings that they felt when they were initiated, but for others it is mere playfulness.

Camwood red is associated with this aggressive mode, where it symbolizes assertion—of initiands toward non-initiates and of initiates toward initiands. There is red not only in the raffia costume and on the boys' in the *ɔka* parade, but on the posts of the rest houses in the second *isubu* stage. There is also the camwood on the initiands' bodies during the *oke aba* masquerade, and on the head, body, and limbs in the earlier part of this second stage of the *isubu* initiation. The several uses of this color all express the idea of fighting and male assertiveness.

Opposing the aggressive theme is the idea that while *ɔka* is a period of harassment of the initiands, it is also one of leisure, play, and a time of good eating, a period of peace, symbolized by the white chalk body markings at the start of this stage. While Afikpo men consider *ɔka* to be the male equivalent of the female fattening period, which is a most leisurely period for girls, an outside observer might also note that the boys look fat and awkward, but eat very well, as infants do; here again is the theme of initiation as a metaphoric return to birth and infancy.

The leisurely life really gets under way in the second stage of *isiji,* when the boys are free of their masquerading duties and live in the compounds, wearing more comfortable dress. But it is in ɔka that the contrasting modes of leisure and aggression occur. These alternations reflect adult male behavior. While women work fairly steadily, men at Afikpo have periods of relaxation alternating with other times of assertiveness, entrepreneurship, conflict, and dispute.

There is another contrast in ɔka. While the initiands feel ashamed of themselves in their bulky dress with the difficulty of movement, there is also a strong sense of competence. They help build their enclosures, make their raffia costumes, produce cord and make net masks, and prepare hunting nets. Shame is matched with confidence. Since the awkwardness can be symbolically associated with babyhood, one message of this stage may be that boys learn to feel ashamed of infancy; they are being directed toward a skillful manhood. Their capability can be contrasted with the aggressiveness of older males towards them; they are put down physically yet their skills in preparing things are recognized; e.g., the father willingly accepts and uses the cord that his son has made for him. Thus we have sets of interrelated and opposing modes in the rites: aggressiveness/peacefulness, competence/shame, and manhood/infancy. The first term of each pair represents desired male qualities.

A simple interpretation of the *omume* sacrifice in the *isubu* initiation as a symbolic act of sexual intercourse is not possible, as it is in the *isiji* initiation sacrifice in the bush, nor is a view of this act as a symbolic return to the womb, only to be reborn again; the signification of the *isubu* sacrifice does not seem as rich as that in the earlier initiation. But some comments are possible. The cock responds to the spirit which resides in the *isubu* shrine pot, associating the maleness of the bird with the female quality of the pots (in their shape and use, and the fact that pots are made by females). This in turn awakens the spirit of the shrine, allowing the sacrifice to be held, and the boys to finish their rites, that is, to mature. The cock and pots together may represent parental intercourse which allows the boy to be born.

Phallic symbolism is also often present in *isubu.* The boy, at the beginning of ɔka is given a bamboo spear by his father; symbolically he is given his sex and his assertiveness, as the father putting him through the initiation symbolically gives him his maleness. There is the broom in the ɔka stage to chase away females, the *okpete* sticks in the *oke aba* masquerade, and the longer sticks as canes at the beginning of the second *isubu* stage. These phallic objects are used assertively by the initiands, especially against inferiors as the Afikpo define them (non-initiates, females). While the sexual symbolism of *isubu* differs from that of the *isiji* initiation, it is present, as we might expect.

The *isubu* feasting differs from the earlier *isiji* initiation; there is little formal eating in *isubu* except for the feast for the title members at the time of the sacrifice by the initiands' fathers, and another feast for them at the earlier divination rite. The father's energies are no longer as concentrated on the initiation, although the son's are. This initiation is more ordinary for the father than the first-son rite; it is not so much of a title for him. The burden is rather on the son's activities, unlike *isiji* where it is more equally spread between father and son. For the boy going through both the *isiji* and the *isubu* initiations the change of the father's role symbolizes the growing autonomy of the boy.

Comparisons

Despite the distinct historical origins of the *isiji* and *isubu* initiations, there are some strong similarities of sequence, action, and symbolism. These suggest that the Afikpo have synthesized both rites around common values and beliefs. Features of the *isubu* rite that carry over from *isiji* include the role of the initiand's mother as food provider, the presence of helpers as protective guides representing the father, and the conning of mothers in the extraction of gifts from them. Also, many of the same symbolic elements appear, including camwood and white chalk. Other features of both include the nature of the relationship of father and son and the presence of sexual symbolism. There is continuity between the *isiji* and *isubu* initiations. While there are differences, there is not a radical change from one to another. I will concentrate on a few common elements of both initiations.

Common organization characterizes the *isiji* and *isubu* initiations, which provides a sense of unity. There are a total of four stages, two in each initiation, and many activities are divided by four-day periods. The number four, as we have seen, associates with the four days of the week and with general Afikpo concepts of the whole. Each stage ideally lasts one Igbo month of twenty-eight days, but all except the very first vary in actual time. This is typical of Afikpo, using the four-day week and the seven-week month as time frames, while modifying the length of time for pragmatic reasons.

Each stage is identified by name, dress, body and head decoration of the initiands, and place of residence. Appearance is diacritical, indicating to others the phase of the initiation, thus how to act toward the initiands and how the initiands should act toward others. One can easily tell what stage a boy is in by looking at him, or by observing where he eats and sleeps.

There are important patterned sequences to the rites. In some villages (but not Mgbom) the initiands' hair is cut at the beginning of the *isiji* rite. At the start of the second stage of *isiji* the hair, which has grown back, is cut in a particular style. At the beginning of the first stage of *isubu* it is cut in certain designs, while at the end of *isubu* it is completely eliminated. These acts occur at key transitions in the initiation, clearly marking them. Hair cutting has multiple referents. The completely shaved head suggests birth, as the head of a newborn child; its growth during the twenty-eight days before it is cut again corresponds to maturation in the bush, the gaining of experience. This is consistent with other features that indicate that the initiation is a replaying of the birth scene and coming out. And if we accept the views of Berg (1951) and Leach (1958, 1973), the head is also symbolic of the penis and hair is rich in meanings according to the manner in which it is treated. Thus the shaved head not only suggests birth but also castration, or at least circumcision (Berg 1951:9–20). Putting the hair that has been cut in the "bad bush" burial grounds in the beginning of the *isubu* rites suggests that the boy's sexuality is undesired, as the hair appears contaminated and has to be disposed of. To quote Leach, "Again and again we meet with the coding convention that the 'cutting of the hair' of the head signifies the imposition of sexual restraints" (1973:228). The cutting may symbolize control of the boys' more general aggressive tendencies associated with the libido by older males (Berg 1951:90). Certainly the whole tone of the initiation is in this direction, with the lack of direct sexual references in the bush, the isolation of the initiands from females, and the holding of the hands over the head.

Through the father's feasting of title members and of other males, as well as the feeding of the spirits through sacrifice, he gains permission to enter his son in the bush. The feasts generalize the father's authority over the boy to other village males, some of whom will go to the bush to help out. Thus the father gives permission for his son to be symbolically castrated and sexually restrained while in the bush, but also to be sexually freed following initiation. The mother, by her continual feeding of the boy, with a big feast before he enters the bush, and good food while in it, acquiesces in these actions. The initiands also present food they have gathered to their parents. These food presentations by both parents and the boys indicate that feeding is very important.*

In both the *isiji* and the *isubu* initiations there is a similar sequence of events. This commences with the father's initial feasts. Then the son goes to live in a special place away from his usual abode, where he is threatened with physical punishment. Then in both cases the initiand has contact with the secret society spirit, in one case in the *isiji* bush and in the other in the *ɔka* stage. Both spirits are projections of the father and his authority, and also of the adult males in the community. Both of these shrines also have feminine and sexual aspects, and represent the mother's womb, out of which the child is symbolically reborn, as a man. After the sacrifice, in both initiation forms, the initiand emerges in public to masquerade. He is now a spirit of the bush, linked to the major bush spirits of each initiation form. The masquerade indicates that the boy has the spiritual forces of the bush and its secret society within him. But he is not yet fully a man; his status is ambiguous. He wears a mask without clear features, it is impossible to tell his sex. In the *isiji* masquerade his mask and headdress embody features of both sexes. He remains in a liminal state until he leaves the initiation.

After masquerading, the initiand in both initiations breaks a calabash with his foot in front of his mother's home, marking the separation from her womb or vagina, and symbolically becoming

---

*Henderson and Henderson, commenting on another Igbo group, state that "Onitsha culture is pervaded by the symbolism of food-giving and eating" (1966:11). LeVine (1973:133) stresses "the emphasis on material transactions in interpersonal relations" for agricultural peoples living south of the Sahara in Africa. Uka (1966:64) suggests that the importance of eating among the Igbo is linked to the oral gratification of the long nursing period, a point I am inclined to agree with.

free from her as a feeding mother and as a sexual being. The two initiations each bring the boy under his father's authority, and by extension under the adult village males, while rejecting dependency on the mother and any covert sexual interest in her. In one initiation he again wears a mask, this time with human features; in the other he does not. In both cases, after a while the initiation simply ends, without any dramatic ritual.

There is a logic to this sequence of events, with their interrelated meanings and the underlying flow of affairs, which has its own rationale and provides a unity of the two initiations taken together. First sons and some other boys, if they complete both initiations, receive many of the same symbolic messages twice. Other boys do so once. The sense of proper order to the initiation replicates the sense of proper order with which the infant and young boy is involved in the rituals and events of his earlier life, as I have already indicated. The idea of proper order is important in both cases. There is order and structure governing the life of an initiand during the rites, although he personally experiences uncertainty and the specific events of the initiation, such as the harassment of the masqueraders, may appear chaotic and disturbing to him. The basic and significant order, however, is present, and has endured even in the course of increasing variation in initiation procedures as a consequence of recent social changes (see Appendixes 1 and 2).

Although the shrines for the two initiations are of distinct historical origin, neither is considered superior to the other. Both represent supernatural forces that have no specific shape or form, whose power goes beyond the sites where they are located. Each can contaminate non-initiates of both sexes. The *isiji* shrine represents male adult power at the village level, while the *isubu* shrine is associated with the compound and the patrilineal aspect of adult male life; the first symbolizes the father in the village, the second in the compound. Most village sons sacrifice to the second in initiation, while first and surrogate first sons sacrifice at both. Either rite gives the boys entrée into the village secret society; both connect the boys with their fathers and with male sexuality. It is not surprising, therefore, that for the Afikpo the two sacrifices and subsequent masquerades form the peak periods of interest in the initiations. For the initiands they are times of intense excitement and sometimes of fear and anxiety. It is unlikely that the boys will ever sacrifice at either shrine again, after the initiation, though they will direct the sacrifice of others at them at later initiations. The spirit of each shrine is forever incorporated in the boy at first exposure. In this they differ from other Afikpo spirits, such as the ancestors, who are sacrificed to over a lifetime. In this sense the function of these initiation sacrifices is to move the boys from one social (and psychological) stage to another. Once done, there is no need for further sacrifices.

Each sacrifice is associated with absolute secrecy from females and uninitiated boys. If there is any aspect of the rites that they—especially females—are likely to know least about, it is their details. Even Western-educated Afikpo men are reluctant to discuss these matters with educated Afikpo women. Similar distinctive roles for the sexes occur in both initiations as well as restrictions on female behavior and observation of the events; both initiations represent, in obvious terms, the marked gender separation at Afikpo. Thus secrecy is linked to gender.

The sexual taboo on the boys during both the *isiji* and *isubu* initiations is consistent with other Afikpo rituals. Priests and other religious persons often refrain from sexual relations the night before important sacrifices or rites. Masqueraders do likewise, and at night after the play they remain in the commons, which is closed to females. No events of the secret society are directly associated with sexuality; females are kept separate although they may sacrifice at one of the secret society shrines to atone for violations of its rules. They may watch public performances, and they will be mocked by masqueraders in the satiric masquerade plays, as others are ridiculed. Close association with women is seen as weakening male secret society activities; unconsciously it probably represents a fear of regression to the infant's dependence on the mother, related to the long infant nursing period (Gilmore 1986). Manly things must be emphatically disassociated from the female at Afikpo.

The taboos on sexuality in the initiations are consistent with the sexual taboos of the secret society, and with the relationship of sexuality and secrecy. The corn taboo, which ends some time after the *isubu* initiation, and following which the boy is expected to have intercourse, represents the sexual restrictions at initiation. It is my interpretation—and not that of the Afikpo—that the corn cob stands for the penis, the kernels for sperm. They are symbolically denied the boy while in the bush. The corn taboo applies to both mother and son, symbolizing the link between them through childhood affective ties and latent sexual feeling. It is the Afikpo women who grow corn, as well as vegetables. Although rarely doing so immediately, the child is free to marry after initiation; he has broken his motherly tie. At the end of the whole initiation he eats corn or greens; he takes them in, and he has a new status, as a sexual adult male.

Two powerful but paradoxically contradictory messages concerning sex appear in the initiation: sexual restraint and sexual awakening. The latter symbolically occurs in the *isiji* bush rites, where the shrine and surroundings have been interpreted as representing the vagina and uterus, which are penetrated by the initiands. This scene clearly suggests the symbolic approval of awakening sexual feelings in the boy by older males, and by extension the fathers, who "own" the bush and conduct the initiation. But the taboos on sexual intercourse while in the bush, the concealing of the genitals from outsiders, the holding of the hands tied over the head away from the genitals, and (by metaphoric extension) the sex-related taboos associated with corn and the teeth, as well as the cutting of head hair, all suggest a denial of sexuality in the context of control by older males.

There is reality to both messages. The initiands, as young men, discover that sexual activity with females does not come easy. Older males, the very males who "own" the bush, have most of the sexual partners, for girls marry older men at adolescence in arranged unions, often also set by older males. Young males thus have to carry out secret liaisons with unmarried girls or with married women, both frowned upon by the community—thus again linking secrecy and sexuality—or they have sex with unattached women who, if considered "loose," may be despised by other Afikpo. The initiation encourages sexual activity while in reality Afikpo society makes it difficult for the new initiands, until they marry in their late twenties or early thirties. These are conflicting signals.

A characteristic feature of these initiations is their restriction on aggressiveness, though there is some channeling of it. As uninitiated boys they have been relatively free of controls and able to actively fight and chase one another. Some have made explorations in the sexual arena. They have talked and argued a lot. But in the initiation the boys are aggressed against; they can respond but only occasionally do they initiate action, nor do they often fight much among themselves; this is frowned upon by others. In the initiations they learn a new, noncombative form of peer-group behavior which will last them their lives. They are restricted not only sexually and vocally but also physically. There are, however, approved and controlled outlets for them: the masquerade plays, the competition over the throwing of the sticks in the *isiji* bush, the construction of the ɔka enclosure in the backyard, the dancing and playing in these structures and the warding off of masquerade figures there, the preparation of fiber and then of net masks and hunting nets, the collection of fruits, and some hunting. Aggression is both denied and permitted under controlled conditions, suggesting that the boys will have to be careful about the direction of their aggression as adults. The restraining quality of the initiation breaks with the pattern of their earlier freedom, placing them within the adult authority structure of their village and compound, within which they will remain all their lives.

So life is made difficult for the initiands. Their hands are tied up, they cannot show their teeth, they are chased by masqueraders, and they wear awkward and strange dress. Adult Afikpo males believe that harassing the boys is important for two reasons. First, it differentiates the initiation from other rites; you simply cannot have a proper initiation without it. Second, they suffered at their own initiations and it is now time for others to be uncomfortable; those who were once put down now put down others. From the anthropological point of view, the suffering can be seen as helping to bring the boys under adult control in the age-hierarchical Afikpo society. The initiation shifts authority over the boys from the peer group to the older men. Certainly, adult controls have always affected the boys in a diffuse manner through parents and older agnates, and peer groups (such as the group of boys who are initiated together, and the age sets they will later join) will continue to be important. But youth in Afikpo is comparatively free and easy, with peer-group controls playing a more significant role than adult authority; after initiation, control by older males becomes the decisive factor.

On the whole there is little differentiation among the initiands; they are dressed alike, they are treated much the same and expected to act similarly, allowances being made for the very small ones. They are forever bonded as a group, and will remember whom they initiated with all their lives. True, boys of the supposed oldest Mgbom compounds have priority to be selected as *isiji* priest, and in *isubu* there is a specific order in which the boys in the masquerade rite enter the compounds. But the major differentiations are between the initiands and the initiated males on the one hand, and the initiands and the non-initiates on the other. The rites stress age differentiation, an important matter at Afikpo. This must make the boys conscious, if they were not before, of their age position and its relationship to authority and control.

Both *isiji* and *isubu* initiations are notable for the absence of direct competition between initiand and father. Whatever tensions exist, their separated roles avoid this. But conflict is symbolically represented in the beating or mock beating of the initiands in the *isiji* bush and through the chasing masqueraders in *isubu*. The aggressors represent the fathers, but tensions are diffused by the absence of the fathers from the bush. The hardship of the boys, the outward denial of sexuality in the bush and of contact with females, indicates that the initiation situation symbolically castrates the boys through their fathers. But again there is a peculiarly diffuse quality involved, since circumcision, the ceremony most directly symbolic of castration, does not occur in the bush at Afikpo, but earlier; the two are usually found together in West African societies. And much of the father-son relationship during the boy's childhood involves avoidance of direct confrontation between the two, through the creation of a social and psychological distance between them.

Some men say that not only the initiand suffers but also his father, especially in the first-son initiation, for the round of feasts to his agnates, village age set members, title holders in the village and in the compound, and his friends and the boy's helpers, are very costly and time consuming, even though he is aided by close male and female relatives. He is likely to be poor at the end of the initiation and under obligation to persons who have helped him. And there is a kind of harassment of the father by the feasting groups, especially of those who have already initiated first sons, in their demands for more wine and food and their complaints over the quality of the meals. The title members set the amounts of food that they wish; for other feasting groups in the initiations the father does so, but this does not preclude demands. Pressure to provide more food is common at other Afikpo eating rites, but here one has the impression that the father is being initiated as well as the son. Thus the father and son are linked by suffering, albeit of different kinds, and also united in achievement, the one moving to manhood and the other moving up the Afikpo title and status system. This link between the two joins them, especially in the context of the agnatic ties in the world of their compound, where they will continue to live their lives together.

The initiation expresses the solidarity of mature and maturing males as against boys and females. The rites act to bring together males of many ages who at other times may be in conflict and hostile to one another (Gluckman 1962), under conditions in which these tensions are kept under control. Young (1965:41) emphasizes this solidarity aspect of initiations and sees it as reflecting more general social solidarity. The introduction of new boys into the adult secret society potentially causes disruption, which the men handle through its rites. The unity of the village at Afikpo as against the outside world is proclaimed in the initiation. The kind of initiation rites found at Afikpo are characteristic of middle-range societies of many cultures (Murphy 1959:96–97; Schlegel and Barry 1980), where the division of labor is mainly based on sex and age, and where the population is large enough for considerable economic cooperation. Secret societies of the Afikpo kind are rare in societies that are more simple organizationally, or in more complex and centralized ones.

How natural and gradual is the evolution of the boy, from his earliest rites of infancy, through the bird-killing rite, the boys' secret societies, the *nwa ulo* relationships, to the initiation itself! In all there is simple and direct symbolism, in the use of the basic colors to the feeding of shrine spirits with kola, wine, and yam, in the separation of the sexes and the emphasis on male skill and assertiveness. There are deeper, more complex symbolic statements as well. In the initiations, the child sees or employs many of the basic symbolic elements of his culture. There is a gradual building up, as the boy matures, of knowledge of sacrifice, the making of dress, masks, and musical instruments, and the use of these.

The child, however, does not learn a great deal about myth and cultural origins as he grows. The secret society of the village, like Afikpo life in general, is not concerned so much with the past and with origins as it is with present and future. Growing up is not a matter of directly learning elaborate conceptions of the world and its past, but is rather growth in experience through doing, making, and performing, in and out of ritual contexts, in developing conceptions of the world through activity.

I turn now to the explicitly artistic aspects of the two initiations. If aesthetics is understood to concern the appreciation of form (Maquet 1979), it can in theory be distinguished from symbolism, though the separation is not always clear in reality. Afikpo initiations are rich in both symbolism and form; it would be hard to say what is not aesthetic in these rites. I have just discussed the common features of sequential form in the two initiations; there is also repetition of elements of color. But what is striking about the rites is the heavy visual element in the initiations, focusing on the human body. This is evident in the emphasis on the dress and appearance of the initiands at different times, the importance of masquerading in the rites, and the obvious enjoyment that viewers have in seeing the masked events. The aesthetic emphasis is mainly on the decorated body of the initiand, the subject of the initiation. There is little attempt to decorate structures; the dressing sheds have simply decorated boards, the *isiji* fence and tower a certain symmetry and elegance, and the men's rest houses in the commons a visual grace, but the shrines are simple and unelaborated with carvings or design. And the decorated body does not stress animality; the masks are not animal forms, they are human faces or faceless human figures in spirit form.

Sound is of less importance, except for signaling (the village gong, the secret society yell, the groans of the boy looking for the *isiji* shrine). The teeth and speech taboos in some initiation rites inhibit the flow of talk; singing and the use of the voice do not loom large. There are no rehearsed speeches, no skillful dialogues by fathers or sons, though on other occasions Afikpo are richly verbal. The initiations focus rather on the appearance and movement skills of the initiands, in and out of the masquerades. It may seem strange that a culture which puts considerable emphasis on men speaking well, with wit, metaphor, and sarcasm, emphasizes speech so little in the initiations. Nor is music a major aesthetic of these rites. There is some singing, but virtually no instrument playing. Thus much of the associated symbolism of the rites is based on visual forms rather than verbal and other sound features. It is a visible initiation, rather than a verbal or a musical one. Verbal skills for males come slowly at Afikpo, often not developing until a man is in his thirties or forties.

As skilled speech among infants comes after visual cues and nonverbal communication, so does it come here only after initiation, again a suggestion that the rites involve a symbolic return to infancy and birth. The nonverbal quality of the masquerades suggests the nonverbal aspects of infant behavior (S. Ottenberg 1982a). But the tactile sense is not emphasized in the initiations, though it is important in infancy. Why, I am not certain. Devereux (1971:214–15) suggests that it is too archaic a sense, so that touch—like certain other senses—is not suitable "for the *sublimated* expression and communication of basic impulses" (italics his). It is certainly not stressed in other aesthetic activities at Afikpo.

Taste is another aesthetic involved in the initiations. The boys eat well in the bush, largely food cooked by their mothers, and their fathers carry out feasts at home. We have seen the importance of eating in the initiation, and its status ramifications. A mother who prepares little or poor food for her initiand son is looked down upon and mocked. A father who neglects his feasting obligations to various groups may have trouble initiating his son. The idea of nourishment in the bush—for the initiands, the "owners" of the bush, and the helpers—is a key one. This again echoes the infant-mother tie, no matter what other social and cultural symbolism it may convey (some of which we have also explored). Taste and sight are key aesthetic aspects of the initiations, and both have links to early childhood.

Humor too is an important aspect of the aesthetics of the rites. True, the initiations are serious enough, with important and meaningful symbolism, necessary activities in the transition from boyhood to manhood. But there is also humor involved. Much of it is of the kidding or conning variety and is not reciprocal, such as extracting presents from mothers to protect their initiand sons going into the bush, the initiates' kidding of the initiands about the dangers of the bush before the rites, and the demanding of gifts to protect them there. A good deal of the humor is visual, such as the ridiculous appearance of the boys in their bush dress, that worn in ɔka, or the black unsmiling faces in *isiji*. Some of it is in the boys' being chased by older and stronger masqueraders, and their dressing in masquerade form, representing spirits while almost everyone knows who they are. Humor arises in seeing the boys perform in public and sometimes not fully succeeding. It is largely of a derisory nature, stressing status differences between two parties. This is not surprising in a rite which emphasizes status change. The simplicity of this humor, its lack of subtlety and complexity, suggests that its genesis is in early childhood rather than in adulthood.

Thus the three major aspects of the aesthetics of the initiation are visual signs, taste, and humor. These three have associations with infancy and early childhood, supporting the idea that the initiation is a symbolic return to birth and infancy. Myth, music, and tactile elements are played down. This is not to say that the initiands' behavior is infantile—far from it—but it does suggest an unconscious reliance on early developed aesthetic forms.

Young (1965) has emphasized, from a cross-cultural sociological viewpoint, that initiations are dramatizations. They are staged publicly like theater, to announce something. They require an audience; they have little meaning without one. Young does not follow this up by looking at the initiations from the viewpoint of theater, but the Afikpo rites are good theater, with drama, excitement, movement, and rich aesthetics and symbolism. Their dramatic qualities fit well with the idea (already discussed) that Afikpo initiations do not involve much formal education but rather a curriculum of symbolic and other less conscious meanings—precisely the stuff of theater.

Precourt (1975:231), in a comparative study of initiations and secret societies, has argued that while there is not much formal education in many initiations that there is a "hidden curriculum," comprised of things that are inculcated without the conscious awareness of those involved, such as authority relationships, or even the three stages of initiation as outlined by van Gennep (1960), of separation, transition, and reincorporation. These comments are applicable to the Afikpo case. Indeed, one of the major aims of the Afikpo rites seems to be to touch on largely unconscious themes, such as the separation from the mother and incestuous wishes, the hostility and affection between father and son, the symbolic castration of the son, the identification of the boy with males, and a breaking of his childhood female identification. Formal education in the initiations is minimal, as it is only occasionally desirable to everyday Afikpo life. There really is no "school in the bush"; the specific knowledge that the boys acquire is not extensive. Initiation is rather an experiential activity, with its excitements, uncomfortable aspects, and fears, a moving toward both new freedoms and new controls.

7

The Final
Initiations

T HE TENDENCY TO ADD NEW RITES TO THE AFIKPO INI-
tiations is affirmed by the presence of another initiation
form, found only in the five southernmost Afikpo villages,
including Mgbom. These villages are known collectively as the Itim
villages, and are indicated on Map 2. The presence of this special
initiation form in the Itim villages has implications for the other
Afikpo communities and it is associated with a more centrally structured form of secret society.

Isubu eda (head initiation [of] Edda Village-Group) derives from
and is named for the neighboring Igbo village-group of Edda. The
first Afikpo communities to obtain it, Kpogrikpo and Anhoia, are
the most southerly of the Itim villages, somewhat isolated from the
rest of Afikpo and physically close to Edda. We have already noted
that these two communities also use a special form of first-son
initiation which is derived from Edda (see page 140; S. Ottenberg,
1971:196).

According to Afikpo tradition, Kpogrikpo and Anohia obtained
the new initiation before Europeans first came to Afikpo in 1902,
probably in the nineteenth century. Shortly afterward it was brought
from Edda by Ogbu of Mgbom to his community, with the assistance of agnates and friends. It then spread to Anohia Nkalo Village,
or was obtained directly from Edda; the reports are conflicting.
Later, when Amuro separated from Mgbom, it obtained its own
society from Edda. Those who brought the initiation became the
first priests of its shrine in their village, for it is a form of secret
society with specific roles for ritual leaders.

From the introduction of this society into the Itim communities to
the present day there has been opposition to it from the leaders of
the rest of Afikpo on the grounds that it is unnecessary, that ade-
quate initiation rites already exist. Yet the Itim villages take great

pride in their own special form of secret society and see it and its initiation as enhancing their status in relation to other Afikpo communities. In the context of a high degree of village autonomy and some intervillage rivalry at Afikpo it is understandable that these Itim communities wish to maintain their own initiation and secret society. In recent years it has become popular for individuals from other Afikpo communities to take this newest form of initiation in an Itim village, thus joining a secret society there. Their presence illustrates the ease with which Afikpo absorb new rites and organizations, leading to greater social complexity. Afikpo is a cumulative culture.

The initiation, which is associated with a more structured form of village secret society than we have seen, is also called *erosi eda* (spirit [of] Edda Village-Group), which is the name for the society's main spirit. A priest, an assistant priest, and a number of male assistants form a special ritual group in each village; in Mgbom they come particularly from Ezi Ume compound and its patrilineage. There is a sacred bush initiation area a little distance from the village, which is distinct from other initiation sites; in Mgbom this is called *ɔhia ogbuji* (*ɔhia,* bush; *ogbuji,* the name of the man who brought this initiation to the community). There is a priests' shrine house, *obu erosi* (house-spirit) at the edge of one of the village commons; in Mgbom it is at the southeast corner of Agbogo common (see Map 3). In former times earth was not used in its walls but it is today, as it is for other houses at Afikpo. Persons who have been initiated into this form of secret society use a special dressing place, *ajaba*—normally one is found in each ward and subvillage—in connection with masquerades; those initiated in other ways dress in the latrines, for they are forbidden to enter the *ajaba.*

The initiation is held annually in each of the five Itim villages and all males in these communities take it in their home settlement, no matter what other form of initiation they do or do not go through. If a boy does the *isiji* and *isubu* initiations one after the other, or only the latter, he cannot do this new form in the same year, for they overlap in time. He is expected to take it the following year; there is no punishment if he fails to take it the very next year, but he should not put it off too long. If he delays, agnates and village elders will pressure the father and boy himself. However, he can go from *isiji* to *isubu eda* in a single year, skipping *isubu;* in this case he goes into the compound for the second phase of *isiji* and stays there until the *isubu eda* begins. Nowadays *isubu eda* is seen as a substitute for *isubu,* though not for first sons; other sons in the Itim communities often do only *isubu eda,* and having done it a boy need not do *isubu* unless he or his father desires it.

Modern conditions have helped to make *isubu eda* increasingly popular, for the major parts of the rite last just an afternoon and a night, interfering little with school, work, or other activities. Males from Afikpo from outside of the Itim villages come to these five settlements, especially Mgbom and Amuro, the two most central ones, and even males from Okpoha, an Igbo village-group northwest of Afikpo, come there or go to Edda Village-Group to do this initiation. Some villages allow boys (other than first sons) to take this as their only initiation, on payment of a fee to their village elders, ranging from less than a pound to over ten pounds. Other villages have refused to recognize the legitimacy of the rite and have forbidden their sons to take it, but facing great pressures they have often had to settle for monetary compensation, which may be interpreted as either a fine or a permission fee (see Appendix 3). The pressure comes not only from the boys, who like to do this short initiation, but from the fathers, for whom it is a less expensive and less troublesome affair. In some communities, boys who first take one of the other forms of initiation at home may then take *isubu eda* in addition in an Itim village, out of interest or for the pleasure taken in this brief and exciting rite. In villages outside Itim those who have taken the *isubu eda* erect their own *ajaba* dressing places at home during their own village secret society season; other secret society members of these villages cannot use these structures. But they do not develop their own initiation bush. It is likely, had not European influence intruded, that in time men from these other villages would have gone to Edda Village-Group to obtain their own shrines and establish their own priesthoods and it would have become a universal village initiation and secret society form at Afikpo.

When an Afikpo from a village outside of Itim wishes to initiate a son, or such a boy has pressured his father to do so, the father goes to any man from one of the Itim villages with palm wine, and sometimes food, and asks him to sponsor the boy. This person is likely to be a matrilineal relative of the father, for a man's uterine kin live all over Afikpo. If the father does not know anyone in an Itim village he takes the palm wine to someone who does and asks him to make the contact. In any case an adult male from the Itim village where the boy is to be initiated has to act as his sponsor, as a surrogate father. With the assistance of the males of his compound, he initiates the boy as if he were a member of that residential group, paying the initiation fees, which he later collects from the father. The surrogate receives no special reward for his role other than the wine and food, but the father pays a higher initiation fee than does the father of a true village son. Some men in Itim villages regularly sponsor boys, almost professionally. In 1952, an Mgbom tailor put six boys through *isubu eda*, three sons of his own and two sons and a sister's son of a friend. The man went into the bush to help supervise the six.

The two most centrally located Itim villages of Mgbom and Amuro try to attract as many of these boys as possible; Mgbom seems particularly successful. To do so brings wealth to the village elders, the two priests, and the members of the priests' group, as well as food and wine and prestige to the community. Consequently this form of initiation, which used to involve genuine physical hardships and the possibility of injury and death from machete wounds, is now much milder. Sometime in the 1940s the Mgbom elders ruled that no one should be injured in the initiation bush; already at an earlier time sticks had been substituted for machetes. The earlier, harsher form was realistic training for warfare.

The Itim villages control the resources received through this initiation, for they do not let an outsider who has been initiated in this form sponsor a boy, whether his own or another lad. Only a man born of an Itim village or living in one regularly can do so.

The popularity of this rite at Afikpo is related to the attitudes of boys and young men. Among them there is nowadays a strong feeling that to be a man one must do all forms of secret society initiation. This was not the view in the past, when initiations were longer and more dangerous. Furthermore, mild whipping with sticks by initiates occurs in the initiation bush and more serious whipping the day before the rite in the village commons. Only *isubu eda* initiates can whip; persons who have taken other initiations do not engage in these contests. This is an enjoyable and attractive sport for young Afikpo males, nearly as popular as wrestling. The other forms of secret society initiation do not involve as much physical competition among persons of equal size or age. The activities of the aggressive masqueraders in the ɔka period of the *isubu* initiation are more one-sided and are between persons at different age levels. And, except for the recent very short form of ɔka, discussed in the last chapter, where boys simply sacrifice at the *omume* shrine and do a bit of masquerading, this *isubu eda* is the shortest initiation of all.

The regulations for proper sponsorship are complicated by another rule; if an uninitiated boy gets into the initiation he cannot be turned back but must finish. In about 1947 members of a young age set from the large village of Mkpoghoro showed up in the Mgbom initiation bush as a lark before it was realized that they had no sponsors in the Itim villages. There already existed a great deal of friction between these two communities over other issues. Mgbom men directing the initiation were angry and beat them with sticks, nearly killing some of them. But since they had gone to the bush and thus knew some of its secrets they were allowed to finish; otherwise, it was believed, harm would come to them and to others through the power of an angered secret society spirit.

Such an act does not have to involve outsiders. In the early 1940s a headstrong fatherless boy from Mgbom—not a first son—appeared at the whipping contest in his village commons the day preceding the initiation. At this time only *isubu eda* initiates and those preparing for the initiation are expected to be there. Secret society members who discovered him were very angry. They told him that he should have informed them and paid the fees in food and money. He replied that he had no money; they then threatened to beat him to death when he went to the bush, to which he replied that he would take as much punishment as possible and then run away into the compounds—which, of course, is forbidden. Men of the society argued with him until his father's brother appeared and offered to pay his fees if the boy would leave the commons for the rest of the day while he collected the requisite items. This was possible, since watching the whipping is optional for a boy planning to take the initiation. Still, the boy refused to leave! Finally everyone acquiesced and the uncle acted as his sponsor. When the boy was in the bush the next day the angry initiates threatened to beat him severely but the youth said that he would tell all the secrets of the bush if they did, so they let him through lightly. Individualism in Afikpo males is strong and sometimes difficult to control.

Schoolteachers, government workers, contractors, and other strangers to Afikpo may take this initiation for business purposes, to improve their image, or to express solidarity with a village. One contractor, who lived at the small stranger's community called Number Two, north of Ukpa village, did so in 1959 in Mgbom where he had close friends. Two Igbo palm-wine tappers from Okposi, north-west of Afikpo, who lived in Mgbom most of the time, became members. The first to join sponsored the other; since he was living in the village he could do so. I went through this initiation in 1952; in 1959 I helped to initiate others. Strangers doing the *isubu eda* initiation do not usually take part in the optional masquerading that occurs in the Igbo weeks following the main rite; they just stay for the night.

The reader will not be surprised, by this time, to discover that there are alternate forms of *isubu eda* in the Itim villages; the prin-ciple of choice operates here as elsewhere at Afikpo.

One special initiation form, *ikwum*, is a more elaborate rite than *isubu eda*, occurring at roughly the same time. The initiands of *ikwum* do some activities with boys taking the other initiations, and some extra ones alone as well. In this chapter I will describe both initiation forms in one account. This longer form is sometimes called "the poor man's *isiji*," for if a first son's parents are dead and other agnatic relatives are poor or simply uninterested, the boy will not go through the first-son initiation of *isiji*, but this special *ikwum* form of *isubu eda*. It is also sometimes taken by a true or surrogate first son the same year he does the *isiji*, rather than *isubu* or *isubu eda*. In this case the boy does *isiji* and then in the compound phase of that form goes into *ikwum*. If a father has wealth and wants to sponsor a son in a fancier form of initiation than *isubu eda*, he puts him through *ikwum*. It is a bit more prestigious for both father and son than the regular form. *Ikwum* is usually done only by boys from the Itim villages, and each lad takes it in his own home village. In Mgbom in a given year there are usually some five to ten *ikwum* initiands, in contrast to the fifty or more boys taking *isubu eda*. Once he has done *ikwum* a boy is considered to have taken *isubu eda* as well.

There used to be a still longer form of initiation into the *erosi eda* society called *ekwa nkpu* (tie–high up, or tie-anthill). It was for the sons of priests, but other boys in Ezi Ume compound in Mgbom, where the priests often come from, generally took this initiation, and still other sons from elsewhere in the village could do so as well if their fathers wished. For fathers from Ezi Ume compound this was not a poor man's form of first-son initiation, for the boys still had to do *isiji*, but a preferred initiation due to their close ties with the priests. These boys might become priests themselves, or join the priests' group as assistants, and maximum knowledge and experience with rituals of this form of secret society was desired.

This special initiation form seems to have disappeared. It is quite secret and I could obtain little information on it. The boys usually went through the two phases of the regular *isiji*. While they were in the compound period, living in the boys' houses, they prepared a raffia costume, *nkpu* (high up or anthill), something like that worn in the enclosure stage of *isubu* except that it projected out horizontally at the waist for about two feet and then dropped low, almost to the ground, having a very bulky appearance; this was worn following the compound stage of *isiji*. Boys did not go through the *isubu* or *isubu eda* initiations but had their own rites lasting some three years. Half of each year the initiands used the special dressing place, *ajaba,* where they bathed and ate, and they slept in the men's houses in the commons. When the *ajaba* was destroyed for the nonceremonial part of the year they lived in boys' houses in the compounds. There they wore their costume all the time, did no masquerades, and followed the usual initiation restrictions on talking to non-initiates and to females.

Preliminaries

I will again describe the initiation rites in Mgbom village. *Isubu eda* is inextricably bound up with two other events: the whipping contests that precede the initiation by a day, and the public song and dance festival *ebu mbe,* the Feast of the Tortoise (Chapter 4), that occurs on the second and third days following the sacrificial part of the initiation (see Table 3). The initiation is also closely related to opening up of this form of secret society for the season, so I will describe this as well.

In Mgbom the rite commences on the fourth *aho* day before the Feast of the Tortoise, when the village elders go to the Rain Controller's house in the village and ask him to ensure that there will be good weather during the feast and initiation. They provide him with money—in 1960 it was two shillings—to *onemi rem nkwo* (give-tongue-palm), that is, to bring down the cabbage part of the palm tree. This is an Afikpo expression for trying to stop undesirable things, such as rain.

On the following *aho* day, called *ere ewowo* (weed-grass), young male age sets under the authority of the elders in each of the wards

TABLE 3

Schedule of the *Isubu Eda* Initiation in Mgbom Village

Time Period	Day of Igbo Four-Day Week	Event(s)
December	*aho*	Village elders consult Rain Controller.
	nkwo	
	eke	
	orie	
	aho	Age sets clean up the commons. Priests' group prepares magical paste. Fathers and sponsors begin to bring palm wine and kola to priests' group. Fathers and sponsors begin to feast members of the age set who helped in cleaning up the commons. Men from villages outside of Itim make contact to secure Mgbom sponsors. These activities continue until the actual initiation.
	nkwo	
	eke	
	orie	Secret society shrine is opened. Construction of *ajaba* dressing place begins, and may continue until the initiation begins, or end before then.
	aho	Whipping day. Priests' *ajaba* is established. Meeting of elders, Rain Controller, and priests' group. *Isiji* first-son initiation is performed.
	nkwo	Initiation in the bush. Everyone spends the night in the commons.

TABLE 3 continued

Time Period	Day of Igbo Four-Day Week	Event(s)
	ɛkɛ	In the morning, the final antidote to the effects of the secret society spirit is given to all villagers, and the priests' group feasts. Ɔkpa masqueraders play about. Ikwum initiands remain restricted and helpers cut materials for their costumes. Priests and elders divide the initiation fees. On this day or afterward, isubu eda initiands are expected to have sex with a non-Afikpo woman.
	orie	Feast of the Tortoise. Ikwum dance in ikpem masquerade. Priests' group divides money received from females for sacrifices.
	ahɔ	Tortoise festival continues.
	nkwɔ	
	ɛkɛ	Ikwum and isubu eda initiands dance in costumes with net masks.
Six-week period	Each orie day	Ikwum and isubu eda initiands dance in costumes with net masks.
	orie	Ikwum and isubu eda initiands play logholo with uninitiated boys.
	ahɔ	Both initiations are complete.

and subvillages of Mgbom clear the grass and debris in their commons; they later build the *ajaba* dressing places. In Mgbom Village lads who are not yet initiated clear around their compound entrances to the commons but not in the commons itself. The men of Mgbom know that it is time for the work because it coordinates with certain activities in Libolo Village in Edda Village-Group, the ritual center of this form of secret society, whence Mgbom derived its *erosi eda* spirit shrine and rituals.

On this day the priest, assistant priest, and their helpers prepare a magical paste (*nsi mano*, strong-oil), not specifically for the initiation but for the entire secret society season. It is made from a special leaf, a red root, dried fish, hot pepper, palm oil, and a little water. The helpers gather the materials and assist the priests in its preparation. This special village ritual group, *nde erosi* (people-spirit) directly controls the rites of this form of secret society, including the *isubu eda* and *ikwum* initiations and that for the priests' sons. In Mgbom the group includes not only the two priests and other interested male adults and friends of the priests, but all adult men of the small compound of the priests, Ezu Ume, next to the shrine house. The priests serve a little palm wine and food to their helpers during the preparation of this magical substance. The work is not sacred; the men talk of politics, scandals, land matters, and other affairs. Women can watch the work, which is carried out openly in the compound, usually in the senior priest's home, sometimes in the home of the other priest as well. When the paste is made people taste it, including female relatives of the priests, for it is said to make those who eat it strong and healthy. Sweet and peppery, it is much liked at Afikpo.

Men who wish to become familiar with the priest and his assistant may take this occasion to drop in and visit, to talk, and to taste. I did so in 1952 since I was shortly to be initiated and wished to meet this group, although normally males to be initiated do not so visit. So did my field assistant, Nnachi Enwo, a rising young politician who had been away from home for years, who was an initiate.

In Mgbom only the priest and his assistant direct the preparation of this paste. I several times heard the story that once in the past an Mgbom priest sold the right to prepare it to another village man. This caused an outcry among Mgbom males and the priest fled to Edda Village-Group where he determined to purify himself by re-initiation into the secret society. He died during this rite, thereby confirming the belief that he had acted wrongly and had angered the society's spirit. The story suggests the importance of the priestly group associated with this form of secret society and their adherence to the society's rules. This centralized village ritual group contrasts with the more general leadership for the other forms of initiation and secret societies at Afikpo. Edda Village-Group, whence this particular initiation and society form derives, is more politically centralized than Afikpo, and the suggestion is that the five Itim villages which took on this new initiation form were moving toward greater central authority until modern times stopped this process. They are historically related to Edda Village-Group as well.

Once the magical paste is prepared the priests and helpers generally remain at their shrine house at the edge of the village commons until the initiation. The father or sponsor of a prospective initiand, or the boy's future helper in the bush, brings a pot of palm wine and some kola as a sign that the boy is to be initiated. This can be done until the time of the rite. The priests do not screen the boys; any lad is free to take this form of initiation as long as he is circumcised, and this is assumed and no inquiries made except of strangers to Afikpo. Whoever is at the shrine house at the time drinks the wine with the priests. This presentation is a way of counting the number who will enter the bush; every year that I was at Mgbom there was anxiety among members of the ritual group and the village elders that the figure was falling off, although this was not so. Villagers see the number as a measure of the community's prestige in Afikpo, and they also wish to gain the maximum economic benefit from the rite.

From the time of the preparation of the paste, men from outside of the Itim villages who wish to initiate someone into the *isubu eda* form make contact with persons in the village to act as sponsors. For example, in 1960, three days before the initiation a man from Ibi village brought palm wine to a friend in a compound of Achara subvillage of Mgbom, leading two young Ibi boys who were not his sons whom he wished to have initiated with this friend as sponsor. Other compound men were called in and they all drank together. Then the Ibi man rose and explained why he had come. He was a "trickster," he said, a bold man who had often come to Mgbom, and who had done many things the Mgbom way, and now he had brought these two boys; the compound men should protect them during the initiation. In this case he acted as intermediary between the boys' fathers, who did not know anyone in Mgbom, and the people of this compound. The only senior man present, who happened not to be from the compound but was visiting friends there, told the visitor that he should pay money to provide a pot of wine for the Mgbom priest, and that he should also feast the compound with yam fufu and wine. A man from the compound rose and said that there was no trickery here, that this is the usual procedure and he should do this. Then the senior man threw out the last of the wine from his cup, held in his left hand, onto the floor. It is usually an insult to employ the left hand in this blessing to the ancestors, but it is generally done in this manner in reference to this form of secret society, especially in drinking in the priests' shrine house. The elder went on to say that he keeps his right hand free to kill any animal; this saying suggests that he is the eldest present and is strong, he can do anything that he wants. The two boys looked quite scared and said nothing; the men there joked with them, making mild threats about the initiation. The feasting of the compound by the visitor who brings one or more charges can be delayed until after the initiation if the man is known to the group, which was the case here.

This procedure secures a sponsor for the boys and ensures that the compound members will assist the youths in the rites. This agnatic group adopts the boys for the event and conceives its role to be to assist all of those it is putting through the initiation. Behind this act lies intercompound competition; each of these residential groupings likes to put through a large number of boys, without any failure or trouble.

Three days after the clearing of the commons, on *orie*, the first day of the four-day period which will take us through the initiation proper, the secret society shrine is opened and work commences on building the *ajaba* dressing places, symbols of this form of secret society. Men call these four days *ɔmuma ajaba* (pin–dressing place), referring to the putting up of the sticks of wood to form the outer edge of this structure. The period is also called *ulomba* (house feast) in popular usage by men, women, and children, referring to the fact that women spend a good deal of time at home cooking at this time, when the commons are closed to them.

The *ajaba* structures are rebuilt every year before the rite and partly burned down at the end of the secret society season some months later. Normally there is one for each ward and each subvillage (if such exist), though the members of a small subvillage may use a neighbor's. Usually located at the edge of the commons and facing it, the *ajaba* fenced enclosure (see Figure 3) has vertical walls seven or eight feet high, with an entrance at one side, near the front, and an exit in the rear. The front section is divided into three roofed parts, the walls and roofing being covered with raffia matting and braided palm leaves, in design something like the front of the en-

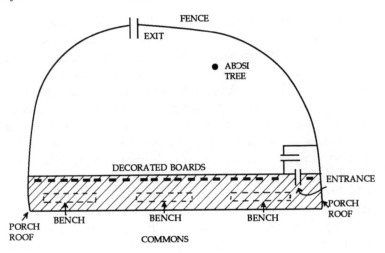

Figure 3. View of *ajaba* dressing house from above

closures in the ɔka stage of the *isubu* initiation. Braided palm leaves are used to form the rest of the structure. There are log benches in the covered front section; here initiates sit and watch society events. In back of the benches, against the wall, are flat vertical boards, some three feet high, which have colored abstract designs on them, called *enwɔrɔ* or *imo*. They are redecorated by those who rebuild the dressing place at this time; when the structure is down they are stored in a house in the village. The Afikpo could not provide me with an interpretation of these boards; they simply said they were decorative.

Somewhere inside the dressing place is an *abɔsi* tree, a small but sacred object. Its leaves are sometimes employed for magical protection at Afikpo. There is generally another one in front of the priests' shrine house. These trees are not burned at the end of the society season; if one dies its stump remains and is maintained.

The dressing houses in the Itim villages are used as places to change for various masquerades. The ɔkpa and ɔtero chasing masqueraders (discussed earlier) do not use them, but dress in the men's houses in the commons. These masquerade figures, probably originally from the non-Igbo Cross River area, are also the only ones who do not have to spend the night in the commons after masquerading. A player may change in an ajaba outside of his own village section, if his own is too crowded or another is more convenient.

These dressing structures are important places of transition in the

Itim villages, for here males change into spirits (*mma*) when dressed in costume, and become human again when through with masquerading. While the priests of the village secret society are nominally in charge of these sheds, they do not enter them; it is believed that if they go into any fenced structure made of palm leaves the spirit of the secret society will kill them. Although the Afikpo offer no other explanation for this taboo, I believe that there is an unconscious one; the belief reinforces the power of the priests in that they cannot be fenced in. Initiates into forms of secret society other than *isubu eda* are forbidden to enter. Uninitiated boys can run by the front of these structures if chased by masqueraders; otherwise they stay clear of them.

The dressing house is built by the same ward age sets who have done the clearing of the commons. In Agbogo ward at Mgbom in 1952, one set was in charge, members of the next two younger sets built the front roofed part, males of the next younger set constructed the back wall of the roofed area, the next set below was responsible for the left half of the side and rear fence (as viewed from the front), and the next lower set the right half. Ward members of this secret society too young to be in sets built the right side entrance. This explicit breakdown of tasks by age is common at Afikpo. The work continues from morning until evening but is not usually finished until the next day, sometimes not until just before the initiation commences.

Also on this *orie* day an adult man of Ezi Ume compound in Mgbom builds a palm frond door at the compound entrance, closing off this residential area from public view. This compound, with its close connections with this form of secret society and its location near the priests' house, is the scene of numerous activities that females and uninitiated boys from elsewhere in the community should not see as they pass by. Those living in the compound see and hear much, but they are believed protected by the power of the society's spirit; it is not thought that harm comes to them from viewing these activities in their compound.

During the morning and afternoon of this day, while the construction of the dressing houses progresses, there is much drinking at the priests' shrine house as boys to be initiated are registered; the lads themselves usually do not appear.

Toward evening, *erosi eda,* also called *egbele,* the shrine spirit of this form of secret society, which is located in the priests' house, is awakened in a major rite, *alota ɔku* (take-fire). Once done this form of secret society is in session and its spirit is active, and it remains so from October or early November until June or July, overlapping with other secret society sessions. *Egbele* is also the name used in Mgbom for the spirit of the boys' secret societies.

The event commences when the priests' helpers, and sometimes the assistant priest, clear the ground in front of the shrine house; then all young and some middle-aged village men who are initiates of this secret society come and sit there. They wear no cloth on the upper part of their body and carry nothing black; shirts are too modern and black is taboo to the society's spirit. Inside the house the priests and their helpers start a fire in the sacred fireplace. Praise singers in the village come and sing of former and present priests. The members of the executive grade of the village, three age sets of young men responsible for communal labor and other village matters (S. Ottenberg 1971: Chap. 4), bring a sacrifice to the priests. In some years this has been a dog, in 1952 it was a white fowl.

The animal is killed by the senior priest and sacrificed at the shrine, with the aid of his assistant; the singers extol the priests and the shrine spirit. The senior priest then calls out the names of all former Mgbom priests of this shrine, in order from first to last, praising them. He then utters certain secret incantations. When he reaches a certain point those sitting outside, who can hear him and who are knowledgeable, know that the spirit of the secret society has appeared. There is a sudden struggle to rush into the house and out the other side; there are always a few strong young men who try to be first, which is an honor. Then everyone goes through the house. It is said that they have touched the fire, though in fact they do not, and thus are associated with the secret society spirit which it symbolizes.

These men then rush from the house to the commons, which has been closed to uninitiated boys and females. The village wooden gong is sounded by some of them. Others shout the typical Afikpo secret society yell, "*hwoh hwoh hwoh*," over and over again, while prancing about, and some of them wave sticks in anticipation of the whipping contests to be held the next day. Men sing old whipping songs and syllables with no known meaning, and they make up new words. In 1952 they came up to me as I was sitting in the commons (a special privilege for a non-initiate) and sang, "If you boast and you fail it is a shame," referring to my forthcoming initiation. Some of the men have a brass bell around their necks, a symbol of power, otherwise worn by senior wrestling grades at Afikpo; this clangs about as they move. The men challenge one another. As Mgbom men say, everyone is very brave at this time for there is little or no actual whipping. After an hour or more all return to the compounds and there is much drinking and merriment.

On hearing the noise other men initiated into this form of society come out of their houses in the compounds and walk through the shrine house. There is no law that they must do this, and if a man is away at the time he is not required to do it later, but it is considered desirable, showing proper respect for the society's spirit and enabling the secret society members to absorb some of its power.

The fire in the priests' house is maintained over the next four days, during which the commons stays closed to females and uninitiated boys. Initiates to the secret society use its special greeting, "*ucay*," rather than the usual forms, especially in the commons and the men's rest houses, there. It is employed throughout the secret society season, though other greetings are not forbidden. When females hear it they are expected not to know its meaning; they generally do but they do not show this. The priest and his assistant remain in the shrine house for these four days, coming out only to relieve themselves, to dance about at the whipping contests, and for the actual initiation.

This rite awakens the secret society spirit, which is said to have been asleep, and it mobilizes the secret society members for the initiation to come. It has analogies to the rite for the *isiji* initiation spirit, with its sacred fire, but in this *isubu eda* initiation the awakening is done before the initiation, not as a part of it. Here we are dealing with a priestly cult and with a shrine spirit which is sacrificed to throughout the secret society season, unlike the case in the other initiations. Now that this spirit is aroused it is possible to proceed with the initiation.

Whipping

The next day, *aho*, whipping contests are held in Mgbom. Older boys and young men view this as one of the exciting events of the year, raising the level of tension for the initiation the next day, a time of spirited aggression. In former years whipping was a form of preparation for warfare, nowadays it is a sport; physical strength and skill are still valued at Afikpo. This is the only time of the year when whipping normally occurs in the village, outside of sporadic contests between uninitiated boys. At Afikpo competitions are generally carried out only by members of the *erosi eda* form of society; thus it occurs mainly in the Itim villages. Persons from elsewhere who have been initiated into the society can come and whip at any of the Itim communities; they usually hold no contests in their own settlements.

Certain activities precede the whipping on this day. Men roast yams to eat in the ward rest houses in the Mgbom commons. If an uninitiated boy has seen or touched anything to do with this form of secret society his father must give yams, perhaps five, to the men there the year the boy is initiated, to "cool the elders." The boy is not punished at the time of the offense, nor does he offer sacrifice. He is merely scolded and chased away. The gift of yams symbolically clears the crimes with the elders so that the boy can be initiated, much as the offense of breaking wind must be cleared before the *isiji* rite commences. Some fathers do this to be on the safe side, even if they do not think their son has committed an offense; this is also a way of showing respect for the elders.

On this *aho* morning the two priests set up their own *ajaba*. Established about the same time as the dressing structures and called by the same name, it can be used by priests because it is not a fenced raffia area. In fact, it is a shrine, although called by the same term as the dressing sheds. In Mgbom this consists of several old pots on some rocks under an *abosi* tree, located outside of the door of the priests' shrine house. A raffia palm branch is placed upright against the tree and tied to it with more raffia. The branch is then plaited with its own leaves to about three quarters of the way up, in the manner done for the dressing shed fencing. During the season the priests sacrifice here to the spirit of the secret society for women's barrenness and other misfortunes; the shrine is a public adjunct to the more private one in the nearby shrine house, where females cannot go.

Also on this morning young initiated boys of each ward recolor the boards for their dressing sheds and place them in the front section of these structures. These sheds should be built by this time, but as we have seen, are not always finished until the next morning.

At Afikpo the whipping contests are called *otiti osi* (whip-stock; *otiosi* in shortened form), a term which covers any sort of whipping. Boys and young members of the *erosi eda* secret society come out for the contests a little after noon. Nonmembers cannot enter the commons at this time, except those who are to be initiated the following day, who now leave their home for good until the rites are over. These initiands sit and watch but do not take part; they will enter the contests next year. They are not attacked by the whippers. The boys to be initiated in the *ikwum* style rub camwood dye on their bodies and wear a camwood colored loincloth called *aji;* the other initiands are in ordinary clothing. Again we see the ritual association of red with aggression in Afikpo initiations.

The contestants range in age from initiated boys to men in their thirties and forties. Older men sit on the benches in the commons or in the men's rest houses and watch and yell out advice. Sometimes the elders challenge one another mockingly (and they did so to me), or jokingly warn the initiands who are watching that they should be careful on the morrow, implying that they will be whipped in the bush. The whippers, dressed as Afikpo wrestlers (see pages 82–87), have white chalk marks down the outside of their arms and the center of their chests. Here I believe that white stands for semen, for male potency. They often wear a loincloth with one end loose at the front and the other at the rear; many wear pants under the cloth, though some wear only pants. Whippers may tie the brass *ikpo* bell at the waist, used by the highest village wrestling grade; they do not have to be members of this group to wear it on this day. The bell clangs as the whipper moves about. Afikpo say that in former times only a strong man wore this bell, for it lead to many challenges, but today anyone who wants to does so. The players also wear a braided and coiled raffia protective headpiece with a raffia chinstrap, *okpu egbese* (cap-hair), though any kind of protective hat can be used; I have seen a German World War I metal helmet so employed. The whipper holds a somewhat flexible whipping stick (*osisi*) about two feet long and half an inch wide in his right hand, made from any kind of tree or bush.

These males run about the commons, strutting, singing songs from warfare days, and challenging one another. Two of them face up and whip at each other's bodies and legs with alternate strikes, each giving three or more blows. Sometimes the contestants become excited and hit many times and not in alternation, flailing at each other. If one breaks off, drops his stick, falls, or grips the other, he is considered the loser, but usually neither does; there is no judgment of the contests except for the comments of onlookers as to who has made the more telling blows. Those with the best form make few but well-placed strikes; to hit lightly many times is poor technique. Cut skin, blood, welts, and bruises are common. It is a test of who can endure pain as well as who can whip strongly. It is bad form to yell out in agony or to grimace or cry. The observing initiands are suitably impressed.

One of the younger adult village age sets voluntarily takes control, trying to regulate the contests by lining up persons of the same size to fight. I have never seen them keep effective order; the situation is much as in wrestling contests. Whippers go off in all directions, challenging as they will, and even members of the controlling sets do so, as there is so much excitement. At times whippers of one village ward move to another ward commons to challenge there, for there is some rivalry between these living units. The village gong sounds intermittently, beaten by any initiate who wishes to do so, calling other initiates to come out of the compounds to fight or watch. In 1952 one young whipper who was prancing around whacked the low roof of a men's rest house in the commons with his stick. He was immediately yelled at and beaten by other whippers, for he had violated a rule of the secret society. He later paid a fine to the elders. These houses are viewed as belonging to them; although any initiate can sit there, to hit the roof is symbolically to hit these men.

Men in the rest houses shout, "Show us how to whip," and while some do so, other contestants decline, saying that they are waiting for Amuro Village later in the day, when the two communities compete. Sometimes members of an age set in a ward collectively give the men sitting at their rest house a shilling or something small as a gift. This is a way of asking the men not to encourage those present to whip one another too much and thus divide themselves; they are thinking of the Amuro contest when they should be united.

A considerable number of at least partially Western-educated Afikpo take part, including teachers, tailors, and government workers. It would be hard to say that all contestants are traditionalists; this is clearly a sport with broad appeal.

Shortly after the whipping starts the two priests come out to the Mgbom commons and dance about, particularly near their shrine, with a running and stopping motion, also used by wrestlers and again by those celebrating the taking of titles. Each priest holds a large white cock in his right hand, wears a traditional white loincloth, has eagle feathers in his hair, and his body is covered with camwood. Feathers and camwood symbolize status and aggression, respectively. They then return to their shrine house, where they perform a sacrifice; the details are unknown to me, although the cocks apparently are not killed until the next day, at the initiation. Some Mgbom men say that the priests come out to raise the spirits of the whippers; this may be so, although they do not seem to need any impetus. Others say that they appear to bless them.

The boys to be initiated watch, sitting on benches and on the ground. Conning occurs as in other initiations. Before they came out they were told by initiated youths and men that today they will see something: "This day you will die!" They are led to believe that they will have to whip without practice and that they will be seriously hit as part of their initiation. Some are frightened until they discover that this does not occur. Others seem to know beforehand that they are not directly involved on this day. In 1956 a boy came out who was not intending to be initiated and was chased away; his father had to give yams to the men in the rest house of his ward at the time of his initiation in a later year, as already described. In 1960 another boy peeped through the fence from the compound, breaking it open. A man in the commons took him to his mother and told him not to do this anymore.

Some whippers drink wine in the compounds before coming out, or they go back to imbibe, and this adds to the boisterous quality of the contests. Men move back and forth between the commons and the compounds, for there is competition in the compounds as well. This is partly to impress the women, who are forbidden to go out to the commons and who are not always certain as to what is happening to their menfolk and to the initiands there. One man explained that if the women see only the marks of the bodies and limbs of their husbands and older sons they will think that they have been defeated in the contests, but if they see them whipping in the compounds they will know that this is not so and that their men can endure great pain. Showing off to females (as well as to other males) is an important part of the event, as it sometimes is at public masquerades. Men drink together, then one challenges the other and they compete.

Mgbom men say that the whipping in the compounds leads women to believe that the initiands are being whipped in the commons; at the end of the day the initiands do not come back but remain in these village centers and women may be anxious about their sons. The deception of females occurs even before whipping, as we have already described for other initiations. Men or initiated boys go to the mother of an initiand, especially if she is considered wealthy, and ask: "What about my kola?" They demand presents to "protect" her son during the contests. In addition, before the event starts, initiated boys speak to the future initiands, asking them for presents from their parents, saying that otherwise they will whip the initiands. The initiands may be scared and run to their fathers for something. This the fathers usually give, as they do not wish to reveal that little will happen; they too are part of the conspiracy. Since normally no initiand is whipped, it looks to the mother as if her gifts—cigarettes, a little food, or some coins—have helped, and she will be pleased.

By midafternoon it is time for the intervillage contest. Mgbom and Amuro alternate village sites each year. The visiting whippers come en masse into the main village commons of their host, followed by older men and elders as spectators, and by the initiands. The visiting players dance and hop about as a group, with the home village gong sounding strongly. Then the contestants from the home community move around in groups by age. After a while the whippers from each village face one another in the main commons, with some space between them; sometimes bamboo poles are placed on the ground to demarcate the areas for the two groups. Men on each side try to determine who should be matched with whom. For Mgbom this is sometimes done by members of a fully established village age set, the set that has already been controlling the event, or a set is appointed by the Mgbom elders. In Amuro it has sometimes been elders themselves and at other times an appointed age set. In either case other interested men assist. These controllers inspect the sticks to make sure that they have no thorns or bad knots on them, and in some years they have made the sticks themselves, since arguments may arise between men of these communities over whether they are properly made or not.

There is an attempt to match up persons of like size and to hold but one contest at a time, in short encounters, starting with the smaller males. But I have never seen or heard of a time when the whippers could be controlled. They soon start to come out and challenge persons from the other side until there are twenty or more contests going on at the same time, with the controllers trying to stop and to organize them, with whippers challenging one another and dancing and shouting. Any controller, or any other man, can run between the whippers and thus stop a contest; some do so because they think that the fighters are unevenly matched or to prevent their favorite from being beaten, and others do so for the sheer delight of breaking up a contest. In the midst of this organized chaos the two priests of the host village again come out with their white cocks and run about to bless the event.

Eventually a few older men come to the center of the commons, pick up dirt from the ground and throw it into the air; this is a sign that all should stop, though contests often continue for some time. Finally, the men of the host village go back to their compounds, inviting friends and relatives from the visiting community to eat and drink with them; other whippers and spectators from the visiting village go home. Though the whipping is aggressive and serious, there is also a great deal of humor and play to it. No village wins or loses. There are no judges to keep score, although individuals have their own impressions, which naturally vary a great deal.

Males from other villages who have been initiated into this form of secret society sometimes come to Mgbom or other Itim villages to whip, for they do not hold contests at home, as we have seen; this would require closing the commons of their villages and making the event an official affair, something their elders would be reluctant to do. For example, in 1952 five youths from the settlement of Ugwuego Elu came to Amuro just at the time that the Amuro-Mgbom contests were breaking up and there were contests involving them.

On this day it is also customary, if a man has an intended bride in another village (especially Amuro if he is from Mgbom, and vice versa), for him to go with friends to visit her and offer her yams. Young men from her compound challenge the husband-to-be there and they whip, considered necessary before the man is allowed to see his intended. The man's friends may whip as well; if there are no challenges the visitors simply whip among themselves in joy. Females are allowed to view these contests, for they are held in the compounds. The qualities of a good husband at Afikpo are said to include boldness and strength; whipping displays these.

Along with eating and drinking, in the evening in the compounds further challenging goes on, with the females remaining quiet. There is much joking, horseplay, and dancing about late into the night. Those who have come out to be initiated remain there; they do not return to the compounds until the day after the initiation. Impressed by the display of physical force, some of them wonder if they will be beaten on the morrow.

Often on this evening the younger male sets in the host village invite their specific counterparts in the other settlement to a feast. This is not required, but the men in their late twenties and thirties enjoy feasting their fellow age mates in the paired village, which they know will be reciprocated at some other time, perhaps the following year. There are usually two or three of these feasts going on this evening, adding to the general merriment; there may be much speech-giving, boasting, and drinking on these occasions. In 1960 the *ogoro* set of Amuro invited *ike agwo* of Mgbom, its equivalent in age. Later, one Mgbom member told me, "On our way to Amuro we were told by them that we were not going to whip in the commons but at their homes in the compound. We never knew what they meant until we got there and they showed us the food and drink and said: 'This is our whip!'" There is a lot of humorous talk and argument on these occasions. It is clear why the activities of the day are so popular with the men.

As the secret society shrine is "awakened" on the previous day, at this time, as a consequence of the whipping, young men of the village are "awakened" into alertness and physical activity, and older men into awareness, feelings, and moods which will carry through to the initiation on the morrow.

Two other events also occur at this time, directly associated with initiation. In the early evening of the whipping day, or sometimes the next morning, the village elders gather in front of the priests' shrine house. The village executive grade supplies wine and food, and a diviner—in Mgbom the Rain Controller—is consulted to ensure the success of the initiation. An *ekike* protective charm (S. Ottenberg 1968b) is made by this man and tied to a tree at the entrance to the path to the initiation bush, near where the men sit. At the start of the initiation a priests' helper will take this object and place it where the senior priest in the bush stands during the initiation. This is to "ensure that the bush is quiet," as one Afikpo said, so that no harm comes to anyone there. The ritual specialist also makes a like charm for each *ikwum* initiand. This is not used in the main initiation but later, when the *ikwum* initiands masquerade, it is tied at the back of each player's waist. And charms are made to place in the shrine house and in each dressing shed to protect people who go there from misfortune. As is usual at Afikpo, the initiation is seen as a time of danger from the powerful spirit of the society, from errant human behavior, or from both.

Then the elders, the diviner, and the priests and their helpers feast.

After this a spokesman from the elders rises, saying roughly the same thing each year. "Well, we are finished. The old laws must hold now. Achara, Ngara, Ameke, Amɔzo, Elogo, Agbogo is the order in which the initiating boys should go through," referring to the sub-villages and wards of Mgbom. Usually the spokesman rules that there should be no roughness in the bush. Here the elders are in a dilemma. They want *some* roughness, for after all this is one of the things that initiations are all about; they went through a good deal of it themselves, more than today. On the other hand they do not wish it to be so rough so as to scare away boys from outside villages who might initiate in Mgbom rather than in other Itim communities. This is an economic and prestige matter. I was told that in the year after the Mgbom *isiji* initiation, when there are plenty of *isiji* initiates doing the *isubu eda* rite, there are so many initiands in the bush that the elders do not care about roughness. On such occasions matters get very violent, for there may be over two hundred initiands.

At night, when things quiet down after whipping, those boys from Mgbom who are to be initiated (including the *ikwum*), who have not done the first-son *isiji* initiation, go through a very short form of it. The commons is closed. An interested senior man leads the initiands of his compound to a spot in front of the *isiji* bush. A reddish orange seed of the type worn on the *isiji* masker's head is tied to each boy's hair, or a number of them are held by each lad in his hands. The *isiji* gourd mask is brought out from the men's rest house in the commons where it is stored, and it is tied onto the boy's face with a string. The man asks the boy to call the name of the *isiji* spirit, which he does, saying something like, "Here, I know you now. Do not worry me any more, I will never be initiated." Then the boy dances about a bit, facing the *isiji* bush and then with his back to it; he does this four times. This is done by each initiand in turn. These boys spend the night in the commons, since technically they have been masked; other initiands do so as well. This is a kind of sacrifice to *isiji*, although the shrine is closed up and the bush unused at this time. There is a feeling in the Itim villages that the initiands should all know the *isiji*, otherwise its spirit might trouble them. The act also reflects respect for the priority of the *isiji* rite, historically and in terms of prestige.

The Mgbom priests take no part in this special event, for they have nothing to do with this spirit, which represents another form of secret society. Nor do boys from villages outside of Itim take part, who come to Mgbom to do the *isubu eda* initiation. It is done on the quiet for Itim people do not want others to know of it, or to be reminded of this very quick and cheap form of *isiji* initiation. The quick initiation is said to be especially important for the *ikwum* boys to do, if they have not done *isiji*. Thus Mgbom men believe that all native sons take the *isiji* initiation in one form or another.

Initiation Day

Afikpo say that the initiands for this rite, as for other initiations, do not like to boast that they will be initiated, but are quiet about it. It is the father who is doing the rite for the boy, and in a rare case he might change his mind, or find he has insufficient resources, and so withdraw his son as a candidate. In *isubu eda,* however, this is unlikely, since the costs are not high, even in the *ikwum* form, and every man is expected to do *isubu eda* for his sons without making a big fuss about it. It is not considered much of a title; it is rather something the father simply does for each son. Nevertheless, he has some feasting obligations; he rejoices over the initiation and is happy for his son.

In the morning and early afternoon of the next day, *nkwɔ,* boys and young men continue to whip, prance, and sing in the commons and the residential areas and there is further feasting and drinking in the compounds. The commons are closed all day to females and uninitiated boys. The whipping matches, however, are more sporadic than on the previous days and few males are involved; the contests are held as much to build interest and excitement for the entrance into the bush in midafternoon as for their own sake. This marks the transition from the sporting quality of the day before to the specialized use of whipping in the initiation bush.

On this morning, also, the *ajaba* structures are completed if they have not been before. Mgbom men say that it is more difficult to finish them on time than in former years, for men do not work as enthusiastically, and this style of communal labor at Afikpo is ending. As one middle-aged Mgbom man put it, "It is hard to get people to finish these things nowadays. They do not care too much." In 1952 some dressing sheds in Mgbom were not completed until this day and in 1960 the roof of the front of the one in Agbogo commons had not been made and that of the year before was used; it had not been burned along with the rest of the structure, perhaps in anticipation of a problem in rebuilding it.

On this morning the Mgbom priests sacrifice a white hen to *ibini ɔkpabe* at one of its shrines in front of their ritual house, to ask for a successful initiation and that no one be hurt. This is a powerful Igbo spirit, which plays important religious roles at Afikpo; the *ibini ɔkpabe* shrine is located at Aro Chuku, some fifty miles south of Afikpo (S. Ottenberg 1958; 1970:41–44; 1971:2–17). (It is possible that this *isubu eda* type of initiation originally derived from Aro Chuku, by way of the Edda Village-Group, as Edda has close ties with that area.)

Also on this morning the Mgbom priests often try cases involving violations of the society's rules. This illustrates how clearly they are in control of activities in the village at this time, and how important the regulation is that there should be no fighting during initiations and no ill feelings or tensions expressed in the village. Such matters can be tried at any time at the priests' discretion; at other times of the year or during other forms of initiation it is the village elders who settle the matter. Fighting at this time, said to anger *egbele*, the *isubu eda* secret society spirit, is the main offense, growing out of whipping. The fine for the guilty consists of sacrificial materials given at the shrine house, usually a dog; the society's spirit is said to enjoy this animal. The priests and their helpers, in fact, feast on much of the animal.

In the early afternoon of this day the fathers or other sponsors of the initiands each bring a pot of palm wine and twenty large yam fufu balls to the male elders of their compounds, part of the initiation fee. These are partially consumed there, but generally some food and wine are brought out to the village commons, where elders group themselves by compound and continue to eat and drink. This goes on during the initiation, for the elders enjoy watching the proceedings. However, they do not usually go into the initiation bush themselves, nor do the sponsors or fathers of the boys, but remain in their compounds or in the commons, eating and drinking. As in other initiations, each boy has one or two helpers from his compound, chosen by the father or sponsor, who enter the bush with the initiand and guide and protect him. Occasionally a sponsor may do this himself, but not usually a father.

In midafternoon the village wooden gong is sounded by interested society members and the initiands come out of the rest houses into the commons, or from the compounds if they did not go to whipping the previous day. They are naked, or wear a crude waist-piece of leaves, or an old and torn pair of shorts brought from home or left in the dressing house, which has been used in previous initi-ations. Some initiated boys and young men go into the bush to raise noise and a bit of action; these are usually the ones who have been whipping in the commons on this day. They carry a stick in each hand which they beat together over their heads as they dance around, often in groups; although frowned upon at this time they occasionally whip one another in the excitement. And they yell the usual "*hwoh hwoh hwoh hwoh*" calls.

The *ikwum* initiands are not permitted to wear any clothes at all; their bodies are dyed with camwood. Mgbom males say this is not for symbolic purposes but to distinguish them from the others in the bush. The boys doing the regular initiation are not so distinguished from initiated males. In former times the initiands charcoaled their faces and thus could be identified; today only some of them do this. I believe the red body represents aggression and struggle, the black face social control, as in previous initiations.

Any clothes or footwear worn into the bush must be left there or in the dressing sheds when everyone returns. This dress cannot go back to the everyday world; it is contaminated with the spirit of the society and is believed capable of harming nonmembers who touch or wear it. For this reason old clothes are used. If a person wears a good cloth or a fine pair of pants it should be torn before being stored in the dressing shed so that there is no chance that it will be stolen and used.

In the year after the *isiji-isubu* initiation sequence in Mgbom there are of course so many initiands to *isubu eda* and *ikwum* that there is a problem in maintaining the usual order in entering the bush. The males line up in Agbogo commons. Initiands like to go early in line, to enter the bush first, but they do not themselves determine the order; the elders do, as we have seen. A few of the priests' helpers go first, followed by the priests. Lined up in back of them at the shrine house in the commons are the first groups of initiands: sons of the priests, sons of friends of the priests, sons of members of the priests' ritual group, and sons from the compound of Ezi Ume. Next are sons of prominent village men, if their fathers have asked the priests to place them there; there is no special fee for this honor but it suggests that there are usually good working relationships between

these "big men" and the religious officials. There will be only a few
of these initiands, if any. Behind them come the camwood-decorated
ikwum.

These first groups of initiands at the front of the line are said to
have it easy. They do not have to struggle to get into the line nor do
they fight to get through the tunnel in the bush. It is said that the
ikwum initiands have to endure special hardship—the familiar arms-
over-head position for a period of time—that other initiating boys
do not, so they should have it a bit easier going into the bush. In the
case of the others at the head of the line there is clearly a status factor
at work, involving their fathers.

Behind these come the bulk of the initiands, lined up with their
helpers, from the subvillages of Achara, Ngara, and Ameke in turn,
and then Amɔzo, Elogo, and Agbogo wards. This order does not
follow the usual view of historical priority of the residential units of
Mgbom as it is reflected in other initiation rites. Afikpo say that in
former times there was no specific order, after the special cases in
front, and the initiands struggled to get ahead of one another, for it
is prestigious to near the head of the line. The struggle was often
very rough, with the boys' helpers fighting to assist and to protect
their charges, and sometimes losing touch with them as they pushed
ahead. By the time I was initiated in 1952 an orderly line had been
introduced to cut down on fighting; this was tied in with attempts
to attract many boys from other villages to initiate in Mgbom. It was
also probably a consequence of changing social conditions, in which
roughhousing and norms of physical strength, although still important, were coming into increasing competition with other values.
The fighting that year may also have been milder as a consequence of
my presence.

The origin of the particular order in line is explained by Mgbom
men simply in terms of geography; boys from the village sections
farthest away from the bush should proceed first, for they have the
farthest to go to get home after leaving it. In fact, the three
subvillages, which go before the wards, are closest to the bush as the
crow flies (see Map 3, page 143), but the boys have to go back to the
main village commons first, which lengthens their trip. Initiands
from outside of Mgbom are placed according to the village section
of their sponsor.

In 1952 the initiands and their helpers tried to crush through the
gate separating Agbogo commons, where most of them were, from

the front of the priests' shrine house, but they were held back by two strong men. In 1960 some of the initiands got out of order, rushing ahead of others along the bush path. Mgbom men say that after the *ikwum* initiates have passed, the order of going into the bush—generally the order in which the boys are initiated—is not really so important and it is all right if there is some mixing.

The initiands and their helpers are followed by initiated males with their sticks, who have been shouting and hopping around the commons of Agbogo and Elogo. There may be over a hundred of these. Again, these males sometimes break ahead of where they should be in line and get to the bush early, and there is little effort to stop them. Behind them are a number of old initiates who wish to go through the initiation again for therapeutic reasons. They may be sick, weak, or old; they hope that contact with the society's spirit will revive them. Such a man may feel, or a diviner may inform him, that in some manner he has offended the secret society spirit and that a return to the bush will appease it.

At the very end of the line are men who bring sacrifices to the bush, each for a particular woman who has troubles, either a Mgbom resident born or married there or a woman born there but now living elsewhere. The woman is barren, or loses her children in childbirth or thereafter; the sacrifice, usually done upon the advice of a diviner, is to correct her condition. In addition, any woman born in Mgbom who has recently had a child should have this done to ensure that it will live. This is so whether she resides in the village, elsewhere in Afikpo, or away from the village-group. In one case a female lived away from Afikpo with her child and had not done this. She was afraid to come to her home village with her offspring for fear that *egbele* would kill it in anger, but she did not want to bother to arrange for the sacrifice. In any case most women born in Mgbom are likely to have this rite performed for them after giving birth, although it does not have to be done in the initiation bush, but can be performed at the priests' shrine house at other times during the secret society season.

If the husband has taken this initiation he usually comes out to sacrifice for his wife, but if he lives elsewhere than in an Itim village and has not done this rite he gets an Mgbom man to do it; he brings that person, perhaps a brother of the wife, wine and fish to share with the sponsor's patrikin, and asks him to help him. In any case the person going to the bush carries a small female dog in a tiny palm-wood basket that he himself builds in the commons. When I asked my friend Tom Ibe whether I could buy such a basket at the market, he laughed: "You don't buy them," he said, "because uninitiated persons don't know about them." A seed (*ehu*) from a certain tree is tied around the dog's neck, as a magical piece. I do not know its purpose.

In addition to the dog the man takes out dried fish and various plants that women grow (corn, okra, long beans, pepper, a plant food called *edo*) and sometimes bits of yams. There is no struggling among the sick males or the men bringing sacrifices for women. In 1960 there were some forty of the latter, signifying the general concern about childbirth at Afikpo. The sacrificers must notify the priests of their intention by giving them a shilling before this event.

The initiands, who are lined up with their helpers in small groups in front of the priests' house, are slowly let through the gate from Agbogo common by two strong men who open and close the entrance with sticks to control the flow. There is struggling for position among the initiands but they are arranged in line by the priests' helpers who guard the entrance to the path to the bush. At this entrance a priests' assistant flicks a magical protective liquid (*ajo*) with a stick from a clay pot, held in a twined wicker frame, on everyone who passes, initiands and initiates. Once this is done a person cannot return to the commons without going to the bush. The fluid, prepared by the priests and their helpers, is believed to "cool" them so that nothing will happen to them in the bush, so that however rough it is there no one will die or be injured—these things have occurred. The society members, especially the younger ones wielding sticks, shout the society cry as they move along the path to the initiation bush clearing, intermingled with the initiands.

In 1952 the route to the bush in Mgbom led between Ezi Ume and Ezi Agbo, following a regular path and then branching off on a special lane leading to the forest area called *Eke Mgbom*, southeast of the main village, where the initiation occurred. In former times there were seven constriction points along this path; at each a fence was built with a small entrance through it. Each point was guarded by one or more strong men holding the initiands back, at least for a while; the initiands had to struggle through these, but not initiates. In 1952 there were only a couple of these barriers and they were unguarded; it was the job of the village executive age grade to build them, and they had been negligent. In 1960, because the growth of

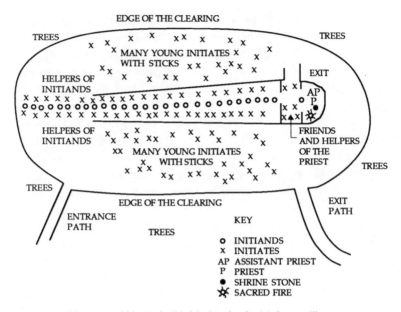

Figure 4. Ɔhia Ogbuji initiation bush, Mgbom village

Ezi Agbo's residential quarters brought the initiands into too close contact with people there, the path to the bush had been changed to include a part of a motor road. There were three barriers on this path. If travelers on the road see anything they should not Mgbom men say it is their business—government does not allow Afikpo to restrict the use of the road—but Mgbom females and children are expected to be home in their compounds at this time.

The initiation area consists of an oval clearing in the forest, some sixty by forty yards. At its center is a trench, about four feet wide and four feet deep, which is covered by branches, twigs, and boughs, built up into a low arch (see Figure 4). The trench is some twenty yards long, often muddy, with biting ants in it; this has been prepared in the morning by the village executive grade. The bush, called ɔhia ogbuji, is also known to society members as *enyum* (river), referring to the wet trench. The boys line up at the north end, where a Mgbom man who lives in Abakaliki Township, some forty miles away, controls their movements; he returns every year because he enjoys this activity. Again there is arguing about places in line, and which boys should enter before others, as the boys struggle against one another, often supported by their helpers. Mgbom men say that if a boy goes ahead of his place he or his helper will later be fined by the priests, but I have never seen this occur, though boys often are in the incorrect order. Forming a line at Afikpo for any purpose is unusual, and given the excitement of the initiation it is not surprising that there are numerous arguments.

Under cover, sitting at the trench sides, with their feet dangling into it, are the members of the priests' group and other interested men. As the boys crawl through the tunnel one by one their helpers go to the south end to await their reappearance; they do not go through the tunnel. The initiands' passage is stopped by the men sitting there, who push them down into the mud with their feet and hands, and try to hold them back. This is especially likely to occur if a man sitting there dislikes a boy's father or feels that the boy is trying to get ahead of others. In one case a boy was held for so long a time that his helper came back and jumped through the bough enclosure, breaking it, in order to free his charge; this caused much palaver. The priests do not like this sort of disruption or confronta-tion and they will cry out for everyone to quiet down. The special status initiands at the head of the initiating line, from the *ikwum* forward, are let through without a struggle.

The boys waiting outside of the trench to go through are admon-ished by initiates to keep their eyes on the ground, although some look up a bit. They are not expected to watch what is going on. They crouch on their knees and huddle close to one another with their hands on their heads, holding a stick given them by a priests' helper as they entered the bush. This is a counter to indicate how many boys are being initiated, which they discard in the tunnel. Some initiands feign a blasé attitude but others look scared. Outside and around the trench the initiates move in a circle counterclockwise, hitting their sticks against one another or occasionally on the ground, shouting the secret society yell, singing society songs, rais-ing a rumpus, threatening to hit the initiands who are not yet in the tunnel, and sometimes whipping one another. Some go off and eat a tasty leaf found nearby, others try to break a nearby beehive to add to the discomfort of all. Some just like to be there without hitting or singing; more aggressive males yell at them, call them weak, and encourage them to participate more fully, though this is not re-quired.

The initiates sing songs deriding other groups; one tells of a cer-tain age set that announced it would go into the bush but then did not do so, which is shameful. Some sing, *"Bababa baaba ejim Mgbom baaba"* (I am going to Mgbom; *bababa* and *baaba* have no particular meaning), referring to boys who come from other villages for their initiations; other society members respond with *"Baaba baaba."* Another song goes:

> ɔnogѳ *ihu mayi baaba*
> one who face wine *baaba*
>
> ɔnogѳ *ihu mayi baaba*
> one who face wine *baaba*
>
> *bianɔ enyum ederi*
> come river flood
>
> ɔnogѳ *ihu mayi baaba*
> one who face wine *baaba*

The term *ihu* refers to the "face" of the wine, that is, the top part, which is often frothy. The song mocks a man living outside of Mgbom, who has contacts in the village, for receiving wine from another outside man who wishes to initiate a son in Mgbom but has no direct links himself. The song asks the man who receives the wine to come to Mgbom himself and see what happens to the boy; i.e., he should participate more fully in Mgbom affairs since he has friends here, and not just make use of his contacts to drink wine. This *baaba* singing occurs only at this initiation.

By my observation, the age of the initiands ranges from five to twenty years, with an average somewhere in the early teens; there is occasionally an older male, usually a stranger. If any male present has a hernia it will be noticed at this time and later the older men will make him go to the Catholic hospital at Afikpo for treatment and possible surgery. This often used to be a fatal condition, but now European treatment is accepted—ritual is tempered by pragmatism.

The tunnel widens a bit at its south end, where stand the two priests, side by side. They have a small fire next to them in which they roast yams, a fire brought from the one in their shrine house, symbolizing the fire of the spirit of the society. Beside them is a magical round stone that they have carried from the shrine house, representing the secret society spirit. The priests' section of the covered area is fenced off with a narrow opening to allow only one initiand at a time through it. On the other side of this opening is another fenced section where friends and helpers of the priests stay. They control the flow of boys into and out of their section, going to the priests. Each initiand goes before the priests for several minutes; the line moves slowly and boys are in the tunnel for a while, sometimes over an hour, most uncomfortably. Every now and then the man controlling the tunnel entrance comes back to the exit at the other end to see how things are going, or someone there goes out to the back to learn how many are left and to see whether there is any trouble. Those in charge take their time; they will not be rushed by stampeding boys. They have a sense of the proper order of things. There is order and disorder here, the former around the priests and those who aid in the rites, the latter around the younger society members, shouting and whipping and gamboling about with sticks. The excitement of the young initiates contrasts with the quietness of the initiands.

When a boy is passed through to the priests he is still crouching. Before him stands the senior priest with the stone, the roasting yams, dried fish (of a kind known as *arera*), chalk, hot pepper, and kola, all on the ground. These items were brought out by the priest in a bag along with a pot of diluted wine which he has carried on his left shoulder, normally a forbidden way to carry wine at Afikpo.

With each initiand before him, the priest touches the boy's lips with a magical preparation. Then giving him a bit of yam to chew, the priest says something like, "Now you have come before *erosi eda*. May you live long. May the power of *egbele* not worry you wherever you go." He gives the boy bits of fish and then hot pepper to chew and has him sip wine four times—the usual reference to the four-day Igbo week. Then the priest takes a small wooden gong (*ekwe*), touches it to the stone and hits it once with a stick, touching the gong to the boy's forehead, left then right shoulder, right then left toes, in between each motion touching the instrument to the stone and hitting it once. Each time he strikes the gong he says "*eeeeeeeee*." The power of the secret society spirit is now in the boy. The assistant priest passes him out to his helpers, who are waiting there for him and go back to the commons with him. If he is an *ikwum* initiand he is told to put his arms up and to keep them that way when he gets back to the commons or he will die. Other initiands are told to keep them that way for the same reason, but only until they get to the commons; this is not always strictly followed, though an initiand's helper may remind him to do so. The belief is that the hands should not touch the ground; other persons coming from the bush do not hold up their hands at all.

For those initiates who follow the initiands through the tunnel due to personal illness or other troubles, a similar ritual is performed. Sometimes a few healthy initiates go through for "good luck," although the *egbele* rite is not done for them; they simply exit at the end of the tunnel. Finally come those men who carry the dog and other sacrificial material for a woman. This is only the first of a series of sacrifices that each has to make on behalf of his female, the others being done at the shrine in the village. If the process is not started at the initiation a man has to offer a larger and more expensive dog later on at the first rite in the village; for this reason it is worth the trouble of coming out to the bush.

The presence of the dog indicates to the priests that the man wants this rite done. He approaches the senior priest, who asks, "Who has the dog?" referring to the woman involved. The man gives her name and the priests takes the animal saying, "Yes, this is [name of woman]. She comes to beg you [the secret society spirit] forgiveness for her. Why has she wronged you? May she have an easy time and good health and children." The words of the priest vary from case to case. In another instance, the 1960 initiation, with a different priest, the assistant priest took the dog and removed its neckpiece, handing the dog to the senior official, who asked the woman's name. Then the senior said, "This is your food that [name of woman] brought you to cook and make use of. You should protect the woman well and not harm her in any way. If the woman has a son let him remain [alive], if she has no son let her conceive as soon as she has done this sacrifice." He mentions her name again. Note here that there is no reference to daughters, only to male children.

Then the priest cuts the dog's neck, dripping blood on the stone and throwing the vegetables and the basket there; the food, having been grown by females, represents the woman. A special knife, stored in the priests' shrine house, is employed for killing animals for the society's spirit. The dead dogs are brought to the shrine house by the priests' helpers at the end of the rites and cooked and eaten by the priests' group that evening or the next day.

Some men of Mgbom feel that this is really a form of initiation for a woman into the secret society; since she is forbidden to come herself, the dog is her representative. *Egbele* is angry at her for some violation; her joining up is seen as the way to appease this spirit, which is calling her. Sooner or later almost all women in Mgbom, those residing there and those born there regardless of where they live, have this sacrifice performed for them. Thus most village females of middle age or older, born or living at Mgbom, can be said in a sense to be members of the society, although they have no direct role in it.

It is said that in former times you had to be a very strong person to take the dog to a bush for the sacrifice, for the young society members were very rough with their sticks; they would knock the dog basket down and kill the animal. The sacrifice could not be done with a dead dog; so another would have to be found.

In 1960 two men came late to the bush with their dogs and other materials, bringing money for the priests, having failed to pay the notification fee ahead of time. The man guarding the tunnel entrance took the coins away and threw them in the bush, saying that this was no good, that they should have brought the money beforehand. For, as in the case of clothes, anything brought to the bush (except people, dogs, the priests' gong, and the sacred stone) cannot be returned; certainly they cannot go back into public circulation but must remain in the bush or the dressing shed areas, the men's rest houses, or the society's shrine house. The two men were permitted to do their sacrifices but had to pay a shilling fine in addition to the regular fee. After this incident a man standing nearby suddenly realized that he had two metal rings on. He disgustedly took them off and threw them away.

These rules stress the separation of the society and its activities from the everyday world; the latter is easily contaminated by the spiritual qualities of the secret bush world. Once in the bush an initiand has to be initiated; there is no turning back, for he knows some of the secrets. To return would place him in an intermediate position, violating the distinction between the two worlds.

In the bush there is sometimes competition between compounds, whose helpers and initiands group together to push ahead of other compounds. The contest can be spirited. If an initiand dies, faints, or gets sick there, men of the village joke with men of the compound that the boy comes from, saying, "Your compound is weak. What have you been doing? Your boy is left behind." These kinds of statements are also made of the initiands who come back last from the bush. Compound males take pride in getting their sons through the rite on time and in good condition. The initiands themselves are well aware of this competitive situation; for them it is an extension of their intercompound fights and competitive events of earlier days, and they are anxious to finish up in good order.

From the initiation bush the exit path runs west to the motor road south of Mgbom and then cuts up to Agbogo ward commons. As the initiands and initiates leave the bush they shout the secret society yell and a priests' helper flicks the *ajo* magical liquid on them from a clay pot. This is an antidote to destroy any harmful influences emanating from the society's spirit before they return to the settlement. At this point the previously initiated males drop their sticks in a pile. Whipping is over for another year.

As the initiands reach the village commons they no longer shout the secret society call but *"yee yee yee ibuɔɔ"* (Ah! Ah! Aah! First!), meaning "I am first to come back from the bush." This is a great honor, usually reserved for a priest's son or the son of some other member of the priest's group, but each new initiate shouts it out, implying that he is first, giving a sense of equality to all initiands. Those who come back last are ridiculed, but they give the shout anyway, even if it sounds funny.

After entering the commons persons who have been in the bush usually go to a nearby dressing house and there spit on the sacred tree, and then come out to the commons again. For initiands this is the first time that they enter this place. This act helps prevent the power of the spirit of the secret society from harming them or from being carried into the village. For most initiands it also means that they no longer hold their hands above their heads, but not so for the *ikwum*.

The returned males congregate in the commons of the three main wards, where much talk goes on; after a while those from the three subvillages go to their own commons. All individuals who have been in the bush sleep the night on the ground or in the men's rest houses in the commons.

Events sometimes occur which alter the normal course of action. In 1952, when I was initiated, some playful initiates broke a beehive in the bush with their sticks after about ten boys had passed through the sacrifice. Rather unbravely the initiands' helpers, other society members, the priests, and their assistants fled the heavy swarm of angry bees by the return path, leaving behind some of the initiands, who had been told that they should on no account leave the bush once there until told to do so. Some eventually found their way back to the village, but the problem was that some initiands who were not from Mgbom did not know their way and wandered off in various directions. Finally the priests' assistants went and collected them. The sacrifices were then held in exactly the same manner in the shrine house, after which they returned to the commons. I was told that this had happened in other years in Mgbom. The young men who broke the beehive were not punished, although the priests and other men helping in the initiation were angry at them. In the 1960 initiation some youths again tried to destroy a hive but were stopped by adults. In the same year the rite started late and the priests were so leisurely that it became dark and the initiands toward the end of the line finished their sacrifice in the priests' shrine house in the village.

As men return from the bush those elders who have remained in the commons put bamboo poles on the ground across the entrance to the compounds, a sign that society members cannot enter the commons from the compounds unless they are willing to sleep the night there. Females and uninitiated boys stay completely away from these gates; they are forbidden even to look into the commons from them. In former times nothing could be passed over the barriers but nowadays men in the compounds send in food, wine, beer, native gin, brandy, cigarettes, clothing, and soap and water for bathing. Money may pass the other way to purchase some of these things, left in the rest houses when the males went to the bush.

Those in the commons eat and drink, but the heavy drinking and whipping has stopped. Further singing of secret society songs occurs and some horsing around, but soon the men sit around, roast yams, and talk; there is much discussion of the experiences in the bush, what one has seen of others' behavior, what went on in past years. There is no separation of initiands from initiates. This kind of talk goes on for weeks as men meet on various occasions. Clearly a major pleasure of the rite is the chance to discuss it later on.

In 1952, following the attack of the bees, two candidates were lost for a very long time. Finally a priests' helper found them and brought them in, completely bewildered and heavily bitten. There was considerable amusement about this and much discussion among the men in the commons but little direct sympathy; rather they were made fun of, perhaps because they were not from the village. Three other candidates had to be carried back from the bush. Two were simply weak, probably ill, and the third had been kicked in the groin.

The first two were dropped to the ground and no particular effort made to revive them other than to remove bee stingers from their skin. Eventually they sat up and then walked around, although too weak to move far. As they grimaced, vomited, looked dazed, and breathed hard, persons crowded around them, poked at and laughed at them, their weakness a source of amusement. The third initiand was walked about by two helpers until he felt better. Some people smiled at him and were amused but said nothing. Eventually all three were taken to the shrine house to finish their initiation. The rites are viewed as a manly situation; to express sympathy or sorrow is to show yourself to be weak. The sense of physical ability and strength, tied to the idea of intercompound and intervillage competition, are directly expressed in this rite and grow out of earlier childhood experience.

I was told that 1952 was a mild year and that at other times people had been seriously injured and had even died. Probably because of the early return from the bush there were fewer injuries that year. Possibly my presence had some effect; there was certainly concern that I might be hurt and I was very well protected by strong men throughout the rite. The 1960 initiation, with fewer initiands, in which I took part as an initiate, seemed less rough. Several men told me on the eve of the 1952 rite that if women knew what went on in the initiation that they would object strongly, and this is why they are excluded from knowledge of it, but, of course, there are other reasons as well, as we shall see.

After the *ikwum* initiates return to the commons, still holding their arms above their heads, older men tie up their hands; they must remain in their own ward commons while the other initiands are free to move about to other commons of the village. The *ikwum* are fed by their helpers or by friends and sit in reclining chairs that friends, agnates, or helpers provide. They are still naked, while others in the commons have dressed, having left clothing there.

In former times in Mgbom the man who was believed to be next in line to be assistant priest, or some other priests' helper, would come out and gather the initiands together, including the *ikwum*, and explain to them the rules and special words of the secret society. I did not see this done in the 1952 initiation; possibly I missed it. In 1960 it occurred late at night, when only some of the initiands were still awake. Men said that they are now reluctant to tell the boys anything for they do not keep secrets well anymore. This is because some boys are now initiated at a very young age and do not understand what is going on and cannot control themselves; they will tell their mothers, other females, and uninitiated boys things they should not. So the priests and elders believe that it is better to be silent. Boys now largely learn the rules and special terms in conversation with others, and by having their behavior corrected as they go along.

Among the regulations are those which are seen as reversals of everyday behavior; it is a mirror world. In the shrine house you drink with your left hand, in the everyday world with the right. If you do so incorrectly in the shrine house you are behaving as if you are in the everyday world and you must present a fowl to the priests to sacrifice to the spirit of the society. Similarly, palm wine is carried on the left shoulder in the shrine house and bush, while normally it is carried on the right. To carry it on the left shoulder in public is to suggest that an initiation is going on. In everyday activities someone should not come from behind a person and put his hands over his eyes or blindfold him with a cloth. This simulates behavior associated with secret society title rites: a man who does this will be sharply rebuked, although there is no punishment. There is also a rule that if a man is out in the commons at night during the secret society season and he wants to go to the compounds he must touch an object—any will do—and spit, to clear the spirit of *egbele* from him.

There are other rules for which I could find no ready explanation. If a leaf falls on the initiate he has to pick it up and slit it silently, doing it in a natural way so as not to attract attention, especially from nonmembers of the society. Also, one should not go down a path when ants are crossing it. Possibly both have to do with the initiation situation, for there are often ants in the tunnel and leaves from the boughs fall down as the initiating boys brush against them there. But this is surmise; the Afikpo simply say that these are the usual practices.

There are also a series of terms employed by secret society members to replace everyday words, especially during the secret society season; boys may have picked them up before initiation, but at any rate they start to use them on this night. They can be employed when talking in private, or even when females are present, for females and noninitiates are expected not to understand them. If they do, as is sometimes the case, they act as if they do not, for to do so would reveal their knowledge. The use of these special terms is seen by men as a way of excluding women and children, either for serious or play purposes. Secret society members may be laughed at by other initiates if they use an ordinary term where a special one exists. In so doing they are talking as small boys, without knowledge. There is pressure to employ these special terms to show that one is manly.

Among the special words are some for masks (S. Ottenberg 1975: Chap. 3), where both public and secret society terms exist. Others include: *adɔ* for the common *ite mini* (pot-water), a big drinking pot; *ɔdo* for *osisi* or for *oosi otara* (stick-fufu), a pestle; *acay* for *unuka*, a general form of greeting, especially to a group; *ncucu mano* for *mkpɵpa mano* (pot-oil), a palm oil storage pot; *etɔtɔ* for *mkpɔkɔrɔdɵ*, a tall straight tree with small branches. Interestingly, there are a number of terms for household objects, such as the pestle and oil pot, and objects used by women, enough to suggest that some of the terms are deliberately designed to exclude females present, even in trivial matters that men would not ordinarily discuss. The men express their manliness and distinctiveness from women even within a female sphere, thus associating secrecy with maleness.

On this evening the priests and many of their helpers remain at the shrine house, eating and drinking. They discuss the day's events, though from a different perspective than that of the initiands, commenting on what went well and what went badly, what was humorous and what was not, who acted foolishly and who behaved intelligently, and how many initiands there were compared to other years. They do not come out to the commons, except for some of the helpers who go there to sleep; the priests remain in the shrine house.

Late at night everyone in the commons quiets down, sleeping on mats in the rest houses, in front of the dressing sheds, on top of compound walls separating the commons from the compounds, or under trees. But young secret society members, excluding those just initiated, are awakened some six times during the course of the night and made to sweep the commons by members of one of the village age sets, who check their work with bush lamps and flashlights. If the job is not good they have to do it again. This mild form of harassment of the young is a reminder that age differentials count for something in the secret society.

The Following Day

Early the next morning, *ɛkɛ* day, everyone who slept in the commons runs to the front of the shrine house, where a priest's helper once again sprinkles the *ajo* antidote on them. In 1960 he also gave out a protective liquid which we cupped in our hands to take back and rub on chairs that we sat on while in the commons, brought out from the compounds. I asked my friends whether I should not also put it on my car, which was parked at the edge of this area; they laughed and said that it was not necessary, but I did so just the same. Again, we see the practice of separating the society's spiritual forces from the everyday life of the compound and village.

Then everyone is free to go, except the *ikwum*. The initiation is finished and those who have done it are considered *isubu eda* secret society members, although they should return to masquerade in the weeks to come. Some do not, or only do so once or twice; this does not affect their membership in the society. Mothers greet their returned sons warmly, but give them no special presents, nor do they do any rite themselves. The *ikwum* also take the antidote for general protection, but they remain in the rest houses in the commons.

Now the commons are open to all. Several young adult secret society members—not new initiates—dress in the *ɔkpa* costume and play about. Fathers and other men bring the male children of the village who are not yet initiated to the priests' house to receive the *ajo* medicine, for their general welfare and to prevent contamination by the secret society spirit, however indirect. The *ɔkpa* stand by the compound entrances and chase after the uninitiated boys going by, grabbing them and swinging them around in the air if they catch them, as if trying to abduct them. Child stealing was a reality during the slave trade in pre-European times at Afikpo. The youngsters attempt to run around the maskers to get to the man with the antidote and then to pass the costumed figures again to return to their compounds. Their fathers or other males protect them a bit but the boys must also fend for themselves. Sometimes small ones are frightened and cry and try to run back to the compounds without the antidote, but they are made to face the silent, graceful, mysterious net-clothed figures. Men, including the fathers, find this amusing. *Ɔkpa* do not chase initiated persons; it is a reminder to the uninitiated of their status; they are both protected and challenged on this day.

Then the *ɔkpa* go into the compounds, dance about, and receive small presents from women there. Their presence in the compounds signifies that the commons are open and the women and girls go and take the same antidote to ensure that the society's spirit will not harm them in the event that they have seen, heard, or touched something that they should not; it is also for their general welfare. The maskers do not bother them. Pregnant women living in the village, and often others born there but living elsewhere, come in traditional dress without a topcloth, bringing the man with the antidote a small present—a yam, three pence, an egg, or a piece of native chalk—which they place on the ground near him. He rubs their bellies with the liquid to ensure a safe delivery. Unmarried girls arrive for their antidote wearing no cloth, only waist beads. It is believed that small children who bring a bit of chalk to the man can be relieved of stomach trouble from which they often suffer (probably dysentery or constipation). The Afikpo say that the chalk is for the spirit of the society to rub on its children, as Mgbom women do on theirs. The application of the antidote to the uninitiated children and to females symbolically broadens the initiation rites to include almost everyone in the community. The end of the initiation becomes a village event for the welfare of all, a total cleansing. Gender distinction through-out the rites gives way to the unity of all.

Then females fetch water, which has been difficult for them to do the past day and a half when they have been restricted to their compounds, and they begin to cook for the Feast of the Tortoise, which begins on the morrow.

The *ikwum* initiands remain naked, covered with camwood dye, hands tied over their heads, sitting at the back of the men's rest houses of their commons, located where they are least likely to be seen by passing females. Even then mats are sometimes placed between them and the front of the house to hide them. When they go to the latrine the commons is closed, for they have to pass through it.

The *ikwum* initiands' helpers go to the bush and cut materials needed for the boys' costumes on the following day. They perform a sacrifice by digging a hole in front of a suitable palm tree, placing a sacrificial pot in it, and breaking an egg into this. Then they chew hot pepper and spit it in the pot, to wake up the spirit of the tree. The pot is covered with earth and they pour palm oil on the ground at the tree's foot. The sacrifice begs permission to cut out the "heart" of the tree—the leaves and palm cabbage—which damages the tree consid-erably. The *ikwum* for whom the material is used must never be shown this particular tree; if this happens it is thought he will become ill or die. This is the only time that I know of when a sacrifice occurs in connection with securing costume material. Taking the heart of the tree for the costume implies imbuing the boys with new life.

The morning of the day after the antidote is given the priests and their helpers drink wine and cook and eat the sacrificial dogs, if they have not done so the night before. In the afternoon they meet with the village elders in front of the shrine house. A relative or a sponsor of each initiand brings nine shillings, the initiation fee for ordinary Mgbom candidates; it is higher for the *ikwum*, for Afikpo from outside of Mgbom, and for strangers to the village-group, including the anthropologist. The money, placed on a mat, is counted and divided by the elders, who get a good share along with the priests and their group. There is often squabbling among the senior village age sets as to how much each set should receive to divide among its members. In 1960 this division of funds was not held until four days later, on *eke* day.

It is believed that on the night of the day the initiation has ended each new initiate, except the *ikwum*, should sleep with a woman foreign to Afikpo, to pass on any evil powers of *egbele* remaining in them and also to show their manliness. Some older boys do this but this is optional; since nowadays some new initiates are as young as four or five this is unlikely to occur with them. This belief clearly connects the power of the society and its spirit with sexuality.

The Feast of the Tortoise

The next day is the first of a two-day singing and dancing event, named after the tortoise, which we have already mentioned in connection with the maturation of boys and girls (see pages 112–14). There is the singing of sexually derisory songs by males and females in the commons in groups organized by sex, with the participation of children. And there are important activities for the *ikwum*, who now take the stage, as their counterparts, the *isubu eda* initiands, are gone. An alternate name for the *ikwum*, *ite mbe* (dance-tortoise), stresses the significance of the festival activities in this form of initiation. The number of *ikwum* is small, yet there is interest in them.

On this *orie* day morning the commons are again closed to uninitiated boys and females and the *ikwum* prepare their masquerade. Their hands, still tied above their heads, are loosened and food is held up to them to eat as they sit in the men's rest houses. One Mgbom man said, "If your hands should touch [the ground] anytime when you are not supposed to people will say that the society's spirit will kill you. You are caught by this spirit. You are unable to control yourself." The initiands are washed by their helpers, who rub white chalk on them from the elbows to the shoulders, on the chest and back, and from the knees down, spreading the chalk with a stick. The helpers and other men of the boy's compound prepare the masquerade costume on this morning in back of the dressing sheds, a convenient place to do this without messing up the commons. Among the items made is *aso*, a braiding of yellow and green palm leaves with *ekɔrθ*, a green leaf from another tree. Also prepared are seven *agbɔsi* leaf bundles tied on a string and another bundle is made of folded *agbɔsi* leaves tied together with more string. These are leaves from the type of tree found in the dressing shed and outside the priests' shrine house, as we have seen. They clearly have strong magical associations with this form of secret society and its initiations.

These items, and other prepared materials—a wrestling bell (*ikpo*) and three chicken eggs—are carried by the boy's helper, who leads the initiand to the spot at the Eke Mgbom initiation bush where the magic liquid was used when everyone left it during the earlier part of the initiation. Initiated boys have cleared the area a bit. Formerly it was not possible for anyone to wear clothes at this spot for this rite, but the helpers and priests do so nowadays.

The two priests arrive, and they ask the helpers to dress each boy. A white palm leaf skirt is tied around each initiand's waist, falling to the knees. One *aso* is tied on the left wrist, another to the right ankle. A third is tied to a specially designated palm tree nearby, one for all the boys. A raffia shirt is put on, and an *ɛkikɛ* charm, prepared by the Rain Controller in Mgbom as we have seen, is tied on the costume at the back of the waist with the magical *agbɔsi* leaves. A cloth is tied on the boy's head and a certain type of mask, *mma ji* (knife-yam), is secured to it to hold it over the face. Two eagle feathers are stuck into the head hair. The mask is the first wooden form that these boys have ever worn. A characteristic Afikpo type, also of the four other Ada village-groups historically linked to Afikpo, including Edda (S. Ottenberg 1975:35–36), it stands for strength and masculinity, having a knife-like top with three or four pegs projecting forward from the vertical center line of the face. The knife and pegs give the mask an assertive quality. The mask carries male symbols, the knife as a symbol of strength in farming and warfare, and the yam as the basic Afikpo food; both knife and yam also probably represent the phallus. The masquerade is called *ikpem*.

The senior priest tells the initiand to take the seven *agbɔsi* bundles, which have been tied up with the bell, and run around and throw these, and then pick them up. The boy does this four times. This chases away any evil forces. The taboo on touching the ground is now over, ending where it began in the initiation bush. The priest then asks the helper for an egg, which he gives the boy, telling him to touch it to his mask and chest seven times, and then to break the egg on a stone near a special palm tree, which is done. The tree and stone are a spirit shrine, *ɔhia ikwum* (bush-*ikwum*), representing the spirit of this particular form of initiation, which, as in the case of other secret society spirits, has no particular form or shape. It is the only time that a sacrifice is made at this shrine; this spirit is not thought to cause "troubles" as the more popular *egbele* spirit is believed to do. The helper then takes the bell and ties it to the boy's back. Each boy does the rite in turn; if there are any priests' sons or boys from the special compound of Ezi Ume in Mgbom they go first, otherwise there is no special order. The ritual not only breaks the taboo on touching the ground, but informs the spirit of the society that the boy is to masquerade and asks it to protect the boy while he performs. The number seven, as in the seven bundles, represents time symbolically, the seven weeks of the Igbo month, as the number four represents the days of the week. The various items involved magically protect the boy. The costume parts from the palm tree, and the sacrifice at the palm tree just described with its stone, represent growth and probably sexual maturity.

Now everyone returns to the *ajaba* shrine next to the priests' house where each *ikwum* sacrifices a second egg in a like manner, this time to the *egbele* spirit. There is a third village shrine near the dressing shed of Elogo commons where the third egg for each boy is given. The *ikwum* then enter the dressing shed of their own ward and rest there. Young initiated men in the commons start to sing the traditional Feast of the Tortoise songs. For example, they sing about women's private parts, that women used to steal away with other men, that they are not good to their husbands. This is a sign to women and others in the compounds that the time for singing and dancing is at hand and that the commons are open; many people hurry out.

The mothers of the *ikwum* are among the first to appear. Each is dressed in a nice waistcloth and headtie, with white chalk on her body, and she carries a stick with a very fine and large smoked fish on it, and a pot of cooked palm kernels prepared to a soft and salty consistency, a delicacy of Afikpo. These are for her son to eat. The mothers join together and sing, "When you see *ikwum* himself you have to see the mother and a stick of fish!" They are very pleased to move about the commons, singing of their offspring.

The masked *ikwum* come out from their dressing shed, join together and dance about in a hopping step, trying to stay in a line, moving from commons to commons. They do not sing or talk. At one point there is a contest in which the initiands go to the west end of Elogo commons and individually turn and run eastward toward the motor road which separates this commons from Agbogo. As each one runs, a man tries to catch him; if he does he hoists him on his shoulders and carries him about. It is a sort of competition among the boys and between them and those who go after them.

After playing about for a while the *ikwum* return and sit in front of the dressing shed, watching and listening to the festival singing and dancing. A boy's father or a helper cuts off the head of the smoked fish and gives it to the priests to eat, along with some of the palm kernels. Then the boys enter the shed again and take off their masks. There, in seclusion from the goings on in the commons, they eat the fish and kernels and drink water provided by their helpers. The food is much enjoyed; it is the only nourishment they receive on this day. Their helpers eat the poorer parts of the fish in the commons outside of the shed; only those who have been wearing masks can eat inside this structure, or else one has to remain there the rest of the day.

After their repast the initiands again don their masks and go out and dance about for some time. Meanwhile their mothers have returned to their houses and each gives the elderly women of her compound a small sum of money, perhaps two shillings and six pence, as a substitute for a gift of corn (as mothers give corn or money in the village commons on the first day that their sons dance in the *isiji* first-son initiation). The gift announces to these elders that the initiands have been seen.

In the late afternoon interested initiates and the initiands' helpers join the masked *ikwum* line, which is again moving about in a row; the initiates move on the sides of the line, the helpers in back and front, guiding the masqueraders. They all dance together seven times through Elogo and Agbogo commons, and through the priests' shrine house. As they move the initiands sing, over and over again,

"*Hwoh hwoh elogo elogo hwoh!*" The first and last words are the secret society yell, as we have seen, used in all Afikpo initiations. *Elogo* refers to the cry, employed by women and uninitiated boys who enter the commons during the secret society season, as a warning in case anything they should not know of is going on (see pages 52–53); *ogo* refers to the commons; it is also a term for village. The words are self-derisive, coupling the initiates yell with that of un-initiated females, suggesting a transitory state. The helpers and fol-lowers do not yell.

These comments are reiterated in another song, sung about the *ikwum* initiands by their helpers and other secret society initiates who move with them. One or more initiates sing as leaders, the rest form a chorus:

Leader(s)
ikpenle le haghayi hayi
ikpenle le haghayi hayi
[no literal meaning]

Chorus
hwoh hwoh hwoh hwoh hwoh hwoh hwoh [etc.]
[secret society yell]

Leader(s)
orie   alagha   haghayi hayi
[day-of-week] gone [no literal meaning]

Chorus
hwoh hwoh hwoh hwoh hwoh hwoh hwoh [etc.]

Leader(s)
nnege   nɔwa ndɵ   ge   tie   nkala-ogo
mother-your   is alive you dance *ikpem*-dancing

Chorus
hwoh hwoh hwoh hwoh hwoh hwoh hwoh [etc.]

Leader(s)
nnage   nɔwa ndɵ   ge   tie   nkala-ogo
father-your is alive you dance *ikpem*-dancing

Chorus
hwoh hwoh hwoh hwoh hwoh hwoh hwoh [etc.]
ɔnwa ewurum   haghayi hayi
this sorry-my [no literal meaning]

The song suggests that "on this *orie* day your mother and father are alive and yet you take the *ikwum* form of initiation," that is, you do the *ikpem* masquerade. It is mockery of boys whose parents are so poor that their first son has to take this form of initiation rather than the longer and more prestigious *isiji*. In fact, most boys who take the *ikwum* are probably not first sons, or if they are first sons the father has already put them or another boy through *isiji*. But this delightful form of initiation is viewed as a substitute for the proper rite. Clearly Afikpo value alternative routes through the initiation process, but they value them differently.

After a while the *ikpem* maskers and their helpers and others move through the compounds of the village, starting with the special compound of Ezi Ume, then Agbogo, Elogo, and Amɔzo wards, in that order, touring in a counterclockwise direction. They do not usually go to the subvillages; I was told it was too far to bother.

The tour of the compounds goes slowly, for the initiands are given presents as they go, usually yams or money. The boys do not hold the gifts until they have removed their costumes; the donors hold them and the helpers announce them to the initiands. Presents are given by both patrilineal and matrilineal relatives, males and females, friends of the initiands, each boy's father and the father's village age set, and his mother. A boy receives his largest gifts in his own compound. In one instance in 1952 a mother gave her son a female goat. In another case a boy whose father was dead received fifty yams from his father's age set—one from each member—when he passed through his own compound. In presenting them, one member of the age set said, "We are your father so we give these yams to you." The men of that compound collectively gave him two pounds and seven shillings, a father's brother gave him two pounds, and members of the father's age set living in his compound also gave him small sums.

The presents mark the *ikwum* initiation as more special than the shorter *isubu eda* form, in which gifts are seldom presented. Descent, kinship, and age ties are jointly reflected in the presentations. While individual matrilineal relatives of an initiand often give presents, especially if they live in the boy's village or compound, the uterine groups do not do so as wholes. As we have seen, these sorts of gifts are frequently offered at the end of other forms of initiation; they reiterate the continuing and actively growing ties of the boy to his compound of birth and its agnates, as well as some uterine ties.

Then the *ikwum* return to the commons, going to the dressing shed where they undress, wash, and remain until night, sleeping in the men's houses. They leave their costumes in the shed and return their masks to their original storage places, usually in these rest houses.

On this day the priests' group meets at the shrine house and divides among themselves the money from the sacrifices for the women at the *isubu eda* bush, and the money, yams, and eggs given by pregnant females the day after the initiation. The priests receive the largest share. Some eggs are saved to sacrifice at the shrine while others are kept to boil and eat; this is an unusual procedure at Afikpo, where eggs are more used for sacrifice than as food, but perhaps this occurs here because there are so many of them.

This day and the following one are known as *Ebu Mbe* (dance-tortoise), or the Feast of the Tortoise. As we have seen this animal is a metaphor for the liminal status of the initiands, being both a land and water creature, as the initiands are neither boys nor men. These days are times of sexual derision, freedom to make sexual criticisms of the other sex, a special kind of liminality in song, to which, however, the *ikwum* initiands are only observers. As the tortoise is a trickster figure in oral literature at Afikpo so the songs of these two days have a trickster quality to them. This particular form of satiric singing is found only in the Itim villages and is clearly linked to the *isubu eda* and *ikwum* initiations; the festival also derives from Edda Village-Group. There is a good deal of aggression in the songs, for women proclaim men's sexual foibles and attempted and completed feats and men sing that women are unfaithful and deceitful in sexual matters. The physical movement of groups of singers and dancers through the commons adds to the sense of assertiveness; I have seen a group of men, clearly bested in song by their female age counterparts, dance close enough to the women to make them lose their steps and confuse their singing. The *ikwum* watch from the men's houses but do not appear, yet all are aware that they are there; they are much a part of the festival. It is as if it is thoroughly appropriate for sexually awakening boys to be part of this scene, to be incorporated ritually into it. It is as if they are forced to reflect on the varieties of sexual experience at this time in their lives. The aggression of males toward other males in the whipping before initiation and in the bush turns to a male-female competition after the bush rites; both are special forms of permissiveness. Boys who have just finished the *isubu eda* initiation can take part as singers and dancers, as they often have done in previous years. Initiation is not a prerequisite for joining in the Feast of the Tortoise for either sex.

By evening the singing and dancing cease and the action shifts to the compound, as is often the case at Afikpo. Adult men and women have each invited friends of their own sex from other villages to visit them and there is much separate feasting. Females eat well, for it is a time when husbands are expected to give their wives fish, yams, and other foods to honor them—not just to cook for others, as on other occasions. A generous husband may also provide his wife with cloth.

In the evening young men hang around the motor road between Mgbom and Amuro villages and accost women who pass by, poking sticks at their genital area and referring to them sexually, in a continuation of the assertiveness of the day. Men and women in separate groups in the large compounds make up further songs for the morrow, here not usually sexual, but making other satirical comments on the behavior of specific individuals and groups in the community. Singers try them out, changing, discarding, and accepting. Each sex sings its own songs. There may be an informal contest between the men and women in a compound to see who prepares the best ones.

The next morning, *aho*, women pass through the commons on their way to the stream or elsewhere; then the *ikwum* in the rest houses know that they are free to go home. This sign (*okpokpo ihu*; first to see–face) occurs the morning after every night or day that there has been masquerading. The *ikwum*, like other maskers in the Itim villages, then go to a dressing shed and spit on the sacred tree there and are then free of the secret society's spiritual forces and able to return home. If a male forgets to do this he can do so in the compound using a piece of wood. In other Afikpo settlements lacking this dressing house the male rubs his neck with his hand to free himself.

The Afikpo say that the *ikwum* initiation has ended, but it is not finished. In former times the boys would put two eagle feathers on their heads and go out and dance and sing with the festival players on the second day of that event; at present this is not required and they are usually content to go home and relax after their adventures. Eagle feathers, normally worn only by men who have taken a head in warfare or who have taken a big title, suggest that they have done an important thing, which from their viewpoint, and that of their parents, they certainly have.

The singing and dancing continue on this day, with a satiric non-sexual slant, and with feasting and drinking. *Ɔkpa* masqueraders appear and prance around the singing groups as they move about the commons. The *ikwum* may come out and watch but generally do not take part. Their initiation ends in an atmosphere of sexual and satiric humor, in sharp contrast to the more serious nature of much of the rite.

Final Masquerades

Two days after the Feast of the Tortoise the new *ikwum* and *isubu eda* initiates masquerade. The former wear the *aborie* style of face covering with a raffia waistpiece and porcupine-quill cap or a headdress of leaves, a costume which also appears in the first phase of the *isubu* initiation (see pages 217–18; S. Ottenberg 1975:196–98), while the *isubu eda* employ a similar body dress but a somewhat different new mask, fuller in form, called *hihi* (S. Ottenberg 1975:195–96). Both forms are featureless net masks. The costumes are prepared in the dressing sheds and the boys put them on in the men's rest houses. Each type makes much the same movements but their wearers move in separate groups, first running through the priests' shrine house, past its shrine for a blessing, then dancing about the commons, and then passing through the compounds of the main village in the same order as the *ikpem* masqueraders three days earlier. Following this each group returns to the commons, dancing and hopping about, shaking their heads, crying "*hwoh hwoh hwoh hwoh*," and singing the songs from the whipping day. The event attracts a large audience of men, women, and children, and the parents send the boys fine food; they eat and sleep that night in the commons.

The play is repeated the next evening and on the five subsequent *orie* days. After the first two times there is less interest, the audience is smaller, and the costumes not always carefully renewed if they become soiled. Some of the *isubu eda* maskers simply drop out; the *ikwum* should remain, as there is a strong commitment to this form of initiation on their part and that of their fathers.

These masquerade figures represent secret society spirits, not powerful or malevolent, simply pleasant forms of spiritual forces. The boys say they do this play to show that they are finishing their initiation; it is their duty to do so, although the *isubu eda* from villages outside of Itim often do not bother to take part. Clearly the masquerading signifies that the boys are now capable members of the secret society, able to take part in its activities, but the faceless quality of the masks suggests that the boys are not yet initiates, that their identity is not yet certain. It is possible for the boy to finish his masquerading the second year. If a boy does not finish it is said that he should not talk about his initiation, for he has not experienced it all, but boys do anyway.

On the seventh *orie* day the initiands doing both forms of initiation who are still taking part perform *logholo*, a masquerade that we have already discussed (see pages 77–78; S. Ottenberg 1975:184–88); this signifies that they are finishing their initiation. They wear wood masks, particularly one form, *acali*, always popular with younger secret society members (S. Ottenberg 1975:16–20), which is a small human male face. The dress is a raffia costume; the player carries a stick in his right hand. The mask is light and easy for boys to handle and to see through, helpful because of the active movement required of this masquerader, who wards off unmasked uninitiated boys who try to throw him. The recent initiands are now secret society members, now perhaps playing with former playmates who have not yet gone through the rites. Both *isubu eda* and *ikwum* initiands are through the next morning when they leave the commons. The new initiates take part in secret society activities later on in the season, including the major satiric masquerade, *ɔkumkpa*, if the village performs it.

Commentary

Many features of behavior and symbolism in the *isubu eda* and *ikwum* rites are similar to the other Afikpo initiations. There is the removal from the village to a special bush nearby, the awakening of the spirit of the secret society, the sacred fire, and the sacrifice. There is the subsequent holding of hands over the head on the part of the initiands and then the masquerading. Sexual activity is encouraged following the rites. There is emphasis on physical strength and bravery. The idea of contamination and danger from the spirit of the secret society is present, involving taboos of separation from everyday life, from females, and from uninitiated boys. There is the importance of certain colors, particularly red and white, and of time concepts, especially the number four for days of the week and seven for the weeks of the month. There is the emphasis on the aesthetic of the observed body, on food, and on humor. The boys' past experience with aesthetics is very helpful here as in the other initiations. There is the role that the agnatic group in the boy's compound plays in supporting and feeding the initiands, the feasts given by the father, the separate role of father and initiand (the father generally staying out of the bush), the attempts to frighten the boys before the rites, and the conning of presents from the boy's mother, who again feeds her son. As in the other initiations there are alternative initiation paths to take, as father and son decide, here the choice is to do either *isubu eda* or *ikwum,* and either continue to the very last masquerade or end participation earlier; *ikwum* may be used as a substitute for the more expensive and extensive *isiji* first-son initiation in the Itim villages, if the father is poor or dead.

The *isubu eda* and *ikwum* rites, like other Afikpo initiations, stress separation by gender and the association of males with secrecy in contrast to females. Male sexuality and power are connected in the initiands' experience with secrecy, as they are for others taking part in the rites. As in other initiations, the initiands bring considerable skill and knowledge in ritual practice and masquerading to these rites, with already formed attitudes toward both sexes. While the initiation is in some ways excitingly new, in certain respects it is a continuation of prior experience and conceptions.

There are also some striking differences from other Afikpo initiations. In the *isubu eda* and *ikwum* rites there are two priests and a ritual group with strong authority, unlike the other initiations, which seem to pretty much run themselves. Of course, the apparent lack of authority in the other initiation forms is an illusion; it is rather that authority is indirect and considerably diffused. In the *isubu eda* and *ikwum* rites the initiands do not provide their own leadership, they are not their own priests, and they are to some extent ranked according to their fathers' positions, perhaps more so than in other initiation forms, although there is some of this in the first-son *isiji* rite. One sees here a contrast between an initiation that involves a priestly cult and one that does not. The balance of events between the roles of the village and of the compound in the *isiji* and *isubu* initiations is pretty equal, but in the *isubu eda* and *ikwum* it is more heavily weighted toward the village—again, evidence of centrality. And the secret society shrine is employed by the priests throughout the secret society season; in the other cases the shrines are not generally used following the initiation. These features are consistent with the strong political position of Edda Village-Group, whence the *isubu eda* and *ikwum* rituals came; probably a more influential regional Igbo group than Afikpo in pre-European times.

The considerable degree of religious centralization around the secret societies in the Itim villages does not seem to have a parallel in the political sphere within these same villages, nor in religious matters unconnected with the secret societies. The rather diffuse leadership of elders in secular matters is common to all Afikpo villages, no matter what form of secret society they may have, and the Itim village secret society priests are not generally the same men as the village political leaders. Also, there does not seem to be much difference between the boys' secret societies in the Itim communities and in other Afikpo villages, despite the differences in the adult secret society structure, nor did I detect any differences in childhood training or experience. The centralization within the Itim village secret societies appears to be a consequence not of childhood experience, but of historical factors.

In contrast, there are fewer tasks for the father in the *isubu eda* and *ikwum* rites than in the other initiation forms; there is little expense and not much sense that the father is taking a title. His authority is less and that of the secret society leaders is considerable; they, as far as the initiating boys are concerned, become strong father surrogates. Conversely, the participation of females in the rites is greater than in other initiation forms, and the initiand does not break a calabash food dish in front of his mother—a gesture which symbolically rejects her during the *isiji* initiation. I have elsewhere suggested (S. Ottenberg 1983) that with greater centralization of authority, as among the Yoruba, females are likely to be more incorporated in male rites than otherwise.

The initiands come into more direct and immediate contact with authority figures than in the other initiations. The father is still absent but is symbolized in the presence of the much respected and not a little feared priests and their associates. There is punishment of the boys in the bush, but little overt conflict between initiands and the secret society leaders; it is the young initiates who threaten the initiands. These *isubu eda* and *ikwum* rites do not seem to exhibit the avoidance of direct authority as much as the other initiations and the boys' previous childhood experience. Despite this direct authority the rites are very popular with youths, but perhaps for other reasons, such as their briefness, and the opportunities to take part in whipping in the years after initiation.

The *isubu eda* initiation rite also differs from other initiations in that it brings to the fore Afikpo intervillage ties. It is the only initiation which boys take outside of their own community, thus creating conflicts, competitions, and problems throughout the village-group, to which various solutions have been reached, as we have seen. It also leads to some intervillage integration. The *isubu eda* rite breaks down the considerable village autonomy at Afikpo, and raises the level of influence of the Itim villages in the village-group as a consequence of their control of this form of initiation. The coming of the British to the area in 1902 and the subsequent changes in social life during and after the colonial period, which also has led to lesser village autonomy, probably has allowed for a more rapid spread of the *isubu eda* form throughout Afikpo than would have otherwise occurred. The politicians of the Itim villages are well aware of the attraction of their initiation and that this gives them some leverage in Afikpo internal affairs.

The *isubu eda* and *ikwum* rites are also more closely tied to non-initiation activities than are the other initiations, although all have important associations of this nature. There are the events of the whipping day and of the Feast of the Tortoise, the sacrifice of dogs for married women, and the blessing of all Mgbom residents, especially pregnant women. The whipping activities pull the community into a social and psychological framework for the initiation. The tortoise festival brings the community back to its usual age, gender, compound, and village orientation, following the bush rites, and returns females to an active role in the village, after their more retired state during the initiation. Whipping moves the community toward the physical assertiveness of the initiation bush; the Feast of the Tortoise marks a shift to an oral and sexual level. Whipping is all male, while the tortoise festival events involve both sexes and the whole village.

The *isubu eda* and *ikwum* initiations have a strong fertility component, more so than other initiation forms, revealed in the dog sacrifices, the special treatment of pregnant females, and the rites at the tunnel itself. The tunnel can be seen as a vagina; the nearly naked youths emerge from it with a blessing and are symbolically reborn, but in a helpless condition, symbolized by their hands being held above their heads. Later the *ikwum* are mystically released from this condition as adults who masquerade in public. While Afikpo initiations generally symbolize the death and rebirth of the initiands, and in this sense fertility in general, as well as being metaphors for the initiands' own actual births, the fertility issue in *isubu eda* and *ikwum* is quite explicit and extends to the village as a whole, even to females born in the community but living elsewhere.

The sexual aspects of the Feast of the Tortoise are explicit, but otherwise the *isubu eda* and *ikwum* initiation rites, like the other initiations, have only symbolic sexual referents, though these are clear. Going through the tunnel can be seen as sexual intercourse as well as rebirth. The shrine at the priests' end of the tunnel, and the fire there, can be seen as the uterus, yet these also represent the father's authority. As with the other initiations these rites symbolize mother and father, sexuality and fertility. The boys are kept down by older men in the tunnel, symbolically their fathers, but they also struggle through and are aided by other males, representing another aspect of their fathers' attitude toward them, who thus play symbolically opposing roles of aiding and thwarting, as boys may perceive the behavior of their fathers in everyday life. The ambiguous, ambivalent image of the father has appeared in other events in the lives of boys at Afikpo.

These two final initiations add rich variation to the pattern of rites and to boys' experiences at Afikpo, and they reinforce past childhood experience, as do the other initiation forms. The boys come well prepared, with strong egos and considerable skill and experience. In terms of the vernacular psychology that has already been discussed, the boys are quite ready for these two final initiation forms, whichever they take, particularly if they have gone through other initiations previously. In terms of depth psychology there is more direct involvement of initiands with senior male authority figures in these last two rites than in other initiation forms, but the same kinds of events and symbolism occur, and similar basic patterns of behavior are found.

Part 3
Conclusions

Part title illustration:
Mba mask of the initiated,
made by Ckukwu Okoro

8
Final
Maturation

A N AFIKPO BOY IS NOT CONSIDERED MATURE UNTIL some ten years after his initiation, when he marries in his late twenties or early thirties. Girls often marry in adolescence, following their "fattening rites," but they too are not considered mature by the Afikpo until a good many years later. The post-initiation period has not been thoroughly described or analyzed by anthropologists working in non-Western societies. Scholars dealing with childhood development in Africa generally stop after analyzing the initiation rites, and those discussing adult life commence with marriage. If the marriage takes place years after initiation, little is said about the period in between. If the marriage occurs shortly after initiation, the concern is with this event and with the subsequent living and social arrangements, but little is written about the continuing maturation process for young persons that occurs early in the married state. Perhaps there is less interest in this final maturation of boys and girls as young adults because there may be no specific rituals to mark it, although individuals of this age are involved in other rites. In any case, this final growth process has suffered anthropological neglect in comparison to the infancy and initiation periods.

My own work reflects this lacuna, for I have considerably less data from Afikpo on the last phase in the maturation of Afikpo males than on other aspects of their growth. This period does not even seem to have a name in the anthropological literature or at Afikpo. Yet it is more than a time of mere continuation in the direction of past maturation. It is an opening-up period, when the maturing male reaches his first autonomy as an adult, when new and diversified social relationships and activities occur.

After a boy's final initiation at Afikpo he is for some years "betwixt and between" the world of children and that of adults. While anthropologists would say that the initiation rites have made him sociologically and psychologically a man—and I would agree with this view—and while Afikpo recognize the social meaning of initiation, he is, after all, still a boy. True, he will now take part in the adult secret society, but for some years he is still living in a boys' house, fed by his mother, dependent on his parents for food, playing some children's games, and still helping his father in farming. The symbolism of the initiation rites is highly significant, but follow-up action is required on the part of the initiand, his relatives, and others, to make the psychological and social program of the rites a reality.

We are dealing with a roughly ten-year period from the time of initiation until the boy reaches young adult maturity in his late twenties, during which gradual rather than sharp changes occur. These alterations extend the maturing male's kinship ties; provide him with wider social contacts and experience in his home village, in other Afikpo villages, and in areas beyond Afikpo; more firmly identify him with adult male culture; and move him on the road to economic independence from his father, not always without some conflict.

One important feature of this final maturation period is that the young man, who could also be called an "old boy," makes much greater direct contact with his matrilineage and his matrilineal clan than formerly. From his matrilineage he secures the farmland to which he is entitled as a member, often through the agency of his mother's brother or brothers. This land will form the bulk of his farm holdings, and is the economic basis of his independence as a maturing adult. He starts to farm the various land plots as soon as they are revealed to him, which will likely be over a period of years. Since his uterine relatives and their matrilineal land holdings are often located in a number of different Afikpo villages, he increases his knowledge of the geography, settlements, and people in the Afikpo Village-Group, as well as meeting numerous relatives. In the process of acquiring his own farm areas, he learns something about land manipulation, so necessary for a male Afikpo adult, for uterine kin sometimes only begrudgingly show him the land that he is entitled to that someone else is using. He may have to press for its release, and he is likely to be involved in his first land disputes while in this final maturation period. He also comes to know members of his matrilineal clan, of which his matrilineage is only a small part, through rituals surrounding the matriclan shrine, *nja*. The strengthening of his matrilineal ties, largely dormant during his childhood years, might be expected to bring him closer to his mother, after years of being distant from her, for she has knowledge of his uterine relatives and of some matrilineal land holdings. But in practice the young man tends to deal directly with his mother's brothers, or his father assists him in this way, and I do not have a sense of mother-son affection growing out of the son's emerging matrilineal links. Perhaps this is because the mother herself does not own matrilineal land (she usually farms some of her husband's land holdings), and certainly because the son has already spent years developing and maintaining social and psychological distance from her. However, mother-son conflict over land or other issues is rare for maturing males at Afikpo.

One of the young man's mother's brothers (sometimes the eldest, though this depends upon geographic location and other factors), becomes a principal guide to his matrilineage and its property and to his matriclan, and in a sense acts as a surrogate father, though the two kinsmen rarely reside in the same compound, and often not even in the same village. The young man may be partly dependent upon this older male for introducing him not only to his farmland but also to his uterine relatives. Sometimes there is a strong and positive relationship between the two but at other times there is suspicion, where the young man feels that his mother's brother is withholding information about matrilineal land, or this man is reluctant to show such land to a new adult, even a uterine relative, especially if he is farming the land himself. The tie between the two is rarely intimate; this mirrors father-son behavior at Afikpo. Perhaps this occurs because the mother's brother plays virtually no role in the childhood rites or activities of the young man; it is principally a link formed in adulthood.

On the patrilineal side there is continuing integration of the young man into his descent group, the group of his compound of birth. He takes part in its many rituals, feasts, and other activities as an adult. He continues to live in a boys' house, though perhaps one with unmarried males of his own age or older. In his twenties he begins to sit with patrikinsmen at their meetings at the compound ancestral shrine house. People gradually come to address him and to act toward him as an adult rather than as a child. This takes time; there is no sharp change immediately after initiation. He is still a dependent in his compound, as his mother continues to feed him, though now he begins to supply food from his farms for her to cook, rather than relying entirely on his parents for his nourishment. He continues to help his father to farm, although as his own farms develop he may increasingly become reluctant to take the time to do so; this may be a source of friction between the two. Another source of difficulty is that the father is farming land of his son's uterine lineage, which has been given to the father to use when the boy was young, or even after the father's marriage to his mother but before the boy's birth; this is land loaned in the name of the son or of a potential son. The father may be reluctant to give up this land to his son as he matures, although eventually he usually does so. The son is also entitled to a small share of land belonging to his patrilineage—about ten percent of the farmland at Afikpo is agnatically owned—and this he gets from his patrilineage elders, sometimes directly but more often with his father's assistance.*

A son is expected to assist his father in taking titles, and to provide food and other help to his parents in various activities, such as arranging funerals for their parents. Before the age of thirty, the son may also take a few lower titles for himself within the secret society, and perhaps one or more outside of it; in these acts his father may assist him. But while his father is alive the son is not expected, indeed not allowed, to do the more advanced titles that his father has not taken; rather he should assist his father to do them. So there are some restraints on the son in regard to his father in land matters and in title taking, areas of some potential conflict. These do not seem seriously disruptive at Afikpo; matters tend to be held in check rather than to flair up publicly. If a dispute occurs the son is usually considered wrong for not respecting his father.

The son may be involved in burying one or both parents during his final maturation period, and the first son of a dead father will have particularly heavy duties in this rite, and considerable responsibility for the father's younger children afterward, although he will be aided by patrikinsmen in both these matters. It should be clear from what I have written that a son's involvement with his parents hardly ceases after his initiation; indeed, it greatly increases for a time.

---

*For further discussion of Afikpo patrilineality and matrilineality, see S. Ottenberg 1968a.

This involvement continues in another way, as well. At the time that I carried out research at Afikpo, the son was usually party to an arranged marriage, usually established by his father when the boy was young but sometimes planned even before his birth. While the son usually does not marry the girl until his late twenties, and she is likely to be still quite young in his last years of maturation, he has an obligation to get to know her parents. This is not always difficult, since the girl's father and his father are often friends or relatives. He occasionally brings presents to the girl and he helps her parents to farm. He is aware that he is under some constraint to marry her, and that to refuse will put him into conflict with his father. This sometimes occurs, but it is my impression that the boy generally accepts his father's choice, and waits to see what joy the marriage brings him and whether there are children before deciding whether to stick with it or not.

At the same time, the son may still be friends with a former *nwa ulo* partner of roughly his own age, now married to someone else. Although this is usually not a sexual relationship, they may become secret lovers, or she may divorce her husband and marry him. More often, however, he seeks sexual satisfaction from divorced or other sexually free females, becomes involved in adulterous affairs with other married women, has sexual relations with "stranger" harlots living in the Afikpo area, or has intimacies with unmarried girls. However, as we have previously suggested, his sexual life in the final maturing years of adulthood until marriage is likely to be uncertain and erratic, and may lead to disputes with other men having claims on a woman who interests him. He is constrained sexually by older men who control most of the females. When he marries he can direct his sexual interests in a regular manner, at least until his wife gives birth; then the post-partum sex taboo goes into effect and he is in difficulties again, which a second marriage may resolve. But a first marriage really establishes the son's independent identity in the eyes of other men, for now he controls a woman himself and he is in a position to produce children. This first marriage symbolizes his true separation from his father, even if the father has arranged it.

During his final maturing years the son is very much involved in the village secret society, which is generally a single organization regardless of what forms of initiation a village makes use of. He is likely to be very active in initiating others into the society, taking delight in conning them and their mothers and, both in and out of masquerade costume, in threatening and harassing the initiands, sometimes wishing to take revenge for the hardships he endured at his own initiation. He may act as a guide or helper to other boys being initiated, and as a secret society member he receives food and money at the feasts associated with the initiations of others. He is likely to be very active in the secret society masquerading, sometimes voluntarily and sometimes at the order of the village elders, and he generally enjoys these activities, as he does acquiring titles and taking part in other rituals in the society. But he is not yet a leader in the secret society, only a participant. His father, of course, is also a member of this society. Through initiation the son has joined his father's group, bringing them closer together, but the relationship is still distant and somewhat patterned by authority; the father is likely to be a leader or nearly a leader in the secret society, while the son is a performer of masquerades and other ritual activities.

Adult secret society activities help to maintain the distancing from females that the maturing male has been involved in before and gives him a sense of full identity with his gender, distinct from women. The secret society activities also bring him into contact with men of various ages in his village, and from compounds other than his own, much more so than before. And in his late twenties his male village age set officially forms (S. Ottenberg 1971: Chap. 3), often with an elaborate set of feasts, rites, and a masquerade, and he takes part in these events. In fact, the set's members have been meeting together for some years to plan this "initiation," as the Afikpo call it, and to drink and eat together in conviviality, and they have been performing village communal labor as a group for some time. The age set, both before and after it is officially formed, supports each member in his marriage rites, title taking, and other activities. Often a large number of members of this group were initiated together, and some belonged to the same boys' secret societies at the same time, so that there is a continuity from childhood into adulthood. These relationships have an easy and familiar quality to them, based on years of peer-group experience. The age grouping is drawn into the age-hierarchical system of authority at Afikpo as well, as it is one of some twenty sets of different ages in the village, ranked by years. While the elders order the communal work as a rule, it is the age sets of middle or slightly younger age which direct the maturing individuals' set or sets to carry out the tasks. It is not done without conflict; the younger sets sometimes dislike the orders of the older age groupings, who seem to do little of the work themselves, and young adult men look forward to the day when they will be in charge of others. A young man's father, of course, belongs to an older age set which may take part in giving orders to his son's set.

The maturing male continues to take part in wrestling into his late twenties, when he passes out of the senior wrestling grade (the one well known for wearing the *ikpo* brass bell, as we have already mentioned). In pre-colonial times he would also have been engaged in warfare a number of times by the age of thirty, defending his home area, fighting against attacking neighboring groups, chasing slave kidnappers, and hiring out as a mercenary to other Igbo groups away from Afikpo. Indeed, in his final maturing years he was often at the peak of his warrior skill. If successful in gathering goods and slaves, and in killing, he was given much praise by males and attracted female interest; his years of boyhood training paid off well. At the time of my research this praise and attention was won largely in the wrestling arena; physical strength and skill are still admired and childhood training in wrestling is important, as we have seen.

Thus by the time the maturing son is thirty he has established strong working ties with his matrilineal and patrilineal descent groups, he has acquired some personal independence from his father, he has recently married and may have a child or two, he has some economic independence from his parents as a consequence of his farming, he is active in the village secret society and his age set, and he has taken some lower titles. He has passed out of his wrestling grade, though he may still act as a wrestling judge. He is likely to be living in his own house in his compound of birth, and to have secured or built another home for his wife; he is no longer being fed by his mother but by his mate, and he has also achieved some regularity in his sexual life. He is to some extent knowledgeable about land matters, on the topic of his various relatives, and concerning the villages of Afikpo and neighboring area, and he may be engaging in some trade. He has had a variety of experiences in making sacrifices at the numerous Afikpo shrines. All of these features point to a man of maturity, but he is still a "small boy" from the point of view of the elders—too young to be seriously involved in politics, to be settling disputes, or to be a priest, and too youthful as yet to have strong economic power through trade or land manipulations.

It is difficult to be certain, without more detailed data than I have, what psychological processes are taking place during these final maturing years. The initiation frees the son to move in the many directions that I have sketched; in this sense initiation is a social catalyst, a stimulus to ego-directed activity. There is no single major move toward final maturation, except perhaps the young adult's first marriage toward the end of this period. Rather there is a gradual unfolding of maturity, and a sense of new activity in many directions: toward his patrilineal and his matrilineal relatives, toward fellow villagers and age set members, toward farming, and toward the village secret society. There is a leisurely, rather than a hurried quality, to this final maturation, allowing the growing male to develop at his own speed without much pressure. There is a sense of sexual constraint and difficulty during much of this time, but there is satisfaction in other areas—farming and increasing economic independence, secret society activities, the senior years of wrestling—and there is excitement as well as frustration in sexual exploration. There is some conflict with the father, and perhaps also with his mother's brother, but generally these are kept under control by the parties involved, or by other relatives. On the whole this seems to be a happy, outgoing, and enterprising time for young men. These males appear to have good ego strength and to be enterprising and occupied with a variety of activities, and they exhibit little evidence of depression or of being heavily restrained. Only occasionally is there a certain brittleness in social relationships, or a tendency to anger quickly, suggesting that there is some stress involved in responding to the contradictory social messages of this gerontocratic society: the pressure to achieve, combined with constraints that keep the young men dependent upon their fathers and other older males. These young adults exhibit some of the typical male anxieties about women that we have alluded to earlier—that a wife will leave the marriage, that she will violate taboos and so fail to have children, that she is adulterous or otherwise deceitful toward her mate—anxieties which I link to the early intimate and dependent tie with the mother and its end, although these fears are by no means totally unrealistic. The male wish to ensure that females reproduce, as evidenced by the use of the secret society to enhance female fertility, is also an expression of male anxiety about the control of women, for if females violate secret society rules the Afikpo believe that they will not bear children unless the proper rituals are performed. Since this means that women potentially have the ability to refuse to have children, men may experience this as a psychological rejection, on the part of the women, of their own ties with them—that bond which is so important to males in their own infancy.

Adulthood moves the boy into constant male relationships that go beyond his boyhood peer group and his links to this father. He now has a surrogate father—a mother's brother—as well as his real *pater;* both are very important in his young adult life. They are not distinguished analytically from one another; there is no father-image split between an authoritarian mother's brother and an amiable father, as often seems to occur in matrilineal societies, or the reverse, as in patrilineal situations. Rather, the young man is under some authority from both, and both are potentially in conflict with him, yet as a rule each is superficially amiable and helpful. In a sense, then, the mother's brother duplicates some of the features of the ties with the father; a split image occurs in both cases.

In summary, the young man is very much involved in male relationships, through the adult secret society, his age set, the senior wrestling groups, as well as his father and his patrilineal grouping, and his mother's brother and other male uterine kin. He is in a thoroughly male world, which he has come to through his many years of boys' secret society activities, wrestling, his initiation, and other activities of youth. He has successfully distanced himself socially from his mother, though male anxieties about female behavior suggest a psychological residue. He maintains friendly, nonconflictual ties with his mother, who often still lives in the same compound as he does. He takes over control of one woman as wife, and then perhaps a second one; and he develops a brotherly, or perhaps a fatherly, concern about the marriages of his sisters, that they fare well and produce offspring, for his sisters' children will inherit his own matrilineal land holdings and continue his matrilineal line of descent. Thus he comes to carry out mature relationships that differ greatly from the mother-child bond of his infancy, and he is involved in a rich panoply of male relationships.

The final maturation of girls is something I know less about, and it is somewhat hidden by marriage, which girls go into in their adolescence, before they are socially fully grown. In a marriage arranged by the parents, the girl sometimes resents the lack of choice and leaves after a short time for another man, but as a rule she will not if she begins to have children, at least not for some time. In any case the girl usually finishes her maturation into adult status as a wife, under the control of an older male, who to a large extent takes on the role of her mother when the girl was single, directing her to carry out household and other duties. Or, if there is a senior wife of her husband, as is likely if he is a much older man, this woman plays something of the role of surrogate mother to the maturing girl, at least for a few years. Yet in other ways the husband is, at a psychological level, a surrogate father figure, particularly as he is likely to be older in age than she, sometimes considerably so. Whether the dual role of father figure and husband produces psychological conflicts in her in this situation is not immediately evident to me from the data that I have, but I suspect that this is one underlying cause of the frequent divorces at Afikpo. The girl marries within her village (but not usually into her own compound), or into a neighboring settlement at Afikpo, but she is rarely far from her parents and she is likely to maintain a close relationship with her mother; her ties with her father have a more distant quality. Her sexual needs are more fully solved by this marriage than are those of males her age, despite long abstentions when she is nursing. Sexual exploration with men other than her husband is difficult and risks rebuke and public punishment, although it is hardly absent at Afikpo. She may have learned skills useful in having love affairs—the rules of secrecy, of doing and of not doing—but unlike males of her age, due to her early marriage she has had little opportunity for free sexual exploration and experiment with a variety of partners.

By the time she is thirty, the typical maturing Afikpo female has had two or three children, at least one of whom has died. She is a well-established domestic, living in her own house and cooking for her family. She works established farm plots, land acquired largely through her husband rather than her matrilineal line, and she may trade food surplus at the Afikpo market or at neighboring ones for a little cash to support her growing family, to spend some on herself, and for presents for her husband. She may have married into a polygynous family, and her relations with other wives are variable but sometimes bitter; she has to learn to hold her own in an uncertain atmosphere of co-wife intrigue, jealousy, and sometimes sorcery (P. Ottenberg 1958), which her childhood experience has not fully prepared her for, though she may have observed her mother in such intersections and heard her talk of them.

By the time she has been married for ten years or so she will have joined a married women's age set in her village of residence and taken part in its dances and feasts; her age set has a male counterpart.

She may also be active in the female communal firing of pottery, which she will make to sell, a popular women's source of income at Afikpo. Pottery firing is an interesting matter, since it involves secrecy from males. The women do this work in specially cleared areas in back of certain compounds in the village, traditionally in the nude and in the absence of men, who are expected not to observe them and can be fined by the elders for so doing. The rationale behind the nudity is a belief that the pots will break if this is not done, and behind the secrecy the idea that males should not see fully nude women. This is the closest to a women's secret group that exists at Afikpo, as far as I know. There are some parallels to the men's secret society, as there is an element of nudity in the men's initiations. The men produce masquerades and the women pots for the public, and in each case there are religious factors involved. However, there is no initiation to these female pot-firing groups as far as I know, and their membership changes as women move into and out of the village upon marriage, divorce, or for other reasons.

The maturing female continues her distant and limited relationships with the boys' and men's secret society that she has been involved in as a girl, and she will start to caution her children about these matters as soon as they are able to understand. As a recently married adolescent, she enters new relationships with the men's secret society; she may sacrifice at its shrine to ensure a good delivery or her husband may do so to help her become pregnant. She is very much aware that her special relationships to the men's secret society are a lifetime matter, although postmenopausal women sometimes violate secret society restrictions and get away with it, for the fear of infertility is no longer an issue. Only after menopause can a woman really become an autonomous being.

The maturing female will also have developed strong familiarity with her matrilineal relatives, especially the women. She keeps in close touch with her brothers, even though she no longer lives with them; they are concerned with her health and marital welfare, and that she produces children for the matrilineal line. She will also have come to know her husband's relatives, particularly on the agnatic side, but her ties with her own patrikin will not expand and in some cases may diminish. She meets many new persons in her community of marriage, establishing lasting friendships. Yet her time is largely taken up with child care, domestic work, and farming.

In contrast to the maturing male, she does not have much autonomy or independence economically or socially, but on the positive side she obtains earlier sexual satisfaction on a regular basis; children bring happiness and prestige to her, as well as an outlet for love in the absence of much close affection from her husband, a characteristic feature of many Afikpo marriages. And she has security in a family, for her husband holds the primary responsibilities. On the other hand, like her male counterpart, she may be under constraints. She may find her husband uninteresting and sexually unstimulating, and she may find her co-wives difficult to get along with.

My sense is that Afikpo females reach maturity as adults somewhat later than males. It is likely that their early marriage delays rather than quickens maturation for them; it moves them from one dependent situation to another without allowing them the kind of freedom that males have as boys, and as young men during the final maturation, a freedom to evolve emotionally. It is often only in their mid-thirties, or even later, that women seem to have a full quality of capability and to have developed the ability to stand up for their own interests in their home. But when they attain this level of maturation they appear to be stronger individuals. Females also do not seem to move out in so many directions after their adolescent initiation as males do; they are more tied down by their early marriage, and by their lesser role in Afikpo political and legal life.

Clearly the final maturation years differ for each sex. This is not surprising, for it is consistent with the presence of marked sex role distinctions in the early years. Yet in both cases there is gentle development in the final period of maturation, rather than hurried or pressured achievement, and there is the eventual reaching of a good sense of self for members of both sexes. It is a long road from birth to maturity, some thirty years or so, which while it has its constraints and frictions, is not a highly repressive or hostile period. Rather it is a slowly unfolding and positive time.

9
An Overview

I N THIS STUDY OF AFIKPO BOYHOOD I HAVE ARGUED
that infants' experience—and in particular the strong mother-
son tie and the relatively absent father—creates conditions that
necessitate special childhood activities to turn mothers' sons into
adult males with strong egos, socially and physically capable. They
must be able to control females; in the past they had to be warriors
as well. This maturation requires (1) psychological and social distancing from the mother, and (2) a reorganization of the distant
father-son tie into an amicable and closer relationship.

Dissociation from the mother is necessary for the maturing male
to function adequately as an adult, and to turn his sexual and other
energies elsewhere. Out of this separation comes the ability to fulfill
the distinctive male roles in relationships at Afikpo, which are
strongly characterized by the separation of male and female activities,
while still functioning in cooperative modes with members of the
opposite sex.

A new man-to-man relationship with the father enables the son to
function as a cooperating adult in his father's compound, where he
will remain for life, with his father and other adult agnates, while
retaining personal autonomy. The father, in turn, comes closer to the
son through his efforts to move the boy ahead in his ritual activities,
his initiation, and in teaching him farming. With this rapprochement
comes the ability of the son as a mature male to operate in the Afikpo
gerontocratic authority structure, thus enlarging his sphere of authority relationships. As a boy he has already had much experience in
male peer groups, which he carries over into adulthood. Now as a
man he engages in both peer-group and hierarchical relationships
and in various combinations of both (S. Ottenberg 1971). The mature male enjoys the autonomy of his peer groups, such as his age set,

and yet accepts the age-hierarchical structure of society, which is concomitant with a closer relationship with his father.

I do not claim that in a society with these infancy features and these adult needs there is any necessary single route to their resolution. I have only explored the particular path that boys at Afikpo travel as they mature, at one point in time, the 1950s and early 1960s. How this pattern of childhood development arose, as against other possible ones, is a question that I cannot answer here. I believe that Afikpo concerns with the health and welfare of infants has been and still is associated with a pattern of extended nursing, and that this has resulted in necessary cultural features of dissociation from the mother and association with the father. Nevertheless, not every culture with the same nursing situation works this matter out in the particular pattern that Afikpo has developed.

Furthermore, I have argued that while adolescent initiation, that rite so fascinating to anthropologists, is a very crucial event in the boys' maturation process, it is only one of a series of ties and activities in a boy's life, from early childhood to adolescence, that contribute to the direction of his maturation. The Afikpo boy comes to this initiation already quite skilled and experienced in many ways. He has also been involved in various rites and activities, such as living in the boys' houses, taking part in the bird shrine ceremony, being a member of the boys' societies and their masquerades, some of which have features similar to his initiation rites, and all of which function to separate the boy from his mother from the age of five or so and prepare him to identify with and to be included in his father's world after initiation. My view is that no initiation can really be understood without examining the child's previous experiences and activities. One must look at the whole road, not just its end.

In this regard two features stand out in the maturation of Afikpo boys: the underlying cultural and social similarities of the various initiations, and the evident relationships of these rites to early childhood experience. The initiations contain key elements and symbols that occur again and again, despite the variety of these rites. There is unity in the order of events and in their form, in the presence of key symbols, and in the major aesthetic qualities of the rites. These features themselves have analogies to, or metaphoric associations with, earlier boyhood experience. At the same time as the initiands look forward to their social adulthood, they refer backward, drawing upon their childhood from infancy onward (S. Ottenberg 1982a:182).

The strength and vitality of these rites lie in the integration of these two views. The initiations emphasize that you cannot look forward without also looking backward. The past has to be integrated with the present, childhood with maturation, in order for the youths to move from adolescence to the future.

A key period in Afikpo boys' lives begins at age five or six and ends with initiation, encompassing all of the latency period and the early part of adolescence. It is important because it is then that the boy learns much of the basic culture of Afikpo, albeit in simplified form: its sociological features, such as the sex role dichotomy and peer-group behavior; its symbols, such as those dealing with color and sacrificial items; its ritual forms; its basic aesthetic qualities; and its emphasis on entrepreneurship and competition. It is the knowledge and experience gained during this period—in various ways a corrective to the experience of infancy and the oedipal period—which makes it possible for the boy to comprehend the variety of meanings of initiation at the time of sexual awakening during adolescence. This period of ten years or so is the bridge between infancy and adulthood. There is not a great deal of distinctive culture of childhood. The boys emulate adult life, and they learn adult social behavior and culture, which draws them away from the infancy mode. In almost every way, the experience of boys during initiation echoes and reaffirms their experiences during latency and early adolescence; there is continuity in sex role relationships, symbolism, and aesthetic experience including masquerading.

Yet initiation has its special consequences. After this adolescent rite, the boy comes directly under the control of older males and is incorporated into Afikpo adult society. Previously, from the age of five or so, he has been largely free from his parents, and his experience of authority has involved his male peers or boys just a little older than himself. I believe that this period of autonomy from parental control allows the boy to develop a strong ego, without engaging him in potentially detrimental conflict arising from the conditions of his infancy. A boy of five years or older has a relationship with his mother which allows for affection between them and support from her, while at the same time freeing his conscious interests to turn elsewhere. Neither is he strongly under the direct authority of his father, though before initiation he associates and identifies with his father indirectly, by emulating adult male behavior in the boys' secret society activities and elsewhere, and he farms under his direction; to a large extent, the authority of the leaders of the boys' peer groups substitutes for that of the father. A boy therefore enters the adolescent initiation with a good sense of his own capability, and is presumably prepared for a psychologically closer tie with his father and the continuation of a distant, but affectionate link to his mother. Looked at in another way, in this middle childhood period, the boy is turned away from his mother, but not yet turned toward direct identity with his father. This is delayed until the initiation.

The middle period in a boy's life is an extremely rich one at Afikpo. Not only does he come to experience many of the basic symbols and metaphors of Afikpo life, but there is almost an idyllic sense of freedom to play, to compete, to aggress, to fantasy, to explore both the social and the natural world. True, the boy is under the authority of his parents in case of serious misbehavior and in any illness or other crisis, and there is a tyranny of conformity in the boys' societies—the peer groups are sometimes demanding in this regard—but on the whole he is free of authoritarian rule. For the boys it is a period marked by much physical and verbal aggression, stimulating fantasies, and considerable learning of cultural norms and skills.

In the process of reworking his relationships with his parents secrecy plays a major role in the boy's life. In the boys' societies and in the adolescent initiation secrecy strongly separates the boy from his mother and other females, putting social distance and barriers between them. Secrecy at Afikpo is associated with maleness and male sexuality; these qualities become metaphorically and symbolically intertwined in the growing boy, and they become associated in his mind, and in practice, with separation from and with control over females. Secrecy distinguishes the boy from his mother but does not end his relationship with her; rather it changes its nature. Secrecy also separates the boy from his father, and yet identifies him with him. The father does not very much involve himself in or intrude into the boys' secret societies, and yet these groups identify the boy with his father culturally and psychologically, in that the boys' secret societies are highly emulative of the adult one, to which the father belongs. The son, mildly dissociated socially from the father, links himself to him psychologically and culturally through the boys' societies. The emulation prepares the boy to accept the father after the adolescent initiation and, in the case of a first son, eventually to replace him in the compound when the father dies. Secrecy is not a break in his ties with his mother and father as much as it is a new way of relating to them. Secrecy for boys (and for adult males) is paradoxically a way of communicating with those excluded from the secrets, a way of relating outside of nonsecret situations (Bellman 1984).

Many of the boys' aesthetic experiences before and during initiation have secrecy aspects to them, even though masquerading occurs in public. Boys' artistic experiences help to distinguish them from females and to identify them with older males. At initiation there is a cultural and psychological identification of boys with their fathers through aesthetics—the boys now mask as their fathers do or have done—leading to a closer social relationship between them and, ideally, to the resolution of emotional tensions surrounding them.

The initiations are crucial as a playing out of the parental theme in the boys' lives. The manner in which the shrine spirit is employed, in every form of initiation, indicates that it represents the authority of the father, as well as the boy's unconscious sexuality towards his mother, and replicates aspects of the birth of the boy and his infancy. All of these features are encompassed in this rite, in which males are reborn under male control in the bush, in contrast to the earlier birth from a female and under female control in the compound. The move to the bush is a move away from the female associations of the compound. Through the villagewide initiation the boy symbolically joins with the father at the village level; previously they have related to one another mainly in the compound. This move to the larger settlement level, paradoxically, allows the boy to develop closer ties with his father in the compound.

I believe that the Oedipus complex is an important issue at Afikpo, as a consequence of infancy conditions and experience, as I have described them, and that many of the steps taken previous to initiation, such as the movement of boys to the boys' houses and the activities of the boys' societies, are steps in its resolution, whether they occur during the oedipal phase of three to six years of age or later. I also think that the anxieties that adult males have about controlling women and female behavior indicate that the Oedipus complex may not be fully resolved after initiation, for at least some, and probably a considerable number of Afikpo. I believe that the disorder at wrestling matches and whipping contests, and sometimes during initiation rites—particularly in the final, short *isubu eda* form, nominally the initiation under strongest direct adult authority—reflects the difficulty that men have in accepting male authority. This is mirrored also in the Afikpo pattern of group decision-making, where usually no single adult or senior bears responsibility for decisions in the compounds, villages, and descent groupings, and in the difficulties of arriving at definite conclusions in group decision-making because of individualism (S. Ottenberg 1971). It may also be that the lack of total isolation of the initiands during certain initiation forms, for example the living in or at the back of the compounds in the first-son and the subsequent *isubu* initiations, and the mother's feeding of the son during his rites, suggests difficulties in isolating the boys from the parental scene.

The problem of achieving full resolution of the Oedipus complex may be indicated by the fact that there is more than one initiation form at Afikpo and that it is popular for boys to go through two or even three, as if one were insufficient. If the father still has oedipal problems or other unresolved issues from his own childhood, the long period of separation from his son may serve him well in keeping down hostilities and conflicts toward the son; both father and son thus appear to benefit from keeping a distance from one another during childhood. The obvious attempts to keep father-son conflict to a minimum through the distancing of boys and fathers during much of the son's childhood, and the displacement of any hostilities a son may have for his father into the boys' societies, wrestling, and other childhood activities and the adolescent initiation, so that virtually no adolescent rebellion occurs at Afikpo, suggests the presence of problems in handling the oedipal situation. We thus have a paradox: Afikpo boys have a very good sense of capability and competence at the same time that they struggle to resolve parental conflicts. I believe that this struggle does not paralyze them, but leads them on to entrepreneurial efforts as adults.

Some of the data presented in this book are liable to another interpretation. I could argue, and marshal some evidence, that it is simply a Western conception that the Oedipus complex is universal, and that at Afikpo oedipal problems are minimal or even absent. For one thing, there is no pattern of adolescent rebellion in either sex. There is also little serious physical punishment at initiation, which seems to mark other initiations in some other cultures (Morinis 1985). Both might be expected in a strongly oedipal situation, although I have given interpretations to explain why not at Afikpo. And circumcision, typical of manhood initiations (Morinis 1985), occurs at Afikpo previous to initiation, in a mild form and with little attention called to it. At the time of my research it did not even occur during adolescent sexual awakening, but earlier. Furthermore, there does not seem to be a great deal of father-son conflict until after initiation and when it does arise it relates to issues of a pragmatic nature, such as farmland holdings. And regardless of psychology, it might be argued that disputes about productive property will occur in any society.

Furthermore, if psychological separation from the mother is such an issue, why does she continue to feed the boy throughout much of his initiation? And why is the bush so close to the village? There is certainly room enough at Afikpo to place the bush farther away, thereby distancing the initiand from his mother, and even from his father, who rarely if ever goes to the bush himself. From this critical viewpoint, male anxiety about controlling females can be seen as realistic: it is indeed difficult to keep women subservient in a society which is so entrepreneurial and which places such an emphasis on status mobility. The strong gender division of roles can be seen as a pragmatic response to the needs of warfare—an efficient division of labor in order to maximize economic and social gains—rather than as a response to infancy conditions. Male anxiety about women might thus be explained as a reaction to the contradiction between basic values, between strong achievement goals and an inferior role for females. Male secrecy might be viewed simply as a mechanism for generating physical strength and order in a warfare society. Using this approach, one could argue that there is no need to invoke the Oedipus complex or other deep psychological interpretations; social and cultural explanations will do.

I have thought about this kind of interpretation a good deal and I believe that if I had written this book twenty years ago I would probably have employed such a nonpsychological viewpoint. But today it goes against my sense of how human beings behave. It defies the telling arguments for the importance of the infancy period (Winnicott 1977) in shaping human behavior and cultural experience. It leaves out the subdued aggressive tendencies in human beings, which all cultures strive to control. It does not offer a powerful enough explanation of secrecy and of repressed or deflected sexual drives at Afikpo. While it is an alternative explanation, I find it to be superficial. It is not a rich enough model to encompass the way humans behave. I do not deny some of its elements—the lack of adolescent rebellion, the minimal father-son conflict until after ini-

tiation of the son, and the contradiction between women's subservient role to men at Afikpo and an entrepreneurial value in the
society. But it seems to me important to interpret these in terms of
the psychological issues in childhood experience, as well as the cultural and social, and this requires accepting some model of psychological maturation in addition to a cultural or social approach. I find
that a Freudian one is the best to explain certain of the facts of
Afikpo boyhood maturation, including the early movement of boys
to live away from home and their rather distant early emotional ties
with their father, the extensive peer-group activity of boys, some of
the symbolism of the initiation rites, the ambivalent attitudes of men
toward women, and so on. I have tried to integrate a psychological
viewpoint with an interpretation of cultural and social features. The
psychological orientation helps me to frame the ethnographic data.
Otherwise fine studies of childhood in West Africa, such as that of
Oppong (1973) on the Dagomba of northern Ghana and that of Leis
(1972) on the Ijaw of coastal Nigeria, suffer from the lack of such a
framework. Other writings, for example, a book by Parin, Morgenthaler, and Parin-Matthey (1980) on the Anyi of the Ivory Coast,
seem to be dominated by a psychological model at the expense of
cultural and social realities. I have aimed at a middle ground in this
book.

What does give me a sense of inadequacy in this study is rather
the lack of data on what Heald (1982) calls the vernacular
psychology and Riesman (1986) refers to in terms of the African's
own views of the psychological processes of Africans, their own
interpretations of human psychological behavior. When I carried
out field research such African studies really did not exist. If I had
discovered an interpretation of this nature I would have a native
model to contrast with the model that I have adopted and this
would be a richer study. The interpretative interplay between the
two psychologies—one derived from Western clinical experience
and the other from African contemplative and philosophical
thought—would be fascinating to work out. I can only pose a
challenge to others, to develop such paired models based on
research and theory (see Ottenberg n.d.).

To turn to another matter: Did a concept of childhood exist at
Afikpo at the time that this book is concerned with? Drawing from
Ariès (1962; see also deMause 1974), I note that this idea was absent
in Western Europe in medieval times, but arose later as a conse-

quence of Christianity, the rise of the bourgeoisie, and the growth of schools, so that childhood as a distinct concept—with its own dress, toys, games, sleeping arrangements and its representation in art, and the idea of the innocence of children—is characteristic of Western life today. Ariès argues that in medieval times there was a perceived stage of infancy and that older children were considered to be adults of sorts, so that there was no real concept of childhood. Children dressed as adults, were not represented in art as children, played with toys that earlier were adult objects, took part in adult activities, slept with adults, and were early exposed to adult sexual experience and language, as well as to open defecation and urination. Thus there was little concept of childhood.

Fortes strikes a similar note for the Tallensi of northern Ghana, stating that "the social sphere of adult and child is unitary and un-divided," and "as between adults and children in Tale society, the social sphere is differentiated only in terms of relative capacity." Even Tallensi children's games are largely emulative of adult behavior (Fortes 1970:204, 205, 244–57).

Some of the features of childhood in medieval Europe and among the Tallensi are found at Afikpo, such as the early exposure of chil-dren to adult sexuality and to public defecation and urination, the lack of portrayal of children in art, the exposure to or participation in adult rituals such as the Feast of the Tortoise, and the emulation of adult rites, as in the boys' secret societies. But other Afikpo child-hood features differ, suggesting the existence of some culture of childhood. Children's traditional dress is not the same as that of adults, as well as girls' hairstyles. Some children's songs and most children's games differ from those of adults, and frequently do not appear to have their origin in adult ones. The idea of innocence in children is not developed at Afikpo as it is in Western society, yet there is the idea of the age of lack of understanding, that children do not always know what they do, that they have not yet reached the age of "sense," thus they are hard to control. If there is no single Afikpo term that translates as "childhood," there are a number of terms, as we have seen, for the stages of childhood, and for types of children. And there is a clear concept of a separate stage for children from roughly five or six years of age, when boys' attachments to their mothers lessen, until initiation, and from when girls begin to help mothers in domestic work at about the same young age until their marriage as adolescents. This period is marked as childhood at

Afikpo, even if it is not denoted by a single term, and even though it differs from that of medieval Europe as explored by Ariès. The heavy initiation rites for boys at Afikpo and the former fattening ceremonies for girls, as entrées into social adulthood, also suggest that there is a clear differentiation of childhood from adulthood and that distinctive conceptions of role behavior exist for each period and for each gender. In medieval times comparable rites were largely absent. I conclude that Afikpo adults have a clear conception of children as being different from themselves; adults recognize the existence of childhood. But childhood behavior is sufficiently emulative of adulthood that there is not a very rich distinctive culture of childhood, as compared to that of adults. This does not mean, of course, that Afikpo childhood is lacking in richness of experience and symbolism.

What was beginning to occur at Afikpo in the 1950–60 period when I carried out research was that the influence of schools, missionaries, and an expanding economy was starting to move Afikpo children toward a more Western European experience, toward a stronger separate culture of children, less emulative of adults—certainly of adults living the traditional life—and surely involving Western conceptions of childhood. This change has greatly accelerated in the post-independence (post-1960) period, especially through schooling, with its emphasis on formal education separated from parents, the promotion of the Christian idea of the innocence of children, the importance placed on the role of the nuclear family, the portrayal of children in art (in religious pictures), the specialized dress for school youths, the delaying of sexual knowledge, and so on. The idea that children do not learn naturally but have to be deliberately taught (Fortes 1970:222) seems to be largely a Western one. The changes occurring at Afikpo do not mean a shift from no traditional conception of childhood to a Western view, but from one view of childhood to another. In this work I have indicated the major features of the traditional view, with particular emphasis on gender and secrecy, peer-group relations and age hierarchy, aesthetics, and the ties between children of each sex and their parents of each sex.

Of course, the period of my study was itself a transitional time. In the pre-1902 British period there was a very strong emphasis on developing warrior skills in boys; fighting with groups outside Afikpo occurred with some frequency, and there was realistic fear of children being kidnapped and traded into slavery to Europeans on the coast (up to mid-nineteenth century), or moved into slavery with other Africans in the region (until some years after the arrival of the British). In pre-British times, the boys' secret societies and other boys' peer groups apparently served not only as training for warfare but as protection against kidnapping by keeping the boys together. In the case of girls, staying at home also helped to avoid capture; in this period women did not often go to the farms without the protection of men.

Strong male controls over women, the necessity of early physical maturity for boys to defend themselves in war, the warrior tradition, all were practices marking the pre-British period at Afikpo. They occurred alongside the efforts to keep down infant deaths through the long nurturing mother-infant tie, with the father kept at a distance so as not to disturb this protective relationship. All these features very strongly marked the pattern of children's socialization. If there was less of a culture of childhood than by the time of my research, perhaps it was because boys had to grow up quickly to protect themselves as well as to guard females. We see this pattern even today in the Moonlight Dancing, where the male *nwa ulo* partner protects his female from boy aggressors. Girls married early in order to maximize the use of their fecundity for a much-desired population growth. These social conditions of earlier times set the pattern of childhood training, introducing the paradoxically opposing needs: to nurture the infant intimately and yet to produce warrior males who stood independent of women and could control them effectively.

The period that I have described in this book thus can be seen as a transitory one between that of the last century, with its particular demands on childhood training, and the 1980s at Afikpo, with its lessening emphasis on the long nursing period, post-partum sex taboo, and warrior tradition, and its greater concern with the culture of childhood. My data and analysis reflect transition between these two childhood conditions separated by eighty years or so, rather than being a simple reflection of "traditional" times at Afikpo, whatever that might mean to the reader and to myself.

But whether we are talking about Afikpo childhood of the nineteenth century or the 1980s, or the transitional period of my research, it is helpful to interpret the data in terms of some universal features of boyhood experience. Children have to be nurtured by their mothers (or by surrogate mothers). Boys have to break their ties with their mothers. The oedipal situation, whether aggravated or mild, must be faced, and boys must achieve independence from their fathers while also identifying with them. In discussing Afikpo at the time of my study, I have tried to show, in terms of the basic processes of maturation in boys, how one society comes to terms with the special needs of infancy, while answering the society's need to produce a certain kind of adult.

Appendix I

Variations in the First-Son Initiation

IN AMAMGBALLA, THE MAJOR VILLAGE FROM WHICH *ISIJI*
spread to the other Ahisu villages of Afikpo, the initiation used
to be performed every year and all village sons had to take it.
First sons remained in the bush a year or more and other sons a
month. But by the 1940s some fathers were buying their sons out of
this initiation form (but not from some other forms) through money
payments and other gifts to the village elders. The number of boys
doing *isiji* yearly became insufficient to warrant its annual performance, and starting in 1952 the rites were scheduled every seventh
year, but with every son expected to go through them.

Certain Afikpo villages lack *isiji* entirely, but have other initiations.
These include the six northern Afikpo communities of Ozizza, which
are somewhat isolated from the rest and which have many rites that
differ (S. Ottenberg 1971:196). And in the central village of Amuro
only one compound, Ezi Onya, does *isiji*; Ezi Onya derives from
Amachi village, from where it obtained the rite. Most of the rest of
Amuro once was a part of Mgbom village but never acquired the
right to *isiji* after separation. Amangwo, a subvillage of the largest
Afikpo settlement, Mkpoghoro, lacks *isiji* entirely. In Mgbom the
subvillages of Achara and Ngara each used to perform *isiji* separately
from Mgbom but do not do so any more.

The division into two *isiji* bushes occurs in several other Afikpo
villages as well as in Mgbom. For example, in Ukpa village one large
compound, Ezi Agbe, does its *isiji* initiation the year before the rest
of the village, with its own bush. The two southern Afikpo villages
of Kpogrikpo and Anohia, somewhat isolated fishing communities
and strongly influenced culturally by nearby Edda Village-Group,
have different initiation forms, called ɔkpo, with slightly different
mask types (S. Ottenberg 1975:193) and the bush is open every year.

The initiation can last up to seven or more years, depending on the wealth of the fathers, but the boys do not spend all that time in the bush. Other variations occur in still other villages.

Appendix 2

Variations in the
Second Initiation

I HAVE ALREADY INDICATED SOME OF THE CHOICES which arise for those involved in the *isiji* rite (Appendix 1), particularly for those taking the *omume* title concurrently and those who put a second son through *isiji*. And at the beginning of Chapter 6, I cited certain options open to fathers for the *isubu* initiation. There are further variations possible in *isubu*.

Time pressures and competition for resources have complicated initiations in recent years. Initiands who are not first sons, who ought to enter the rites at the *ɔka* stage nowadays wait until the end of it, perform the sacrifice, perhaps do some subsequent masquerading, and then break off. While traditionally *isubu* occurs only once every seventh year, nowadays in some villages, though not in the Itim settlements, boys do the sacrifice and subsequent masquerade every year.

I know of two sons in Mgbom who did the *isiji* initiation, but not the *isubu*. However, both took the special, short, yearly initiation called *isubu eda,* discussed in the Chapter 7. One boy is the son of a rising middle-aged politician, the other of a slightly older man, a wood carver and member of the special ritual group in the secret society associated with this yearly initiation. Both men are respected and of good status.

In recent years the pressures of Western education and of other modern interests have affected those who do not do the first-son form. Here are some case histories.

About 1943 a schoolboy in Ukpa village went into *ɔka* only the second day before the initiating boys left the backyard enclosures. He remained with the others only a few days, until the day after the *omume* spirit sacrifice, when he left the initiation for good, not bothering to masquerade. Everyone thought that the wrath of the *omume* spirit would turn on him, but nothing happened. An Ukpa elder said to me, "This was an eye-opener." Other sons started to do the same. The village elders did not object, as they could have, due to pressure from the fathers to allow this new form. Ukpa is the nearest village to the Afikpo Government Station, the Afikpo community most influenced by change.

A few years later a prominent leader from the same village had several sons whom he wished to put into the *isubu* initiation the year it was done, following the *isiji* phase. But the sons were away and did not arrive home until the initiation was over. So one day he brought them out to the commons, without special dress, and that evening performed the *omume* sacrifice for them. The sons stayed in the rest house in the commons that night, leaving the next morning. Nothing terrible happened to him or them, as some had predicted. Then other fathers began to do the *omume* sacrifice for sons in violation of the seven-year cycle, on *nkwɔ* day preceding the first day of the Dry Season Festival—the proper time but not the proper year. This practice is now common outside of the Itim villages, that is in most Afikpo communities, especially for boys in school and for those who live away from Afikpo. However, the father must still pay the proper fees. Since the sacrifice is based on the compound, if initiated male agnates do not object to this arrangement it is difficult for the village elders to do anything about it; the agnates own the shrine and compound autonomy in the village is considerable.

Thus the number of boys who now do the full *isubu* from beginning to end has decreased considerably. There is a humorous expression for a male who takes any of the short forms of *isubu:*

| *ite* | *nne* | *oko ogeri* | *ɔkɔrɔ* | *ta* | *ɔhɔrɔ* | *ta* |
| pot | mother | [female name] | build pot | today | fires | today |

The name changes according to the situation. The expression refers to someone in a hurry, as a woman who fires her pots the very day that she makes them; usually a woman prepares pots over a number of days and then treats them all together. The saying also suggests that the person has acted in a womanly and not a manly way. Nevertheless, shortened forms of initiation are increasingly popular at Afikpo.

Other variations occur. In villages having the first-son rites, a father should not put sons into *isubu,* either in the regular or shortened form, until he has done the first-son initiation. But since the *isubu,* at least in its shortened form, is now carried out every year in the villages outside of Itim, a father in one of these settlements may wish to start initiating sons before the seven-year cycle for the first-son rite comes around. He does one of two things. He "begs" the *isiji* title holders to let him put a son through *isubu* first, promising to do the first-son rite later on. This usually requires a payment of perhaps five pounds and some food and wine to the village *isiji* title holders. Or, in the year that he initiates his first son he enters another son at the ɔka stage to do the *isubu* in full or shortened form, where the boy joins the first child. Here it is considered that the eldest son is first, for he has started in the *isiji* stage; priority should be given to the first son whenever possible.

In the five Itim villages, including Mgbom, there are no shortened forms of the *isubu* initiation, and it occurs only every seventh year, following *isiji*. Boys take the full form of *isubu* at the prescribed time or not at all. But another initiation, *isubu eda,* a brief annual type, has to be done by all boys of these villages, regardless of what other forms they do (see Chapter 7). First sons do *isiji* and *isubu eda;* they can omit *isubu*. If they do *isubu* they have to wait until the following year for *isubu eda,* since there is a time overlap in the rites of *isubu* and *isubu eda*. Other sons than the first can do *isubu* one year and then *isubu eda* the next year. Or they take *isubu eda* and nothing else; then there is very little press for them to do *isubu*. In all initiation forms fathers tend to initiate their boys at an earlier age than formerly.

The point of these comments on variations in the initiations is that there is not, and has not been for some time, uniformity in these procedures. The Afikpo seem to delight in choice and variation within a general procedural order. Villages and compounds have considerable autonomy to go their own way. Fathers make choices, and may even be innovative, as we have seen. What form of initiation is done depends upon the father's resources, competing interests in the expectations of status gains for himself, and possible advantages for the son. Sons also, nowadays, pressure their fathers to allow them to do shorter forms. What had once been a fairly set and routinized procedure, in which the father made a simple decision, has now become a matter of calculation on the father's part, with input from the son. The decision reached may reflect not only the father's needs, and those of his son, but also the state of the ties and tensions between them. But all boys go through some initiation; the idea that they might not is abhorrent at Afikpo.

Despite alternative forms of initiation experience for the sons, their common membership in the village secret society, with equal rights, strongly binds them together, to the exclusion of females and non-initiates. And many of the basic events and symbols of the rites show similarities, even in the midst of variation.

Appendix 3

Variations in the
Isubu Eda *Initiation*

IN 1952 THE ELDERS OF UKPA, A VILLAGE OUTSIDE OF Itim, forbade all their sons to go through *isubu eda* in any village, fining some of them heavily for doing so. In 1960 the penalty was greatly reduced and viewed more as a permission fee. At Amamgballa in 1952 a son (other than a first son) could do the *isubu eda* rite in an Itim village if his father paid the Amamgballa Village elders thirty shillings; he would then be exempt from any other initiations in Amamgballa. A first son had first to do *isiji* and *isubu*, and after that could take the Itim initiation without a fine. In the far northern Afikpo villages of Ozizza, by 1952 all communities had their own *ajaba* dressing places, indicating that even in this relatively isolated and culturally autonomous area of Afikpo the *isubu eda* rite was popular. First sons had to go through *isubu,* which was the only other initiation practiced in these settlements; other sons could take *isubu eda* as their only initiation if they preferred. These examples suggest the increasing popularity of this new form of initiation at Afikpo.

Bibliography

Afikpo District Office. 1935. "The Cult of Arisi Edda by D.O. [District Officer] Afikpo." In Afikpo Native Authority file no. 106, Vol. 2, p. 41. Manuscript in archive of the Afikpo District Office (seen there by the author in 1960; present location unknown).

Allen, M. R. 1967. *Male Cults and Secret Initiations in Melanesia*. Melbourne: Melbourne University Press.

Ariès, Philippe. 1962. *Centuries of Childhood: A Social History of Family Life*. Translated from the French by Robert Baldick. New York: Knopf.

Babcock, Barbara, ed. 1978. *The Reversible World: Symbolic Inversion in Art and Society*. Ithaca: Cornell University Press.

Barry, Herbert, III, and Alice Schlegel. 1980. "Early Childhood Precursors of Adolescent Initiation Ceremonies." *Ethos* 8:2, 132–45.

Barry, Herbert, III, Margaret K. Bacon, and Irvin I. Child. 1957. "A Cross-Cultural Survey of Some Sex Differences in Socialization." *Journal of Abnormal and Social Psychology* 55:327–32.

Basden, G. T. 1938. *Niger Ibos*. London: Seeley, Service.

Bateson, Gregory. 1972. *Steps to an Ecology of Mind*. New York: Ballantine.

———. 1973. "Style, Grace and Information in Primitive Art." In *Primitive Art and Society*, edited by Anthony Forge, 235–55. London: Oxford University Press.

Bellman, Beryl. 1984. *The Language of Secrecy: Symbols and Metaphors in Poro Ritual*. New Brunswick: Rutgers University Press.

Berg, Charles. 1951. *The Unconscious Significance of Hair*. London: Allen and Unwin.

Bettelheim, Bruno. 1962. *Symbolic Wounds*. Revised ed. New York: Collier.

———. 1977. *The Uses of Enchantment: The Meaning and Importance of Fairy Tales*. New York: Vintage.

Bourguignon, Erika, ed. 1980. *A World of Women: Anthropological Studies of Women in the Societies of the World*. New York: Praeger.

Brain, James L. 1977. "Sex, Incest and Death: Initiation Rites Reconsidered." *Current Anthropology* 18:2, 191–208.

Brown, Judith K. 1963a. "Adolescent Initiation Rites in Preliterate Peoples." In *Studies in Adolescence*, edited by Robert E. Grinder, 75–85. New York: Macmillan.

———. 1963b. "A Cross-Cultural Study of Female Initiation Rites." *American Anthropologist* 65:4, 837–52.

Butt-Thompson, F. W. 1929. *West African Secret Societies: Their Organisations, Officials and Teaching.* London: Witherby.

Cannizzo, Jeanne D. 1978. *"Alikali* Devils: Children's Masquerading in a West African Town." Ph.D. diss., University of Washington.

Cohen, Yehudi. 1964. *Childhood and Adolescence: Cross-Cultural Studies of Initiation Ceremonies, Legal Systems and Incest Taboos.* Chicago: Aldine.

d'Azevedo, Warren L. 1973. "Mask Makers and Myth in Western Liberia." In *Primitive Art and Society,* edited by Anthony Forge, 126–50. London: Oxford University Press.

deMause, Lloyd, ed. 1974. *The History of Childhood.* New York: Psychohistory Press.

Devereux, George. 1971. "Art and Mythology: A General Theory." In *Art and Aesthetics in Primitive Societies,* edited by Carol F. Jopling, 193–224. New York: Dutton.

———. 1978. *Ethnopsychoanalysis: Psychoanalysis and Anthropology as Complementary Frames of Reference.* Berkeley: University of California Press.

Dike, K. O. 1956. *Trade and Politics in the Niger Delta 1830–1885.* Oxford: Clarendon.

Duru, Mary S. 1980. "Socialization Among the Igbo: An Intergenerational Study of Cultural Patterns, Familial Roles and Child Rearing Practices." Ph.D. diss., University of Maryland.

Eliade, Mircea. 1965. *Rites and Symbols of Initiation: The Mysteries of Birth and Rebirth.* New York: Harper.

Erikson, Erik H. 1963. *Childhood and Society.* 2d ed. New York: Norton.

Finnegan, Ruth H. 1965. *Survey of the Limba People of Northern Sierra Leone.* Great Britain, Department of Technical Co-Operation, Overseas Research Publication no. 6. London: Her Majesty's Stationery Office.

Forde, Daryll, and G. I. Jones. 1950. *The Ibo and Ibibio-Speaking Peoples of South-Eastern Nigeria.* Ethnographic Survey of Africa, Western Africa, Part 3. London: International African Institute.

Fortes, Meyer 1970 (1938). "Social and Psychological Aspects of Education in Taleland." In his *Time and Social Structure and Other Essays,* 201–59. London: Athlone.

Friedl, Ernestine. 1975. *Women and Men: An Anthropologist's View.* New York: Holt, Rinehart and Winston.

Gilmore, David D. 1986. "Mother-Son Intimacy and the Dual View of Woman in Andalusia: Analysis Through Oral Poetry." *Ethos* 14:3, 227–51.

Gluckman, Max. 1962. "Les Rites de Passage." In *Essays on the Ritual of Social Relations,* edited by Max Gluckman et al., 1–52. Manchester: Manchester University Press.

Goffman, Erving. 1959. *The Presentation of the Self in Everyday Life.* Garden City: Doubleday Anchor.

Golde, Peggy. 1970. *Women in the Field: Anthropological Experiences.* Chicago: Aldine.

Granzberg, Gary. 1973. "Twin Infanticide: A Cross-Cultural Test of a Materialist Explanation." *Ethos* 1:4, 405–12.

Hammond, Dorothy, and Alta Jablow. 1976. *Women in Cultures of the World*. Menlo Park: Cummings.

Hardman, Charlotte. 1973. "Can There Be an Anthropology of Children?" *Journal of the Anthropological Society of Oxford* 6:2, 85–99.

Hay, Margaret J., and Sharon Stichter. 1984. *African Women South of the Sahara*. London: Longman.

Heald, Susette. 1982. "The Making of Men: The Relevance of Vernacular Psychology to the Interpretation of a Gisu Ritual." *Africa* 52:1, 15–36.

Henderson, Joseph L. 1967. *Thresholds of Initiation*. Middletown: Wesleyan University Press.

Henderson, Richard L. 1972. *The King in Every Man: Evolutionary Trends in Onitsha Ibo Society and Culture*. New Haven: Yale University Press.

Henderson, Richard L., and Helen K. Henderson. 1966. *An Outline of Traditional Onitsha Ibo Socialization*. Institute of Education Occasional Publication no. 5. Ibadan: University of Ibadan.

Herdt, Gilbert H., ed. 1982. *Rituals of Manhood: Male Initiation in New Guinea*. Berkeley: University of California Press.

Jones, G. I. 1985. "A Memoir of Early Field Photography." *African Arts* 18:4, 64–67.

Kanner, Leo. 1935. *The Folklore of the Teeth*. New York: Macmillan.

Leach, Edmund R. 1958. "Magical Hair." *Journal of the Royal Anthropological Institute* 88:147–64.

———. 1973. "Levels of Communication and Problems of Taboo in the Appreciation of Primitive Art." In *Primitive Art and Society*, edited by Anthony Forge, 221–34. London: Oxford.

Leis, Philip E. 1972. *Enculturation and Socialization in an Ijaw Village*. New York: Holt, Rinehart and Winston.

LeVine, Robert A. 1961. "Africa." In *Psychological Anthropology: Approaches to Culture and Personality*, edited by Francis L. K. Hsu, 48–92. Homewood, Ill.: Dorsey.

———. 1966. *Dreams and Deeds: Achievement Motivation in Nigeria*. Chicago: University of Chicago Press.

———. 1973. "Patterns of Personality in Africa." *Ethos* 1:2, 123–52.

Maquet, Jacques. 1979. *Introduction to Aesthetic Anthropology*. Malibu: Undena.

Marsh, A. T. E. 1934. "The Cult of Arisi Edda." In Afikpo NA 106/Vol. 2, pp. 2–8. *See* Afikpo District Office 1935.

Meek, Charles K. 1937. *Law and Authority in a Nigerian Tribe*. London: Oxford University Press.

Miller, Phoebe. 1982. "Sex Polarity Among the Afikpo Igbo." In *African Religious Groups and Beliefs: Papers in Honor of William R. Bascom*, edited by Simon Ottenberg, 79–94. Meerut and Berkeley: Archana and Folklore Institute.

Morinis, Alan. 1985. "The Ritual Experience: Pain and the Transformation of Consciousness in Ordeals of Initiation." *Ethos* 13:2, 150–74.

Murphy, Robert F. 1959. "Social Structure and Sex Antagonism." *Southwestern Journal of Anthropology* 15:1, 89–98.

Murphy, W. P. 1980. "Secret Knowledge as Property and Power in Kpelle Society: Elder versus Youth." *Africa* 50:2, 193–207.

Nigeria, Census Superintendent. 1953–54. *Population Census of the Eastern Region of Nigeria, 1953.* 8 parts. Port Harcourt and Zaria: C.M.S. Niger Press and Gaskiya Corporation.

Norbeck, Edward, Donald E. Walker, and Mimi Cohen. 1962. "The Interpretation of Data: Puberty Rites." *American Anthropologist* 64:3, pt. 1, 463–85.

Nunberg, Herman. 1964. *The Problems of Bisexuality as Reflected in Circumcision.* London: Imago.

Nzimiro, Francis I. 1962. Family and Kinship in Ibo Land. A Study in Acculturation Process. Ph.D. diss., University of Cologne.

Okafor-Omali, Dilim. 1965. *A Nigerian Villager in Two Worlds.* London: Faber and Faber.

Opie, I., and P. Opie. 1959. *The Language and Lore of Schoolchildren.* Oxford: Clarendon.

———. 1969. *Children's Games in Street and Playground.* Oxford: Clarendon.

Oppong, Christine. 1973. *Growing Up in Dagomba.* Accra: Ghana Publishing Corporation.

Oppong, Christine, ed. 1983. *Female and Male in West Africa.* London: Allen and Unwin.

Ortner, Sherry B., and Harriet Whitehead, eds. 1981. *Sexual Meanings: The Cultural Construction of Gender and Sexuality.* New York: Cambridge University Press.

Ottenberg, Phoebe. 1958. "Marriage Relationships in the Double Descent System of the Afikpo Ibo of Southeastern Nigeria." Ph.D. diss., Northwestern University.

———. 1959. "The Changing Economic Position of Women Among the Afikpo Ibo." In *Continuity and Change in African Cultures,* edited by W. R. Bascom and M. J. Herskovits, 205–23. Chicago: University of Chicago Press.

———. 1965. "The Afikpo Ibo of Eastern Nigeria." In *Peoples of Africa,* edited by James L. Gibbs, Jr., 1–39. New York: Holt, Rinehart and Winston.

Ottenberg, Phoebe, and Simon Ottenberg. 1964. "Ibo Education and Social Change." In *Education and Politics in Nigeria,* edited by Hans N. Weiler, 25–56. Freiburg im Breisgau: Rombach.

Ottenberg, Simon. 1958. "Ibo Oracles and Intergroup Relations." *Southwestern Journal of Anthropology* 14:3, 295–307.

———. 1959. "Ibo Receptivity to Change." In *Continuity and Change in African Cultures,* edited by W. R. Bascom and M. J. Herskovits, 130–43. Chicago: University of Chicago Press.

———. 1965. "Inheritance and Succession in Afikpo." In *Studies in the Laws of Succession in Nigeria,* edited by D. M. Derrett, 39–90. London: Oxford University Press for the Nigerian Institute of Social and Economic Research.

_____. 1968a. *Double Descent in an African Society: The Afikpo Village-Group.* American Ethnological Society Monograph Series, no. 47. Seattle: University of Washington Press.

_____. 1968b. "An Ibo Protective Shrine." *International Archives of Ethnography* 51, 143–62.

_____. 1970. "Personal Shrines at Afikpo." *Ethnology* 9:1, 26–51.

_____. 1971. *Leadership and Authority in an African Society: The Afikpo Village-Group.* American Ethnological Society Monograph Series, no. 52. Seattle: University of Washington Press.

_____. 1972. "The House of Men." *African Arts* 5:4, 42–47, 85–88.

_____. 1975. *The Masked Rituals of Afikpo: The Context of an African Art.* Seattle: University of Washington Press.

_____. 1982a. "Illusion, Communication, and Psychology in West African Masquerades." *Ethos* 10:2, 149–85.

_____. 1982b. "Boys Secret Societies at Afikpo." In *African Religious Groups and Beliefs: Papers in Honor of William R. Bascom,* edited by Simon Ottenberg, 170–84. Meerut and Berkeley: Archana and Folklore Institute.

_____. 1983. "Igbo and Yoruba Art Contrasted." *African Arts* 16:2, 48–55, 97–98.

_____. 1985. "Thirty Years of Fieldnotes: Changing Interpretations of the Text." Paper presented at the annual meeting of the American Anthropological Association, Washington, D.C., December 6.

_____. 1988. "Psychological Aspects of Igbo Art." *African Arts* 21:2, 72–82, 93–94.

_____. n.d. "The Dancing Bride: Art and Indigenous Psychology in Limba Weddings." *Man: Journal of the Royal Anthropological Institute,* forthcoming.

Ottenberg, Simon, and Linda Knudsen. 1985. "Leopard Society Masquerades: Symbolism and Diffusion." *African Arts* 18:2, 37–44, 93–95, 103–4.

Paige, Karen E., and Jeffrey M. Paige. 1981. *The Politics of Reproductive Ritual.* Berkeley: University of California Press.

Parin, Paul, Fritz Morgenthaler, and Goldy Parin-Matthey. 1980 (1971). *Fear Thy Neighbor as Thyself: Psychoanalysis and Society Among the Anyi of West Africa.* Translated from the German by Patricia Klamerth. Chicago: University of Chicago Press.

Parsons, Anne. 1969. *Belief, Magic, and Anomie: Essays in Psychosocial Anthropology.* New York: Free Press.

Paul, Robert A. 1980. "Symbolic Interpretations in Psychoanalysis and Anthropology." *Ethos* 8:4, 286–94.

Precourt, Walter E. 1975. "Initiation Ceremonies and Secret Societies as Educational Institutions." In *Cross-Cultural Perspectives on Learning,* edited by Richard W. Brislin, Stephen Bochner, and Walter J. Lonner, 231–50. New York: Wiley.

Reik, Theodor. 1964 (1914–15). "The Puberty Rites of Savages." In his *Ritual: Four Psychoanalytic Studies,* 91–166. New York: Grove.

Riesman, Paul. 1986. "The Person and the Life Cycle in African Social Life and Thought." *African Studies Review* 29:2, 71–138.

Rosaldo, M. Z., and Louise Lamphere, eds. 1974. *Women, Culture and Society*. Stanford: Stanford University Press.

Sarnoff, Charles. 1976. *Latency*. New York: Aronson.

Saunders, George R. 1981. "Men and Women in Southern Europe: A Review of Some Aspects of Cultural Complexity." *Journal of Psychoanalytic Anthropology* 4, 413–34.

Schlegel, Alice, and Herbert Barry III. 1979. "Adolescent Initiation Ceremonies: A Cross-Cultural Code." *Ethnology* 18:2, 199–210.

———. 1980. "The Evolutionary Significance of Adolescent Initiation Ceremonies." *American Ethnologist* 7:4, 696–715.

Schurtz, Heinrich. 1902. *Alterklassen under Mannerbunde: Eine Darstellung der Grundformen der Gessellschaft*. Berlin: Reimer.

Shelton, Austin J. 1969. "Igbo Child-Raising, Eldership, and Dependence: Further Notes for Gerontologists and Others." *The Gerontologist* 8:4, 236–41.

———. 1971. *The Igbo-Igala Borderland: Religious and Social Control in Indigenous African Colonialism*. Albany: State University of New York Press.

Simmel, Georg. 1950. *The Sociology of Georg Simmel*. Translated by Kurt Wolff. New York: Macmillan.

Simmons, Donald C. 1960. "Sexual Life, Marriage and Childhood Among the Efik." *Africa* 30:2, 153–65.

Spiro, Melford E. 1982. *Oedipus in the Trobriands*. Chicago: University of Chicago Press.

Stephens, William N. 1962. *The Oedipus Complex. Cross-Cultural Evidence*. Glencoe: Free Press.

Talbot, P. Amaury. 1926. *The Peoples of Southern Nigeria*. 4 vols. London: Oxford.

Tefft, Stanton K. 1980. *Secrecy: A Cross-Cultural Perspective*. New York: Human Sciences Press.

Turner, Victor. 1967. *The Forest of Symbols*. Ithaca: Cornell University Press.

———. 1969. *The Ritual Process: Structure and Anti-Structure*. Chicago: Aldine.

Uchendu, Victor. 1965. *The Igbo of Southeast Nigeria*. New York: Holt, Rinehart and Winston.

Uka, Ngwobia. 1966. *Growing Up in a Nigerian Culture*. Institute of Education Occasional Publication no. 6. Ibadan: University of Ibadan.

van Gennep, Arnold. 1960 (1909). *The Rites of Passage*. Translated from the French by M. B. Vizedom and G. L. Cafee. Chicago: University of Chicago Press.

Webster, Hutton. 1908. *Primitive Secret Societies: A Study of Early Politics and Religion*. New York: Macmillan.

Whiting, John M. 1961. "Socialization Process and Personality." In *Psychological Anthropology: Approaches to Culture and Personality*, edited by Francis L. K. Hsu, 355–80. Homewood, Ill.: Dorsey.

———. 1964. "The Effects of Climate on Certain Cultural Practices." In *Explorations in Cultural Anthropology*, edited by Ward H. Goodenough, 511–44. New York: McGraw-Hill.

Whiting, John M., Richard Kluckhohn, and Albert Anthony. 1958. "The Function of Male Initiation Ceremonies at Puberty." In *Readings in Social Psychology*, edited by Eleanor E. Maccoby et al., 359–70. 3d ed. New York: Holt, Rinehart and Winston.

Winnicott, D. W. 1971. *Playing and Reality*. London: Tavistock.

Young, Frank. 1965. *Initiation Ceremonies: Cross-Cultural Studies of Status Dramatization*. Indianapolis: Bobbs-Merrill.

Index